911200601 40
1/49

JEWISH IDEAS AND CONCEPTS

STEVEN T. KATZ

JEWISH IDEAS
AND
CONCEPTS

SCHOCKEN BOOKS · NEW YORK

First published by SCHOCKEN BOOKS 1977

Copyright © 1977 Keter Publishing House Jerusalem Ltd.

Library of Congress Cataloging in Publication Data

Katz, Steven T.   1944–
    Jewish ideas and concepts.

    Bibliography: p. 309
    1. Jewish theology.   2. God (Judaism)   3. Ethics,
Jewish.   I. Title.
BM601.K37   296.3   77–75285

Manufactured in the United States of America

Table of Contents

Introduction

In the preparation of this volume two goals were kept in mind. The first was to present an accurate, informative, rich picture of Jewish thought which could serve as the basis for a proper understanding of Judaism. Accordingly, we have endeavored to extract the salient features of those Jewish concepts which form the building blocks of the Jewish intellectual tradition, especially as they concern the relationship between God and the Jew, which is the cornerstone of the Jewish experience. Our second related but distinct goal was to bring to the surface the uniquely *Jewish* understanding of concepts which Judaism shares with its theological offspring, Christianity and Islam, as well as with most of the world's great religions. This second purpose emerges not out of a case of "theological one-upmanship," the "our view is better than yours" kind of attitude found in apologetic literature, but rather out of the essential intellectual requirement that insists that concepts, like languages in general, do not exist independently of their environment. Except for a narrow class of scientific, logical and mathematical terms, the concepts we embrace in order to give expression to our understanding of the world and our place in it are deeply bound to specific cultural and intellectual milieus and receive their intelligibility within definite social contexts. Every theological concept, like all linguistic idioms, is informed and re-inforced by a wide range of specific ideas and more broadly by a unifying *weltanschauung* (world view) which defines the nature and limits of the language spoken in a given culture.

Jewish thought is no exception to this rule. The concepts and language which Jewish thinkers employ reflect the value-laden outlook of their unique religious civilization. Jewish philosophers and theologians do not philosophize in a vacuum; their problems, data and solutions emerge from the specific realities and pre-suppositions of

Judaic experience. Thus, to understand Judaism accurately one has to examine the meaning of each given idea in its various and specific Jewish contexts and not simply rely on vague notions, available in our more general culture as to what a certain concept means or, even worse, trying to establish the meaning of a Jewish idea by refracting it through the influential non-Jewish prisms of other theological or ideological traditions. Consequently, in this volume we are engaged in the exploration of the meaning of fundamental philosophical and theological concepts as they are specifically employed in classical Jewish sources such as the Bible, the rabbinic materials, medieval Jewish philosophy, Kabbalah and modern Jewish thought.

Our stated first goal of presenting a coherent introduction to Jewish thought will hopefully unfold as the reader makes his way through the present volume. Likewise, it is hoped that our second goal will also be realized through the material discussed. Recognizing, however, the somewhat more complex philosophical character of this second aim, I should like to emphasize in an introductory way the significance of making correct distinctions in the use of ideas and of placing these in their proper social-ideological milieu. Two well-known examples will help us achieve this desired clarification, the first being the medieval attempt to synthesize Aristotle and the Bible, and the second being the more contemporarily relevant discussion of the compatibility of Jewish and Christian theology.

The medieval encounter between Aristotle and Judaism (12th century onward) drove Jewish thinkers, like their Muslim colleagues before them and their later Christian colleagues, to try to integrate biblical and Aristotelian thought. So, for example, Jewish biblical exegetes of the period began to translate the difficult verse in Genesis regarding "*tohu vavohu*" (Genesis 1:2; translated by J.H. Hertz as "unformed and void")[1] in light of Aristotle's metaphysics as "form and matter." Now whatever "*tohu vavohu*" means it certainly does not denote the technical Aristotelian doctrine of "form and matter" which stems from, and is only intelligible within, Aristotle's complex ontology. This may be an issue of marginal importance but it gives a first lucid indication of the issue. A simple and exact translation of Aristotle into the imagery of Genesis or Genesis into the metaphysics of Aristotle is not possible without ignoring or distorting basic differences between them.

Again, a more complex, but far more important example can be found in the attempt made in these same circles to render equivalent the "Prime Mover" of Aristotle's *Metaphysics* and the God of biblical faith. Both are agreedly the "first cause" of things, but this common feature is far less significant than the unbridgeable conceptual chasm which separates the two. The "Prime Mover" of Aristotle is conceived of as an amoral reality of whom it is logically impermissible to predicate attributes of personality or relation with humankind. On the other hand, the God of the Bible and of Judaism is most importantly and markedly distinguished by the fact that He is conceived as a moral being who does, in some sense, manifest what men know as "personality" and whose outstanding quality is that He willingly has relations with humans, even to the point of entering into covenants with them. It will not do to say that both Aristotle and Genesis teach a monotheistic doctrine (even if it were absolutely true in the case of Aristotle) and go away happy at the universality of this idea, for in fact the God-ideas of the two are utterly distinct and many of the differences between the Greek world-view and the Hebraic can be considered corollaries of these two mutually exclusive views of Divinity.[2]

More interesting perhaps and even more pertinent are the differences between Judaism and Christianity. Today we are accustomed to speak of a Judeo-Christian tradition as if there really were such a common tradition and shared ecumenical perspective. In fact, the "Judeo-Christian tradition" is, in Arthur Cohen's phrase, "a myth,"[3] and realistically speaking, from the Jewish side at least, there is little on which such a tradition could be built. If, first of all, we pursue the example discussed above, we shall see that, despite talk of Judaism and Christianity as "monotheistic" religions, the God-ideas of Judaism and Christianity are very different. Jews conceive of God's unity in such a way as to rule out multiplicity, while Christianity speaks of God in the language of a trinitarian or tri-une conception (claiming of course that this tri-unity is the profoundest understanding of God's monotheistic unity). We are not concerned here with resolving or evaluating these alternative concepts. Our only purpose is to indicate that what Jews rule out as impermissible in describing God, Christians permit, indeed insist upon.[4] Hence it seems accurate to note that Jews and Christians cannot both be correct, though both could be wrong, and that there is much to suggest that Judaism and Christianity, far from sharing a common conception of the Deity, have very different God-concepts. (Islam, of course, thought that both Judaism and Christianity were insufficiently rigorous in protecting the unity and perfection of God!)

If we pursue the topic of Judaism and Christianity a little further it will also become clear that not only the understanding of God is different, but that almost every central term in the religious vocabulary is different. This difference is caused by the fact that the Church, quite correctly from its perspective, defines and understands every major concept through the prism of the life, teaching, death and resurrection of Jesus. Thus, for example, the crucifixion and resurrection and their imputed soteriological (salvific) function caused the Church to reconsider its inherited Judaic understanding of the nature and destiny of man and its account and expectation of messianism. With regard to the anthropological situation, the crucifixion requires that in some real sense the human condition be interpreted as "fallen" in order to make a place for the type of soteriological function played by Jesus' death (i.e., Jesus' death as a "vicarious atonement" and a "gift" of God for the sins of mankind). So, most notably, the concept of "original sin" becomes an essential element in the Christian account of man. Judaism, however, does not have to account for an event similar to that of the Easter event (vicarious atonement of the sort claimed for Jesus), and thus need not interpret the human situation in terms of "original sin" and all that this entails. This difference in the accounts of the human situation colors every feature of the respective outlooks of Judaism and Christianity, for example, their understanding of human freedom, the nature of man and sin, the efficacy of human repentance, and the role of divine grace in the cosmic economy. Indeed, that strain in the Christian tradition which came closest (though remaining dissimilar) to the Jewish perspective of a majestic image of humanity possessing a totally free will and stressing the importance and value of human action, was branded a heresy by the Church (the "Pelagian" heresy) and traces of these elements were branded pejoratively as "Judaizing" or "Jewish" error.

Moreover, the events surrounding the death of Jesus and the later understanding of these events by the Church dramatically altered the conception of "messianism" in Christianity from what it was, and still is, in Judaism.[5] Without pausing too long over this issue here, it is important to state that Judaism and Christianity can never reach any theological rapprochement over this crucial issue because the concepts of "Messiah" the "messianism" mean something different in the two religions. It is not a matter, as it is usually considered, of whether or not some biblical prophecy has been fulfilled, as if Judaism and Christianity agreed on what "messianism" is and only differed on whether or not it had come to pass; rather it goes much deeper than that, differing over what to count as "messianic" activity and purpose; that is, differing over the very essence of the messianic idea. The clearest and most important example of this difference is found in the fact that the personal soteriological function which is at the very center of Christian messianism, i.e., "Jesus died for our sins," is totally absent from Jewish messianism, which accords the Messiah no role in the drama of personal salvation and judgment.

Our brief remarks about the contextual nature of language and the few examples discussed bring out the essential point that concepts have to be closely scrutinized in their contexts, and that changing the latter may radically alter the meaning of the concept. If this is true (and it is hoped that we have shown, however briefly, that it is), then it becomes of paramount importance in trying to understand Judaism, and Jewish thought in all its forms, to examine closely the particularly Jewish exegesis or exegeses of the basic terms and concepts which Judaism shares with its Christian and Muslim neighbors. How does Judaism view the nature and activity of God? How does Judaism view the nature and activity of mankind? What is its outlook on God's relation to mankind and especially Israel? These and like questions become the indispensable first step in trying to render Judaism intelligible and in trying to evaluate Judaism's relations with other religions.

II

The approach used in organizing this volume has been a topical one, examining the use of each concept under discussion as it is found in the different historical strata of Jewish thought, i.e., biblical, talmudic, medieval and modern. Arranging the material this way causes some asymmetry in its presentation, as there is a change in philosophical styles and concerns from one period to another. In the medieval world, for example, great pains were taken to disentangle the issues related to proving God's existence and the nature of His attributes, while in the modern period there is relatively little discussion of these themes. In their place one finds, among other things, more concern with technical issues raised by the subjects of morality and freedom.

In addition to the topical treatment, the individual subjects, e.g., anthropomorphism, sin or Torah, are further organized as entries under three broad headings: (i) God, (ii) Man, (iii) God and the Jew. A further word is required about this arrangement. It was originally intended to conclude this work with a final section on "Jewish Eschatology." However, publishing practicalities intervened and forced the deletion of this section. In leaving out the eschatological material two considerations weighed heavily. The first was that the subject is too important and all too often ignored to treat only cursorily as would of necessity have been required if the subject were to be raised at all in the present context. Secondly, it is hoped that the lacunae caused by the exclusion of this material here will be filled by the publication of a separate volume dealing with this issue in the near future.

It might also be noted that in making the difficult decisions as to what topics to include in the present volume two alternative methods of organization and selection suggested themselves. The first was to try to be "encyclopedic," i.e., to include *every* relevant topic even if very sketchily. The second was to treat fewer but more inherently cohering and intrinsically significant topics in greater detail. My own dissatisfaction and the general dissatisfaction I have often heard expressed by colleagues with works of the former sort led me to adopt the latter alternative. I believe readers will concur with the wisdom of this choice.

Although each discussion is largely complete in itself it is also important to recognize that in an organic phenomenon such as Judaism, concepts are integrally inter-related and the various topics discussed ought not to be treated as vacuum-sealed containers, but rather as open-ended discussions, each specific debate involving and having implications for every other. It should also be noted that this has meant some overlapping between the various discussions, but this was unavoidable, and actually serves to reinforce the discussion rather than detract from it. The attention of readers is also drawn to a companion volume of the present work, which entitled *Jewish Philosophers*,[6] contains a chronological history of Jewish thinkers throughout the ages and further discussions of the concepts examined in this volume.

III

It is hoped that this book will serve, among other purposes, as an introductory work for those seeking to learn the history of Jewish thought. With this audience in mind special care has been taken in the preparation of the Notes, Glossary, Biographical Index and Bibliography. The organization of the notes presented something of a problem due to the very different sorts of material covered, and this was especially true of the notes for the biblical and talmudic materials which at times became too numerous to handle as individual references. To solve this problem resort was made on occasion to the device of listing all relevant source material for an entire paragraph in one extended note. Though this meant a slight stylistic inconsistency in the organization of the notes it also meant a much more readable text, and the gains far outweighed the issue of formal consistency which, in any case, should not become a fetish when comprehension and intelligent organization are involved. The Glossary contains religious and philosophical terms which it was felt would be unknown to readers at an introductory and intermediate level. The Biographical Index lists the majority of the thinkers discussed in this volume so that the reader can easily gain some basic idea of who someone is, what historical period he belongs to, and what philosophical and theological tradition he is associated with.

The Bibliography is quite extensive. It has been prepared to provide the reader with a more than adequate starting point for future research. It is felt that a good bibliography is one of the most valuable parts of a book to students of a subject and it is hoped that all who have occasion to use the present one will find it useful. Special effort has been made to include more specialized and technical works, as well as the more general ones, so that it will be of help both to advanced students of the subject as well as to those at an introductory or intermediate level.

Lastly, a pictorial representation of the standard arrangement of the Kabbalistic *Sefirot* has been placed at the end of this volume to give those not familiar with the details of Kabbalistic thought (for which the theory of the *Sefirot* provides the basic skeleton) assistance in understanding its complex structure.

IV

I should like to acknowledge five debts incurred in the preparation of this volume. The first is to Dartmouth College which through its "Research Committee" helped defray part of the typing costs of preparing this volume. The second is to the always helpful, willing and friendly library staff of the Dartmouth College Library who assisted in various projects connected with the preparation of this work. The third is to Rabbi Laurence Edwards of Dartmouth Hillel who kindly read over Section III of the work in manuscript. The fourth is to the contributors to the *Encyclopaedia Judaica* whose work formed the basis of this volume, and whose names and contributions are listed at the end of this volume. Finally, my last and greatest debt which words cannot adequately express is to my wife Rebecca, who was a constant source of encouragement and a loving coworker in this as in all my other endeavors.

Steven Theodore Katz
Dartmouth College

[1] The Torah, Jewish Publication Society of America, Philadelphia, 1962.

[2] For further remarks on this and related issues see the Introduction to *Jewish Philosophers,* ed. S. Katz (1975).

[3] This is the title of A.A. Cohen's book, *The Myth of the Judeo-Christian Tradition* (1971).

[4] I recognize that some forms of Christianity are "unitarian" and reject Trinitarian formulae, but these groups are marginal both historically and theologically in the history and life of the Christian community. Moroever, this difference itself reinforces the point being made, namely that even the term "Christian" or "Christianity" is not monolithic or univocal; indeed, if space permitted we would have to deal with the use of the various concepts here being discussed in relation to 'Christianity' and the 'Church' much more concretely in their specific and variegated Christian contexts.

[5] It is important to note that though we have referred to 'Judaism' in our brief remarks on Judaism and Christianity we do not want the reader to lose sight of the fact, stressed in the treatment of the specific issues dealt with in this work, that Judaism too is a multi-faceted reality, allowing of diversity and differences from historic era to historic era, and from culture to culture. Our very sensitivity to this fact has caused us to approach each of the issues in the main text in a chronological way, drawing attention to the treatment of a specific topic in the various strata of Jewish thought.

[6] S. Katz (ed.), *Jewish Philosophers* (1975).

PART I

GOD

God in the Bible

Despite its outward appearance the Bible is a very complex book. One must remember that it is not the product of a single author but a work made up of many volumes written by different authors living in various countries over a period of more than a millenium. Under such circumstances, differences of emphasis, such as those found between Jonah and Nahum, and even differences of fact, like those in Genesis 26:34 and Genesis 36:2–3, are to be expected. Nor is it surprising that these factors should also have affected the biblical presentation of the concept and understanding of God. There are passages in which Israel's monotheism is portrayed in unalloyed purity and incomparable beauty, such as I Kings 19:12 and Isaiah 40:18; and there are other verses in which folkloristic echoes and mythological reflexes, though much transmuted and refined, appear to be present—for example, in certain details of Genesis 2 and 3.

One must be careful, however, in evaluating these discrepancies, for in the main the biblical concept of God is more homogeneous and harmonious than heterogeneous or discordant. In addition, one must recognize the absolutely fundamental differences between the biblical concept of God and other ancient Near-Eastern notions of divinity. The borrowings, similarities and overlap in certain details do not alter the fact that the nature of the God of the Bible and the God of Israel's faith is unique, a reality which is, in its most essential characteristics, *sui generis.*

God, the One and Incomparable, is the hero of the Bible. Everything that is narrated, enjoined or foretold in biblical literature is related to Him. Yet nowhere does the Bible offer any proof of the Deity's existence or command belief in Him. There are two possible reasons for this: Hebrew thought is concrete and intuitive rather than speculative and systematic, and secondly, there were no atheists in antiquity in the

3

sense that we use the term today. When the psalmist observed: "The fool hath said in his heart 'There is no God' " (Psalms 14:1), he was referring not to disbelief in God's existence but to the denial of His moral governance of the world. That a divine being or beings existed was universally accepted.

There were those, it is true, "who did not know YHWH" (Exodus 5:2), but all people acknowledged the reality of the Godhead. What was completely new was not the idea of a divine Being but Israel's idea of the nature of that Being. This idea is expounded in numerous, though not necessarily related, biblical passages which build up, facet by facet, a cosmic, awe-inspiring spiritual portrait of a Being of infinite magnitude. Paganism is challenged in all its aspects. God is One; there is no other. Polytheism is rejected unequivocally and absolutely. There is no pantheon; even the dualism of Ormuzd and Ahriman (of the Zoroastrian religion) is excluded. Apotheosis is condemned. Syncretism (as distinct from identification, which plays a historical as well as a theological role in paganism) is necessarily ruled out. Verses like Exodus 15:11—"Who is like Thee, O Lord, among the gods?"—do not support polytheism but expose the unreality of the pagan deities. Beside the true God, how can these idol-imposters claim divinity?

God is also unique in all His attributes. The prophet asks: "To whom then will ye liken God? Or what likeness will ye compare unto Him?" Although the question is rhetorical, the Bible provides a series of answers, scattered throughout the entire range of its teaching, which elaborate in depth the incomparability of God. He has no likeness; no image can be made of Him. He is not even to be conceived as a spirit; the spirit of God referred to in the Bible alludes to His energy.[1]

Idolatry, though it lingered for centuries, was doomed to extinction by this new conception of the Godhead. It is true that the Torah itself ordained that images like the cherubim should be set up in the Holy of Holies, but they were meant to represent the divine throne rather than God itself.

No human eye can see the occupant of the divine throne, yet the invisible God of the Bible is not a philosophical abstraction. He manifests His presence in a variety of ways: His theophanies are accompanied by thunder, earthquake and lightning, which indicate that strength which none can resist.

God's greatness, however, does not lie primarily in His power but rather in His wisdom. He is omniscient; true wisdom is His alone. Only He envisions and reveals the future. He alone is the source of human understanding, and only He endows human beings with their skills and knowledge. God is also omnipresent, but not in any pantheistic sense, for the God of the Bible transcends the world of nature which is His creation. It is He who has brought the world into being, established its laws and given it its order. Likewise He has His being outside of time and space, which are also His creations. Everything which has been created must perish, but He alone who preceded the universe and brought everything else into being will remain after it has disappeared. In a world of flux He alone does not change; He is the immutable foundation of all existence.[2]

God's power and wisdom find their ultimate expression in the work of creation. The specific miracles to which the Bible attests highlight the divine omnipotence, but the supreme miracle is the universe itself. There is no biblical theogony, but there is a cosmogony, designed and executed by divine fiat (Genesis 1). The opening verses of the Bible do not conclusively point to *creatio ex nihilo*; the primordial condition of chaos (*tohu* and *bohu*) mentioned in Genesis 1:2 could conceivably represent the *materia prima* (fundamental matter) out of which the world was fashioned. But Job 26:7 appears to express poetically the belief in a world created out of the void,[3] and both prophets and psalmists seem to substantiate this doctrine (Isaiah 42:5; Jeremiah 10:12; Psalms 33:6–9). It is true that the greatest of medieval Jewish philosophers, Maimonides, did not believe that the Bible provided incontrovertible proof of *creatio ex nihilo (Guide to the Perplexed)*. Nonetheless, it is correct to argue that biblical thought generally regards the existence of uncreated matter as a grave diminution of the divinity of the Godhead, for God must precede all matter in order to be the sole creator (Isaiah 44:24).

The celestial beings ("sons of God") referred to in Job 38:7 and the angels who, according to rabbinic *aggadah* and some modern exegetes, are addressed in Genesis 1:26 (cf. 3:22) were themselves created forms and not co-architects or co-builders of the cosmos. Angels are portrayed in the Bible as constituting the heavenly court, and as taking part in celestial consultations (I Kings 22, 19ff; Job 1:6ff; 2:1ff). These heavenly creatures are not independent and autonomous beings, but rather act as God's messengers or agents (the Hebrew *mal'akh* and the

Greek αγγελος. from which the word "angel" is derived, both mean
"messenger" or agent). For the most part they perform various tasks
without being individualized or named, except in the later books of the
Bible.

Nor are these heavenly creatures God's only messengers; natural
phenomena like the wind (Psalms 104:16) or man himself may act in
that capacity (Numbers 20:16). It has been suggested that since the
Bible concentrated all divine powers in one God, the old pagan deities,
which represented various forces of nature, were demoted in Israel's
religion to the position of angels. The term *shedim* (Deuteronomy
32:17; Psalms 106:37), on the other hand, when applied to the gods of
the nations, does not, according to Y. Kaufman, denote demons but
rather "no-gods"—i.e., beings devoid of both divine and/or demonic
powers.[4] It should also be noted that the fantastic proliferation of the
angel population found in pseudepigraphical literature (4th century on)
is still unknown in the Bible, and that even in this post-biblical Jewish
angelology these celestial beings are God's creatures and servants. They
fulfill the divine will rather than oppose it. The pagan notion of demonic
forces that wage war against the deities is wholly alien and repugnant to
biblical theology. Even Satan is no more than the heavenly prosecutor,
"The Accuser," serving the divine purpose. The cosmos is thus the
work of God above, and all nature is seen to declare His glory and to
belong to him.

This creation theorem has a corollary of vast scientific and social
significance: the universe, in all its measureless diversity, in all its
irreducible complexity, nevertheless remains a homogeneous whole.
Nature's processes are the same throughout the world, and underlying
them is "One Power, which is of no beginning and no end, which has
existed before all things were formed, and will remain in its integrity
when all is gone—the Source and Origin of all, in Itself beyond any
conception or image that man can form and set up before his eye or
mind." There is no cosmic strife between antagonistic forces, between
darkness and light, between good and evil. By the same token, mankind
constitutes a single brotherhood. And yet the ideal is not that of
unvarying uniformity. Differentiation is an essential element of the
Creator's design—the Tower of Babel is necessarily doomed to
destruction—but the family unity of mankind, despite racial, cultural and
pigmentary differences, is clearly stressed in mankind's origin (Adam is the

human father of all people) and in its ultimate destiny at the end of days (Isaiah 2:2–4).

The course of creation is depicted in the opening chapter of the Bible as a graduated unfolding of the universe, and more particularly of the earth, from the lowest levels of life to man, the peak of the creative process. God, according to this account, completes the work in six days (that "days" here means an undefined period may be inferred from Genesis 1:14, where time divisions are mentioned for the first time).[5] The biblical account of the days, however, is not intended to provide the reader with a science or history textbook but to describe the ways of God. Running like a golden thread through all the variegated contents of the Bible is the one unchanging theme—God and His moral law. Thus, of far greater significance than the time span of creation is the fact that it is crowned by the Sabbath (Genesis 2:1–3), bringing rest and refreshment to the toiling world. The concept of the creative pause, sanctified by divine example, is one of the greatest spiritual and social contributions to civilization made by the religion of Israel. (The attempts to represent the Assyro-Babylonian *sabattu* or *sapattu* as the forerunner of the Hebrew Sabbath are without foundation.[6] The former is a designation for the ill-omened 15th day of the month, and the notions associated with it are as different from those of the Sabbath—with its elevating thoughts of holiness and physical and spiritual renewal—as a day of mourning is from a joyous festival.)

The Sabbath does not mark the retirement of the Deity from the world that He has called into being. God continues to care for His creatures, and human beings—all human beings—remain the focal point of His loving interest (Psalms 8:5[4]ff.). The divine providence encompasses both nations and individuals (the Patriarchs, for example). Cosmogony is followed by history, and God becomes the great architect of the world of events, even as He is of the physical universe. He directs historical movements, and the peoples of history are in His hands as clay in the hands of the potter (Jeremiah 18:6). There is, however, a vital difference between the two spheres of divine activity: creation encountered no antagonism. Thus, for example, the monsters that in pagan mythology are the mortal enemies of the gods become in the Bible creatures formed in accordance with the divine will (Genesis 1:21).

Alternatively, unlike creation, history records endless acts of rebellion against the Creator. Man is not an automaton: he is endowed with free will. The first human beings already disobey their Maker; they acquire knowledge at the price of sin, a condition that reflects the discord between the will of God and the action of man. The perfect harmony between the Creator and His human creation, which finds expression in the idyll of the Garden of Eden, is disrupted and never restored. The revolt continues with Cain, the generation of the Flood, and the Tower of Babel.

Human history is a rhythm of rebellion and retribution, of oppression and redemption, of repentance and grace, and of merit and reward. Israel is the first people to write history as teleology, to discover that history has a moral base. The Bible declares that God judges the world in righteousness; that military power does not presuppose victory; that the Lord saves the humble and dwells with them; and that the moral factor determines the time as well as the course of events. Thus, the Israelites will return to Canaan only when the moral iniquity of the Amorite is complete. Similarly, the children of Israel must wander in the wilderness for forty years as punishment for accepting the pessimistic report of the ten spies rather than trusting in God. On the other hand, Jehu is rewarded with a dynasty of five generations for his punitive action against the evil house of Ahab; and to Daniel is revealed the timetable of redemption and restoration. It is this moral direction in history that makes God both Judge and Savior.

God's punishment of the wicked and salvation of the righteous are laws of the divine governance of the world, comparable to the laws of nature: "As smoke is driven away, so drive them away; as wax melts before fire, let the wicked perish before God . . . " Nature and history are related in the ultimate plan of God (Jeremiah 33:20ff), and He rules over both. The divine design of history, marked by universal peace, human brotherhood, and knowledge of God, will be accomplished in "the end of days" (Isaiah 2:2–4; 11:6ff) even as the cosmos was completed according to the divine plan. Man's rebellions complicate the course of history, but they cannot change the design. God's purpose, despite human straying, shall be accomplished, and in the end there will be a new heaven and a new earth (Isaiah 66:22). Then human beings will return to the proper relation with God and act co-operatively with Him.[7]

Within the macrocosm of world history there is the microcosm of

Israel's history. It is natural that in their own national literature the people of Israel should receive special and elaborate attention, although the gentile world is never lost sight of, particularly in prophetic teaching. The Bible designates Israel as an *am segullah*, a "treasured people," which stands in a particular relationship to the one God: He recognizes Israel as His own people, and they acknowledge Him as their only God (Deuteronomy 26:17–18). In return, He redeems them from Egyptian bondage, brings them to the promised land, and comes to their aid in times of crisis.

Israel's election is not, however, to be interpreted as a form of favoritism; the Exodus from Egypt is paralleled by similar events in the histories of other peoples, including Israel's enemies (Amos 9:7). Rather, Israel's election dictates greater responsibility, with corresponding penalties as well as rewards: "You only have I singled out of all the families of the earth; therefore I will visit upon you all your iniquities" (Amos 3:2). The Bible suggests that the choice of the children of Israel as God's people is not due to their power or merit, but is rather a divine act of love and the fulfillment of a promise given to the Patriarchs (Deuteronomy 7:7–8; 9:4–7). The Lord declares that the spiritual and moral way of life pioneered by Abraham will be transmitted to his descendants as a heritage, an assurance that finds material expression in the covenant solemnly established between God and His people at Sinai (Exodus 24:7ff.).[8] This everlasting covenant demands wholehearted and constant devotion to the will of God (Deuteronomy 18:13): to be a chosen people it is therefore incumbent upon Israel to become, as the English writer Israel Zangwill phrased it, a choosing people. Despite the recurring pattern of human rebellion and divine retribution, the fulfillment of God's purpose is not in doubt. God's chosen people will not perish (Jeremiah 31:26–27). He will be restored to faithfulness, and through her redemption she will bring salvation to the whole earth, leading all human beings to God (Jeremiah 3:17–18). Until that far-off day, however, Israel endures her suffering and the trials of her historical existence in order to remain God's witness in the midst of history (Isaiah 44:8).

Ultimately the covenant that binds the children of Israel to their God is the entire Torah, not only Sinai. Although God rules all nations, the Torah is obligatory as a covenant only for Israel. Even idolatry, the constant butt of prophetic irony, is not regarded as a gentile sin

(Deuteronomy 4:19). At the same time the Bible assumes the existence of a universal moral code that all peoples must observe. The talmudic sages in fact identify the seven Noachian laws (San. 36a) as the basis of this universal ethic. Although the Bible does not specify the ethical principles incumbent upon all mankind, it is clear from various passages that murder, robbery, cruelty, and adultery are considered major crimes no matter who commits them, and are to be recognized as such by all human beings.[9]

The Bible seems to postulate an autonomous basic human sense of right and wrong, unless it is supposed that a divine revelation of law was vouchsafed to the early saints of the pre-Sinaitic period, such as that suggested by the apocryphal and rabbinic literatures (and perhaps by Isaiah 24:5). At the same time, the Torah—which means "teaching" or "instruction" rather than "law"—does not, in the strict sense, contain a properly formulated legal code. Nevertheless, detailed regulations concerning religious ritual as well as civil and criminal jurisprudence are an essential part of pentateuchal teaching. The centrality of these regulations is reinforced by the prophets: Isaiah (58:13), Jeremiah (34:8ff), Ezekiel (40ff) and Malachi (1:8; 2:10) among others lend their authority to the maintenance of various religious observances.

Yet within the Bible there also seems, at least on the surface, to be a paradoxically "anti-halakhic" current. Thus, in Isaiah the Lord is said to cry: "What to Me is the multitude of your sacrifices . . . I have had enough of burnt offerings of rams and the fat of fed beasts . . . who requires of you this trampling of My courts? . . . Your new moons and your appointed feasts My soul hates . . . When you spread forth your hands, I will hide My eyes from you; even though you make many prayers, I will not listen." Jeremiah not only belittles the value of the sacrifices but derides the people's faith in the Temple itself: "The temple of the Lord, the temple of the Lord, the temple of the Lord are these." Even the Book of Psalms, though essentially devotional in character, seems to make an anti-ritual protest: "I do not reprove you for your sacrifices . . . I. will accept no bull from your house . . . For every beast of the forest is Mine, the cattle on a thousand hills . . . If I were hungry, I would not tell you; for the world and all that is in it is Mine. Do I eat the flesh of bulls, or drink the blood of goats?"

These and similar passages seem to represent a negative attitude towards established cultic practices. No less inconsonant with Torah law seems the positive prophetic summary of human duty formulated by Micah: "He has told you, O man, what is good; and what does the Lord require of you but to do justice, and to love lovingkindness, and to walk humbly with your God?" A similar note is sounded by Hosea: "I will espouse you with righteousness and with justice, with steadfast love, and with mercy. I will espouse you with faithfulness; and you shall be mindful of the Lord"; by Amos: "Seek good, and not evil, that you may live"; and by Isaiah: "Learn to do good; seek justice, correct oppression; defend the fatherless, plead for the widow." The emphasis here is on moral and spiritual conduct over against the ceremonial and ritualistic aspects of religion, which are conspicuously left unmentioned.[10]

The anti-halakhic paradox, however, is generated only through a misunderstanding of the intention and language of the biblical text. Inherently there is no contradiction between the ritual and moral aspects of biblical religion. The ostensibly antinomian statements do not oppose the offering of sacrifices, prayer, or the observance of the Sabbath and festivals, but instead are concerned to condemn the hypocrisy that substitutes ceremony for intention, ritual for morality. Isaiah (1:13) expresses the thought in a single phrase: "I cannot endure iniquity and solemn assembly." Organized religion must necessarily have cultic forms, but unaccompanied by inwardness and unqualified sincerity they are an affront to the Deity. The underlying purpose of the *mitzvot* is to purify and elevate man, to bring man and God together rather than to set up barriers between them. It is heartfelt devotion that saves the *mitzvah* (the religious deed) from becoming a meaningless convention. The specific commandments are pointers and aids to that larger identification with God's will that informs human life: "In all your ways acknowledge Him" (Proverbs 3:6). Biblical religion is an indivisible synthesis of moral and spiritual principles with practical observances and concrete application of God's will.[11]

The claim to a moral providence, as implied in the ethic of the Torah, raises the problem of justifying biblical theodicy. In the Bible itself Abraham challenges the divine justice: "Shall not the Judge of all the earth do right?" and Moses echoes the cry in another context: "O Lord, why hast Thou done evil to this people?" The prophets are no less perplexed: "Why does the way of the wicked prosper? Why do all who are treacherous thrive?" The psalmist speaks for the individual and the nation of many generations when he cries: "My God, my God, why hast Thou forsaken me?" Likewise, the Book of Job is a heroic attempt to solve the problem of unwarranted human suffering.[12]

The biblical answer appears to point to the limitations of man's experience and understanding. History is long, but individual life is short. One person's view is necessarily fragmentary; events justify themselves in the end, but the person concerned does not always live to see the dénouement. In the words of the psalmist: "Though the wicked sprout like grass and all evildoers flourish, they are doomed to destruction forever" (92:8–10). Moreover, not only is man all too finite but he is further limited by his lack of complete insight. Of necessity God's purpose is beyond his comprehension: "For as the heavens are higher than the earth, so are My ways higher than your ways and My thoughts than your thoughts" (Isaiah 55:9). In the final analysis, biblical theodicy recognizes, indeed emphasizes, human limitations and calls for faith: "But the righteous shall live by his faith" (Hab. 2:4); "They who wait for the Lord shall renew their strength" (Isaiah 40:31). However, this faith is not intended to be an irrational one—Certum est quia impossible ("it is certain because it is impossible")[13]—but rather a faith necessitated by man's existential limitations and the inherent intellectual boundaries imposed by the human situation.

There are other occasions of which the Bible speaks in which God's ways are even more difficult to justify. God, the Bible states categorically, hardened Pharaoh's heart; nevertheless the Egyptian ruler was punished for the actions that ensued. Indeed, his obduracy was induced in order to provide the occasion for his punishment (Exodus 7:3).[14] Here the norms of justice by any standards seem to be flagrantly violated. The explanation in this sphere of biblical theodicy is not theological but semantic. Scripture ascribes to God phenomena and events with which He is only indirectly concerned. However, since God is the author of all natural law and the designer of history, everything that occurs is, in an ultimate sense, His doing. Even in human affairs the king or the government is said to "do" everything that is performed under its aegis. Thus God declares in Amos 4:7: "And I caused it to rain upon one city, and I caused it not to rain upon another city," although the next clause uses passive and impersonal verbal forms to describe the same occurrences. The processes of nature need not be mentioned independently, since the laws of the universe are dictates of

God. Similarly Exodus states indiscriminately that "Pharaoh hardened his heart" (8:28), that "the heart of Pharaoh was hardened" (9:7), and that "the Lord hardened the heart of Pharaoh" (9:12). In the end it is all one; whatever God allows to happen can be seen as His actions, in some ultimate sense.

This interpretation does not, however, explain another area of divine conduct. Uzzah, the Bible states, was struck dead for an innocent act that was motivated by concern for the safety of "the ark of God" (II Samuel 6:6–7). Wherein lay the iniquity? Here the reason appears to be that in certain circumstances even innocent actions may be disastrous. Uzzah's attempt to save the ark from falling was well meant, but it led to irreverence. The moral of this very difficult story seems to be that man needs God's help, but God does not require the help of man.[15] In one thoughtless moment Uzzah could have reduced the sacred ark in the eyes of the people to the impotent level of the idols, which the prophets depicted with such scathing mockery. The same principle appears to operate in the tragedy of Nadab and Abihu, in which Moses speaks for God in explanation of what occurred: "I will show Myself holy among those who are near Me" (Leviticus 10:1–3).

Another fundamental question about the biblical view of God is whether the Godhead is subject to restriction. Biblical teaching seems to imply that such a limitation exists: man's freedom to resist or obey the will of God is a restriction of the Deity's power that is totally unknown in the physical universe. However, this restriction is voluntarily self-imposed by God. In His love for man God has set aside an area of freedom in which man can elect to do right or wrong (Deuteronomy 5:26; 30:17). In rabbinic language: "Everything is in the power of Heaven except the reverence for Heaven" (Ber. 33b). The human power to choose adds a totally new dimension to the relationship between God and man. Man may defect, but when he takes the path of loyalty, he does so from choice, from true love. Without this freedom there can be neither sin nor punishment, neither merit nor reward. The divine humility, which permits human dissent, is also the grace to which the dissenter succumbs in the end. Man is a faithful rebel, who is reconciled with his Maker in the final crowning period of history. God's self-limitation is thus an extension of His creative power.

Other biblical concepts that likewise might be viewed as restrictions of God's infinitude prove not to be real limitations. The association of the Lord with holy places like the Tent of Meeting, the Temple, Zion, or Sinai does not imply that He is not omnipresent. In prophetic vision Isaiah sees the divine train fill the Temple, and at the same time he hears the Seraphim declare: "The whole earth is full of His glory" (6:1–3). God's geographical association or His theophany at a given place signifies consecration of the site, which thus becomes a source of inspiration to man; but no part of the universe exists at any time outside God's presence.

God is sometimes depicted as asking man for information (Genesis 3:9; 4:9); on other occasions He is stated to repent His actions and to be grieved (Genesis 6:6). Alternatively, and more in keeping with the biblical view, is the claim that the Lord knows all (Jeremiah 11:20; Psalms 7:10), and that unlike human beings He does not repent (Numbers 23:19). Genesis 6:6 is not a contradiction of this thesis; its "human" terminology does not signify a diminution of God's omniscience, but rather emphasizes the effect which the moral freedom granted to man has upon God.

In addition to spiritual choice the Creator gives man knowledge. That knowledge sometimes finds expression in magical powers which, in as much as they are "supernatural," constitute a challenge to God's will. In Moses' protracted struggle with Pharaoh, the Egyptians actually pit their magical powers against the Almighty's miracles. In the end they acknowledge their relative weakness and admit that they cannot rival "the finger of God" (Exodus 8:15). Nevertheless the use of all forms of sorcery, even by non-Israelites, is strongly denounced (Isaiah 44:25), and witchcraft is totally forbidden in Israel (Deuteronomy 18:10–11). Related to this negative view of magic, sorcery and witchcraft is the important distinction between magic and miracles which has deep roots in Hebrew monotheism. To the pagan mind magical powers are independent forces to which even the gods must have recourse. Miracles, on the other hand, are regarded in the Bible as a manifestation of God's power and purpose. When performed by a prophet they authenticate his mission (Isaiah 7:11), whereas pagan divination and sorcery are either forms of deception (Isaiah 44:25), or where magic is effective, as in the episode of the witch of Endor (I Samuel 28:7ff), are an abuse of man's God-given knowledge. Moreover, even in those rare cases where magic succeeds it is not proof of an independent realm or power which witchcraft can control; for all power, natural and supernatural, emanates from God.

God is portrayed throughout the Bible as a person, in contradistinction to the pagan idols, who are "dead." He is called the living God (II Kings 19:4, 16). He is neither inanimate nor a philosophical abstraction; He is the living source of all life. Anthropomorphisms abound in the Bible, but it is not by these that the divine personality is to be known. Anthropomorphic figures were intended to help early man grasp ideas that were beyond his philosophic understanding. God's essential personality is primarily reflected in the attributes that motivate His deeds. He is King, Judge, Father, Shepherd, Mentor, Healer, and Redeemer—to mention only a few of His aspects in His relationship to man.

Biblical teachers emphasized different facets of God's character. Amos is conscious of God's justice. Hosea focuses on the Lord's love, and sees forgiveness and compassion as the measures of divinity: "I will not execute My fierce anger . . . for I am God and not man" (11:9). Ezekiel stresses that God does not desire the destruction of the wicked, but that through repentance they may live (18:23). The Torah clearly states: "The Lord passed before him (Moses), and proclaimed, 'The Lord, the Lord, a God merciful and gracious, slow to anger, and abounding in steadfast love and faithfulness, keeping steadfast love for thousands, forgiving iniquity and transgression and sin, but who will by no means clear the guilty . . . '" (Exodus 34:6–7). Maimonides may have been philosophically justified in insisting that God has no attributes and that the epithets applied to Him in the Bible really represent human emotions evoked by His actions (*Guide*, 2:54). The Bible, however, manifests little interest in the speculative approach to the Deity; it teaches practical wisdom and religion-as-life without using catechism or formulated dogmas, and prefers to endow God with personality.[16] Consequently, the divine nature is seen to be composed of both justice and love, because without justice love becomes a form of injustice, but justice in itself is not enough.

To sum up: the biblical conception of God was revolutionary both in its theological and its moral implications. The pagan world may occasionally have glimpsed in primitive form some of the higher truths inherent in Israel's ethical monotheism. Egypt briefly attained monolatry (Akhenaton's heresy); Babylon had a glimmering of a unified cosmic process; Marduk, Shamash, and Aton punished evildoers; and some Greek philosophers commended the imitation of the godhead. Yet no cult in antiquity even remotely approached the elevated conceptions associated with the one God of the Bible. This spiritual revolution eventually brought paganism to an end. It also gave birth to two daughter religions, Christianity and Islam, which, despite their essential differences from Judaism, are deeply rooted in biblical thought and owe a great debt to their mother faith.

God in Talmudic Literature

Abstract philosophical concepts, like those found in the hellenistic Jewish philosopher Philo, and in Greek thought more generally, are foreign to the thought-system of the rabbis who created the Talmud and Midrash. There is, however, a marked tendency among them to present an exalted picture of God, and to avoid expressions that could throw the slightest shadow on the conception of His absolute Oneness. This feature of rabbinic thought can be clearly appreciated if, to begin, we take one example from the Targum. In the Targum, the early Aramaic translations of Scripture, the name of God is frequently rendered *memra* (word) of God. No connection whatsoever is intended between this term and the concept "logos," or the idea of an intermediary between God and the world. In that case the word *memra* would have been used in the Targum to translate such verses as "The Lord sent a word unto Jacob" (Isaiah 9:7); "So shall My word be that goeth forth out of My mouth" (ibid., 55:11); "He sent His word and healed them" (Psalms 107:20). It is precisely in these verses that the Targum employs the word *pitgam* (word) or *nevu'ah* (prophecy). Even in the verse "By the word of the Lord were the heavens made" (Psalms 33:6) "word" is rendered by the Targum as *milta*. Nor is there any mention of the expression *memra* in the Targum's account of creation. We can therefore conclude that this word, which occurs in the Targum but not in the Talmud or the Midrash, was used only to guard against any idea which might diminish the pure conception of the Divinity in the minds of the common people for whom the Targum was intended.

For the same reason many euphemisms are employed as substitutes for the names of God, such as *Ha-Gevurah* (Might), *Rachmana* (the Merciful), *Ha-Kadosh Barukh Hu* (The Holy One, blessed be He); or such terms as *Shamayim* (Heaven), *Ha-Makom* (Omnipresent), *Ribbono shel Olam* (Lord of the Universe), *Mi-she-Amar ve-Hayyah ha-Olam*

17

(He who spoke, and the Universe came into being), *Avinu she-ba-Shamayim* (Our Father in heaven), *Mi-she-Shikken Shemo ba-Bayit ha-Zeh* (He who caused His name to dwell in this house).

The rabbis give special significance to the Tetragrammaton, YHWH—denoting God's attribute of mercy—and to Elohim—which indicates the attribute of judgment. As they understand it, God's mercifulness does not negate the principle of divine justice, but rather complements it and reinforces its efficacy. In analyzing the 13 attributes by which God manifests Himself to us the rabbis point to the positive interaction of mercy and justice in God's relation to the world. Moreover, God is seen to resolve the tension between strict judgment and mercy in favor of the latter. That this was a time-honored distinction is evident from its occurrence in Philo, who lived in Alexandria, as well as in the teachings of the Sages of Palestine. In Philo, however, in conformity with the tradition of the Septuagint that translates the Tetragrammaton by the Greek word κυριος, which corresponds more closely to the concepts of rule and judgment, YHWH is seen to symbolize the attribute of judgment, whereas Elohim (translated in the Septuagint by θεος is a symbol of the attribute of mercy.

The idea of the unity of God, which was widely discussed in non-Jewish circles at the time, receives strong emphasis in the *Aggadah*. The discussion is on the premise that the cosmos, with all the activity it contains, is inconceivable without the existence of a single power that determines and directs it in accordance with a preordained plan and with a definite purpose. In order to give concrete expression to this idea the rabbis of the *aggadah* cite various parables, whose prototypes can be found in Philo and other classical sources. They are particularly fond of the parable of "the ship and the captain," "the building and its owner," or "the building and its director."[17] Just as it is impossible for the ship, for example, to reach its destination without a captain, so administration of the cosmos and of individuals is impossible without a directing and supervising force. Other parables frequently found in the *aggadah* are intended to inspire reverence for the might of God, whose awesomeness is rendered even greater for the very reason that it defies man's powers of comprehension. If the brilliance of the sun blinds the human eye, how much more so the light of God. Man is unable to observe more than a particle of His grandeur and sublimity. The rabbis of the *aggadah* also teach this doctrine of Divine mysteriousness by pointing to the human soul. If a man's own soul, the source of his life, is beyond his intellectual comprehension, how much less can he comprehend the creator of the universe and the source of its life.[18]

It should be emphasized that the recognition of the oneness of God is regarded by the scholars of the Talmud as a cardinal principle of religion for mankind as a whole. Their strongest argument in favor of this view was the fact that among the Noachide laws—the seven precepts held to be binding upon all mankind—is one forbidding idolatry.

One finds no echo in the *aggadah* of the arguments for and against idolatry that occur in the Greek literature of that period. On the contrary, the *aggadah* consistently attacks idolatry even more vigorously than the earlier biblical material. Its sages express contempt and disdain for those who presume to desecrate in a degrading and crude manner that which is most holy in human life—the service of God. In their violent attacks on idolatry the rabbis do not shrink from denouncing with equal vehemence the cult of hellenistic or Roman emperor-worship, a type of idolatry for which Nimrod, Sisera, Sennacherib, Hiram, and Nebuchadnezzar served as prototypes.

If there is any difference between the biblical concept of God and that of the Talmud, it lies in the fact that the God of the Talmud is presented as more accessible to people than the God of the Bible. He is nearer to the masses, to the broken-hearted, to the ordinary person in need of His help. In this sense He appears at times as an even greater epitomization of ethical virtues than the God of Scripture.

The nearness of God is the predominating idea of the Talmud and Midrash. God mourns because of the evil decrees He has pronounced upon Israel; He goes into exile with His children; He studies Torah and gives His view on *halakhic* topics, and is overjoyed if the scholars triumph over him in *halakhah*.[19] Every generation of Israel has been witness to the nearness of God. God revealed Himself at the Red Sea as a warrior; at Sinai as a sage filled with mercy; after the incident of the golden calf as a congregational reader draped in a *tallit* (prayer shawl), instructing the people how to pray and repent. These metaphors are not intended anthropomorphically, but are rather devices for driving home the idea of God's closeness to his people by the use of striking and daring images.

The sages see no difference between God's closeness to Israel in the past and in the present. In both, the idea of the selection of Israel and the greatness of its destiny stands at the very center of the relationship between God and His people. Israel may therefore have complete confidence that God will answer them whenever they seek Him. The concept of God's nearness to man is also enshrined in the central ethical teaching of the Talmud, wherein the rabbis enjoin man to imitate the attributes of God as the essential feature of Jewish religiosity: "Just as He is merciful and compassionate, be thou too merciful and compassionate."

God in Medieval Jewish Philosophy

Medieval Jewish philosophy[20] concentrated largely on problems concerning the existence and nature of God, His knowability, and His relationship to man and the world. Neither the Bible nor rabbinic literature present systematic philosophic treatments of these topics, and it was only under the stimulus of Greek and Arabic philosophy that Jews began to engage in such inquiries in philosophically structured ways. In natural philosophy, metaphysics, and theology Jewish thought was influenced by Arabic Kalām theology and by Arabic versions of Neoplatonism and Aristotelianism.

Fundamental to Jewish philosophic speculation about God was the conviction that human reason is reliable (within its proper limits), and that biblical theology is rational. Thus most medieval Jewish philosophers considered intellectual inquiry essential to a religious life, and were convinced that there could be no real opposition between reason and faith. Consequently, Saadiah Gaon could hold that, "The Bible is not the sole basis of our religion, for in addition to it we have the fountain of reason . . . " (*Book of Beliefs and Opinions,* 3:10). Likewise, Bahya ibn Paquda believed that it is one's religious duty to apply the methods of rational investigation to such questions as God's unity, because of the three avenues which God has given us to know Him and His law, "the first is a sound intellect" (*Hovot ha-Levavot,* Introduction; cf. 1:3). Even Judah Halevi, who distrusted philosophy, said, "Heaven forbid that there should be anything in the Bible to contradict that which is manifest or proved" (*Kuzari,* 1:67). This attitude toward the relationship between reason and faith dominated medieval Jewish philosophy. It reached its highest, most elaborate, and most familiar formulation in the thought of Maimonides, and was reaffirmed by later philosophers, such as Levi ben Gershom and Joseph Albo.

The first task of medieval philosophical theology was to prove the existence of God, though this topic did not always feature at the beginning of contemporary treatises. Of the familiar philosophic arguments for the existence of God, the ontological argument—i.e., that God's existence follows necessarily from a definition of what He is—seems to have been unknown to medieval Jewish thought. Instead, emphasis was placed on the cosmological argument, according to which the existence of God was derived from some contingent aspect of the world, such as the existence of motion or causality. Attention was also given to the teleological argument, according to which the existence of God was derived from the order existing in the world, which it was argued was too purposeful to have arisen accidentally.

The simplest form of the teleological argument—the argument from design—was adopted by Saadiah[21] and Baḥya.[22] Both derided those who claim that the world arose by chance, without an intelligent and purposive creator. They pointed out that it was highly improbable (in their view, incredible) that the extremely complex and delicately balanced order of the universe could have come about accidentally, since even ordinary artifacts are known to require an artisan. A more sophisticated version of this argument was proposed by Levi ben Gershom.[23] From the teleological nature of all existing things, i.e., the fact (as he supposed) that each thing is moved toward the realization of its own proper end, he concluded that all things together move toward their common, ultimate goal. This is the final cause of the world, namely, God.

In Saadiah's versions of the cosmological argument,[24] which closely follow the Kalām, the existence of God is deduced from the creation of the world. He first demonstrated that the world must have been created in time out of nothing, and then showed that such a world could have been created only by an omnipotent God whose essence is an absolute unity. Baḥya followed a similar method. His basic argument was that since the world is composite, it must have been put together at some point in time; it could not have made itself, because nothing can make itself. Hence, it must have been created, and its creator we call God.

The earliest Jewish philosopher to turn away from the Kalām in favor of a stricter Aristotelianism was Abraham ibn Daud (12th Century), and the most prominent by far was Maimonides. In contrast to the followers of the Kalām, Maimonides[25] rejected the view that proofs for the existence of God are contingent on proofs of the creation of the world.

He showed that in principle one cannot prove either that the world is eternal or that it was created, but went on to argue that even if the eternity of the world is conceded, it is still possible to demonstrate the existence of God. The arguments he used, two of which had already been set forth in Abraham ibn Daud's *Emunah Ramah*,[26] are basically cosmological. The most familiar of these is the argument from motion. It posits that since all objects in the world are in motion, and no finite thing can move itself, every motion must perforce be caused by another; but since this leads to an infinite regress, which is unintelligible (according to Maimonides, and medieval thinkers in general), there must be an unmoved mover at the beginning of the series. And this unmoved mover is God.

Another of Maimonides' arguments begins from the fact that the existence of all things in our experience is contingent, i.e., their existence begins and ends in time, so that each thing can be conceived as not existing at some time. Now such a series of contingently existing things is unintelligible for it means that at some time nothing would be, and hence our world could never have begun, unless there is at least one necessarily existing Being whose existence is eternal and independent of all cause, standing behind the entire process. Maimonides, it can be seen, laid great stress on the philosophically interesting conception of God as necessary existence.[27] It should be finally noted that this last argument was the only one that Hasdai Crescas[28] found acceptable, though he was a severe critic of the Aristotelianism of his predecessors.

In addition to the cosmological and teleological arguments, Saadiah and Judah Halevi offered a non-philosophical argument for God's existence that became a standard feature of Jewish theology. Since the revelation at Sinai took place in the presence of 600,000 adults, there is public evidence that places the fact of God's existence beyond all reasonable doubt.[29]

For Judaism, the proof of God's existence is incomplete unless it also establishes His absolute unity. Though Jewish philosophers never deviated from the fixed belief in God's unity they perceived the meaning of this doctrine in different ways. In reflecting on this question, practically all Jewish philosphers of the Middle Ages came to the conclusion that the unity of God necessarily implies that He must be incorporeal. This conclusion then required them to posit figurative or metaphorical interpretations of the many biblical passages that ascribe bodily characteristics to God, because no proper philosophical understanding of God can accept a literal reading of these anthropomorphisms. As Abraham ibn Daud pointed out, Jewish philosophers were particularly sensitive to this problem because many non-Jews held the slanderous opinion that the Jews believe in a corporeal God. This explains why Jewish philosophers of the period devoted so much of their attention to arguments for God's incorporeality and the detailed exegesis of anthropomorphic passages in Scripture. Some scholars even suggest that the primary purpose of Saadiah's philosophical work was to refute all claims of the Deity's corporeality. Likewise, Maimonides began his *Guide of the Perplexed* with an elaborate and comprehensive effort to refute all literal interpretations of biblical passages that speak of God as possessing corporeal features.

Having rejected the literal meaning of biblical statements about God, the next step for these philosophers was to determine what constitutes a legitimate description of God. Can such attributes as goodness, mercy, wisdom, and justice be predicated of Him positively? The bulk of medieval opinion held that one cannot properly say anything positive about God, for two reasons. First, ascribing multiple attributes to Him compromises His unity. Second, human language reflects the limitations of the human perspective, so that describing God by way of human predicates reduces Him to the finiteness of man. Therefore, a majority of the medieval philosophers held that nothing positive can be said about God. However, since there is no choice but to talk about God in some way, despite the limitations of human language, they had to find some interpretation of the divine attributes which would not be a positive one.

The most widely accepted solution was to regard all the essential attributes of the divine nature, such as living, wise, powerful, in the negative sense, so that every seemingly positive assertion about God only says what He is not. For example, the statement, "God is wise," can only mean that He is not ignorant. In this way one may describe God's nature in human language without compromising His unity and without reducing Him to human form. Because God transcends all knowledge and all experience, one can only affirm that He exists, and even this must be interpreted as negating that He *lacks* existence and describes what He is solely in terms of negative attributes. This view was held with minor variations by Saadiah, Bahya, Joseph ibn Zaddik,

Judah Halevi, Ibn Daud, and Maimonides, who gave this doctrine its classical expression.

Besides these descriptions of God's nature which were interpreted as negative attributes, there are others, such as "merciful" and "just," which appear to describe what God does rather than what He is. A positive interpretation of these adjectives was also ruled out on the grounds that a positive predication of these descriptions would likewise impair the correct understanding of God's unity. These descriptions were therefore understood as attributes of action or, put differently, as describing certain divine effects without, however, attempting to account for what specific characteristic or property in the Deity accounts for these effects. Divine unity has thus been safeguarded once more.

Maimonides provided the most subtle and comprehensive treatment of the problem of attributes. While holding vigorously to the negative interpretation of essential attributes, he also followed some of his predecessors in affirming the doctrine of attributes of action.[30] Thus, a great calamity may be interpreted by men as an expression of God's anger, and a seemingly miraculous rescue of men from danger will be understood as an instance of God's love and compassion. These however must be understood as human constructions placed upon God's actions rather than literal statements about God in Himself. Two major figures of the late medieval period rejected the doctrine of negative attributes. Both Levi ben Gershom and Ḥasdai Crescas argued in favor of the view that if God is to be intelligible, then some of His attributes at least must be understood as positive predications. They did not fear that such an approach would compromise the concepts of divine unity and perfection. Moreover, Levi ben Gershom believed that positive predicates could be applied to God literally because their primary meaning derives from their application to God, while their human connotation is secondary. The position of Joseph Albo, the last of the medieval Jewish philosophers, is ambiguous. Although affirming the doctrine of negative attributes, he maintained simultaneously that the divine attributes possess a descriptive-positive significance.[31]

God in the Kabbalah

The kabbalistic view of God is in principle derived from the desire to abolish the contradiction between the two concepts: God's unity and God's existence. The emphasis on God's unity leads the philosopher to reject any attribute, or quality, that might be interpreted as an addition to His unity or, conversely, as evidence for plurality in His nature. On the other hand, the emphasis on God's life which is characteristic of religious faith endangers His unity, since life is variegated by its very nature: it is a process and not a state. As a consequence, in the opinion of many kabbalists, the divinity should be conceived of in the following two fundamental aspects: God in Himself, hidden in the depths of His own being; and the revealed God who creates and preserves his creation. For kabbalists these two aspects are complementary, and not contradictory. Regarding God in Himself, the first aspect suffices, and in the opinion of some,[32] doubt might arise, whether seen thus, anything at all exists apart from God. It is precisely the second view, however, that is required by religious faith: namely, a revealed God who can be recognized by His action and revelation.

God in Himself has neither a name nor any sort of attribute and nothing can be said of Him except that He is. This absolute divinity is usually called in the Kabbalah *Ein-Sof* ("the Infinite"). The *Ein-Sof* lacks all attributes, in a sense even more so than does the God of Maimonides, if it is possible to say this. From the sayings of some early kabbalists, it is apparent that they are careful not even to ascribe personality to God in any sense. Since He is beyond everything—beyond even imagination, thought, or will—nothing can be said of Him that is within the grasp of our thought. He "conceals Himself in the recesses of mystery"; He is "the supreme cause" or "the great existent,"[33] appellations which contain a negation of the personal nature of God.

There were also kabbalists, however, who wished to imbue the *Ein-Sof* with a personality, though they too maintained that this personality was indefinable. According to them, *Ein-Sof* is *ba'al ha-razon,* "the possessor of will,"[34] hence it is possible to say of Him, as do faithful, pious Jews, "Blessed be He"; "May He be blessed and exalted," etc. Both these conceptions are encountered in the pages of the Zohar.[35] In favor of the personal character of *Ein-Sof* was the argument that even without the existence of emanations, the *Sefirot,* and the worlds, His perfection would not lack anything, hence one should not think that God acquired personality through the emanation of the "attributes" or the *Sefirot,* which determine for us the personal character of God. It should be noted that, in the opinion of all kabbalists the *Ein-Sof* is divinity itself, but some kabbalists doubt whether it is also the "God" of traditional religion. For the life of the *Ein-Sof* lies concealed within itself and thus remains unrevealed, whereas the religious man seeks the relevation of this Being and deals with a Deity who has seen fit to reveal Himself and enter into relations with men. This revelation comes about through the emanation of the *Sefirot* which are the domain of the life of the revealed God as compared to the utter isolation of the inaccessible *Ein-Sof.* This emanation is not a necessity, according to the nature of the *Ein-Sof;* it is a voluntary activity of the emanator.

The special difficulty in connection with this view is that according to kabbalistic doctrine the ten *Sefirot* or worlds of heavenly *Parzufim* ("configurations," in the Lurianic Kabbalah) are not created regions distinct from the *Ein-Sof,* like other creations, but are included within the divine unity. The *Sefirot* are also attributes (and some kabbalists explicitly indentify them with the "attributes of action" of the philosophers), but in actual fact they are more than this: they are the various stages at which God reveals Himself at the time of creation; they are His powers and His names. Each quality is one facet of his revelation. Hence every name applied to the divine is merely one of these qualities: *Eheye, Yah, El, Elohim, Zeva'ot, Adonai*—each points to a special aspect in the revealed God, and only the totality of all these qualities exhausts the active life of God. It is this totality, its order and its laws, in which the theology of the Kabbalah is fundamentally interested. Here the personality of God is manifested even if it is not developed: God revealed himself not only at Mount Sinai, but in all things since the beginning of creation, and will continue to reveal

Himself thus until the end of time. His act in creation is His main revelation.

From this position stems a certain dualism in the realm of the revelation of the divine: on the one hand there is *Ein-Sof*, which is transcendental and its traces are not discernable in the creatures; yet on the other hand the traces of the living God, who is embodied in the world of the *Sefirot,* are found in everything and are discernable in everything—at least to the mystic who knows how to interpret the symbolic language of outer reality. God is in His creation, just as He is outside of it. And if the *Sefirot,* active in the creation, are the "souls" and the inwardness of everything, then the *Ein-Sof* is the "soul of all the souls." By the mere fact of being a creature, no creature is divine, though nevertheless something of the divine is revealed in it. The world of the *Sefirot* then is the region of divine revelation *per se,* for the flow of divine life rises and descends in accordance with the stages of the *Sefirot.* The divine revelation also emanates outward into the region of creation, through the "clothing" of the *Sefirot* in the mundane world.[36]

God in Modern Jewish Thought

Jewish thinkers in the modern era have continued to ponder the nature and existence of God. In the modern period such speculation has not only transmitted and developed elements already found in the medieval philosophical tradition, such as the classical proofs for the existence of God; but has reflected as well the new philosophical currents of the times, especially Kantianism, German Idealism and, more recently, existentialism and naturalism.

It is customary to date the modern era in Jewish philosophy as beginning with Moses Mendelssohn (1729–1786). Mendelssohn shared the view current in 18th-century Enlightenment circles that certain metaphysical truths, including some knowledge of God's existence and unity, could be arrived at by rational demonstration and were thus available to all men. In his *Morgenstunden*, Mendelssohn tried to provide a valid metaphysical proof for the existence of God. Significantly, however, Mendelssohn's Deity is not simply the "God of the philosophers," i.e., a highly rarefied abstraction, devoid of personality and of the other essential aspects of the God of Judaism. Rather, Mendelssohn's rational arguments were intended to prove the existence of a God very much like that held sacred by the Jew. Hence, God is seen to possess, as a necessary corollary of His perfection and reality, perfect qualities of personality and morality. Above all else, Mendelssohn's God is a supremely moral and just God who deals with humankind and all of creation according to the highest standards of benevolent justice.

Moreover, according to Mendelssohn's position, these attributes of God are truths of natural religion which are available to all humanity, and through which all people can regulate their lives so as to achieve salvation. Thus, all men can know God, love God, and achieve immortality. Were this not so the Deity would be capricious, arbitrary and less than perfectly just.

Accordingly, Mendelssohn redefined the nature of Judaism. Its unique teaching is now no longer seen as a set of metaphysical truths unavailable to the rest of mankind, but rather as a very special type of revealed legislation—the Torah. What God, in his unfathomable love, has peculiarly revealed to the Jewish people, and what sets Judaism apart from other religions, is the specific body of laws transmitted to Moses at Sinai. This revealed legislation (Torah) is binding solely on the Jewish people by virtue of their special covenantal status vis-à-vis the Lord. As such, Torah is necessary for their salvation, but theirs alone. It does not obligate non-Jews in any way, nor does it impinge on the universal truths of natural religion. For Jews, Torah-law supports and enhances their moral sensitivity, enabling them to live up to the highest standards of universal morality. But it does not transcend or contravene these universal standards.[37]

Mendelssohn attempted to synthesize the demands of Enlightenment metaphysics and moral sensitivity with the uniqueness and continuing validity of Judaism. However, his efforts were destined to have only limited success and Jewish philosophical thought in the modern era is, in the final analysis, primarily influenced by the metaphysical and epistemological program suggested by Kant and the neo-Kantians and by Hegel, Schelling and the Idealists. Kantian thought, with its emphasis on ethics, was compatible and synthesizable with the ethical dimension of Judaism and suggested rich philosophical possibilities in this direction. Similarly, Hegel's, and to a lesser extent Schelling's, metaphysics of spirit suggested a variety of sophisticated metaphysical theories which attempted to portray Judaism as the religion of spirit par excellence.

Among the first figures of the post-Kantian age in Jewish philosophy is Solomon Formstecher (1808–1889). He was especially indebted to the idealist philosopher Schelling for the metaphysical foundations of his theology, though it is open to question how much of Schelling he actually understood. Nonetheless, like Schelling, he conceived God as the "world-soul" which is the ultimate ground of the unity of all reality and that which lies behind all appearances and contingencies. While nature is the open manifestation of God in the world of our experience, the Divinity is also manifest in spirit, and it is in this form alone, i.e., as spirit, that God can truly be conceived. Yet even in this form we do not learn of His essence, which is necessarily beyond all human knowledge. Alternatively, restricting God to the necessarily anthropomorphic conceptions of humankind borders on paganism and the distortion of any true understanding of the Deity. For Formstecher, the "world-soul" is not the world but anterior to and independent of it; God is that autonomous spirit whose absolute freedom is most patently evident in His self-willed activity as creator of the world. Because of His absolute freedom, God is comprehended as the ultimate ethical being and as the ideal that should serve humankind as the source to be imitated and realized in its own ethical life.[38]

Samuel Hirsch (1815–1889) propounded a doctrine similar to that of Formstecher, although he was more dependent on Hegel's system for his inspiration. Even more than Hegel or Formstecher, however, Hirsch emphasized the centrality of ethical considerations in human and divine existence alike. According to Hirsch, man discovers his freedom in his own self-consciousness. He knows himself not as part of nature but as an "I" who confronts the universe in freedom. God is conceived, on the basis of this anthropological model, as absolutely free being reigning supreme over all that exists and, who, simultaneously, is the source and creator of all freedom. Through his deeds, and especially through the miracles which He performs for Israel, God exhibits to all His absolute power and autonomy. Accordingly, for Hirsch, Judaism is, above all, the religion of the spirit, that is, the religion of uncoerced ethical action. Its highest purpose is the actualization of human freedom in the ethical life because only in self-willed moral behavior does man emulate and truly serve God.[39]

Unlike most of his contemporaries, Solomon Ludwig Steinheim (1789–1866) thought that philosophy and religion are radically antithetical. He held that true knowledge of God can be acquired only through revelation, while insisting at the same time that scriptural revelation contradicts the canons of human reason. In Kantian-like manner he argues that if God is conceived in purely rational terms, His freedom must necessarily be denied, because rationality entails causal necessity. The God of reason is subject to causal rules since, even as first cause, He is limited to that which reason finds possible. Such a God is not absolutely free. Neither is He a true creator, for according to the principle that "nothing comes from nothing," He could not have created the world freely and *ex nihilo*. However, this unfree and limited God of reason is not the God of religion, and thus Steinheim rejects reason in favor of revelation. Steinheim denies that the principle of causality applies to God and represents the Divine, as demanded by an authentic religious concept of Him, as the true and free creator who stands above the limitations of rational necessity and nature. This true knowledge of God and His freedom, moreover, comes only from revelation. In addition, it is only through revelation that human beings attain freedom, and then only when they recognize the limits of reason and subordinate their reason to the God of revelation, whose creative freedom provides the sole ground of genuine human existence.[40]

Nachman Krochmal (1785–1840), although living in Eastern Europe, was more fully Hegelian than his Western Jewish contemporaries. They had modified the prevailing philosophical systems to accommodate the personal God of traditional Judaism while Krochmal developed a doctrine bordering on pantheism. He conceived God, in strict Hegelian fashion, as the Absolute Spirit, containing within itself all reality. Now this Absolute Spirit has none of the characteristics of a personal God. Even as cause, He is impersonal: He causes the world to be only in the sense that He is its totality. The world is derived from God through a process of emanation, which Krochmal understood as a form of divine self-limitation. In this, Krochmal was affected by certain elements in medieval Jewish thought and kabbalistic doctrines, which he combined with Hegelianism, in order to generate his own complex metaphysical schema.[41]

Three major thinkers appeared in the late 19th and early 20th centuries: Hermann Cohen (1842–1918), Franz Rosenzweig (1886–1919) and Martin Buber (1878–1965). In his early years Cohen thought of God only as a philosophical construct that served as the guarantor of morality and moral progress. The existence of God, according to this conception, is unverifiable. The Deity is beyond all positive descriptions, and is thought of only as an "idea" in the technical Kantian sense. Though His nature is absolutely unknown to us, God as "idea" is the one essential ground of morality. His reality—at least as an "idea of pure reason"—is thus ultimately affirmed because the alternative of denying morality cannot be accepted. In his later years, however, Cohen adopted more traditional language as he became increasingly concerned with Judaism and with the problem of the relation of religion and philosophy, and in addition came more and more to see "God" as an ontological reality rather than as only an "idea." He then spoke of God as Creator, God of love, and the source of all being, who is absolutely one and unique.[42]

In Franz Rosenzweig's view, God is not known at all through philosophic inquiry or rational demonstration. He is met only in direct existential encounter, which distinguishes true revelation. Mankind, in the anguished consciousness of its own contingent character, encounters God, the creator of the universe. Above all it becomes cognizant of its dependence on God as the Creator, Sustainer, Redeemer and caring father whose love for humankind results in commandments that bind and guide every individual for whom the divine-human encounter is a reality.[43]

Like Rosenzweig, Buber stressed, above all, the personal quality of God. For Buber, God is the Eternal Thou, whom one meets as the supreme partner in the I-Thou dialogue. God as met in this encounter is not the depersonalized Deity of the philosopher-theologian, whose nature is expressed in a set of formal propositions and whom Buber terms an "It." Indeed, no effort to provide a consistent definition of God outside the encounter can succeed. What Buber does tell us, in his poetic-paradoxical way is: "Of course God is the 'wholly Other'; but He is also the wholly Same, the wholly Present. Of course He is the *Mysterium Tremendum* that appears and overthrows; but He is also the mystery of the self-evident, nearer to me than my I" (*I and Thou* (1937), 79).[44]

In the United States, Mordecai Kaplan, the founder of what is called Reconstructionist Judaism (1887–   ), developed a naturalistic view of God in conscious opposition to the traditional, supernatural views. Convinced that modern science makes it impossible to believe in a transcendent, personal God, Kaplan nevertheless saw value in retaining the idea and the appellation "God." He conceived God, following certain tendencies in Kant and even more especially the neo-Kantianism of Hermann Cohen, simply as that power in nature which makes possible the fulfillment of man's legitimate aspirations. Despite his commitment to scientific naturalism, Kaplan believed that the world is so constituted that valid human ideals are supported and helped toward realization by the cosmic process. It is this force making for human salvation that Kaplan called God.[45]

God

In the period following the close of the Second World War, Jewish philosophers have continued to be exercised by the problem of God. However, despite a considerable quantitative output in this sphere, few new insights of importance, with regard to the conception of God have so far emerged. During this period Buber's personalistic dialogical position has unquestionably been the major influence. It is noticeably represented, with slight modifications, in the work of such otherwise diverse thinkers as A. J. Heschel in whose thought it is most notably and profoundly presented; Emil Fackenheim, who uses it to wrestle with problems raised by the Holocaust; Will Herberg, where it is tied to a Jewish "neo-orthodoxy" adapted from the thought of the great Protestant theologian Karl Barth; the orthodox thinker Eliezer Berkovits; and Eugene Borowitz, where it takes on a decidedly Reform viewpoint, to name but a few. In his most recent book, *A Jewish Theology,* Louis Jacobs is the latest to endorse this position and claims to find it "extremely helpful in extracting meaning from the whole concept of God as a person."[46]

The only serious alternative to this existentialist approach to God in recent Jewish thought has been a continuation of Mordecai Kaplan's naturalism. Kaplan himself has continued to write on this theme and it has been adapted by a variety of younger Reform and Reconstructionist thinkers. Most notable in this respect is the work of rabbis Levi Olan of Dallas and Roland Gittelsohn of Boston, and to a lesser degree the work of Alan Miller, I. Eisenstadt and J. Cohen.

Lastly, and completely anachronistic, is the position of Richard Rubinstein, a self-professed "God is dead" theologian who, on the basis of his sensitive and serious reflections on the Nazi Holocaust, felt himself forced to the conclusion that "God is dead" if He did not prevent Auschwitz. Rubinstein's position, however, has been widely and tellingly criticized, and he has found few followers.[47]

Names of God

Various Hebrew terms are used for God in the Bible.[48] Some of these are employed in both the generic and specific sense; others are used only as the personal name of the God of Israel. Most of these terms were employed also by the Canaanites, to designate their pagan gods. This is not surprising; since on settling in the Promised Land the Patriarchs and early Israelites made "the language of Canaan" their own (Isaiah 19:18), the Hebrew language would naturally use the Canaanite vocabulary for terms designating their own Deity. It must be noted, however, that in the Bible these various terms, when used by the Israelites to designate their own Deity, refer to one and the same god, the sole God of Israel. At least from the time of Moses on this is certainly true, and it is probably true even from the time of Abraham. When Joshua told the tribes of Israel, assembled at Shechem, that their ancestors had "served other gods" (Joshua 24:2), he was referring to the ancestors of Abraham, as is clear from the context. The God who identified Himself to Moses as YHWH said He was "the God of Abraham, the God of Isaac, and the God of Jacob" (Exodus 3:6). Therefore, the terms "the Fear of Isaac" or perhaps rather, "the Kinsman of Isaac" and "the Mighty One of Jacob" are synonymous with YHWH, even though these terms may have been specific titles by which the God of these patriarchs was known as their individual tutelary deity.[49]

EL

The oldest Semitic term for God is 'el, the etymology of which is obscure. It is thought that the term may derive from a root 'yl or 'wl, meaning "to be powerful," but the converse may also be true since power is an essential element in the concept of deity.

35

In the Bible *el* is seldom used as the personal name of God, e.g., *El-Elohei-Yisrael*, "El, the God of [the Patriarch] Israel" (Genesis 33:20). Almost always, *el* is an appellative, with about the same semantic range as *elohim*. In contrast, however, to the extremely common word *elohim*, *el* occurs relatively infrequently, except in archaic or archaizing poetry, as in Job and Psalms. But *el* and, in rare instances, *elohim* are used when the terms are modified by one or more adjectives, e.g., "an impassioned God," as for example in Exodus 20:5, or "a God compassionate and gracious" as in Exodus 34:6. Moreover, it is *el*, not *elohim*, which is employed in contrasting the Divinity with humankind, as for example in Numbers 23:19 and Isaiah 31:3. In theophoric names, it is once again *el*, not *elohim*, that often serves as the prefatory element, e.g., Elijah, Elisha, and Elihu, and more frequently as the suffix, e.g., Israel, Ishmael, and Samuel. Of special interest are the divine names of which *el* is the initial component.

EL ELYON

The Hebrew word *elyon* is an adjective meaning "higher, upper." When used in reference to God, the word can rightly be translated as "Most High." Since, as a lone reference to the Deity *elyon* is never preceded by the definite article *ha*-("the"), it must have been regarded as a proper noun, a name of God. Thus, it can be used as a divine name meaning "the Most High," as in Deuteronomy 32:8, or in parallelism with the Tetragrammaton YHWH (Psalms 18:14), *El* (Numbers 24:16) and *Shaddai* (Psalms 91:1). Whereas for the pagans, furthermore, the term signified the god who reigned supreme in the Pantheon, in Israel it referred to the transcendent nature of the one true God.[50]

EL OLAM

According to Genesis 21:33, "Abraham planted a tamarisk at Beer-Sheba, and invoked there the name of YHWH, the everlasting God." The Hebrew for "the Everlasting God" is *el olam*, literally, "the God of an indefinitely long time." This may have been the title of *El* as worshiped at the local shrine of Beer-Sheba.

EL SHADDAI

According to the Torah YHWH also "appeared to Abraham, Isaac, and Jacob as *El Shaddai* (Exodus 6:3). The traditional English rendering of the obscure Hebrew term *El Shaddai* as "God Almighty" reflects ancient usage. The Septuagint renders *Shaddai* as *Pantokrator,* "All-powerful"; this is followed by the Vulgate's *Omnipotens,* "Omnipotent." This connotation is apparently based on an ancient rabbinic interpretation which renders *sha* as "who," and *dai* as "enough," and thus translates the appellative as "He who is self-sufficient."[51]

In the Bible the full name, *El Shaddai,* is used only in connection with Abraham, Isaac and Jacob.[52] However, the latter word alone occurs as God's name in the ancient oracles of Balaam (Numbers 24:4), in poetic passages such as Isaiah 13:6 and Ezekiel 1:24, and 31 times in Job. Moreover, Shaddai is an element in ancient Israelite names, such as Ammishaddai ("My Kinsman is Shaddai"), and Zurishaddai ("My Rock is Shaddai"), both mentioned in Numbers 1.

EL BERIT

The divine name *El Berit,* "God of the Covenant," occurs only in Judges 9:46, where mention is made of "the house [i.e., temple] of *El Berit*" at Shechem.

ELOHA, ELOHIM

The word *eloha,* "God," and its plural, *elohim,* is apparently a lengthened form of *El.* The singular, *eloha,* is of relatively rare occurrence in the Bible outside of Job, where it appears about forty times. It is very seldom used in reference to a pagan god and then only in a late period as in Daniel 11:37ff. In all other cases it refers to the God of Israel. *Elohim,* however, is used not only in the plural sense as in Exodus 12:12 and 18:11, but also of an individual pagan deity as seen in Judges 11:24; in one case—Kings 11:15—it even denotes a "goddess."

As a reference to Israel's "God" it finds extremely frequent expression—more than 2,000 times—and often with the definite article, as in *ha-elohim,* "the (true) God." Occasionally, the plural form *elohim,* even when used of the God of Israel, is construed with a plural verb or adjective, as for example in Genesis 20:13, especially in the expression *elohim ḥayyim*, "the living God." In the vast majority of cases, however, the plural form is treated as if it were a singular noun.[53]

ADONAI

The Hebrew word *adon* is correctly rendered in English as "lord." In the Bible it often denotes any human being in a position of authority, such as the ruler of a country (Genesis 42:30). In formal polite style a man, not necessarily a superior, was also addressed as "my lord," *adoni*, as in Genesis 23:6. Since God is "Lord [*adon*] of all the earth" He is addressed and spoken of as *Adonai*, literally "my Lord."

YHWH

The personal name of the God of Israel is written in the Hebrew Bible with the four consonants YHWH and is referred to as the "Tetragrammaton." At least until the destruction of the First Temple in 586 B.C.E. this name was regularly pronounced with its proper vowels, as is clear from the Lachish Letters[54] written shortly before that date. But by the third century B.C.E., if not earlier, the pronounciation of the name YHWH was being avoided. *Adonai*, "the Lord," was substituted for it. This is evidenced by the use of the Greek word *Kyrios*, "Lord," for YHWH in the Septuagint, the translation of the Hebrew Scriptures begun by Greek-speaking Jews during that century. Where the combined form *Adonai* YHWH occurs in the Bible, this was read as *Adonai Elohim*, "Lord God."[55]

In the early Middle Ages, when the consonantal text of the Bible was supplied with vowel points to facilitate its correct traditional reading, the vowel points for *Adonai* (with one variation—a *sheva* with the first *yod* of YHWH instead of the *ḥataf-pataḥ* under the *aleph* of *Adonai*) were used for YHWH, thus producing the form YeHoWaH. When Christian scholars of Europe embarked on their study of Hebrew, they failed to grasp the meaning of the combined form, and thus introduced the hybrid "*Jehovah*." In order to avoid pronouncing even the sacred name *Adonai* for YHWH, the custom was later introduced of saying simply in Hebrew *ha-Shem* (or in Aramaic, *Shema*, "the Name") even in such an expression as that in Psalms 118:26, "Blessed be he that cometh in the name of YHWH" (leading to the repetitious *be-shem ha-shem* in Hebrew). The avoidance of pronouncing the name YHWH is generally ascribed to a sense of reverence. However, it may have been caused by a misunderstanding of the Third Commandment as meaning "Thou shalt not take the name of YHWH thy God in vain," whereas it must really be interpreted as "You shall not swear falsely by the name of YHWH your God."

The true pronunciation of the name YHWH was never lost despite popular views to the contrary. Several early Greek writers of the Christian Church testify that the name was pronounced *Yahweh*. This is confirmed, at least for the vowel of the first syllable of the name, by the shorter form *Yah*, which is sometimes used in poetry as in Exodus 15:2 and the *-yahu* or *-yah* that serves as the final syllable in very many Hebrew names. In the opinion of many scholars, YHWH is a verbal form of the root *hwh*, which is an older variant of the root *hyh* "to be." The vowel of the first syllable shows that the verb is used in the form of a future-present causative *hiph'il*, and must therefore mean "He causes to be, He brings into existence." The explanation of the name, as given in Exodus 3:14, *Ehyeh-Asher-Ehyeh*, as "I will be what I will be," offers a folk etymology, common in biblical explanations of names, rather than a strictly scientific one.[56]

Like many other Hebrew names in the Bible, the name *Yahweh* is no doubt a shortened form of what was originally a longer name. It has been suggested that the original, full form of the name was something like *Yahweh-Asher-Yihweh*, "He brings into existence whatever exists"; or *Yahweh Zeva'ot* (I Samuel 1:3, 11), which really means "He brings the hosts [of heaven? or of Israel?] into existence." "The Lord of Hosts," the traditional translation of the latter name, is doubtful.

DIVINE EPITHETS

Besides the above-mentioned divine names, the God of Israel is also given several epithets or appellatives that are descriptive of His nature. Only a few of these can be mentioned here.

Basic to Israel's concept of its God is the divine title given Him of "Creator of heaven and earth" in Genesis 14:19. He is also called "the Creator of Israel" (Isaiah 43:15); for His creative activity was regarded, not only as His initial bringing of the world into existence, but also as indicating His continuous governing of the world. To stress His transcendent sanctity, He is called "the Holy One" in Isaiah 40:25; and especially, "the Holy One of Israel," as for example in Isaiah 1:4. In order to indicate His loving care for His flock, His Chosen People, He is known as "the Shepherd of Israel" in Psalms 80:2, or "the Rock," in Deuteronomy 33:4, thus comparing Him to a high crag, symbolic of refuge and safety.

The God of Israel is very often spoken of, or addressed as "King" or "King of Israel," thus describing His sovereign rule over His Chosen People, and his power to give them peace, happiness and salvation. The so-called "Enthronement Psalms of YHWH" (Psalms 47:93;96–99) emphasize this aspect of the divine kingship over Israel. Prophetic oracles are proclaimed as pronouncements made by His Royal Majesty as one can see for example in Jeremiah 46:18. It should also be noted that although before the time of Saul, Israel generally rejected the idea of human kingship as an encroachment on the Lord's sole rule over his people, at a later period the Chronicler did not hesitate to speak of the Davidic kings as the Lord's representatives, seated on the royal "throne of YHWH" (i.e., I Chronicles 17:14).[57]

IN THE TALMUD

The subject of the names of God in the Talmud must be considered under two heads, the prohibition of using the biblical divine names, and the additional names evolved by the rabbis.

The prohibition on employing the names of God applies both to their pronunciation and committal to writing, apart from their use in sacred writings. In addition, there was a special prohibition against the pronunciation of the name of God as represented by the Tetragrammaton, which could be pronounced by the high priest only once a year on the Day of Atonement in the Holy of Holies, and in the Temple by the priests when they recited the Priestly Blessing.[58] As the Talmud expresses it: "Not as I am written am I pronounced. I am written *yod he vav he* (YHWH) and I am pronounced *alef dalet (Adonai)."* The prohibition of committing the names of God to secular writings belongs to a different category. Basing themselves on Deuteronomy 12:4, the Sifrei and the Talmud have ruled that it is forbidden to erase the name of God from a written document, and since any paper upon which that name appears might be discarded and thus "erased," it is forbidden to write the name explicitly.

The Talmud gives an interesting historical note with regard to one aspect of this. Among the decrees of the Syrians during the persecutions of Antiochus Epiphanes (175–167 B.C.E.) was one forbidding the mention of the name of God. The Hasmonean victors not only naturally repealed the decree, but demonstratively ordained that the divine name be entered even in monetary bonds, the opening formula being "In such and such a year of Johanan, high priest to the Most High God." The rabbis, however, forbade this practice since "tomorrow a man will pay his debt and the bond (with the name of God) will be discarded on a dunghill"; the day of the prohibition was actually made an annual festival.

It is, however, specifically stated that this prohibition refers only to seven biblical names of God. They are *El, Elohim* (also with personal suffixes), *Ehyah-Asher-Ehyeh, Adonai,* the Tetragrammaton, *Shaddai* and *Zeva'ot.* The passage in *Shevuot* states explicitly that all other names and attribute-descriptions of God may be freely written. Despite this, it became the accepted custom among Orthodox Jews to use variations of most of those names in speech, particularly *Elokim* for *Elohim,* and *Ha-Shem* (('the Name" and, for reasons of assonance, *Adoshem*) for *Adonai.* The adoption of *Ha-Shem* is probably due to a misunderstanding of a passage in the liturgy of the Day of Atonement, the *Avodah.* It includes the high priest's confessional formula on that day. Since on that occasion he uttered the Ineffable Name, the text has "Oh, *Ha-Shem,* I have sinned," etc. The meaning is probably "O [here he mentioned the Ineffable Name] I have sinned," and from this developed the custom of using *Ha-Shem* for *Adonai,* which is in itself a substitute for the Tetragrammaton.[59]

The rabbis evolved a number of additional names of God. All of them, without exception, are references to His attributes, but curiously enough they are not included in the list of the permitted names enumerated in the passage in *Shevuot:* "the Great, the Mighty, the Revered, the Majestic," etc. The most common is *Ha-Kadosh barukh Hu* ("the Holy One, blessed be He"; in Aramaic, *Kudsha berikh Hu*). It is an abbreviation of "the Supreme King of kings, the Holy one blessed be He." The full formula is found in Mishnah *Sanhedrin* 4:5 and *Avot* 3:1 but more often the abbreviation is found; it is by far the most common appellation of God in the Midrash.[60] Another name is *Ribbono shel Olam* ("Sovereign of the Universe"), normally used as an introduction to a supplication, as in the prayer of *Honi ha-Me'aggel* for rain, recorded in *Ta'anit* 3:8.

One of the most interesting names is *Ha-Makom,* which literally means "the place," i.e., the Omnipresent, and it is explained in the Midrash: "R. Huna in the name of R. Ammi said, 'Why do we use a circumlocution for the name of the Holy One, blessed be He, and call him *Makom*? Because He is the place of His world, but this world is not His [only] place'" (Gen. R. 68:49). The name *Ha-Rahaman* ("the All-Merciful") is commonly used in the liturgy, particularly in the Grace after Meals. In the Talmud, the Aramaic form, *Rahmana,* is also present, and it is found in several prayers from the geonic period. So also *Shamayim* ("heaven") as in *Yirat Shamayim* ("Fear of God"), and *Avinu she-ba-Shamayim* ("Our Father in Heaven"). According to the Talmud, *Shalom* ("Peace") is also one of the names of God, as is the word *Ani* ("I") as in Hillel's statement "If *Ani* is here, all is here."[61]

In *Kiddushin* (71a) reference is made to a "Name of 12 letters" and a "Name of 42 letters." Of the former, it is stated that "it used to be entrusted to everyone, but when unruly men increased, it was confided only to the pious of the priesthood and they used to pronounce it indistinctly ("swallowed it") while their priestly brethren were chanting the benediction." R. Tarfon, who was a *kohen* (of priestly descent), states that he once heard the high priest thus muttering it. Similarly the 42-lettered Name is entrusted only to those of exceptionally high moral character. Rashi in his comment on this passage states that these names have been lost. According to the kabbalists the prayer *Anna be-Kho'ah,* found in the prayer-book, and consisting of 42 words, is connected with this latter name. Finally we repeat what has been mentioned earlier in this study: to the rabbis it is definite that the Tetragrammaton denotes God in His attribute of mercy and *Elohim* (which can mean a "judge," as in Exodus 22:8, 27) in His attribute of justice.

IN MEDIEVAL JEWISH PHILOSOPHY

The multiplicity of divine appellations in the Bible posed a special problem for medieval Jewish philosophers. Concerned to defend and explicate God's absolute unity, they found it necessary to treat these names in a way that eliminates any suggestion of plurality in God's being. To achieve this they either reduced the multiple names to a single common meaning or attempted to show that, among the numerous designations, one alone was the proper and exclusive name of God. Saadiah Gaon held that the two most widely used scriptural names, YHWH and *Elohim* have a single meaning. This is in marked contrast to the general talmudic teaching that one name stands for God's attribute of mercy and the other for His attribute of justice. Judah Halevi, Abraham ibn Daud, Maimonides, and Joseph Albo, all emphasized the Tetragrammaton as the only proper name of God. Thus Judah Halevi argues that all the other names "are predicates and attributive descriptions, derived from the way His creatures are affected by His decrees and measures" (Kuzari, 2:2; 4:1–3).

Maimonides declared that, except for YHWH, "All the names of God that are to be found in any of the books derive from actions" but only the Tetragrammaton "gives a clear and unequivocal indication of His essence," a view which is shared by Albo.[62] For Halevi the meaning of YHWH is hidden, and for Ibn Daud it refers to God as master of the universe. The philosphers identified God as creator, first cause, prime mover, first being, or necessary existence, but none of these technical philosophic terms can be considered names of God.

IN THE KABBALAH

All kabbalistic systems have their origin in a fundamental distinction regarding the problem of the Divine. In the abstract, it is possible to think of the Deity either as God in Himself with reference to His own nature or as God in His relation to His creation. However, all kabbalists agree that no religious knowledge of God, even of the most exalted kind, can be gained except through contemplation of the relationship of God vis-à-vis His creation. God in Himself, the absolute Essence, lies beyond any speculative or even ecstatic comprehension.

The attitude of the Kabbalah toward God may be defined as a mystical agnosticism, formulated in a more or less extreme way and close to the standpoint of Neoplatonism. In order to express this unknowable aspect of the Divine the early kabbalists of Provence and Spain coined the term *Ein-Sof* (lit. "without end" or "Infinite"). This expression cannot be traced to a translation of a Latin or Arabic philosophical term. Rather it is a hypostatization which, in contexts dealing with the infinity of God or with His thought that "extends without end" *(le-ein sof* or *ad le-ein sof)*, treats the adverbial relation as if it were a noun and uses this as a technical term.

In this sense *Ein-Sof* first appears in the writings of Isaac the Blind and his disciples, particularly in the works of Azriel of Gerona, and later in the Zohar, the *Ma'arekhet ha-Elohut,* and writings of that period. While the kabbalists were still aware of the origin of the term they did not use it with the definite article, but treated it as a proper noun; it was only from 1300 onward that they began to speak of *ha-Ein-Sof* (the *Ein-Sof)* as well, and to generally identify it with other common epithets for the Divine. This later usage, which spread through all the kabbalistic literature, indicates a distinct personal and theistic concept in contrast to the vacillation between an idea of this nature and a neutral, impersonal concept of *Ein-Sof* apparent in some of the earlier sources. At the outset it was unclear whether the term *Ein-Sof* referred to "Him who has no end" or to *"that* which has no end." This latter, neutral aspect was emphasized by stressing that *Ein-Sof* should not be qualified by any of the attributes or personal epithets of God found in Scripture, nor should such eulogies as *Barukh Hu* or *Yitbarakh* (found only in later literature) be added to it. In fact, however, there were various attitudes to the nature of *Ein-Sof* from the very beginning; Azriel of Gerona, for example, tended toward the impersonal interpretation of the term, while Asher ben David employed it in a distinctly personal and theistic way.

Other terms or images signifying the domain of the hidden God that lies beyond any impulse toward creation occur in the writings of the Gerona kabbalists and in the literature of the speculative school. Examples of these terms are *mah she-ein ha-mahshavah masseget* ("that which thought cannot attain" sometimes used also to describe the first emanation); *ha-or ha-mit'allem* ("the concealed light"); *seter ha-ta'alumah* ("the concealment of secrecy"); *yitron* ("superfluity"—apparently as a translation of the neoplatonic term *hyperousia*); *ha-aḥdut ha-shavah* ("indistinguishable unity," in the sense of a unity in which all opposites are equal and in which there is no differentiation); or even simply *ha-mahut* ("the essence"). The factor common to all these terms is that *Ein-Sof* and its synonyms indicate a Deity above or beyond thought.

A certain wavering between the personal and the neutral approach to the concept of *Ein-Sof* is also detectable in the main part of the Zohar with its neutral stress, while in the later stratum, in the *Ra'aya Meheimna* and the *Tikkunim,* a personal concept is paramount. *Ein-Sof* is often (not always) identified with the Aristotelian "cause of all causes," and, through the kabbalistic use of neoplatonic idiom, with the "root of all roots." While all the foregoing definitions have a common negative element, occasionally one encounters in the Zohar a remarkable positive designation which applies the term *Ein-Sof* to the nine lights of thought shining forth from the Divine Thought, thus bringing *Ein-Sof* out of its concealment and down to a more humble level of emanation.

In addition to these, and still other references to the unknowable God, the kabbalists also associated God's names with the various aspects of His being which were progressively revealed in the unfolding of the *Sefirot.* Thus the *Sefirot* were conceived both as attributes and names of God. In this way a set of equivalences between the *Sefirot* and the various names of God was established; it is usually presented in this manner:

	Ehyeh	
YHWH		*Yah*
(vocalized as *Elohim*)		
Elohim		*El*
	YHWH	
Elohim Ẓeva'ot		*YHWH Ẓeva'ot*
	El Ḥai or *Shaddai*	
	Adonai	

According to the Kabbalah these are "the ten names which must not be erased," seven of which are mentioned in the Talmud *(Shevuot,* 35a), and compared with them all other names are mere epithets. The Zohar designates *Shaddai* as the name particularly related to the *Sefirah Yesod,* while Joseph Gikatilla associates this *Sefirah* with *El Ḥai.*

Finally, the kabbalists also used a variety of special magical names of God composed of long combinations of Hebrew letters. There were "names" containing 45, 52, 63 and 72 letters; all were composed of various elaborations of the Tetragrammaton according to the numerical value of the four possible spellings of the fully written names of its letters, viz., the "name" 45 (יוד, הא, ואו, הא), the name 52 (הה, וו, הה

יוד), the "name" 63 (הי, ואו, הי, יוד) and the "name" 72 (הא, ויו, הי, יוד).
The kabbalists also provided alternative explanations for these "names,"
but the numerical values remained constant. For example, another way
of arriving at the "name" 45 was deriving it from Proverbs 30:4, "What
(mah) is His name," 45 being the numerical value of the Hebrew word
mah. Or again the "name" 72 was arrived at by a combination of the
numbers of the letters in the names of the twelve tribes, the Patriarchs,
and the nine letters of the words *shivtei Yisrael* ("The Tribes of Israel").

IN MODEN JEWISH PHILOSOPHY

From Moses Mendelssohn through Martin Buber, modern Jewish
philosophy exhibits two main tendencies with respect to the names of
God. One line, moving from Mendelssohn through such thinkers as
Solomon Formstecher, Samuel Hirsh, Nachman Krochmal, and Hermann Cohen, treats the names of God as primarily metaphysical. In his
German translation of the Bible, Mendelssohn renders YHWH as "the
Eternal"; Formstecher speaks of God as the "World-Soul"; and
Krochmal conceives Him as "Absolute Spirit." Hermann Cohen, in an
extensive discussion of the traditional divine names, interprets all of
them as pointing to God's unity and uniqueness. YHWH refers to God
as absolute Being; *Ehyeh-Asher-Ehyeh* (Exodus 3:14) relates to His eternal and unchanging nature; and *Shekhinah,* translated by Cohen as
"Absolute Cause," refers to God's absolute power.

In contrast, Franz Rosenzweig and Martin Buber view the names as
primarily religious and personalistic. In their translation of the Bible,
they render YHWH by the personal pronouns YOU or HE. *Ehyeh*
denotes the God who is ever-present to man and constantly participates
in human concerns. Thus, Buber interprets Exodus 3:14 as saying, "I
again and again stand by those whom I befriend; and I would have you
know indeed that I befriend you." They consider the philosophic interpretation of the names as seriously inadequate in its failure to grasp
the personal-religious reality which is fundamental to Judaism.

The Rosenzweig-Buber position has been widely influential and is
generally accepted by all their disciples and all the modern Jewish existentialist theologians, ranging from A. J. Heschel to Louis Jacobs and
Eugene Borowitz.

Veering off in a radically different direction, Mordecai Kaplan developed what he considered to be a purely naturalistic conception of God which, it was contended, was consistent with modern science and values. He refers to Him as "The Power that makes for salvation" and interprets this as "The Power that makes for the fulfillment of all valid ideals." This position has been generally adopted by Reconstructionists, though it has been severely criticized by Eliezer Berkovits and Emil Fackenheim. Kaplan's naturalistic stand has also been further and more radically developed by Levi Olan and Roland Gittelsohn.[63]

Attributes of God

The discussion in Jewish philosophy of the attributes or predicates (Hebrew, *te'arim;* Arabic, *sifat*) of God is based on the problem of how God, whose essence is presumed to be unknowable and who was said to transcend all human categories of thought and language, can be spoken of in meaningful terms.

As a philosophical problem this issue dates from Philo, who was the first to introduce the doctrine of the unknowability of God, which he claimed to derive from the Bible.[64] Philo interprets Moses' prayer, "Reveal Thyself to me" (according to the Septuagint version of Ex. 33:18) as a plea for a knowledge of God's essence, and God's answer to Moses' plea as pointing out that only His existence, and not His essence, can be known.[65] Philo argues that from God's unlikeness to any other being follows His simplicity, i.e., essential unity, indivisibility, and His being "without quality," i.e., without "accidents" such as inhere in corporeal objects and without "form," such as inheres in matter. Moreover, God belongs to no class. He is without genus or species, and consequently no concept can be formed of Him.[66] The scriptural passages describing God in anthropomorphic and anthropopathic terms must, therefore, be understood as serving a merely pedagogical purpose aimed at the spiritual education of men. Since God's essence is unknowable, all the predicates of God in Scripture describe Him only by what is known of Him through the proofs of His existence, and they refer only to the causal relation of God to the world.

Philo bequeathed this problem to future western thought and the philosophical discussion of the problem of God's attributes continued in the early Christian centuries and especially gained new impetus under the influence of Muslim philosophy, especially the Kalām school.

The most elaborate Jewish Kalām discussion of attributes is found in Saadiah's *Emunot ve-De'ot (Book of Beliefs and Opinions)*. Saadiah finds in Scripture the following attributes assigned to God: He is one, living, omnipotent, omniscient, and unlike any other being. His unity and incomparibility follow logically from the notion of "Creator" (1:1), as do the notions of existence, omnipotence, omniscience. The latter three attributes do not imply diversity in God. Just as the attribute of "Creator" does not add anything to the essence of God, but merely expresses His causal relation to the world, so do these three attributes, which explain the term Creator, add nothing to His essence, but merely denote the existence of a world created by Him (1:4). It would seem to follow that these three attributes are active, not essential attributes, but this is not Saadiah's ultimate meaning. Since these attributes, when applied to God (unlike the case when they are applied to man) are not distinct from God's essence, Saadiah upholds positive essential attributes (existence, omniscience, omnipotence), but reduces their meaning to that of God's causality as Creator. He does, however, distinguish between these essential attributes and attributes of action. Attributes such as merciful, gracious, jealous, and avenging are attributes of action in the sense that they express a certain affection for the creatures produced by the causality of God (1:12).

As compared to Kalamic thought, Jewish neoplatonic writings are marked by a new emphasis on the unity of God. At the same time the notion of the will of God was injected into the discussion. The extant writings of Isaac Israeli, the earliest Jewish neoplatonist, contain few references to the attributes[67] and make little contribution to the discussion. However, somewhat later, the most important Jewish neoplatonist Solomon ibn Gabirol expressed more explicit and more interesting views on the subject. In his *Mekor Hayyim*[68] and his poem *Keter Malkhut,* Ibn Gabirol emphasizes God's unity (*Mekor Ḥayyim,* 3:4, 5:30). Negative terms are used particularly with reference to the "mystery" *(sod)* of the divine unity, concerning which we do not know "what it is," but which may be described as unaffected by plurality or change, or by attribute *(to'ar)* and designation *(kinnui)*. His negative interpretation of the divine attributes is, however, complicated by Ibn Gabirol's doctrine that matter and form, the two principles which constitute all created beings, derive from the essence and the will of God respectively. Matter (which is originally "spiritual" matter) proceeds from the very essence of God, and form is impressed upon, and diffused in matter by virtue of God's will. According to Ibn Gabirol's view the divine will tends to assume the

character of an intermediate between God and the world and, in certain
respects, shares in the divine absoluteness (*ibid.,* 5:37–9; 4:20).

Bahya ibn Paquda's elaborate treatment of the attributes in the
"Sha'ar ha-Yihud" ("Chapter on Unity") of his *Hovot ha-Levavot* starts
from the thesis that from the existence and order of the universe, the existence of one single creator can be inferred. Like Aristotle
(*Metaphysics,* 5, 5, 1015b, 16–7), Bahya distinguishes between the "accidental" and "absolute" senses of the term "one" and concludes that
the truly One is God alone, who is incomparable and unique (1:8–9).
Having established God's unity in the neoplatonic sense, Bahya
proceeds to discuss the meaning of the attributes, which he holds may
again be classified under two heads: essential attributes and attributes
of action. The essential attributes are existence, unity, and eternity.
However, these attributes do not imply a plurality in God's essence, but
must be interpreted negatively. That is, God is not nonexistent: there is
no plurality in Him; He is not a created thing. Alternatively the attributes of action found in the Bible which describe God's actions either
in anthropomorphic terms or in terms of corporeal motions and acts are
used by Scripture in order to establish a belief in God in the souls of
men (1:10), i.e., for pedagogical reasons.

In Jewish Aristotelianism the discussion of the divine attributes
reached a new level, reflecting the influence of Avicenna and, subsequently, of the greatest Arab philosopher Averroes. The notion of God
as the "necessary being" which was introduced by the Arabic thinker
Avicenna, contested by the Arabic thinker al Ghazali, and modified by
the Arabic thinker Averroes replaced, in some measure, the neoplatonic
concept of the One. Moreover, the problem of the meaning of terms like
"one" and "being" came to the fore, for even though these terms were
predicated of God in a peculiar sense, they seemed also to bear a
generic sense in which they were predicated of other beings as well. Al-
Fārābī held the notion that common terms of this kind are predicated of
God "firstly" or "in a prior manner," and of other beings "secondly" or
"in a posterior manner," i.e., that the perfections implied by the particular predicate derive from God as their cause or exemplar. According
to Avicenna, the term "one" is predicated of God and other beings "in
an ambiguous sense,"[69] which implies the doctrine of the "analogy" of
being, a view which was not adopted by the first Jewish Aristotelians.
Abraham ibn Daud and Maimonides substituted for Avicenna's

doctrine the notion that terms like "one" have a purely homonymous character, that is, that terms that are applied to both God and other beings share only the name but not the meaning of the predicate. Only under the influence of Averroes did the doctrine of the "analogy" of being eventually command the assent of Jewish Aristotelians, most notably Levi b. Gershom (see below). Abraham ibn Daud, in his *Emunah Ramah*,[70] follows Avicenna in establishing the existence of God as "the necessary being" in the sense that God's essence necessarily implies His existence, while in the case of all other beings their existence is only "possible" and extrinsic to their essence. True unity is therefore established in the case of God alone by virtue of His intrinsic necessary existence. Ibn Daud enumerated seven positive attributes: unity, truth, existence, omniscience, will, omnipotence, and being. These neither imply definitions of God nor constitute a plurality in Him. They have to be interpreted as either negations or as asserting God's causality. Unlike Avicenna, he asserts the homonymity of the term "being" in the case of God as compared with its application to all other beings. God's being is true and necessary because it alone has an underived and independent existence. The other eight attributes are explained by Ibn Daud as negative.

The most incisive treatment of the problem of attributes is found in Maimonides' *Guide of the Perplexed* (1: 50–60). Maimonides argues that every attribute predicated of God is an attribute of action or, if the attribute is intended for the apprehension of His essence and not of His action, it signifies the negation or privation of the attribute in question (1: 58). There cannot be affirmative essential attributes, i.e., affirmative predications relating to the essence of God which is unknowable (1:60). The anthropomorphic and anthropopathic descriptions of God in Scripture have to be understood as attributes of action, or as assertions of God's absolute perfection (1:53).

Novel elements in Maimonides' discussion of attributes are his fivefold classification of them; his rejection of relational attributes; and his interpretation of negative attributes. Maimonides lists and discusses five kinds of attributes: (1) A thing may have its definition and through it its essence is predicated of it. In the case of God, who cannot be defined, this kind of attribute is impossible. (2) A part of a definition may be predicated. This, again, is inapplicable to God; for if He had a part of an essence, His essence would be composite. (3) A quality subsisting in an essence may be predicated. None of the genera of quality is applicable to God. (4) A relation to something other than itself (to time, place, or another individual) may be predicated of a thing. This is inadmissible in the case of God who is not related to time or place and not even to any of the substances created by Him. (5) The action performed by a certain agent may be predicated of him. This kind of attribute makes no affirmation of his essence or quality and is therefore admissible in the case of God (1:52). The "13 attributes of mercy" revealed by God to Moses (Ex. 34:6–7) are attributes of action. They do not denote affections (e.g., compassion) on the part of God, but merely express the actions proceeding from Him in terms drawn from analogous human experience. Maimonides makes the point that not only the many attributes of God used in Scripture, but also the four intellectually conceived attributes of existence, omnipotence, omniscience, and will are attributes of action and not essential attributes (1:53). Because of God's absolute uniqueness and unlikeness to anything else, God's essence is unknowable (1:55). The only correct way of speaking of God's essence is that of negation.

Maimonides lists eight terms (existence and life, incorporeality, firstness, omnipotence, omniscience, will, and unity), all of which are interpreted as negative in meaning and as expressing the dissimilarity between God and all other beings, e.g., "God exists" means "God is not absent"; "He is powerful" means "He is not weak." The negation means that the term in question (e.g., "weak") is inapplicable to God. It also means that the affirmative term (e.g., "powerful") is equally inapplicable, and that it can only be used in an equivocal sense. Maimonides' doctrine of attributes reflects, fundamentally, Avicenna's position as represented by al-Ghazāli in his *Tahāfut al-Falāsifa'* (i.e., denial of essential attributes based on the concept of God's "necessary existence," which, in turn, is based on the Avicennian ontological distinction between essence and existence in the cases of all beings except God), but goes beyond Avicenna in rejecting relational attributes.

In post-Maimonidean Jewish philosophy the influence of Averroes became increasingly pronounced. Averroes' attack on Avicenna's ontological distinction between essence and existence achieved particular prominence and led to the adoption of the theory that the divine attributes did not imply homonymous terms, but rather that essence and existence are identical in all beings, including God.

The full implications of Averroes' critique of Avicenna appear in the doctrine of Levi b. Gershom (*Milḥamot Adonai*, 3:3). The attributes are not to be interpreted as equivocal in meaning. They are to be understood *secundum prius et posterius* (both by a priori and a posteriori reasoning). They do not thereby imply a kind of relation and similarity between God and other beings, nor do they involve plurality: "For not every proposition in which something is affirmed of something implies plurality of that thing."[71] Levi ben Gershom quotes scriptural passages affirming God's oneness (Deut. 6:4) and existence (Ex. 3:14), and he concludes from them the attributes of intellect, life, goodness, omnipotence, and will must likewise be predicated of God in a positive sense.

The last significant development of the doctrine of divine attributes in medieval Jewish philosophy is found in Ḥasdai Crescas (*Or Adonai*, 1:3, 1–6). He distinguishes between the essence of God, which is unknowable, and essential predicates which are knowable. The latter are neither identical with God's essence nor merely accidental to it, but inseparable from it in the sense that the one cannot be thought of without the other. This distinction is not in conflict with the notion of God's absolute simplicity. Nor is God's unlikeness to any other being thereby denied. The attributes of omnipotence and omniscience may be predicated of God *secundum prius et posterius*. There are, however, some attributes which are, in the final analysis, negative in meaning, namely existence, unity, and eternity. These too apply to God and all other beings *secundum prius et posterius* and are thus not equivocal. Crescas thus firmly rejects denial of affirmative attributes, and suggests that such denial may be interpreted as really referring only to God's essence, where it is legitimate, but not to His essential attributes (1:3,3 end).

In modern Jewish philosophy the divine attributes are no longer discussed with the stringency imposed by the medieval tradition as inherited from Philo and the neoplatonists and modified by the Aristotelians. Nevertheless, the concepts evolved by the medieval thinkers are not entirely lost. Both Moses Mendelssohn and Hermann Cohen reflect in different ways, according to their respective positions, essential elements of the earlier discussion. Mendelssohn deals with the attributes particularly in his small treatise *Die Sache Gottes oder die gerettete Vorsehung* (1784). He asserts in the name of "the true religion of reason" the conjunction in God of his "greatness" and His "goodness." The greatness of God contains two parts: His power or omnipotence and His wisdom or omniscience. Mendelssohn's discussion of the divine attributes (he does not use this term) is directed towards the problem of theodicy. The essential point is that the infinite wisdom of God is allied to His infinite goodness, which constitutes God's "justice." In its highest degree justice is "holiness' in which equity and mercy are included. The concept of the goodness of God implies that God's punishment of the sinner is meant for the sake of the sinner's improvement.

Hermann Cohen presents his concept of the attributes of God in much closer dependence on the medieval Islamic and Jewish philosophers, particularly on Maimonides. The concept of the unity of God in Judaism, according to Cohen, must not be confounded with that of mere "oneness," which is merely negative in meaning. Cohen adopts the term "uniqueness" *(Einzigheit),* which denotes God as the only Being in the true sense of the word, and signifies also His incomparability, eternity, and causality,[72] as well as the concept of God as creator. He interprets Maimonides' theory of negative attributes as the absolute negation of negativity and the affirmation of positivity. Thus, propositions such as "God is not weak" are given in the logical form "God is not non-active." Moreover, he links this interpretation with his own concept of *Ursprung (principium,* Gr., *arche)* as the thinking which alone can produce what may be considered an adequate notion of being, and one which is independent of the data of sense experience. Cohen interprets Maimonides' attributes of action as expressing the "correlation" between God and men;[73] as such they denote exemplars for human action rather than qualities or predicates of God. Furthermore, according to this view, the attributes of action can be reduced to those of love and justice which, in Cohen's ethical monotheism, become "concepts of virtue for man." The moral activity of humankind, rather than metaphysical speculation about God's character and nature, is the end of all religion, and the implication of the divine attributes. The purpose of the biblical, and other, references to God's attributes, in this view, is primarily to point man back to his own ethical obligations to his "fellow men."

Post-idealist Jewish philosophy, which has mainly been either existentialist or naturalist, has paid little sustained attention in the classical manner to the question of the divine "attributes." However, they have of necessity had to deal with the issue, if only obliquely, and we conclude our discussion of this theme with a brief look at some of the more important of these positions.

Franz Rosenzweig, though not concerning himself directly with the question of attributes, does pay indirect attention to the problem insofar as it affects his theory of revelation between God and humankind. Positing revelation as a fact, Rosenzweig argues that it requires a medium of communication and this medium, by the very nature of things, can only be that of human language. Though man is not God and recognizes his limits, he can still address God in meaningful language, with the Divinity doing the same in relation to man. In such a situation Rosenzweig does not see why human language to and about God, even if anthropomorphic, should be considered inauthentic or impermissable, given the revelatory situation which exists between God and humankind. The attribution of certain qualities and characteristics to God is justified by the quality and nature of the meeting which transpires between the Deity and man, nor can it be otherwise, insofar as the dialogue is constituted between them.

Buber, in related fashion, has argued that it is proper to talk of God in personal *(I-Thou)* rather than impersonal *(I-It)* ways. In the course of this *I-Thou* thinking, Buber has had to face the question: in what sense is it more appropriate to predicate personal attributes of God, such as that God is loving, caring, concerned, etc., than to say of Him, for example, that He is the Creator and First Cause, as did all the medieval philosophers. His reply has been ambiguous. On the one hand he maintained that all language is, strictly speaking, inappropriate to God, but it seems that "personal" language is somehow less so, although just why is never specified. However, Buber has claimed in his work *I and Thou,* and elsewhere, that "Thou is no metaphor," i.e., when we refer to God as the *Absolute Thou* we are in some literal and meaningful sense saying something true about Him. This contradictory position was never resolved by Buber, though in fairness it should be noted that he was aware of this contradiction, but was not troubled by it, as he believed that the most suitable language for talking to and about God, insofar as any language is appropriate, is that which embraces paradox rather than tries to escape it.[74]

A similar view was taken by Abraham Joshua Heschel. Heschel, an excellent student of Jewish philosophy who was thoroughly familiar with the detailed discussion of the medieval thinkers on this theme, freely used anthropomorphic and especially anthropopathic expressions, such as the "Divine Pathos," yet still held that God transcends all language. For Heschel, God is forever mysterious and "ineffable." Like Maimonides he asserts that all attempts to predicate anything positive of God must fail and, at best, can eventually only point beyond themselves to the realm where language no longer performs any function. However, religious language, whose vocabulary contains the attributes of God, is of value in that it helps "point" humanity in the direction of the mysterious which is the foundation of existence, and helps evoke in it the proper sense of awe before its God. Like Buber, Heschel does not object to stating his views in paradoxes.[75]

Other disciples of Buber and Heschel, where they have expressed themselves about this question at all, have adopted similar views.

The major alternative position has again been that suggested by Mordecai Kaplan. Kaplan argues that human reason can never discover the nature of God. At best, man has to adopt an agnostic position about such ultimate metaphysical questions as the nature and essence of God. All questions about the attributes of God and His essential being are likewise unanswerable. Instead, Kaplan suggests that a radically different analysis of religious language and God's attributes has to be undertaken. We must understand these terms, not as divine or transcendental referents, but rather as elements which humans create and project onto their God because of the social, psychological and natural needs held by themselves and their society. Hence the essential meaning and value of the Deity's attributes are to be found in human society. Thus, for example, and most importantly, the moral attributes of the Divine, so basic to the Judaic God, are actually articulations of Israel's enduring demand for ethical behavior and the attempt to encourage in its adherents the highest standards of moral action. In this sense Kaplan, at one and the same time, rejects anthropomorphic attributes as being metaphysically inaccurate, while accepting and advocating them as sociologically and psychologically, i.e., pragmatically, valuable.

Kaplan's position has been influential among those who favor a translation of religion into the categories of the social and natural sciences. However, it is not philosophically adequate and in recent years has declined in influence and persuasiveness.[76]

Providence of God

Providence is the term used to describe God's guidance or care of His creatures, a concomitant of His constant concern for them and for the achievement of His purposes. This aspect of the Divinity includes both supervision of people's acts and the meting out of just retribution aimed at establishing the rule of justice in the world. Hence an intimate connection also exists between providence and the principle of reward and punishment. The term providence is Greek in origin (πρovia, lit. "perceiving beforehand") and first appears in Jewish literature in the Wisdom of Solomon, 14:3; 17:2.

IN BIBLE AND APOCRYPHA

The biblical conception of God is the basis of the Jewish belief in a constant and eternal divine providence. In polytheism there is generally a belief in a fixed "order" of nature, which is above the gods. This "order" serves to some extent as a guarantee that right prevails in the world.[77] However in this type of belief the right is, as it were, a product of blind and necessary action (this is also the case in the Buddhist belief in "karma") and is not dependent on a divine providence with a universal moral purpose. On the contrary, through the use of certain magical acts, one can even overcome the will of the god. In any case, there is a basic belief in fate and necessity. By contrast, the belief in providence is in the first instance a belief in a God who has cognition and will, and who has unlimited control over nature as well as a personal relationship with all men—a relationship which is determined solely by their moral or immoral behavior. Biblical belief does not deny the existence of a fixed natural order—"the ordinances" of heaven and earth, of day and night (Jer. 31:35–36; 33–25)—but it sees God as the creator of nature and therefore not subject to its laws. God can guide man and reward him according to his merit, even at times using the supernatural means of miracles to this end.

God's providential concern is both individual—extending to each and every person (Adam, Abel, Cain, etc.), and general—over peoples and groups, especially Israel, His chosen people. Thus we see the guarding and guidance of the Patriarchs Abraham, Isaac, and Jacob and their families (Sarah in the house of Pharaoh, Hagar in the desert, Joseph in Egypt, etc.) aimed at the ultimate purpose of creating an exemplary people. We also view the whole history of Israel according to the biblical conception, beginning with the Exodus from Egypt, as a continuous unfolding of the guidance of the people as a whole by divine providence, in the way marked out for it. Even the sufferings undergone by the people of Israel through history are regarded as the mysteries inherent in this providential sphere.[78]

It can be said that the entire Bible is a record of divine providence, both in the general and individual realm. While the Pentateuch and the Prophets emphasize general, national providence, the Psalms and Proverbs are based on the belief that God is concerned with the individual, hears the cry of the wretched, desires the well-being of the righteous, and directs humankind, even against its will, to the destiny which He has determined for it. Thus the author of Proverbs notes: "The lot is cast into the lap, but the whole disposing thereof is of the Lord," (16:33). The Prophets and Psalmists sometimes question the ways of God and the nature of divine justice, but ultimately they always affirm the traditional belief in divine providence. In the last analysis, this position is even maintained by the author of Ecclesiastes—who otherwise expresses the gravest doubts regarding providence: "But know that for all these things God will bring thee to judgment" (11:9)—as well as the author of Job.

Though the unlimited belief in providence would seem to conflict with the biblical doctrine that man can freely choose good and evil (for which God rewards or punishes him), both doctrines were affirmed by the biblical authors. The philosophical problems arising from this seeming contradiction were left to religious philosophy in the Middle Ages.

In the Apocrypha, as in the Bible, the belief is widespread that God watches over the deeds of mortals in order to requite the wicked and the righteous according to their actions. The suffering of the righteous is but a temporary trial in order that they be well rewarded in the end. Tobit, for instance, is persecuted by the authorities for dealing kindly with the living and with the dead, and it even appears as if the hand of God was turned against him. But finally his righteousness is rewarded, and Tobit is vindicated and vouchsafed the victory of righteousness. The same applies to the community of Israel—the enemy invariably receives his punishment and the righteous nation is saved, almost unexpectedly. Thus according to I Maccabees (9:46), Judah Maccabee urged the people to pray because he knew that God pays attention to prayer: "Now therefore cry unto Heaven that you may be delivered out of the hand of your enemies." Similarly, the inhabitants of Jerusalem were convinced that in Hasmonean times as in ancient days, their prayer saved them in time of trouble (II Macc. 1:8). God is even seen to continue to save His people by means of angels and other intermediaries sent by him.[79]

In the concept of providence in the apocalyptic works, particularly in the writings of the Dead Sea sect, one can detect a tendency toward an important innovation. In these works the idea is expressed that God, who has foreknowledge of everything, decrees all in advance; both the wicked and the righteous are formed at their creation. So we read in the Dead Sea sect's Manual of Discipline, "all the sons of light each one to his fortune according to the counsel of the Lord . . . ; all the sons of darkness each one to his guilt according to the vengeance of the Lord" (1:9–10) and again "From the Lord of Knowledge, all is and was . . . and before they came into being he prepared all their thought . . . and it is unchangeable" (3:15–16). Likewise, according to the Book of Jubilees, everything is written beforehand in the "tablets of the heavens" (3:10).

Josephus, too, distinguishes between the different sects that arose in the time of the Second Temple, primarily on the basis of the difference between them in the concept of providence.[80] According to him, "the Pharisees say that some things but not all depend on fate, but some depend upon us as to whether they occur or not. The Essenes hold that fate rules everything and nothing happens to man without it; while the Sadducees abolish fate, holding that it does not exist at all, that human actions do not occur through its power, and that everything is dependent upon man himself who alone is the cause of the good, and evil results from man's folly."

God

IN THE TALMUD

The outlook of the scholars of the Mishnah and Talmud on the nature and purport of divine providence is summarized in the dictum of Akiva (Avot 3:15): "All is foreseen, but freedom of choice is given; and the world is judged with goodness, and all is in accordance with the works." It is apparent that the first part of this dictum expresses an attempt to reconcile the principle of providence on the one hand with freedom of choice on the other; but it is possible that the idea here expressed is identical with that contained in the dictum: "Everything is in the hand of heaven except for the fear of heaven" (Ber. 33b), which is intended to build a bridge between freedom of choice and the idea of predestination.

From various dicta in the Talmud it is possible to infer that the idea of providence during this era embraced not only all men but even all creatures. The Talmud, for example, teaches that for the gazelle that is wont to cast its seed at parturition from the top of the mountain, the Holy One prepares "an eagle that catches it in its wings and places it before her, and were it to come a moment earlier or a moment later [the offspring] would die at once" (BB 16a–b); again, in similar vein is the statement: "The Holy One sits and nourishes both the horns of the wild ox and the ova of lice" (Shab. 107b). Likewise, God's providence directly affects human action and thus it is said of man: "No man bruises his finger on earth unless it is decreed in heaven" (Hul. 7b). The rabbis even see God involved in the role of matchmaker: "The Holy One sits and pairs couples—the daughter of so-and-so to so-and-so" (Lev. R. 8).

The continuation of Akiva's dictum "that the world is judged with goodness" accords with the traditional outlook of the Talmud. Thus, for example, it was said that even if 999 angels declare someone's guilt and only one speaks in his favor, God assesses him mercifully, and God is seen to be distressed at the sad lot of the righteous, while also finding no pleasure in the downfall of the wicked. Through the whole of talmudic literature God is pictured as a benevolent father who sits and awaits the errant son's return, and does not punish him until his measure is full in the hope that right up to the last he will repent.[81]

IN MEDIEVAL JEWISH PHILOSOPHY

The concern with providence (now called in Hebrew *hashgaḥah*) in medieval Jewish philosophy reflects the discussion of this subject in late

Greek philosophy, particularly the writings of the second-century Aristotelian commentator, Alexander Aphrodisias, and the theological schools of Islam.[82]

The first major treatment of this theme in medieval Jewish thought is found in Saadiah, who deals with the problem of providence in treatise 5 of his *Emunot ve-De'ot*. In chapter 1, he identifies providence with the reward and punishment meted out by God to the individual in this world, which is "the world of action"; ultimately, however, Saadiah sees reward and punishment as reserved for the world to come. Further echoes of the philosophical debate on the problem of providence may be found in other parts of Saadiah's work. Thus, he asks how it is possible that God's knowledge can encompass both the past and the future and "that he knows both equally" in a single, eternal, and immutable act of knowing (*ibid.*, 2:13). His reply is that it is impossible to compare man's knowledge, which is acquired through the medium of the senses, with God's, which "is not acquired by any intermediate cause" and is not derived from temporal facts, but rather flows from His essence. This linking of the problem of providence with that of the nature of God's knowledge originated with Alexander of Aphrodisias, as did the question of the reconciliation of God's prescience with man's freedom of the will. Saadiah, in his solution to the latter problem however, is careful to point out that the Creator's knowledge of events is not the cause of their occurrence. If that were the case, all events would be eternal, inasmuch as God's knowledge of them is eternal (*ibid.*, 4:4).

Abraham ibn Daud devotes an entire chapter of his book *Emunah Ramah*[83] to the problems involved in the concept of providence. Ibn Daud, too, was considerably influenced by Alexander of Aphrodisias, who upheld "the nature of the possible," thereby allowing for human choice, in opposition to the absolute determinism of the Stoics. Like Alexander, he limits God's knowledge to that which stems from the necessary laws of nature through natural causes, to the exclusion of the effects of accident of free will which are only "possible" events. He argues that God's ignorance of things that come to be as a result of accident or free will does not imply an imperfection in His nature, for whatever is "possible" is also only possible for God, and hence He knows these things only as possible, not as necessary.

Maimonides deals with the question of providence in light of the philosophic teachings on "governance" *(hanhagah)*, which identify providence with the action of the forces of nature (*Guide*, 2:10). He also fully discusses individual providence (*hashgaḥah, ibid.,* 3:16–24), listing five main views on the matter: those of Epicurus, Aristotle, the Ash'arites, the Mu'tazilites and, lastly, of the Torah, which affirms both freedom of the human will and divine justice. According to Maimonides' account, the good and evil that befall man are the result of this divine justice, "for all His ways are judgment," and there exists a perfect correspondence between the achievements of the individual and his fate. This is determined by the level of man's intellect, however, rather than by his deeds, so that it follows that only he whose perfected intellect adheres to God is protected from all evil (*Guide,* 3:51). Such a man realizes that governance, providence, and purpose cannot be attributed to God in a human sense, and he will, therefore, "bear every misfortune lightly, nor will misfortunes multiply doubts concerning God . . . but will rather increase his love of God."

Maimonides further argues against Alexander of Aphrodisias and Ibn Daud that God's knowledge instantaneously encompasses the numerous things subject to change without any change in His essence; that God foresees all things that will come to be without any addition to His knowledge; and that He therefore knows both the possible ("privation," i.e., that which does not yet exist but is about to be) and the infinite (i.e., individuals and particulars which are unlimited in number). The philosophers such as Ibn Daud, he states, arbitrarily asserted that it is impossible to know the possible or the infinite, but they overlooked the difference between God's knowledge and human knowledge. Just as man's intellect is inadequate to apprehend God's essence, so it cannot apprehend His knowledge (*ibid.,* 2:20).[84]

Maimonides' position that God's providence was directly proportional to the level of development of man's intellect, was however, not a characteristic position in Jewish thought and seemed to many of his contemporaries to be out of keeping with more classical Jewish teaching. Perhaps the first to raise the consideration of Maimonides' position was Samuel ibn Tibbon, who in a letter to Maimonides calls attention to what seems a contradiction between the latter's philosophical exposition of the doctrine of providence in chapter 3 of the *Guide,* and his seemingly less philosophical exposition in chapter 51 of the same work. In chapter 51, departing from his view that providence is only relevant to the welfare of the soul, Maimonides argues that the devout man will never be allowed to be harmed. Shem

Tov ibn Falaquera, Moses ibn Tibbon, Moses of Narbonne and Efodi (Profiat Duran), in their commentaries on the *Guide,* all raise this same point, noting the seeming contradiction and trying to resolve it in a variety of ways. More severe critics, such as Shem Tov ibn Shem Tov in his *Emunot* and Isaac Arama in his *Akedat Yizhak,* take Maimonides to task for having made the degree of providence exercised over man dependent on the development and level of intellectual perfection rather than on moral behavior and performance of the *mitzvot.* On a different note, another critic, the Karaite theologian Aaron ben Elijah, devotes several chapters of his work *Ez Hayyim* to the subject of providence and in the course of his discussion on this theme criticizes Maimonides. He argues that once the position has been taken that God's knowledge cannot be restricted, the activity of providence likewise cannot be made to be dependent solely upon the degree of the development of man's intellect. Just as God knows everything, so He watches over all things (Ch. 88).

Among later Jewish philosophers Isaac Albalag, in his *Tikkun De'ot,* discusses providence in the course of his critique of the opinions of Avicenna and al-Ghazālī. It is impossible, he contends, to comprehend God's mode of cognition, but it is possible to attribute to Him a knowledge of things which are outside the realm of natural causation, i.e., free will and chance. God's knowledge and providence also provide the subject of a penetrating analysis in the *Milhamot Adonai* of Levi b. Gershom (treatises 2 and 3), who returns to the Aristotelian position as understood in the light of Alexander of Aphrodisias' commentary. It is inadmissible, he states, that God should know the possible and the numerically infinite, that is, the particulars qua particulars, but He does know all things through the order embracing them all.

In contrast to this view, Hasdai Crescas argues in his *Or Adonai* (2:1–2) that the belief in individual providence is a fundamental principle of the Mosaic Law, according to which God's knowledge "encompasses the infinite" (i.e., the particular) and "the non-existent" (i.e., the possible) "without any change in the nature of the possible" (i.e., without His knowledge nullifying the reality of free will). Crescas maintains that the biblical and talmudic faith in providence is based on a belief in individual providence. His disciple, Joseph Albo, also deals extensively with God's knowledge and providence in his *Sefer ha-Ikkarim* (4:1–15), during the course of his discussion concerning reward and punishment. However, Albo advances the discussion very little, if at all, largely repeating the views of predecessors.

IN THE KABBALAH

The question of divine providence almost never appears in the Kabbalah as a separate problem, and therefore few detailed and specific discussions were devoted to it. The idea of providence is identified in the Kabbalah with the assumption that there exists an orderly and continous system of government of the cosmos, carried out by the Divine Potencies—the *Sefirot*—which are revealed in this government. The Kabbalah does no more than explain the way in which this system operates, while its actual existence is never questioned. The world is not governed by chance, but by unceasing divine providence, which is the secret meaning of the hidden order of all the planes of creation, and especially in the world of man. He who understands the mode of action of the *Sefirot* also understands the principles of divine providence which are manifested through this action. The idea of divine providence is interwoven in a mysterious way with the limitation of the area of action of causality in the world. For although most events which happen to living creatures, and especially to men, appear as if they occur in a natural way which is that of cause and effect, in reality these events contain individual manifestations of divine providence, which is responsible for everything that happens to man, down to the last detail. In this sense, the rule of divine providence is, in the opinion of Naḥmanides, one of the "hidden wonders" of creation. The workings of nature ("I will give you your rains in their season," Lev. 26:4 and the like) are coordinated in hidden ways with the moral causality determined by the good and evil in men's actions.

In their discussions of divine providence, the early kabbalists stressed the activity of the tenth *Sefirah,* since the rule of the lower world is principally in its hands. This *Sefirah* is the *Shekhinah,* the presence of the divine potency in the world at all times. This presence is responsible for God's providence for His creatures; but according to some opinions the origin of divine providence is actually in the upper *Sefirot.* Symbolic expression is given to this idea, particularly in the Zohar, in the description of the eyes in the image of *Adam Kadmon* ("Primordial Man"), in his two manifestations, as the *Arikh Anpin* (lit. "The Long

Face" but meaning "The Long Suffering") or *Attikah Kaddishah* ("The Holy Ancient One"), and as the *Ze'eir Anpin* ("the Short Face," indicating the "Impatient"). In the description of the organs in the head of *Attikah Kaddishah*, the eye which is always open is taken as a supernal symbol for the existence of divine providence, whose origin is in the first *Sefirah*. This upper providence consists solely of mercy, with no intermixture of harsh judgment. Only in the second manifestation, which is that of God in the image of the *Ze'eir Anpin*, is the working of judgment also found in the divine providence. For ". . . the eyes of the Lord . . . range through the whole earth" (Zech. 4:10), and they convey his providence to every place, both for judgment and for mercy. The pictorial image, "the eye of providence," is here understood as a symbolic expression which suggests a certain element in the divine order itself. The author of the Zohar is also here refuting those who deny divine providence and substitute chance as an important cause in the events of the cosmos. He considers them to be fools who are not fit to contemplate the depths of the wisdom of divine providence and who lower themselves to the level of animals (Zohar 3:157b). The author of the Zohar does not distinguish between general providence (of all creatures) and individual providence (of individual human beings), though the latter is, of course, more important to him. Through the activity of divine providence, an abundance of blessing descends on the creatures, but this awakening of the power of providence is dependent on the deeds of created beings, on "awakening from below."

In later kabbalistic thought a detailed consideration of the question of providence is set forth by Moses Cordovero in *Shi'ur Komah* ("Measurement of the Body"). He, too, agrees with the philosophers that individual providence exists only in relation to man, while in relation to the rest of the created world, providence is only directed toward the generic essences. But he enlarges the category of individual providence and establishes that "divine providence applies to the lower creatures, even animals, for their well-being and their death, and this is not for the sake of the animals themselves, but for the sake of men," that is to say, to the extent to which the lives of animals are bound up with the lives of men, individual providence applies to them as well. "Individual providence does not apply to any ox or any lamb, but to the entire species together . . . but if divine providence applies to a man, it will encompass even his pitcher, should it break, and his dish, should it crack, and all his possessions—if he should be chastized or not" (p. 113). Cordovero distinguishes ten types of providence, from which it is possible to understand the various modes of action of individual providence among the gentiles and Israel. These modes of action are bound up with the various roles of the *Sefirot* and their channels which convey the abundance (of blessing) to all the worlds, in accordance with the special awakening of the lower creatures. He includes among them two types of providence which indicate the possibility of the limitation of divine providence in certain instances, or even its complete negation. Also, in his opinion, things may happen to a man without the guidance of providence, and it may even happen that a man's sins cause him to be left "to nature and to chance," which is the aspect of God's hiding his face from man. In fact, it is uncertain from moment to moment whether a particular event in an individual's life is of this latter type, or whether it is a result of divine providence: "And he cannot be sure—for who will tell him if he is among those of whom it is said: 'The righteous man is as sure as a lion'—perhaps God has hidden His face from him, because of some transgression, and he is left to chance" (p. 120).

Only in the heretical Kabbalah is divine providence seen once again as a serious problem. Among Shabbetai Zevi's disciples was handed down his oral teaching that the Cause of Causes, or the *Ein-Sof* ("the Infinite") "does not influence and does not oversee the lower world, and he caused the *Sefirah Keter* to come into being to be God and *Tiferet* to be King.[85] This denial of the providence of *Ein-Sof* was considered a deep secret among the believers, though the Shabbatean Abraham Cardozo, who was opposed to this doctrine, wrote that the emphasis on the secret nature of this teaching arose from the Shabbateans' knowledge that this was the opinion of Epicurus the Greek.

The "taking" *(netilah)* of providence from *Ein-Sof* (which is designated in these circles by other terms as well) is found in several Shabbatean schools of thought, such as the Kabbalah of Baruchiah of Salonika, in *Va-Avo ha-Yom el ha-Ayin,* which was severely attacked for the prominence it gave to this opinion, and in *Shem Olam*[86] by Jonathan Eybeschuetz. The latter work devoted several pages of casuistry to this question in order to prove that providence does not actually originate in the First Cause, but in the God of Israel, who is emanated from it, and who is called by Eybeschuetz, the "image of the ten *Sefirot.*" This "heretical" assumption, that the First Cause (or the highest element of the Godhead) does not guide the lower world at all, was among the principle innovations of Shabbatean doctrine which angered the sages of that period. The Orthodox kabbalists saw in this assumption proof that the Shabbateans had left the faith in the absolute unity of the Godhead, which does not permit, in matters pertaining to divine providence, differentiation between the emanating *Ein-Sof* and the emanated *Sefirot*. Even though the *Ein-Sof* carries out the activity of divine providence through the *Sefirot,* the *Ein-Sof* itself is the author of true providence. In the teachings of the Shabbateans, however, this quality of the First Cause of the *Ein-Sof* is blurred or put in doubt.

HASIDISM

As in the earlier Kabbalah, the *Hasidim* were interested in the issue of providence as   part of their general theological concern with God. However, unlike the general view of the philosophers, and unlike even the expanded view of providence found in Cordovero, the Hasidim extended God's providential concern and action to every element and every individual in the world, even to every inanimate entity. Thus the Hasidim were generally of the opinion that nothing, whether it be the individual events in the life of men, or the historic events governing Israel and the nations, down to the blooming of a flower or the falling of a stone, occurs without the assent of the divine will. It was, moreover, the accepted hasidic view that the Baal Shem Tov opposed Maimonides' position on special providence, arguing that this divine concern extends to the whole of reality—there is no arbitrariness in reality, the whole of which is in God by whom all things are intended and ordered by his own divine requirements.

It should be noted that this emphasis on the part of the Baal Shem Tov and his disciples flows naturally from their panentheistic metaphysics in which the world is not separate from God but, in kabbalistic-emanationist fashion, flows from the *Ein-Sof* while yet remaining inseparably part of the life and character of the Divine. As a result, this emanationist position generates and reinforces the hasidic view on divine providence. Thus the Rabbi of Koretz, one of the Baal Shem Tov's earliest colleagues, teaches the following: "A man should believe that even a piece of straw that lies on the ground does so at the decree of God. He decrees that it should lie there with one end facing this way and the other end the other way.[87] It would be hard to think of a more vigorous defense of God's providential concern with particular and seemingly irrelevant detail than that found in this teaching of R. Pinhas. In similar fashion, and with Maimonides' limitation of special providence focussed before him, R. Hayyim of Sanz taught: "Although Maimonides has a different opinion in this matter the truth is that not even a bird is snared without providence from above."[88]

Justice and Mercy of God

God's primary attribute of action is justice, referred to by the Hebrew terms *mishpat* and *Ẓedek*. His commandments to all, and especially to Israel, are essentially for the purpose of the establishment of justice in the world. One helps fulfill this purpose by acting in accordance with God's laws and more generally in imitating the divine quality of justice. This struggle for a just society requires constant effort, and the entire process of establishing justice in the world is to be completed only in the messianic future.[89]

The two main biblical terms for justice are *ẓedek* and *ẓedakah*. They refer to both divine and human justice, as well as to "the works of justice" as in Ex. 9:27 or Prov. 10:25. In biblical thought, moreover, justice is essentially synonymous with holiness (Isa. 5:16) and is consistently paired with "mercy" or "grace" (*ḥesed;* Isa. 45:19; Ps. 103:17ff.). So common is this association that by talmudic times the term *ẓedakah* comes to mean almost exclusively "charity" or "works of love" (BB 10b), and the notion of "justice" is rendered by the terms "truth" *(emet),* "trust" *(emunah),* and "integrity" *(yosher).* In addition, throughout the rabbinic literature, other values, particularly peace and redemption, are consistently associated with justice, as its components or products, so that ultimately virtually the entire spectrum of ethical values is comprised within the notion of justice and its exercise.

There is, however, a problematic element in the traditional understanding of the working of divine justice and this critical issue emerges in the form of a question over the issue of theodicy: if God rules the world justly, why do the righteous suffer and the evil prosper? The problem of theodicy, a recurrent theme in Jewish literature, is raised by the Psalmist and by Job, and appears in much recent post-Holocaust literature. In the history of Jewish thought many solutions have been suggested. For example, Maimonides advances the essentially neoplatonic notion that evil is privation, i.e., that it is not something positive in itself but merely the absence of good (*Guide* 3:18–25). Others have argued that evil and suffering constitute trials of the just; while still others argue that suffering is, in the language of rabbinic literature, an "affliction of love", i.e., God tests and purifies the righteous by causing them to suffer in this world. Finally, and most commonly, it is said that God's ways are justified by reference to the doctrine of reward and punishment in the world to come when God will requite each man according to his merit. Nevertheless, no one answer, nor any combination, is a completely satisfactory answer to the problem.[90]

It must also be noted, however, that the biblical account of God's actions and nature constantly relates God's attribute of justice to His attribute of mercy. Justice is not contrasted with love, but rather correlated with it. In rabbinic literature, Jewish philosophy, and Kabbalah, God is described as acting out of the two "attributes of lawfulness and compassion."[91]

Both God's justice and mercy are affirmed in His proclamation to Moses at Sinai before the giving of the Decalogue: "The Lord, the Lord, a God compassionate and gracious, slow to anger, abounding in kindness and faithfulness, extending kindness to the thousandth generation, forgiving iniquity, transgression, and sin; yet He does not remit all punishment, but visits the iniquity of the fathers upon children and children's children, upon the third and fourth generations" (Ex. 34:6–7). Justice and mercy are thus seen to be the bases of the covenant between God and the Israelites. God's mercy is revealed in the fact that He redeemed the people of Israel from slavery in Egypt to make them His people and contract a covenant with them: "When Israel was a child, I loved him, out of Egypt I called my son" (Hos. 11:1). His justice is revealed in the fact that He punishes the Israelites if they sin and do not uphold their covenantal obligation: "You only have I known of all the families of the earth; therefore I will punish you all your iniquities" (Amos 3:2). Both the justice and mercy of God are evident in and central to the biblical portrayal of God's relationship with Israel; "I will betroth you to me in righteousness and in justice; in steadfast love and in mercy" (Hosea 2:19). To ignore either is to make a caricature of the reality of God's covenantal relation with Israel.

IN POST-BIBLICAL JUDAISM

This same intermingling of justice and mercy is to be discerned in the works of Philo and other post-biblical writings.[92] In rabbinic Judaism a vivid expression of this intermingling is found in a parable in Genesis Rabbah (12:15) comparing God to a king who in order to prevent a fragile goblet from shattering must mix hot and cold water when filling it. Thus the world exists because of the admixture of the attributes of mercy and justice *(middat ha-raḥamim* and *middat ha-din)*. Behind this parable lies a complex development of biblical ideas in which the two divine appellations, the Tetragrammaton (YHWH) and *Elohim,* were understood to refer to the two main manifestations of God's providence: the first, to express the attribute of mercy; the second, that of justice.[93] The presence of both names in Genesis 2:4 signifies that mercy and justice were both necessary in order to make creation possible. Genesis Rabbah 39:6 expresses a similar notion: "If thou desirest the world to endure, there can be no absolute justice, while if thou desirest absolute justice the world cannot endure..." Insofar as God's justice and mercy are necessary for creation it is not only the community of Israel that is the major object of these divine activities but the world as a whole. Nonetheless, it must be recognized that rabbinic Judaism was more concerned with the divine activities of mercy and justice as they were directed toward the community of Israel. The fate of the Jewish people in the Roman period was a tragic impetus to this discussion. Faced, too, with the problem of the suffering of the righteous and the prosperity of the wicked, the rabbis examined the concept of divine justice and advanced a number of new interpretations of it in an effort to justify the apparent imbalance of suffering and prosperity in the world. It was suggested that ultimate reward and punishment would take place in the afterlife, that suffering was a process of purification *(yissurin shel ahavah),* and that the individual often suffered for the sins of his ancestors or of the community at large.

This issue was carried over and discussed in medieval Jewish philosophy, but, on the whole, the medieval discussion added little that was new or innovative to the earlier understanding. Of those philosophers who did consider the issue, special mention should be made of Saadiah, who carried forward the rabbinic debate in his discussion of theodicy and the question of the suffering of the righteous.

Saadiah adamantly defends His ways and argues that, in fact, there is no unjust suffering, and further, in the final balance, God's justice is subordinated to His mercy.[94] Judah Halevi gave a further philosophical explication of this basic distinction in his *Kuzari* (IV: 1–17), but again his discussion is not radical or especially innovative, while Maimonides took up the theme in a somewhat different though still derivative way in the opening section of the *Guide*, where he discusses the names of God.

This distinction was also central to kabbalistic theology and its understanding of the nature and interaction of the *Sefirot* and the origin of evil. According to the classical kabbalistic schemata, the fourth *Sefirah* of *Hesed* (love) and the fifth *Sefirah* of *Din* (judgment), which in kabbalistic imagery can be said to represent respectively the attributes of mercy and justice, are intended to work harmoniously together and to contribute to the general orderliness of the world of the *Sefirot* and the proper interdependence of the upper and lower worlds. However, due to complex causes within the world of the divine *Sefirot* these two are separated, and in their separation lies the cause of evil. Gershom Scholem sums up this process in a lucid passage in his *Major Trends in Jewish Mysticism:* "The totality of divine potencies forms a harmonious whole, and as long as each stays in relation to all others, it is sacred and good. This is true also of the quality of strict justice, rigour and judgment in and by God, which is the fundamental cause of evil. The wrath of God is symbolized by His left hand, while the quality of mercy and love, with which it is intimately bound up, is called His right hand. The one cannot manifest itself without involving the other. Thus the quality of stern judgment represents a great fire of wrath which burns in God but is always tempered by His mercy. When it ceases to be tempered . . . then it breaks away from God altogether and is transformed into the radically evil, into Gehenna and the dark world of Satan."[95]

In later Kabbalistic thought, especially in the work of Isaac Luria and his disciples, this notion undergoes further refinement and development, although the same essential notion of the required interaction of God's attributes remains. The same may be said of the use of these notions in ḥasidic thought, both in their more esoteric and mystical manifestations and in the more popular ḥasidic literature.

Modern Jewish thinkers have made no substantial addition to this discussion. Instead, they have utilized the classical understanding of these notions, and the distinctions built upon them, for their own philosophical purposes.

Manifestations of God

In traditional Jewish sources, for a variety of reasons, the concept of God, and references to Him, were replaced or complemented in the texts by new terms and referential designations. The three most famous "synonyms" of this kind are the Hebrew terms *Ru'ah ha-Kodesh, Shekhinah,* and the Greek term *Logos.* In this section the meaning and significance of these terms will be developed more fully.

RU'AH HAKODESH

The term *Ru'ah ha-Kodesh* literally means the "Holy Spirit." Although the phrase occurs in the Bible (cf. Ps. 51:13; Isa 63:10), its specific connotation as divine inspiration is wholly post-biblical. In rabbinic thought the phrase is used to indicate the spirit of prophecy which comes from God, a divine inspiration giving man an insight into the future and into the will of God (cf. Yoma 9b). Traditionally the Pentateuch was said to have been given directly by God to Moses, while the other canonical writings were produced under the inspiration of *Ru'ah ha-Kodesh.* Thus the determination of what should be included as canonical scripture turns on whether or not a given work was understood to have been composed with the aid of the Holy Spirit.[96] Further elaborating on this theme, the sages held that this power of the spirit was given to the prophets in unequal measure[97] and could be passed on to a disciple, as for example in the case of Joshua inheriting it from Moses, and Elisha from Elijah. On the other hand, there are a number of references in rabbinic literature pointing to the cessation of the *Ru'ah ha-Kodesh* in Israel, some dating it from the end of the First, some from the end of the Second Temple (cf. Yoma 21b). The generally accepted view is the one given in Yoma (9b): "When the last of the prophets, Haggai, Zechariah, and Malachi, died, the Holy Spirit ceased from Israel."

Apart from its function as prophetic inspiration the Holy Spirit is also seen to rest on charismatic or exceptionally holy individuals, who are not prophets in the accepted sense. They are thus possessed of exceptional qualities and of an ability to divine the future (Er. 64b). Thus, for example, when the rabbis were gathered in Jericho a divine voice announced to them that there were two among them who were worthy of *Ru'ah ha-Kodesh*. The Holy Spirit is also promised to other categories, e.g., those who teach Torah in public, those who study from pure motives, and those who perform even one *mitzvah* in complete faith. The Midrash says: "All that the righteous do, they do with the power of *Ru'ah ha-Kodesh*." The Holy Spirit may be attained by the saintly man, and the spiritual stages toward its attainment are found in the Mishnah: "Phinehas b. Jair says: 'Heedfulness leads to cleanliness, and cleanliness leads to purity, and purity leads to abstinence, and abstinence leads to holiness, and holiness leads to humility, and humility leads to the fear of sin, and the fear of sin leads to saintliness, and saintliness leads to [the gift of] *Ru'ah ha-Kodesh*.' "[98]

In addition to the gift of the Holy Spirit to individuals, the people of Israel as a whole were in some way guided by the power of *Ru'ah ha-Kodesh*. Thus, for example, when the problem arose among the rabbis as to whether the Paschal offering should be brought on the Sabbath, it was to how the ordinary people would act concerning the Sabbath restrictions that the rabbis turned for a decision. Hillel declared: "Leave it to them, for the Holy Spirit is on them. If they are not in themselves prophets, they are the sons of prophets" (Tosef. Pes. 4:2).

A more problematical use of the term *Ru'ah ha-Kodesh* is found when the term is in some way hypostatized, or used as a synonym for God. This tendency toward hypostatization is already apparent in such expressions as "*Ru'ah ha-Kodesh* resting" on a person or a place or someone "receiving *Ru'ah ha-Kodesh*." But it is most pronounced in descriptions of the Holy Spirit speaking (Pes. 117a), acting as defense counsel on Israel's behalf (Lev. R. 6:1), or leaving Israel and returning to God (Eccles. R. 12:7). This hypostatization is essentially the product of the free play of poetic imagery, and should not be taken to denote that the *Ru'ah ha-Kodesh* is an entity separate from God, and neither here nor elsewhere are there any overtones of the *Ru'ah ha-Kodesh* as somehow forming part of the Godhead, as is found in the Christian concept of the Holy Ghost, which is a Christian translation of *Ru'ah ha-Kodesh.* The problems centering around this use of the term *Ru'aḥ ha--Kodesh* are the product of its different uses fusing into one another. Sometimes it is used merely as a synonym for God, and at others it refers to the power of prophecy through divine inspiration. In order to maintain a perspective on the matter, the monotheistic background and the vivid image character of rabbinic thinking must always be kept in mind.

In Jewish Philosophy.
To Philo the Divine Spirit is that which inspires the prophet to prophecy. In *De Specialibus Legibus* (4:49) he writes that: "no pronouncement of a prophet is ever his own; he is an interpreter prompted by Another in all his utterances, when knowing not what he does he is filled with inspiration, as the reason withdraws and surrenders the citadel of the soul to a new visitor and tenant, the Divine Spirit (τοῦ θείου πνεύματος) which plays upon the vocal organism and dictates words which clearly impress its prophetic message." Influenced by Plato's notion of divine inspiration or frenzy, Philo interprets Abraham's "deep sleep" (Gen. 15:12) as a form of ecstasy which the prophet experiences: "This is what regularly befalls the prophets. The mind is evicted at the arrival of the Divine Spirit, but when that departs the mind returns to its tenancy" (Her. 265). According to Philo, the Divine Spirit "comes upon" man, "fills" him, visits him, or speaks to him only occasionally. But in an exceptional case, such as that of Moses, the Divine Spirit remains continuously in man's soul. Philo apparently did not know or perhaps did not accept the tradition of the Palestinian rabbis that there is a difference in degree between the divine inspiration of the prophet and that of post-biblical authors.

Philo maintains that the Divine Spirit is a separate spiritual entity—a "unique corporeal soul" whose function is to act as an "intermediary of divine communications to man." While unique, it is of the same nature as the incorporeal soul of man or as the angels, which are unembodied souls. Although Philo does not apply the term Logos to the Divine Spirit, he does refer to it as Wisdom, which he identifies with the Logos. Though one must be careful with such comparisons, it can be said that Philo's Divine Spirit corresponds, though not exactly, to the rabbinic *Shekhinah.*

Philo however uses the term Divine Spirit in several other senses as well: in the sense of the rational soul, as in *De Specialibus Legibus* (4:123), where he identifies the Divine Spirit with the "breath of life breathed upon the first man"—which is the rational soul; in the sense of air, the third element, as in Genesis 1:2: "the spirit of God was moving above the water" (Gig. 22); and in the sense of the "pure knowledge in which every wise man naturally shares." Philo bases this last sense of the term on Exodus 31:2 in which Bezalel is said to have been filled by God ". . . with the Divine Spirit, with wisdom, understanding, and knowledge to devise in every work" (Gig. 23).

The concept of the Divine Spirit in the Dead Sea Scrolls is similar in many ways to that of Philo, insofar as it is regarded as a spirit that "comes upon" man or "speaks" to him. In the scrolls, man, as a result of purification from carnal pollution (connected with baptism) is reborn and receives a new spirit. While there are many Platonic and Gnostic elements in the conception of Divine Spirit found in the Dead Sea Scrolls, it has been maintained that the origin of the concept as used in the Scrolls is Jewish.[99]

In medieval Jewish thought the concept of the Holy Spirit played a relatively small role, possibly as a reaction to the Christian trinitarian understanding of the notion. It is primarily used to denote a low type of biblical prophecy, but it also describes a kind of prophecy that could still be attained even after prophecy proper had come to an end with Haggai, Zechariah, and Malachi. A. J. Heschel in an interesting study of the concept in the medieval period enumerates many early thinkers who believed that the door to prophecy was not completely closed, and that there was still a possibility for revelation that takes place by means of the Holy Spirit in a dream, a lower type of prophecy, or through a *bat kol* (a heavenly voice).[100]

Among important discussions of the concept that did exist in medieval Jewish literature mention should specifically be made of Judah Halevi and Maimonides. Judah Halevi discusses the *Ru'aḥ ha-Kodesh* in several contexts. He opposes the opinion of the Islamic Aristotelians that prophecy comes through the intermediary of the active intellect, also called (by them) Holy Spirit or Gabriel, holding instead that prophecy comes directly from God (*Kuzari* 1:87). In another context he maintains that the spiritual forms called Glory of God arose from a spiritual substance called Holy Spirit (*ibid.* 2:4). The Glory of God is a fine substance by means of which select individuals see God (*ibid.*, 4:3).

In still another context he states that the Holy Spirit envelops the prophet when he prophesies as well as the Nazirite, the Messiah, and the high priest when he consults the Urim and Thummim (*ibid.,* 4:15). Finally, in explaining the *Sefer Yeẓirah,* Judah Halevi states that the angels are created from the Spirit of God and that spiritual souls are connected with them (*ibid.,* 4:25).

Maimonides in his discussion of prophecy in the *Guide of the Perplexed,* enumerates 11 degrees of prophecy, of which the second from the lowest stage is prophecy through the *Ru'aḥ ha-Kodesh.* This type of prophecy is ascribed to Balaam, to the high priest when he consults the Urim and Thummim, and to the 70 elders, as well as to David while he composed Psalms, and Solomon while he composed Proverbs, Ecclesiastes, and the Song of Songs. In Maimonides' view the other works of the Hagiographa were also composed through inspiration, i.e., by means of the *Ru'aḥ ha-Kodesh.* In describing the latter he writes that "it consists in the fact than an individual finds that a certain thing has descended upon him . . . so that he talks in wise sayings . . . concerning governmental or divine matters" (*Guide,* 2:45).

In Modern Thought.
Compared to the other terms used to indicate God's activity and presence, the term *Ru'aḥ ha-Kodesh* became increasingly less frequent in the post-medieval period. This is probably due to the use of the term 'Holy Spirit' in Christianity. However, one does find the term used in various ways. In the 19th century, Jewish thinkers, influenced by German Idealism, especially those following the thought of Hegel, sometimes used the term in relation to various aspects of the Absolute Spirit and its manifestations. In this way, traditional Jewish perspectives were blended with Hegelian ones in order to show that Judaism was compatible with the philosophical values of the day and, even more, that it was the religion of spirit (in the idealist sense) par excellence.

In the 20th century the term has been further revised in order to make it useful in various modern interpretations of Judaism. Hermann Cohen, for example, makes considerable use of it in developing his theory of correlation between God and man, which is the basis of his account of Judaism. Cohen objects to Philo's conception of the Logos as an intermediary reality standing between God and man; instead, he maintains that the Holy Spirit is, when understood properly, the characterization of the correlation that exists between man and God. For Cohen, the 'Holy Spirit' is something that God and man share between them. Furthermore, in line with his general neo-Kantian position with its stress on ethics, Cohen relates the Holy Spirit to the goal of ethical purification in human life, that finds its expression and instrumentality in the active moral life rather than in the passive receptivity of grace. Through his ethical action man attains a new spirit and moves towards his potential as "Imago Dei." The Holy Spirit therefore cannot be understood either as an aspect of God alone or of man alone but emerges from the correlative relation that obtains between them and is a common, shared aspect of this relationship.[101]

In a very different mood, the liberal thinker, Kaufman Kohler, understood the 'Holy Spirit' as the gift of reason given by God to man. In line with the optimistic views of Liberal Judaism, and its 19th-century faith in the growing and evolving role of reason in history and human life, Kohler equated the 'Holy Spirit' with the dynamic processes inherent in history and man which makes this progress and evolution possible. In Kohler's phrase, the 'Holy Spirit' is that which propels all forms of human life "toward the highest of goals."[102]

In additon to Cohen's and Kohler's views, there are other mentions of the 'Holy Spirit' in modern Jewish thought, for example, in the writings of Rosenzweig, Heschel and Buber, three leading Jewish existentialist theologians. However, in their thought, as in most other 20th-century thinkers, the preferred term to describe God's presence and activity in the world is *Shekhinah* (see below). Moreover, the technical distinction between *Shekhinah* and *Ru'aḥ ha-Kodesh* has largely been lost and the two terms are used interchangeably, usually without any recognition or sense that in former periods the terms had distinct meanings.

SHEKHINAH

The term *Shekhinah* (literally "dwelling," "resting") or Divine Presence is a rabbinic term used most often to refer to the numinous immanence of God in the world. For the sages, the *Shekhinah* is God viewed in spatio-temporal terms as a presence, particularly in a this-worldly context: when He sanctifies a place, an object, an individual, or a whole people—a revelation of the holy in the midst of the profane. The rabbinical material, however, also uses the term simply as an alternative way of referring to God himself, similar in this usage to such phrases as "The Holy One Blessed be He," or "The Merciful One." Thus, for example, on the verse, "After the Lord your God shall ye walk . . ." (Deut. 13:5), the Talmud comments: "And is it possible for a man to walk after the *Shekhinah?* . . . Rather this means that one should follow (emulate) the virtues of the Holy One Blessed be He" (Sot. 14a). However one must be careful in using this term, for though seemingly hypostatized in certain rabbinic passages, the Talmud scholars never thought of the term as representing a separable aspect of God or as being in any sense a separate part of the Godhead. Those references to the *Shekhinah* which are open to misinterpretation, e.g., those which talk of God placing His *Shekhinah* in the midst of Israel (cf. Sif. Num. 94), or where the *Shekhinah* is pictured as talking to God (Mid. Prov. to 22:28), must be understood as the product of homiletic license. Nor should it be thought that the rabbis themselves were unaware of the dangers of misinterpretation; indeed, it is for this reason that they occasionally preface their remarks with the phrase *kivyakhol,* "as if it were possible,"[103] i.e., as if it were possible to take these phrases and attributions literally.[104]

In addition to its use in Rabbinic material, the term *Shekhinah,* in its Aramaic forms, is also frequently found in the Targums (the Aramaic translations of the Bible), particularly in Targum Onkelos. In this literature it is employed together with other "intermediary" terms such as *memra yakara* ("noble word"), to paraphrase certain references to God, thus attempting to avoid the overtly anthropomorphic[105] implications of various biblical expressions. For instance, the verse "the Lord is not in your midst" (Num. 14:42), Onkelos translates "the *Shekhinah* of God is not in your midst" and the verse "you cannot see My face, for man shall not see Me and live" (Ex. 33:20) is rendered, "You cannot see the face of My *Shekhinah*" (see also Ex. 33:14–15).

The talmudic and midrashic usage of *Shekhinah* does not have quite the same apologetic overtones which are apparent in the Targums; on the whole it is wider in extension and in texts of different dates it varies considerably in nuance. In origin *Shekhinah* was used to refer to a divine manifestation, particularly to indicate God's presence at a given place. This did not imply a limitation of God's omnipresence, however, since it is said that the *Shekhinah* is in all places (BB 25a), and that just as the sun radiates throughout the world so does the *Shekhinah* (Sanh.

39a). Even those special places and objects which God imbues with an extra holiness by His presence—such as the thorn bush in which He revealed Himself to Moses, or Mount Sinai, or the Tabernacle in the wilderness—in connection with which the term *Shekhinah* is most often used, teach us that no place is devoid of His presence: neither the lowliest of trees, nor the barest of mountains, nor a wooden sanctuary (Shab. 67a; Sot. 5a; Ex. R. 34:1).

Though the presence of God is seen to be everywhere, the *Shekhinah* is believed to rest preeminently on Israel (Ber. 7a). For Israel is a people chosen and sanctified by God to be carriers of His will to the world. However, Israel's sins affect the relation to the *Shekhinah* and as such Israel's sins led to the destruction of the Temple, where the *Shekhinah* was always present. According to one view the destruction of the Temple caused the departure of the *Shekhinah* to heaven (Shab. 33a; Ex. R. 2:2). In opposition to this, however, we find it said that even while Israel is unclean the *Shekhinah* is with them (Yoma 56b); and when they are exiled the *Shekhinah* goes into exile with them, and when they come to be redeemd the *Shekhinah* will also be redeemed (Meg. 29a).

The *Shekhinah* not only rests on the people of Israel as a whole, but also on a wide variety of subgroups, each of which are said to influence the *Shekhinah* for good or for ill. For example, where ten are gathered for prayer, or where even only one learns Torah, the *Shekhinah* is present (Ber. 6a). The *Shekhinah* is also said to watch over the sick, to rest between man and wife if they are worthy; and to rest on one who gives charity. On the other hand, he who is proud is said to push against the feet of the *Shekhinah* as does he who sins in secret or who is sad, lazy, playful, light-headed, or engages in idle conversation; nor can scoffers, flatterers, liars and slanderers be recipients of the *Shekhinah*.[106]

The *Shekhinah* is also commonly associated with the charismatic personality and is said to rest on specific outstanding individuals. "The *Shekhinah* only rests on a wise, rich, and valiant man who is tall of stature" (Shab. 92a). Several of the talmudic rabbis were considered to deserve that the Divine Presence rest on them, except that their generation was unworthy (Sot. 48b). This charismatic association seems to be connected with the idea already discussed in the previous section, that certain individuals possess *Ru'aḥ ha-Kodesh,* the Holy Spirit. The use of the term *Shekhinah* would thus seem to range from the numinous revelation of God, as in the theophany at Sinai, or the awe-inspiring presence speaking to Moses from the Tabernacle, to the more mundane idea that a religious act, or *mitzvah,* draws man nearer to God. Sometimes the term is simply an alternative for "God," while at others it has overtones of something separate from the Godhead; it may be used in a personalized or depersonalized way. From the point of view of Jewish theology it would be a mistake to overemphasize any given use to the exclusion of the others, and it is important to view it in the perspective of the Jewish monotheistic background as a whole.

Unlike the rabbinic sages, who generally identified *Shekhinah* with the presence of God, or even with God Himself, the medieval Jewish philosophers were concerned with avoiding any possible anthropomorphic interpretations of this concept, and therefore went to great lengths to point out that *Shekhinah* refers not to God Himself, nor to any part of His Essence, but rather to an independent entity, created by God.

Three discussions of the *Shekhinah* in medieval Jewish philosophy especially deserve a brief comment. First that of Saadiah. According to Saadiah, the *Shekhinah* is identical with *kevod ha-Shem* ("the glory of God"), which served as an intermediary between God and man during the prophetic experience. He suggests that the "glory of God" is the biblical term, and *Shekhinah* the talmudic term for the created splendor of light which acts as an intermediary between God and man, and which sometimes takes on human form. Thus, when Moses asked to see the glory of God, he was shown the *Shekhinah,* and when the prophets in their visions saw God in human likeness, what they actually saw was not God Himself but the *Shekhinah.*[107] By emphasizing that the *Shekhinah* is a created being which is separate from God, Saadiah avoids any possible compromising of the divine unity and any hint of anthropomorphism.

Judah Halevi follows Saadiah in interpreting the *Shekhinah* as an intermediary between God and man, maintaining that it is the *Shekhinah,* and not God Himself, which appears to prophets in their visions. Unlike Saadiah, however, Judah Halevi does not speak of the *Shekhinah* as being a created light. It seems that he identifies the *Shekhinah* with the Divine Influence *(ha-Inyan ha-Elohi),* about whose meaning there is much disagreement among scholars. According to Judah Halevi, the *Shekhinah* dwelt first in the Tabernacle, then in the

Temple. With the destruction of the Temple, and the cessation of prophecy, the *Shekhinah* ceased to appear, but will return with the coming of the Messiah (*Kuzari,* 2:20, 23; 3:23). Furthermore, Judah Halevi distinguishes between the visible *Shekhinah* which dwelt in the Temple, and was seen by the prophets in their visions, and which disappeared with the destruction of the Temple, and the invisible spiritual *Shekhinah* which has not disappeared but is "with every born Israelite of virtuous life, pure heart, and upright mind" (*ibid.,* 5:23).

Maimonides accepts Saadiah's view that the *Shekhinah* is a created light, identified with glory. He too associates the *Shekhinah* with prophecy, explaining that it is the *Shekhinah* which appears to the prophet in his vision (*Guide* 1:21). Explaining prophecy as an overflow from God through the intermediation of the active intellect (*ibid.,* 2:36), Maimonides writes that man apprehends God by means of that light which He causes to overflow toward him, as it is written, "in thy light do we see light." Some interpreters of Maimonides believe that the *Shekhinah* corresponds to the active intellect itself, which is the lowest of the ten intellects, and which communes with the prophets (*Yad, Yesodei ha-Torah,* 7:1). However, there are also passages in which Maimonides takes a more traditional approach and identifies the *Shekhinah* with God Himself rather than with some other being. For example, in his exegesis of Exodus 24:10 (*Guide,* 1:28) Maimonides interprets the "feet" of God as the throne on which sat the *Shekhinah* (i.e., God).

In the Kabbalah.

The concept of the *Shekhinah* played a very prominent role in kabbalistic thought and the basic elements of this concept of the *Shekhinah* are already to be found in the earliest kabbalistic work, the *Sefer ha-Bahir.* In this work the *Shekhinah,* or *Malkhut,* is described and identified as the daughter, the princess, and more generally as the feminine principle in the world of the divine *Sefirot* (Divine Emanations). These motifs were later developed in kabbalistic circles in the late 12th and 13th centuries and were mingled with a variety of philosophical ideas in the works of the Gerona circles and in the writings of Abraham Abulafia. Still later and most importantly, most of these motifs were drawn together by the author of the Zohar, Moses de Leon, and his circle, and especially by his colleague and disciple Joseph

Gikatilla. From this period at the end of the 13th century the basic concept of the *Shekhinah* remained constant up to the time of Isaac Luria and his disciples in Safed (16th century) and even persisted into the teachings of Ḥasidism (18th century). Although certain modifications of the concept can be found in the work of every single kabbalist, our brief remarks here deal with its basic elements common to all the mystical authors.[108]

The *Shekhinah,* or *Malkhut,* is the tenth and last in the hierarchy of the *Sefirot.* In the divine world it represents the feminine principle, while *Tiferet* (the sixth *Sefirah*) and *Yesod* (the ninth) represent the masculine principle. All the elements and characteristics of the other *Sefirot* are represented within the Shekhinah. Like the moon, she has no light of her own, but receives the divine light from the other *Sefirot.* The main goal of the realm of the *Sefirot* (and of religious life as a whole) is to restore the true unity of God, represented as the union of the masculine principle (mainly *Tiferet*) and the feminine *Shekhinah,* which was originally constant and undisturbed, but which was broken by the sin of Adam, the sins of Israel, by the machinations of the evil power (know as the *sitra aḥra*), and by the exile. This goal of the restoration of the original divine harmony can be effected by the religious acts of the people of Israel through adhering to the Torah, through keeping the commandments and through prayer.

The symbolism describing the *Shekhinah* is the most developed in kabbalistic literature. Most of the many and varied symbols refer to aspects of the *Shekhinah's* relationship with the other *Sefirot* above her—such as her acceptance of the divine light from them, her relationship to them as a lower aspect of themselves which is nearer to the created world, and her coming close to the masculine element or moving further away from it. In another group of symbols the *Shekhinah* is the battleground between the divine powers of good and evil; because of her femininity and closeness to the created world she is the first and the main target of the satanic power. If the evil powers could fill the *Shekhinah* with their own evil essence, the unity of the divine powers would be broken, constituting an enormous victory for the powers of evil. It is therefore the duty of man and the *Sefirot* to protect the *Shekhinah* from the designs of the powers of evil.

The *Shekhinah* is the divine power closest to the created world, of which it is the source and the sustaining power, and through her passes the divine light which maintains the created world. Accordingly the angels and the world of the *Merkavah* are all her servants. Furthermore, in kabbalistic theology the *Shekhinah* is the divine principle of the people of Israel. Everything that happens to Israel in the earthly world is therefore reflected upon the *Shekhinah* who waxes and wanes with every good deed and every sin of each individual Jew and of the people as a whole; on the other hand, everything that happens to the *Shekhinah,* her relationship with *Tiferet* and other *Sefirot* and her battle against the evil powers, is reflected in the status of Israel in the earthly world. Study of the Torah and prayer bring a Jew near the *Shekhinah,* for she is symbolized as the Oral Law.

The *Shekhinah* is also the divine power usually revealed to the prophets, though sometimes higher divine powers may take part in such a revelation, and she is the first goal of the mystic who tries to achieve *devekut,* communion with the divine powers; though a mystic may reach higher divine powers through *devekut,* the *Shekhinah* is the first and the closest for mystical contact. Finally, the idea of the exile of the *Shekhinah,* resulting from the initial cosmic disaster and from Adam's fall, became of great importance in Lurianic Kabbalah. To fulfill every commandment for the purpose of delivering the *Shekhinah* from her lowly state and reuniting her with the Holy One, blessed be He, became the supreme goal and in the process the notion of redeeming the *Shekhinah* from exile acquired new eschatalogical content. This Lurianic doctrine of redeeming the *Shekhinah* was active in the theology of Sabbateanism, as it was still later in Ḥasidism. In more recent Jewish mystical teachings the doctrine has continued to exercise an important influence.

LOGOS

The term *"logos"* meaning specifically the word of God in all its manifestations appears in Jewish and Christian theological texts in Greek from the Hellenistic period onwards. It can first be found in Aristobulus of Paneas, the Wisdom of Solomon, and Philo among the Jewish sources, while the Gospel of John is the earliest representative of the Christian material. The development and later history of the term belongs essentially to Christian theology, where, following John, *logos* is used as a synonym for the Son, or the preexistent Messiah.

The doctrine of the *logos* as an independent entity appeared in Jewish literature suddenly in the writings of Philo. Because of the connection between Philo's use of the term and the Johannine innovation, according to which *logos* is an intermediary between God and the world, scholars sought parallels elsewhere in Jewish writings, both for the word of God as a distinct concept and for its appearance as a divine intermediary. The *memra* ("word") of the Lord, one of the terms used to paraphrase the name of the Lord in the Targums, has been mistakenly viewed as such a parallel, as has *Ru'aḥ ha-Kodesh* (Holy Spirit).

Among early Greek philosopers Heraclitus (fifth century B.C.E.) considered *logos* as (1) the order of the universe, (2) the organizing force that originates and maintains that order, and (3) human apprehension and reasoned expression of it. All these things for him are one and the same, and are, it seems, to be identified with heat. Plato used the term primarily for logical discussion. However, in *Epinomis* (986c4), a dialogue almost certainly not written by Plato himself, *logos* is identified with the intelligence that governs and imposes rational structure in the world; in the Sixth Letter (323d2f.), whose authenticity is also disputed, the son of the true god is identified as "the divine governor and origin of all things present and future," which may point to some notion of the *logos* as an intermediary between true reality and the world in Greek sources. In Stoic thought *logos* again has the threefold role of (1) being responsible for fashioning things (2) accounting for the disposition of things (and so for the rational faculty in man), and (3) expressing reality in language.

In the Bible, by comparison, the word of God *(devar Adonai)* appears as divine teaching, i.e., the medium of revelation and guidance and as the instrument that controls nature. This multiple usage parallels in some ways the threefold, normative Greek philosophical identification of *logos,* except that the biblical emphasis is on moral, instead of natural, philosophy.[109]

Against this dual Jewish-Greek background, we find that the Jewish Hellenistic philosopher Aristobulus (fl. circa 160 B.C.E.) speaks of the voice of the Lord as the natural law, according to which the universe functions[110] and thus suggests a rapprochement of the Jewish and Greek notions. Likewise, in the *Wisdom of Solomon* (7:17–21), Wisdom *(logos)* teaches natural philosophy to man. In the same work *logos* also personifies divine Mercy (Wisdom 16:12) and slays the first-born of Egypt. The uses of the term *logos* in Aristobulus, the *Wisdom of Solomon* and other Jewish Hellenistic writings, however, are all of minor consequence compared to the centrality and importance that the notion gains in the work of Philo, and through Philo in Christianity.

It is in Philo's work that the *logos* emerges as a central concept. Influenced by neo-Platonic notions of reality and Stoic doctrines about the *logos* and the world, Philo held that God, in His perfection, could not deal directly with the impure and deficient world of material things. Therefore some means of bringing God and the material world together while not diminishing the distinction between them or alternatively, breaking them apart, needed to be found. Philo believed that this bridging operation is played by an entity known as the *logos*. The *logos* has three quite distinct meanings in Philo's thought: it is an attribute of God, at times seemingly the same as God Himself; it is an incorporeal being existing between God and the world and bringing the two together; and it is the immanent principle of order and rationality in the world itself. As an attribute of God it is pictured as God's chief power which unites His strength and His goodness and, more generally, which reconciles all tensions in His being. As an incorporeal intermediary it serves to bring God and man together and is the representative of God to His creations. In this respect it is also pictured as a copy or model through which the world was created and on which human intelligence is based. As such it is likened by Philo to God's Wisdom which is correspondingly associated with the pre-existent Torah. As the immanent principle of order and rationality in the world it is the pattern of creation which directs and maintains the material world.

The doctine of the *logos* is found infrequently in post-Hellenistic Jewish thought. This is due to the fact that this doctrine was used by Christian writers to express their trinitarian concerns and christological interests which made the doctrine suspect to Jewish thinkers. After this early period, Jewish thinkers, when trying to express the concept of God's immanence in the world and related notions, preferred to use other terms, especially that of the *Shekhinah,* as we have seen. However it must be noted, so as to avoid any confusion, that the concept of the *Shekhinah* is not equivalent to the later christological and trinitarian uses of the *logos*. That is to say, Judaism did not develop notions similar to those of Christianity, separated only by the use of a

Hebrew rather than a Greek vocabulary: after the rise of Christianity the two religious traditions went off in very different directions in the development of their notion of God. Thus, for example, the prologue to the Gospel of John follows apocryphal sources in portraying the preexistent *logos* dwelling on earth; but the presentation of *logos* as an independent agent and, furthermore, as the preexistent Messiah is a radical Christian innovation. It is most likely correct to say that even Philo did not think of either notion in connection with the *logos*.[111] Moreover, the *memra* of the Targums, whether it is used in an attempt to express the otherness of God or to avoid anthropomorphisms, or for some other reason, was not thought of by the sages as an intermediary between man and God and it was certainly not personified in rabbinic thought. The *memra* was also not identified with Torah regularly in rabbinic literature. In later rabbinic writing *ha-dibbur* ("the speech") is used to refer to God, but that phenomenon seems unrelated to the Jewish-Hellenistic understanding of *logos*.[112]

Anthropomorphism

Anthropomorphism, a Greek term meaning the attribution to God of human physical form or psychological characteristics, is a normal phenomenon in almost all religious literature. In Jewish literary sources from the Bible to the *aggadah* and Midrashim, the use of anthropomorphic descriptions and expressions (both physical and psychical) is also widespread. Yet at the same time it is accepted as a major axiom of Judaism, from the biblical period onward, that no material representation of the Deity is possible or permissible. The resolution of this apparent contradiction requires consideration and understanding of virtually every anthropomorphic expression. In every instance it should be asked whether the expression is an actual, naively concrete personification of God, or a fresh and vital form of religious awareness resorting to corporeal imagery, or an allegorical expression, in which the anthropomorphism is not merely an aesthetic means for the shaping of a particular perception or utterance, but is rather a conscious method of artificially clothing spiritual contents in concrete imagery.

The evolutionary approach to the study of religion, which mainly developed in the 19th century, suggested a line of development beginning with anthropomorphic concepts and leading up to a more purified spiritual faith. It argued, among other things, that corporeal representations of the Deity were more commonly found in the older portions of the Bible than in its later books. However, this view does not distinguish between the different possible explanations for anthropomorphic terms and it especially fails to account for the phenomenon common in the history of all cultures, that sometimes a later period can be more primitive than an earlier one. In fact, both personifications of the Deity as well as attempts to avoid them are found side by side in all parts of the Bible. The paucity of anthropomorphisms in certain works is not necessarily proof of any development in religion, but may well be due to the literary characteristics and intentions of certain biblical narratives, e.g., the narratives designed to express the growing distance between God and man through describing His relationship to Adam, the patriarchs, and the early and late prophets, etc.

Let us consider the problem as it presents itself in the Bible first. An obviously anthropomorphic expression is found in Genesis: *ẓelem Elohim* ("the image of God") and there are references to actually "seeing" God. The limbs of the human body frequently serve as allegorical descriptions of the acts of God as perceived by man. Thus divine providence is referred to as "the eyes of the Lord" and "the ears of the Lord" (very common in Prophets and Psalms); "the mouth of the Lord" speaks to the prophets (both in Torah and Prophets); the heavens are the work of His fingers and the tablets of the covenant are written by the finger of God. Striking figurative expressions are *af* ("nose"; i.e., "the wrath of the Lord"), "His countenance" (which He causes to shine or, alternatively, hides), *yad* ("hand," "His right hand," "His arm," "His sword"). At times the personification is startlingly extreme: God (or His voice) "walks about in the garden"; He "goes down" in order to see what is being done on the earth or in order to reveal Himself there, and He "goes up again"; He goes through the land of Egypt and passes over the houses of the Israelites; He sits on a throne, causes His voice to be heard among the cherubim who are over the ark of the tabernacle, dwells in Zion and in Jerusalem; the hair of His head is as wool; Moses sees "His back." In addition, anthropomorphic expressions abound in the song at the Red Sea and in the song of David.[113]

More important from a theological perspective are the anthropopathisms, or psychical personifications of the Deity. Scripture attributes to God love and hate, joy and delight, regret and sadness, pity and compassion, disgust, anger, revenge, and other feelings. Even if one explains these terms as being nothing but picturesque expressions, intended to awaken within man a sense of the real presence of God and His works, nonetheless they remain personifications. The basis for such terms is the conception of God as a Being who wills in a personal (though not exactly in a human) way. This personalized conception of the Deity, in conjunction with the axiomatic belief in His absolute transcendence, leads to unusual boldness in the use of anthropomorphic imagery.

Ultimately, every religious expression is caught in the dilemma between the theological desire to emphasize the absolute and transcendental nature of the Divine, thereby relinquishing its vitality, immediate reality and relevance, and the religious need to conceive of the Deity and man's contact with Him in some vital and meaningful way. Jewish tradition has usually shown preference for the second tendency, and there is a marked readiness to speak of God in a very concrete and vital manner and not to recoil from the dangers involved in the use of apparent anthropomorphisms.

However, this anthropomorphic style is frequently accompanied by mitigating expressions indicating reservations. The basic opposition to all such personifications is decisively formulated in the Decalogue. In addition, it finds expression in many verses which maintain that nothing can be compared to God, who has no form or shape, cannot be seen, is eternal and without end (very frequent in the Pentateuch, Former and Latter Prophets, Psalms, Job, and Chronicles). Yet, many of these verses appear to contradict others which describe God in corporeal terms (for example, Ex. 20:4; Deut. 4:15, as against Gen. 1:26, and Num. 23:19 and I Sam. 15:29 as against Gen. 6:6). These verses emphasize the transcendent nature of the Divine, not in philosophical abstractions but in vivid descriptive expressions. In other places one finds attempts to avoid such personifications and to substitute less daring imagery; if it is said, on the one hand, that the Lord dwells in His sanctuary (Ex. 35:8), and also appears in the cloud over the cover of the ark (Lev. 16:2), there are, on the other hand, verses which speak instead of God's *kavod* "glory" or *Shemo,* "His name." [114]

It should also be noted that there is no evidence of any physical representation of God in Jewish history (in contradistinction to the worship of Canaanite and other foreign gods by Israelites). Even the golden calves of Jeroboam represented, according to the view of most scholars, only a footstool for the invisible God. In archaeological excavations no images of the God of Israel have been unearthed and, interesting, biblical Hebrew is the only fully developed language which has no specific term for the notion "goddess."

The method of mitigating offensive anthropomorphisms by means of small emendations, described by the *tannaim* (Sages of the Mishnah) as "biblical modifications of expression," is also prevalent in the early translations of Scripture. The Aramaic translation Targum Onkelos often renders the name of the Lord in such substitutes as "the glory of the Lord," "the Word of the Lord," and "fear of the Lord." Similarly, he translates "He saw" or "He knew," referring to the Deity as "it was revealed before Him"; "He went down" becomes "He revealed Himself"; "He heard" becomes "it was heard before Him," and other similar examples.[115] If the same verb is used in the Bible to describe an action of God and of man, Onkelos uses two different words in order to distinguish clearly between the Divine and the human as, for example, in Gen. 32:29, 40:8 and Ex. 14:31; He is less hesitant, however, about attributing man's psychical qualities to God, and he translates such expressions as hatred, love, anger, and the like without making any changes for those words which indicate regret and sadness on the part of God (Gen. 6:6). Yet Onkelos is not consistent in his treatment of anthropomorphism, as Maimonides already observed (*Guide,* 2:33), and it has been suggested that he prepared his translation with the simple worshipper in mind: expressions whose metaphorical meaning was obvious, were translated literally; where misunderstanding and error were likely, his translation circumvents the anthropomorphism by a paraphrase. The other Aramaic translators follow a similar course, although the Aramaic translation known as "Targum Yerushalmi" goes even further in avoiding anthropomorphisms than does Onkelos and Targum Jonathan to the Prophets.

The same sentences and point of view generally also apply to the Greek translations of the Bible. For instance, *temunah* ("likeness") is always translated in the Septuagint as μορφή ("form") or ὁμοίωμα ("likeness"), and, if it refers to the Deity (Num. 12:8), it is rendered δοξα ("that which appears"). The Septuagint is also extremely careful with God's "wrath," "anger," and similar terms, which the Aramaic Targums never hesitate to translate literally. Yet even within the Septuagint one ultimately finds no consistency in handling anthropomorphisms. Among the other Greek translations, of which only fragments are extant, Symmachus[116] is the most consistent in avoiding personifications of the Deity. For example, in Genesis 1:27, he separates the terms "in the image of God," reading instead: "in the image—God created him" (the Targum Yerushalmi attributed to Jonathan treats this verse in a similar manner).

Among the Hellenistic philosophers, Aristobulus[117] deals in a systematic way with the "true" (that is, the allegorical) interpretation of anthropomorphic verses in Scripture, basing himself on the methods and ideas of Greek thinkers and poets. The consistent avoidance of any personification of God led Philo of Alexandria to the concept of a Deity who neither acts nor creates, who is without attributes or qualities and hence no kind of positive relationship to this world could be attributed to him. Yet at the same time Philo could not be unaware of the dynamic vitality and activity of God as portrayed in the Bible and this contradiction caused him to posit an intermediate being between God and the world, the *logos*. Philo's biblical exegesis is an attempted allegorization of Scripture to coincide with this view. Hence we must be careful to distinguish the *memra* ("word") of Onkelos and the *logos* of Philo, which despite their terminological similarity cannot in fact be equated.

As compared to the Targum and Hellenistic Jewish literature, rabbinical *aggadah* essentially follows the biblical manner of boldly using anthropomorphic imagery, while at the same time qualifying it. In the *aggadah* the number of substitute terms for God increases. To the *memra* of the Targum are now added other names and circumlocutions, such as *gevurah* ("strength"), *shamayim* ("heaven"), *makom* ("place"), etc. Sentences in which personifications occur are softened by means of the qualifying term *kivyakhol* ("so to speak," "as it were") or by means of sayings such as "if it were not written in Scripture, it would be impossible to utter it." Occasionally, anthropomorphic personifications of God are justified for didactic reasons and by the need to make divine truth accessible to human understanding: "The Torah speaks in the language of man."[118] At times the rabbis resort to anthropomorphic language in order to drive home a moral lesson. Thus God's "descent" on Mount Sinai is used for the following exhortation: "Let a man always learn from his Creator, for here the Holy One blessed be He forsook all of the mountains and high hills and caused His presence to rest on the lowly Mount Sinai" (Sot. 5a). Similarly, on the third day after the circumcision of Abraham, "the Holy One blessed be He said to the ministering angels: Let us go down and visit the sick man."

However, definite attempts to qualify anthropomorphic tendencies are evident in other homilies on the revelation at Sinai: "The Divine Presence never descended, nor did Moses and Elijah ever ascend to heaven" (Suk. 5a). Likewise, the commandment to cleave to the Lord is explained in the Talmud in this way: "As He is compassionate, so should you be compassionate; as He visits the sick, so should you visit the sick" (Shab. 133b). But the original version of the Midrash read: "As He is called compassionate and gracious, so should you be compassionate and gracious," thereby avoiding the potential personification involved (Sif. Deut. 11:22). The rabbis did not recoil from such terms whenever they thought them useful to impress man with an awareness of the existence of God, His love and His fear, and, hence, aggadic literature abounds in statements to the effect that the Holy-One-blessed-be-He studies the law (Hag. 15b), puts on *tefillin* (Ber. 6a), weeps over the destruction of the Temple, and the like.

As we enter the medieval period we see that the proper explanation of the anthropomorphic passages in biblical and aggadic texts became a major problem in Jewish theological thought. Generally one may discern three main trends of thought with regard to it, although there are no clear lines of demarcation, and the number of intermediate positions is considerable: (1) Allegorization: every anthropomorphic description of the Deity is explained simply as a metaphor. This approach developed chiefly through the influence of Greek and Arabic philosophy. (2) Talmudic orthodoxy: a well-nigh literal understanding of the sayings of the rabbis. Philosophical, i.e., allegorical, exegesis was considered a danger to religion, since the whole biblical, halakhic, and aggadic tradition might easily evaporate into allegorical ideas. (3) The mystical view: there are intermediate beings between God and the world (or stages of God's self-manifestation, i.e., the *Sefirot*), and all anthropomorphic expressions refer to these emanations from the Deity. Further support for this line of thought is found in the *Targumim* and *aggadah,* which make frequent use of such names as *Shekhinah* ("Divine Presence").

In the medieval period the discussion of the problem reached its zenith in the philosophical work of Maimonides, who insisted upon a nonliteral, allegorical understanding of all anthropomorphic expressions, both physical and psychical, and ruled that every anthropomorphism was outright heresy.[119]

The violence of Maimonides' polemic against anthropomorphic beliefs and doctrines suggests that these were fairly widespread, and that a great many people were affected by "the *aggadot* ("homilies") which confuse one's mind."[120] The influence of Maimonides, however, was both powerful and lasting. Even against the vehement opposition of more conservative thinkers of his day, most notably Abraham ben David of Posquières, Maimondes' *Guide* determined what was to become the accepted Orthodox concept of God within Judaism. There is evidence (e.g., Jedaiah ha-Penini of the 13th century, Moses Alashkár of the 15th) to show that it was the writings of Maimonides which finally did away with all anthropomorphic notions amongs Jews. It is interesting here to note that whereas in Maimonides' own lifetime his orthodoxy was suspected in some quarters because of his opposition to anthropomorphic beliefs, Spinoza was equally strongly denounced in the 17th century for his rejection of Maimonides' principles of exegesis and for his contention that scriptural anthropomorphisms were originally meant to be taken literally.

Turning from philosophy to Kabbalah, we find a different and far more extensive and positive employment of anthropomorphic language. Thus, for example, in the talmudic *Merkavah* (the heavenly throne-chariot) mysticism, which taught the ascent of the ecstatic soul into the realm of the divine throne, there is a description of the revelation of the divine majesty in the form of a human figure (following Ezekiel 1:26), which became the focal point of this vision. This description is found in fragments of a tract called *Shi'ur Komah*,[121] literally "the measure of the body," i.e., the body of God as He appears, revealing Himself in this form. The text, attributed to the two mishnaic rabbis R. Ishmael and R. Akiva, gives enormous figures for the measurement of each organ of that divine primordial man on the throne. Such measurements are preserved, for example, of God's right and left eyes, of His lips, and other parts. The description of God's organs is designedly linked with the description of the beloved one in the Song of Songs 5:11–15, and it is certainly connected with some esoteric doctrine about the Song of Songs as a mystical text. It constitutes a major piece of theosophy, no longer clear, evolved precisely within the circle of strict rabbinical Orthodoxy. The age of these fragments, which were forcefully attacked by the Karaites as a profanation and degradation of the religious concepts about God, was for long debated. Some philosophic apologists of the Middle Ages, for whom the existence of these doctrines was a source of embarrassment, tried to explain them away as late forgeries, though, in contradiction, Judah Halevi justified the *Shi'ur Komah* "because it brings the fear of God into the souls of men" (*Kuzari* 4:3). Later Maimonides ruled that it was unquestionably an idolatrous work and should be destroyed.[122]

The term *Shi'ur Komah* appears as the keyword of an esoteric doctrine connected with the Song of Songs in the hymns of Eleazar ha-Kallir, which are pre-Islamic, and the existence of an esoteric doctrine about the Song of Songs is attested in the third century by the church father Origen who lived at Caesarea. By this reference Origen cannot have meant the openly accepted allegorization of the Song of Songs as the relationship between God and Israel, but must have had in mind a doctrine about the appearance of God in the form of the beloved one, such as is taught by the *Shi'ur Komah*. Saul Lieberman[123] has shown that in the earlier *aggadah* the revelation of God on His *Merkavah* at the exodus from Egypt and the revelation on Mount Sinai, are in fact attested in a manner which fits into the traditions of the *Shi'ur Komah*. However, it is clear from the extant fragments that this extreme form of anthropomorphism was not really meant to describe the Divine Being as corporeal. The description here is of a visionary apparition, however exotic, but not the appearance of God Himself.

In medieval kabbalistic literature, *Shi'ur Komah* was interpreted as a symbol for the revelation of the Divinity in the *Sefirot* (Divine Emanations) and therefore it was favorably appraised. Important parts of the Zohar, in particular the Great and Small *Idras,* represent a kind of kabbalistic adaptation or imitation of the *Shi'ur Komah*. In them, the theosophic beliefs of the kabbalists are quite consciously expostulated in the form of concrete descriptions of the features of the head of the Divinity, in order to doubly stress their symbolic character.[124]

PART II

MAN

Man in the Bible

NATURE AND PURPOSE OF MAN

A proper understanding of Judaism requires an adequate appreciation of the human situation. Man, no less than God, is an inescapable datum of the Jewish life of faith—indeed, God and man are dialectically related and the understanding of one colors and helps create an understanding of the other. In Jewish anthropology this human-divine dialectic is especially evident in Judaism's fundamental affirmation of the majesty of both God and His creature/co-partner in history—man. The Bible witnesses to this anthropological understanding and its centrality: the Bible, after all, is not about God alone or about man alone but about God and man together. This inter-relationship finds its paradigmatic expression in the fundamental biblical notion of Covenant and especially in the covenantal relationship of God and Israel, the story of which occupies the main stage in the biblical narrative to which everything and everyone else is subordinate.

A helpful way to begin to gain some substantial appreciation of the biblical idea of man is to examine briefly the most important terms used by the Scriptures to describe different aspects of his nature. First of all there is the term *adam* which the Bible usually employs as a collective term meaning "men," "human beings" or "mankind" in distinction to other creatures or to God. Secondly, there is the term *ish* meaning "individual (man)," "male" or "husband" (and sometimes "servant" or "soldier"). Thirdly, we find the term *enosh* which is used mainly to denote the human race collectively or to indicate frailty or mortality, as opposed to the term *gever,* which is used to indicate a strong man. Finally, we also find the term *metim,* which is used only in the plural and indicates "males" or "men" or "people."[1] From this variegated terminology we can see that the Bible suggests a complex image of man which recognizes and encompasses his activity as both an individual and a member of the human race, as a single person and as a member of a family, as both strong and weak (and this in both the physical and spiritual sense), and as both Lord and servant. In this way the biblical narrative does justice to the richness of human experience and also to the manifold and differing roles man is called upon to play in his concrete historical situation. The biblical authors thus avoid any simplistic rendering of the human situation or of man's place in history and cosmos.

Further insight into the nature of man is furnished by certain terms that describe different aspects of the human personality. The term *nefesh* can denote the essence of any living creature and may even be equated with the life blood. It signifies the "individual," "ego," "person" and hence even at the times the body (Exodus 21:23). Synonymous at times with *nefesh* but also distinguished from it is the term *ru'aḥ,* "spirit." It represents the power and energy that come to man from without; it provides the impulse to higher life and finds expression in special skill, might, or leadership. The concept of *neshamah,* "breath," is not only the vitalizing element breathed into man by God, but the divine spirit and lamp—the soul—within him. In contrast to these spiritual aspects of man, *basar* signifies his physical nature, the living body and, as such, it symbolizes human frailty, sensuality and mortality.[2]

The Bible also regards certain organs as the seat of given psychological attributes. Thus, *lev,* the "heart," is the center of thought, conscience and emotion (love, joy, hatred, courage, and the like). The heart also represents the whole inner life of man. The *kelayot,* "kidneys" (in stylized "biblical" English "veins"), are likewise the source of emotion and conscience, and in conjunction with "heart" describe the fundamental character of man. Overpowering feelings finds their partial expression in *me'ayim,* "bowels," modern versions sensibly substitute "heart" for "kidneys" or "bowels" in such contexts. The word for "liver," *kaved,* also means "being" while *raḥamim*—from *reḥem,* "womb"—means "compassion." *Yad,* "hand," is often used in the sense of "power." Other shades of psychological significance are also expressed by other parts of the body, e.g., face, eyes, ears, head, and so forth.[3]

This extensive nomenclature, though pointing to the complexity of the human personality, is not exhaustive. The complete picture of man's nature as envisaged by the Bible can only be seen in the full context of scriptural evidence.

The key is to be found in the story of man's origin. He is not a descendant of the gods (as in certain pagan mythologies); the term child(ren) used in Scripture with reference to man in relation to God (Deuteronomy 14:1; Psalm 2:7) has a metaphorical connotation. Nor is man the product (as some philosophical systems hold) of the blind forces of nature. He is the artifact of God, fashioned purposefully out of two diverse elements: his body is of the earth, but it is animated by the divine breath of life. Yet man is not a dichotomy of body and soul (a view characteristic of Orphism and Platonism), and certainly not a trichotomy of elements. His is a multifacted unitary being—*nefesh hayyah,* "a living person" (Genesis 2:7).

Of particular significance is the concept that all humans, irrrespective of ethnic and cultural differences, stem from two common ancestors, Adam and Eve. Humanity, despite its diversification, is essentially a single family, and men remain brothers even in the face of hatred and murder (Genesis 4:9–10). To this inherent brotherhood and equality of all there were no exceptions. Furthermore, the world was divinely planned to be one of creaturely peace, harmony, and understanding; mankind, as well as other living things, was not to destroy its fellow creatures even for food. The permission granted to Noah to eat flesh was a sad concession to a world that had lost its original idealism (Genesis 9:3). Finally monogamy is clearly viewed in the creation story as the proper marital state.

However, the Bible does not merely stress the creatureliness of man. It depicts him as the peak of creation. He climaxes the ascending course of the six days of the Beginning. He is formed by special resolve (Genesis 1:26) and in a unique manner (Genesis 2:7). However, his crowning glory is that he was made in the divine "image" and "likeness,"[4] which endow him with unique worth. Man alone among the creatures is capable of sustained thought, creativity, and awareness of God; the spirit of God is immanent in him. Hence he is given dominion over the earth (Genesis 1:26, 28) and is privileged to commune with God and enjoy His fellowship (Genesis 2–3). In the language of later rabbinic literature, he became a "partner" of the Creator.[5] The dualism of man's status and significance within the unified framework of his psychophysical being is given unmatched expression by the Psalmist:

"What is man that Thou art mindful of him . . . Yet Thou hast made him little less than the angels" (8:5–6).

There is still another aspect of the divine image reflected in man, which plays a crucial role in the profound parable of the Garden of Eden. In a supreme act of self-limitation the Absolute God gave man freedom of moral choice. He could will to do right or wrong, to obey or disobey his Maker. It was heaven's greatest gift to man: he was not to be an automaton. However, the immediate consequences were calamitous. Man rebelled against the Creator: he introduced disharmony into the universal harmony. Sin was born and in turn begot suffering and death. History had begun.

While the Bible is unequivocal in its assertion of the reality of human responsibility for evil and in condemning sin trenchantly as estrangement from and treason against God (this is the meaning of the story of Eden), it is no less emphatic in its affirmation of God's grace and readiness to forgive. Sin is never final. It is punished, or rather punishes itself. However, retribution is part of the divine redemptive process. It helps man to seek atonement, which the divine love never fails to vouchsafe.

The road of redemption, however, is hard and long. Outside the Garden of Eden man's iniquity reaches new depths. Brotherhood as well as "sonship" are made difficult. Cain's example was widely imitated. It almost seemed that the making of man was a divine error which only the Flood could expunge. At this point, however, a new providential principle manifests itself—the elective factor. The family of Noah is chosen from a doomed generation to be saved and to save the world. Later Abraham is elected to be a source of blessing to all mankind (Genesis 12:3). Israel, the seed of Abraham, were chosen to be "a kingdom of priests and a holy nation" (Exodus 19:6). Though themselves far from perfect, they were destined to become a light to the world, illuminating the way of ethical and spiritual truth. To this end God made a covenant with Israel at Sinai (Deuteronomy 5:2), which found detailed expression in the Torah. Religious and secular precepts are inextricably intermingled in the Law, for human life is a unity and must be dedicated to God's will in all its diversified aspects. God is served in the righteousness of human relationships—in love between man and man, which reflects God's image—as well as in divine worship: the two are inseparable. When the "image" is wronged, religious service becomes an abomination, as the Prophets so vividly testify.

The path toward God is further delineated and interpreted by the Prophets, and even by figures (like Abraham and Job, and some of the Psalmists) who question God's moral government of the world. Revelation—the word of God understood in its broadest sense—is the great antidote to sin, leading man to repentance and regeneration. The relevance of this biblical teaching is not confined to Israel. In a profound sense, the Bible tells the story of Everyman in all generations. Even when Israel is the focal point of the Bible's concern, the universal concept of mankind is never ignored. Israel's significance, in turn, flows from man's relation to God. History is thus seen as the moral and spiritual drama of the human species.

NATURE AND PURPOSE OF WOMAN

The biblical image of woman, in contra-distinction to that held more widely in the Ancient Near East, was generally favorable in the context of both society as a whole and the family in particular. The Bible uses the term *ishah* both for the generic meaning of "woman" and also for "wife." Interestingly, the term, despite the wordplay in Genesis 2:22–23, probably does not derive from either the Hebrew word *ish* (man) or *enosh* (man or mankind).

The biblical view of woman's origin and purpose is expressed in Genesis 2:23–24. She is said to have been created from a rib taken from the first man in order to be a partner and assistant to man. The story of the rib is meant to indicate her inseparable connection to man and her essential character as man's companion. In the biblical anthropology it is clear that she manifests these attributes primarily in the role of mother. Two sexes were required for reproduction and continuation of the human race. Especially and ideally, the woman fulfilled this role as wife and mother in marriage and the good wife and mother are lavishly praised.

Womanly traits, both good and bad, were much commented upon. The foolish, the contentious, the fretful, as well as the fair but indiscreet, were all censured. On the other hand, the gracious woman *(eshet ḥen)* was honored. Likewise, the highest praise was given to the *eshet ḥayil*—the virtuous woman extolled in Proverbs (31:10ff) and who is described as industrious, thrifty, diligent in household skills, and generous in her concern for others.

The surest evidence of a society's estimation of the position of woman is found in its legislation. Here we find clear evidence of the Bible's concern and regard for woman. Thus a girl's wishes were not to be ignored when a marriage contract was made, and the sensitivities of a female war captive were to be respected. Likewise, quite out of keeping with the normal practice of ancient legal codes, the owner of an ox paid the same penalty if his animal gored a man or a woman or a child. Special attention was paid to injury suffered by a pregnant woman during a brawl between men. Likewise both parties guilty of adultery, the man and the woman, were subject to the death penalty and both faced capital punishment for stepmother-stepson incest and a higher punitive measure for sibling (or half sibling) incest. The regulations pertaining to food were incumbent on women as well as men and the law demanded equal respect for the father and the mother.[6]

Within the Covenant women had the same moral responsibility as men. The man or the woman who apostasized would suffer the death penalty. Lesser infractions, atonable by sacrifice and restitutions, were also charged against both men and women; this also proves that the latter could offer their own sacrifices, and though the three annual pilgrimages were incumbent on men only, it is clear that women often accompanied their husbands. Moreover the assembly of the seventh year did require the presence of the women and children. In addition women were eligible to take the Nazirite vow, but a woman's competence to make religious vows was limited, being valid only if her guardian (father or husband) did not intervene.[7]

Nevertheless, there were certain laws that reveal that some inferior status was assigned to women in Israelite society. A man could sell his daughter as payment for a debt but he was forbidden to force her into prostitution. If she were sold into bondage (concubinage seems to be the only object sanctioned by the law), her master was forbidden to resell her. If he were not satisfied with her, she could be redeemed; if he gave her to his son, he was to treat her as a daughter. She might be released if her master did not provide for her proper maintenance but the automatic rule of release in the seventh year was not applicable to her (Exodus 21:7–11) as it was to a man. The divergent law of Deuteronomy 15:12–17 seems to contemplate the possibility of an Israelite woman being sold into bondage for service only (perhaps as the wife of a man who sells himself into slavery because of his poverty).

Woman's role in organized worship was limited to secondary

functions. There was no order of priestesses in Israel. However, women were credited with contributions for the Tabernacle and when David brought the ark to Jerusalem, there were women in the joyous procession. Likewise, young girls with tambourines also took part along with the musicians on festive occasions. In addition, women were commonly associated with magic and divination (Exodus 22:17; I Samuel 28:3ff.).[8]

Furthermore, apart from the laws of ritual impurity to which both men and women were subject, a woman was additionally regarded as ritually impure both during her menstrual flow and for seven days thereafter. She was also regarded as ritually impure for the first seven days after giving birth to a male child and forbidden to touch consecrated objects or visit a sanctuary for the next 33 days; both figures are doubled if the child was a female (Leviticus 12:2–5).

Despite some of these seemingly negative features, women play an important part in the public life of Israel in the biblical narrative. Deborah stands out for her political and military leadership in a confrontation with Israel's enemy. Miriam, the sister of Aaron and Moses, is the paradigm of a female prophetess who plays an important national-religious role. Deborah, likewise, is seen as a true prophetess, as is Huldah who prophesied during the reign of Josiah and who is consulted in matters of national policy (II Kings 22:12–20). On the other hand, Ezekiel (ch. 13) complains of unworthy female as well as male prophets, and Nehemiah (6:10–14) refers to a prophetess among the false prophets who tried to discourage him from completing the restoration of the walls of Jerusalem.

Given these various, often seemingly contradictory, elements, it is hard to generalize about the biblical view of woman. Nonetheless, on balance, and especially given the role played by some admittedly extraordinary women, it seems clear that though a social sense very different from ours was operative at the time, the role of woman was not seen negatively in the Bible.

SIN

In biblical Hebrew there are about 20 different words which denote "sin." It may be inferred therefore, that the ancient Israelites had more concepts expressing various nuances of sin than are prevalent in

Western thought and theology. A study of the biblical concept of sin, therefore, cannot disregard the diversity of words by which it is expressed. These words must be examined in their context, i.e., in the formulas and literary units in which they occur. The three most commonly used terms are: *het, pesha,* and *avon.*[9]

The root *ht* occurs in the Bible 459 times. The original meaning of the verb *hata* is "to miss" something, "to fail."[10] In its evolution, the root came to signify a failure of mutual relations, corresponding, thus, to the modern idea of "offense" rather than to that of "sin," which is a theological concept. One who fulfills the claims of a given relationship or agreement is righteous, *zaddik;* one who does not, offends his partner. "What is my offense that you have so hotly pursued after me?" Jacob asks Laban. David puts a similar question to Jonathan in connection with his relation to Saul which was of such a nature that it required of David that he devote all his abilities to the service of Saul, and of the latter that he treat David as his loyal subject. The obligation was mutual as long as it was upheld by both parties. When Saul and David were in the same cave, and David was content to cut off the skirt of Saul's robe, he called out to Saul that it was now clear that he had not "offended" him. Then Saul acknowledged that David was righteous and that he himself was the offender, since he had not fulfilled his obligations.

All lack of obedience toward superiors is "offense," because in the relations between subordinates and superiors, the former are expected to obey the latter. The Egyptian baker and cupbearer who were in prison with Joseph had been sent there because they had "failed" to obey the orders of Pharaoh. The people of Pharaoh were accused of "failing" *(ht)* in their duty, when they did not give any straw to the Israelites so that they might make bricks. The same applies to every deed that is in conflict with, or causes the dissolution of, a community. So Reuben acknowledged that his brothers "sinned" against their brother Joseph. When the king of the Ammonites attacked Israel, Jephthah sent him word explaining that there had always been a relation of peace between the two peoples, and he addressed to him the following reproach: "I have not 'sinned' against you, but you do me wrong to war against me." The "sin" is here a breach of the covenant relation between the peoples. When Sennacherib threatened Judah in 701, King Hezekiah sent a messenger to him, saying: "I have 'sinned'."

The "sin" of Hezekiah consisted in a violation of his vassal duties.[11]

According to I Samuel 2:25, failure in carrying out one's duty can concern the relations between men or between God and man: "If a man offends against a man, God will mediate, but if a man offends against God, who shall act as mediator?" This passage indicates that the "sin" against God was also conceived as an "offense," as a failure to fulfill one's obligation toward God. Since the root *ht* denotes an action, that failure is neither an abstraction nor a permanent disqualification but a concrete act with all its consequences. This act is defined as a "failure," an "offense," when it is contrary to a norm regulating the relations between God and man. So, for instance, the infringement of the law of the ban *(herem)* appears in Joshua 7:11, 20 and I Samuel 15:3–19 as an "offense" or "sin" against God in view of the traditions partially recorded in Deuteronomy 20:10–18. That adultery is a "sin" against the Lord results from a law such as Exodus 20:14. Social mischiefs stigmatized as "sins" by the prophets[12] are, in fact, contrary to commandments of the divine law such as Exodus 20:16 (13) and Deuteronomy 27:17–19. The concept of *het* extends not only to juridical, moral, and social matters, but also to cultic obligations, and even to involuntary infringements of ritual prescriptions (Leviticus 4–5) or of occasional divine premonitions (Numbers 22:34).

The second most common term for sin, based on the root *pesha* occurs in the Bible 136 times. Its basic meaning is that of "breach." In terms of international law, the breach of a covenant is thus called *pesha.* In the realm of criminal law, *pesha* is the delict which dissolves the community or breaks the peaceful relation between two parties. This is also the meaning of *pesha* when used to express the sinful behavior of man toward God.[13] Next there is the verb *avah,* found in the Bible 17 times, which basically expresses the idea of crookedness, and thus means "to wrong" (Lamentations 3:9), and in the passive form *(nif'al),* "to become bent" (Psalms 38:7). The noun *avon,* from the same root, is found 227 (in variants 229) times, and designates "crookedness." The use of these words in a figurative sense to denote the transgression, the guilt incurred by it, or the punishment, is of popular origin.

The nouns *het, hata'ah* or *hattat, pesha,* and *avon,* and also the corresponding verbs, denote a "sin" in the theological sense of the word when they characterize a human deed as a "failure," a "breach," or a "crooked" action with reference to prescriptions that proceed ultimately

from the stipulations of the Covenant. It is not the external nature of the
act that makes it sinful. In biblical thought, the relation that creates the
right to God's protection also creates the sin. There would be no sin if
there were no covenantal law. The sinner is one who had failed in his
relation to God, insofar as he has not fulfilled his obligation to God. In
other words, it is a "sin" to violate, or to break, the Covenant. The
biblical doctrine of sin is thus described in Jeremiah 16:10–12 in the
following way: "When you tell this people all this, and they say to you:
'Why has the Lord threatened us with such terrible misfortune? What is
our crime? What is the offense *(ht)* we have committed against the Lord
our God?'—then answer them: 'It is because your fathers forsook Me.
They followed other gods, worshipping them and doing obeisance to
them, and forsook Me and did not keep My law. And you have done
even worse than they did, each following his own stubbornly wicked
inclinations and refusing to listen to Me.'"

Even the sin of Adam and Eve, although not described as such in the
Bible, was an act that destroyed a special relation between God and
man (Genesis 3). The original sin does not appear in the Bible as an
innate depravity common to all human beings in consequence of the fall
of the first parents. Rather, the biblical tradition knows that "there is no
man who does not sin" (I Kings 8:46). The hyperbolic language in
which the psalmist describes his own sinfulness, "I was even born in iniquity, my mother conceived me in sin" (Psalms 51:7) only stresses the
ineluctable character of sin. Nobody can escape from it, as sin can
also be involuntary or proceed from ignorance, and yet a man is
responsible for all his actions. This does not mean, however, that the
ancient Israelites did not make a distinction between an inadvertent sin
and one that is committed wilfully. This distinction clearly emerges in
Numbers 15:27 and 30 and the psychological sentiment of guilt is also
expressed in various texts. Moreover, the subjective aspect of a deed is
clearly taken account of by the Torah, for example in Exodus 21:13–14
and Deuteronomy 19:4–5.

The idea of "deadly" or "mortal" sin originates in biblical expressions
connecting *ht* with *mvt*[14] ("to die" or "death"). The oldest text linking
the two is probably Amos 9:10, dating from the eighth century B.C.E.:
"All the sinners of my people shall die by the sword." The connection of
the formula expressing the death sentence with such an indefinite word
as "sin" or "offense" cannot be original. It must be regarded as a

generalization proceeding from theological reflection. Its original "setting in life" *(sitz im leben)* is still visible in Deuteronomy 21:22 and 22:16, which refer to the proceedings of the civil tribunal. Numbers 18:22 and 27:3, both of which belong to the Priestly tradition, reflect instead the sphere of sacral law. The remaining passages use the concept of "mortal sin" in a context of "prophetic" preaching.

In a certain sense, every sin may be regarded as "deadly"; for, if all people die, it is because all have sinned, and not in consequence of the "the original sin." That the sinner must die is stated or assumed by many texts.[15] Stereotyped formulas say even that "each man shall die because of his sins" or "because of his transgressions." The sinner must indeed "bear *(nasa)* his sin." The expression means practically "to take the blame upon oneself," and it normally refers to the sinner himself.[16] The law of retaliation demands, in fact, that the offender should be punished according to his sin. However, the same expression also occurs in early pleas for forgiveness, in a Thanksgiving Psalm, in a predication and in a song of The Suffering Servant in Deutero-Isaiah.[17]

In these texts, the one who takes the blame upon himself is God, the offended person, or a substitute of the sinner. There are still other cases when one's *avon* is borne by another person: by the priests, by Aaron, by the prophet Ezekiel, by the community, by the scapegoat, or even by a sacrificed goat.[18] It means that there was a possibility that the sin might not work its consequences upon the sinner. Accordingly, there was sense to the prayer for forgiveness of sin or the intercession of the prophet.[19] The ancient remedy, the sin-offering *(hattat),* also worked both for the purification of the person and to obtain the forgiveness of the Lord. It is probable that the slaughtered animal was originally regarded as a substitute for the sinner. The confession of sins was another means of winning forgiveness. In this way the sinner expels the sin from his heart; he shows at the same time that he does not intend to conceal his sin and to deceive the Lord.

The formula of the individual's confession of sins, expressed by the verb *hatati* ("I have sinned"), is found in the Bible 30 times. It has beyond any doubt a ritual character, even if it is used twice in a rather colloquial way (I Kings 18:9; Nehemiah 6:13). In the other instances, it is employed with reference to sacral judicial proceedings, as shown by the juridical terminology of the context. It is used not only when someone has sinned against God but also against man.[20] After the sinner was designated by the sacred lots, Urim and Thummim, he had to present a public confession of his sin, which was confirmed by an inquiry. The sin could be forgiven or not, it could be expiated by a sacrifice or by putting the sinner to death. On the other hand in I Samuel 15:24 and II Samuel 12:13 the casting of lots and public confession are dispensed with, the sin being confessed before the cultic prophet who accused the sinner in God's name. This procedure was probably characteristic of the early monarchical period.[21] These confessions occur in many different contexts: prayer, praise, interrogation, etc.; the confession of sins is thus often indirect.

The formula of the national confession of sins is expressed by the verb *hata'nu* ("we have sinned"). This verbal form occurs in the Bible 24 times, but only twice in texts that are definitely ancient, i.e., pre-seventh century. All these texts have a cultic or sacral character. Other formulas of national confession of sins, expressed by the word *pesha'enu* ("our sins") and *avonenu,* can be found in a wide variety of texts, all of which are exilic or post-exilic (i.e., 586 B.C.E. onward).[22] It seems, therefore, that contrary to the individual confession, the national one is a relatively late innovation in Israel's penitential liturgy.[23]

When God "forgives" one's sin, He "covers" or "hides" it. Though it is merely said that the sin is forgotten, covered, not imputed to the sinner,[24] God's forgiveness of sins is identical with the curing of the man and with the regeneration of his strength. It means, indeed, that God will not take him away "in the middle of his days (Jeremiah 17:11), but will permit him to spend on earth the full span of human life, i.e., "70 years" (Isaiah 23:15). Then He will cut him off by death, for "there is no righteous man on earth who does good and never sins" (Ecclesiastes 7:20).

REPENTANCE AND FORGIVENESS

The biblical concept of forgiveness presumes, in its oldest strata, that sin is a malefic force that adheres to the sinner, and that forgiveness is the divine means for removing it. This is demonstrated by the vocabulary of forgiveness which, in the main, stems from the cultic terminology of cleansing.[25] Even the most common verb for forgiveness, *salah,* probably derives from the Mesopotamian cult where it connotes sprinkling in purification rites. More significantly, the most prominent epithet of God in His role of forgiver is *nose avon/het/pesha* (lit., he who "lifts off sin").[26]

In the religion of ancient Israel, however, in contrast to that of its neighbors, rituals are not inherently efficacious. This point is underscored by the sacrificial formula of forgiveness. Whereas the required ritual is carried out by the priest, its desired end, forgiveness, is granted solely by God, e.g., "the priest shall make atonement for him for his sin and he shall be forgiven," i.e., by God (Leviticus 4:26). Another limitation placed upon sacrificial means of obtaining forgiveness is that it can only apply to inadvertent errors (Numbers 15:22–29). Blatant contempt of God cannot be expiated by sacrifice or any other means. Moreover, contrition and compassion are indispensable coefficients of all rituals·of forgiveness, whether they be expiatory sacrifices or litanies for fasting.[27]

Indeed, man's involvement both in conscience and deed is a *sine qua non* for securing divine forgiveness. It is not enough to hope and pray for pardon: man must humble himself, acknowledge his wrong, and resolve to depart from sin. The Psalms provide ample evidence that penitence and confession are integral components of all prayers for forgiveness.[28] The many synonyms for contrition testify to its primacy in the human effort to restore the desired relationship with God, e.g., seek the Lord (II Samuel 12:16; 21:1), search for Him (Amos 5:4), humble oneself before Him (Leviticus 26:41), direct the heart to Him (I Samuel 7:3), and lay open the heart (II Kings 22:19). The rituals of penitence, such as weeping, fasting, rending clothes, and donning sackcloth and ashes, are unqualifiedly condemned by the prophets if they do not correspond with, and give expression to the involvement of the heart.[29]

At the same time, inner contrition must be followed by outward acts: remorse must be translated into deeds. Two substages are involved in this process: first, the negative one of ceasing to do evil, and then the positive step of doing good.[30] Again, the richness of the biblical language used to describe man's active role in the process testifies to its centrality, e.g., incline the heart to the Lord (Joshua 24:23), make oneself a new heart (Ezekiel 18:31), circumcise the heart (Jeremiah 4:4), wash the heart (Jeremiah 4:14), and break one's fallow ground (Hosea 10:12). However, all these expressions are subsumed and summarized by one verb which dominates the penitential literature of the Bible, *shuv,* ("to turn," "to return") that develops ultimately into the rabbinic doctrine *teshuvah* ("repentance"). This doctrine implies that man has been endowed by God with the power of "turning." He can turn from evil to the good, and the very act of turning will activate God's concern and lead to forgiveness.

What is the source of the biblical optimism that man's turning will generate divine movement to pardon him? This confidence resides in a number of assumptions concerning the nature of God, as presumed by the unique relationship between God and Israel, the bond of the covenant. Covenant implies mutuality of obligation, that Israel's fidelity to God's demands will be matched by God's response to Israel's needs, particularly in his attitude of forgiveness.[31] That is why in the wilderness traditions, Moses can continue to plead with God despite the lapses of his people, because of his certainty that God's forgiveness is a constant of his nature.[32] Again, the profusion of idioms expressing divine forgiveness (in addition to the cultic expressions, mentioned above), e.g., overlook sin (Micah 7:18), not reckon it (Psalms 32:2), not remember it (Psalms 25:7), hide his face from it (Psalms 51:11), suppress it, remove it (Psalms 103:12), throw it behind his back (Isaiah 38:17) or into the sea (Micah 7:19), points to the centrality of this concept.

Another covenant image that invokes God's attitude of forgiveness is His role of Father and Shepherd. A father's love for his children can lead them to hope that their sins will be forgiven. Furthermore, this parental relationship shows that Israel's suffering is not inflicted as retribution for their sins, but as corrective discipline—"afflictions of love"—so that Israel may correct its ways.[33]

Another component of the covenant is that God will accept the mediation of an intercessor. He is, however, not bound to comply with the plea of the intercessor—in contradistinction to the coercive claims of the pagan magician—for God will reject even the mediation of the most righteous when Israel's sins have exceeded the limit of His forbearance. Intercession is, first and foremost, the function of Israel's prophets. Indeed, the only time Abraham is called a prophet is at the precise moment when his intercessory powers are invoked (Genesis 20:7). Moses' main concern, to judge by the narratives of the Exodus and the wandering in the wilderness, is to intervene on behalf of others.[34] The psalmist singles this out in his eulogy of Moses: "He (God) said He would have destroyed them, had not Moses, the chosen one, stood in the breach before Him" (Psalms 106:23). To "stand in the breach" is for Ezekiel the main function of the prophet (Ezekiel 13:5; 22:30).

An equally significant concomitant of God's covenant is His promise to the forefathers that the people of Israel will exist forever and that they will be in eternal possession of Erez Israel. This aspect of the covenant is constantly invoked in pleas for forgiveness.[35]

This promise to the forefathers bears a final corollary. Because of the covenant, God's honor is at stake in the world. Israel's woes will not be comprehended by the nations as divine punishment for its violations of the covenant, but as God's inability to fulfill His covenantal obligations. This argument features prominently in Moses' intercession and is mentioned repeatedly in subsequent prayers for Israel's pardon. Conversely, the argument continues, it is important for God to redeem Israel for the glorification and sanctification of His name throughout the world, even if Israel itself is undeserving of forgiveness.[36]

DEATH

The Hebrew word for death is *mavet,* from the root *mvt.* This term is borrowed from the Canaanites, for whom *Mot (Mvt)* was the god of the underworld.

In the Bible there are two reasons given for man's death: the first states that God made man from the dust of the earth, and to dust he must return. Genesis 3:22–24 gives a second reason: that of sin. By his expulsion from paradise, man was deprived of access to the tree of life, and thus eternal life was lost to him. The sentence of death as expressed in Genesis 3:19, "By the sweat of your face shall you get bread to eat until you return to the ground. For from it you were taken. For dust you are, and to dust you shall return,"[37] is opposed to other biblical passages that speak of the dead who go down into the tomb and enter the region of the dead.[38]

Many names are given to this netherworld in the Bible. The most common is *she'ol,* always written in the feminine form and without a definite article as is usual in proper nouns. This term has no parallels in other ancient languages and is peculiarly Hebraic. Other biblical terms for this region include *erez* ("earth," "underworld"); *kever* ("grave"), whose Akkadian parallel *gabru* normally designates the world of the dead; *afar* ("dust"); *bor* ("pit"); *shahat nahalei beliyya'al* ("the torrents of Belial"). Moreover, this region is said to be in the depths of the earth and is therefore called "the nether parts of the earth," "the depths of the pit" and "the land of darkness."[39]

Furthermore in the Bible great importance is placed on burial, especially in the family tomb.[40] On the other hand, not to be buried at all is a serious punishment.[41] Burial and care of the dead are also inspired by self-interest because they can affect the world of the living either for good or for evil and can even foretell the future (I Samuel 28:15–20).

The reticence of the Torah on matters concerning the dead is easily understandable when one/appreciates the importance the cult of the dead played in other, especially Egyptian, religions, and the desire of the Torah to separate Israel from these practices. Thus, there is nothing in the Torah about honoring the dead; on the contrary, there are prohibitions about mourning certain persons, and it is forbidden to give them alms (Deuteronomy 26:14) or to consult them. The sacrifices to the dead, forbidden by Deuteronomy 26:14, are linked by Psalm 106:28 to idolatry: "They joined themselves also unto Baal-Peor, and ate the sacrifices of the dead." The custom of bringing meals to the dead did not however disappear, and during the Second Temple period, at least in certain devout circles, it was considered a pious work: "Pour out thy bread on the tomb of the just and do not give it to sinners" (Tob. 4:7). Ben-Sira, however, attacks this belief (Ecclus. 30:18). All these prohibitions are linked to the general biblical concern to wean the people of Israel away from the religious practices of the idolatrous nations around them, especially the Egyptians with whom they had lived for hundreds of years first as neighbors and then as slaves. This concern is also generally credited by later authorities as the reason for the Bible's reticence to speak of eschatological matters such as immortality of the soul and resurrection of the body.[42]

Man in Talmudic Literature

NATURE AND PURPOSE OF MAN

The sages of the Talmud continued where the Bible left off. Thus they discussed, debated and developed the major anthropological themes already mentioned in, and central to, biblical thought. Beginning with a concern for man's physical nature the sages were prompted to teach, while reflecting on the process of human gestation and especially the preservation of the embryo, that man's creation clearly reflected both God's skill and solicitude. This reflects the general rabbinic respect and awe for man and the love of God they saw evidenced in him.[43]

The fact that every hair of man's head is fed through a separate root is cited, for example, as further evidence of God's careful workmanship. It was taught that from each of his parents man receives five parts of his body, and ten parts from God. From his father, he receives bones, veins, nails, brain, and white of the eye; from his mother, skin, flesh, blood, hair, and the pupil of the eye. To his formation, God contributes breath, soul, light of countenance, sight, hearing, speech, touch, sense, insight, and understanding. Hence, the rabbinic saying that there are three partners in man—his father and mother and God.[44] A late Midrash[45] describes the human body as possessing ten orifices, including the navel. The marvel is, the Midrash continues, that when the child is in the embryonic state, the navel is open and the other orifices are closed but when it issues from the womb, the navel is closed and the other orifices are opened.

In the totality of his physical structure, man constitutes a microcosm.[46] An elaborate parallel, covering 30 items, is drawn between the various components of the human body and similar features in the physical world. A hardly less complex parallel is found to exist between the organs of the human body and the structure and ves-

115

sels of the Tabernacle.[47] A simpler summation of man's physical being is deciphered in the word *adam* ("man") as being an acronym for "dust" *(efer)*, "blood" *(dam)* and "gall" *(marah)*. In their deliberations the rabbis also give a remarkably accurate enumeration of the 248 organs of the human body. It may be fairly said that the rabbinic reflection on the complex mechanism of man's physical structure served as occasion for the admiring reverence for the skill and wisdom with which God created him. Indeed, its unknown aspects suggested the argument that if man does not know his own body, he certainly cannot fathom God's acts. But for all its marvelous mechanism, it is destined, save for the soul, to return to the earth from which it originally came. Only one tiny bone remains indestructible and, in the time of resurrection, will serve as the nucleus out of which the body will be restored.[48]

Nowhere in rabbinic literature is there any denigration of the human body so characteristic of contemporary Platonic, Stoic, and Gnostic thought. On the contrary, since even the body is conceived as having been created in the image of God, man is duty bound to honor it by maintaining it in a state of cleanliness. No less an authority than Hillel termed such action a religious duty. Since Genesis describes Adam as having been both created in God's image (1:27) and formed out of the dust of the earth (2:7), the sages declare that man possesses both heavenly and earthly qualities. In four respects, he is said to resemble the animals and the angels respectively. Like the angels, he possesses the power of speech, intelligence, upright posture, and glance of the eye. In his physical aspects, he resembles the animals. Indeed, God created man because he was not completely satisfied with either the angels or the animals. The former failed to satisfy him because they lacked the evil inclination. The animals, on the other hand, lacked the good inclination. God therefore created man, who possesses both a good and evil inclination and is confronted with the need to exercise free will.

This is the origin of the ambivalent character of man. If he pursues evil, he is likened to an animal: if he chooses the good, he is likened to an angel. The contradictory nature of man is highlighted by the legend describing the sharp difference of opinion evoked by God's taking counsel with the angels as to whether or not man should be created. The angels that favored his creation contended that man would be affectionate and a doer of justice. Those who opposed his creation claimed that he would be quarrelsome and ridded with falsehood. This ambivalence, the Rabbis argued, derives from the two inclinations within man: the good inclination *(yezer tov)* and the evil inclination *(yezer ra)*[49] which compete within mankind for domination.

In their attitude toward wealth and possessions, men fall into four distinct categories, ranging from the wicked to the saintly. It is assumed, as a legal principle, that all men become excited when their property is at stake, and it is assumed further, as a matter of legal principle, that in money matters no man is likely to regard himself as culpable. However, the rabbis look askance at one who has an excess of material things. They conclude that such a situation can only produce deplorable moral consequences. Indeed, when a man is poor, he can be relied upon to have trust in God while riches incline him to trust in his money and thus displace his piety. Nonetheless, for all the rabbinic recognition of the powerful influence of the economic motive on human conduct, a certain basic honesty is assumed as characteristic of all men. Hence, the assumption is made that a man makes no legal monetary claim unless there is some substance to it, and that a man is not so brazen as to deny outright the existence of his debt in the presence of his creditor.[50]

More generally it is taught that a man's basic character is recognizable by his drinking (how he behaves when under the influence of liquor), by his rectitude in financial transactions (Rashi's interpretation) and by his anger (to what extent he is able to control his temper). To this generalization, some also add, by his good humor (Eruv. 65b).

The sages relate the biblical acount of the creation of man in the image of God—which acknowledges a resemblance between man and his Creator—to their doctrine of the imitation of God *(imitatio dei)*. The main biblical sources for the injunction to imitate God are found in the command to be holy as God is holy and to walk in God's way. Man is to be God-like in his actions, but he cannot aspire to be God. This distinguishes the biblical notion from the pagan attempts to achieve apotheosis or absorption in the deity.[51] Man is to imitate God in loving the stranger, in resting on the Sabbath, and in other ethical actions.

The idea of the imitation of God finds clear expression in rabbinic writings, especially the statements of the *tanna* Abba Saul. On the verse, "This is my God and I will glorify Him" (Exodus 15:2), he comments: "Be like Him. Just as He is gracious and merciful, so be thou also gracious and merciful." Abba Saul also comments on the verse, "You shall be holy as I the Lord your God am holy" (Leviticus 19:2)—"The household attendants of the king, what is their duty? To imitate the king." Another classic expression of the ideal of imitating God in rabbinic literature is that of Hama bar Hanina, who expounded the verse, "After the Lord your God ye shall walk" (Deuteronomy 13:5): "How can man walk after God? Is He not a consuming fire? What is meant is that man ought to walk after [imitate] the attributes of God. Just as the Lord clothes the naked, so you shall clothe the naked. Just as He visits the sick, so you shall visit the sick. Just as the Lord comforted the bereaved, so you shall also comfort the bereaved; just as He buried the dead, so you shall bury the dead." The rabbis admonish the people to imitate the qualities of divine mercy, forbearance, and kindness. They *do not* counsel imitating God in His attribute of stern justice. In this way the actions of the Lord served the rabbis as ideals of conduct.[52]

The sages were very interested in man's destiny. They interpreted the phenomena experienced in the revelation of the Divinity afforded the prophet Elijah (I Kings 19:11–12) as symbolic of the four worlds through which man must pass. The wind symbolizes the evanescent quality of the life of this world. The earthquake represents the day of death, since on it man quakes and trembles. Fire is the symbol of man's judgment in Gehenna. The "still small voice" is the Last Judgment. A more elaborate Talmudic articulation describes seven distinct phases through which man passes in this life. Each phase is marked by its own characteristics, few of which are flattering. All of life is seen as clouded over by uncertainty, for a man goes on his way and knows not whether good or evil awaits him.[53] Moreover, a trace of a tragic view of human destiny is to be discerned in a few rabbinic statements. Throughout his lifetime, man is caught in the impossible dilemma of either obeying his Creator (*yoẓer*) or his evil inclination (*yeẓer*). Whichever he follows, he finds himself perpetually at odds with the other. Moreover, the ultimate vanity of human ambition is expressed in the observation that man comes into the world with his fists clenched, as if to say, "The whole world is mine"; he leaves with palms outstretched, as if to say, "I have inherited nothing from this world."

Perhaps the most unusual view of man's worth is found in the talmudic debate over whether or not it would have been better had man never been created. This subject was the cause of a prolonged controversy between the schools of Shammai and Hillel. The debate terminates with the decision that it would have been better for man never to have been born. But once having entered the world, "let him scrutinize his deeds." This very pessimistic conclusion is unique and has no parallel in rabbinic literature and most talmudic commentators have sought to temper it by interpretation.[54]

As compared to this minority negative view, rabbinic thought considers all creation as having been called into being for the sake of man who is the only creature formed directly by the hand of God, and who was created last because he was to have dominion over all. The sages teach that one man is worth the whole of creation while Rabbi Akiva is moved to exclaim: "Beloved is man who was created in the image (of God); still greater was the love in that it was made known to him that he was created in the image of God." The notion of man's likeness to God, which we have already discussed, is a doctrine meant to emphasize the singular position of man in the world. Man is even commonly held to be superior to the angels by virtue of his superior wisdom and in his possession of free will. In poetic fashion, man is termed God's candle in the world.[55]

NATURE AND PURPOSE OF WOMAN

The rabbinic attitude towards women is complex and, like almost everything else in talmudic literature, contains conflicting views representing the whole spectrum of possible opinion. This variety notwithstanding, it is a fair generalization to say that the sages took a positive view of women and their role, though their social context and concerns were very different from those of the modern period.

To begin with, all available evidence suggests that on the level of personal experience and behavior the rabbis seemed to have loved their wives, that they all, apparently, had only one wife each, and that the position of the wife was one of much influence and importance. That the rabbis themselves did not practice polygamy is fairly well established. Indeed, it has been convincingly argued that while polygamy was legally sanctioned in rabbinic times it was rarely practiced by Jews. The oriental Jews who, in the Middle Ages and later, had more than one wife, were influenced by Islamic practice rather than by talmudic legislation.

On the legislative and religious level one must be careful in weighing up the rabbinic evidence and in not overinterpreting the material. Nowhere is this caution required more than in the analysis of the daily benediction in which men praise God for not having made them women. This has been the subject of a great deal of misunderstanding. It is clear from the context in which this prayer is found that the thanks to God are offered because of the greater opportunity a man has for carrying out the *mitzvot* (religious precepts), women being generally exempt from those positive precepts which depend for their performance on a given time of the day or year. Thus, this prayer is not a denigration of women but a recognition of the religious difference between the obligations incumbent on men and on women. Likewise women were exempt from the precept of studying the Torah, and as a result few women were learned. However the saying that women acquire merit by sending their sons to study and by encouraging their husbands to study is very revealing in this connection, and points back to the crucial social role which women were seen to hold in maintaining the family, and through the family the community at large. The needs of the community were the preeminent concerns, and it was in relation to them that both male and female defined their roles. From this social perspective the role of the woman is seen as both positive and necessary.

The sages elaborated on these themes in a variety of ways. Thus they held that a man without a wife lives without joy, blessing, and good, and that a man should love his wife as himself and respect her more than himself. Again, when Rabbi Joseph heard his mother's footsteps he would say: "Let me arise before the approach of the *Shekhinah.*" It was also taught that Israel was redeemed from Egypt by virtue of its righteous women. We also learn that a man must be careful never to speak slightingly to his wife because women are prone to tears and sensitive to wrong; that women have greater faith and greater powers of discernment than men; and that they are especially tenderhearted.

Perhaps the clearest positive evaluation of the woman's role can be further seen in the fact that the Torah, the greatest joy of the rabbis, is frequently hypostatized as a woman and is represented as God's daughter and Israel's bride.[56]

FREE WILL

The doctrine of free will, expressed in the idea that man is free to choose between good and evil, was at the core of the rabbinic outlook. Josephus indeed characterizes the differences between the Pharisees and their Sadducean and Essene opponents as between those who accepted both the freedom of man and divine providence (the Pharisees); those who ascribed everything to chance, denying providential guidance (the Sadducees); and those who denied human freedom, maintaining a doctrine of predestination (the Essenes). Though some doubt has been cast on Josephus' account because of his tendency to explain matters in terms of Greek philosophical schools, there seems to be no ground for rejecting the main outlines of his characterization.[57]

Though both the doctrine of man's freedom and that of divine providence were adhered to by the rabbis as central to their faith, they do not seem to have been integrated in any systematic way in the talmudic texts which deal with the subject. On the one hand, one finds constant reference to the notion that nothing happens in this world which is not in some way determined from on high: "No man can touch that which has been prepared in advance for his friend"; "No man injures his finger here below unless it has been decreed for him on high"; "Never does a snake bite . . . or a government interfere in men's lives unless incited to do so from on high"; "Everything is in the hands [i.e., control] of heaven except cold and heat"; "Forty days before a child is formed a heavenly voice decrees so-and-so's daughter shall marry so-and-so."[58] On the other hand the whole rabbinic theological structure of reward and punishment turns on the idea that man is free to do evil or good. As Josephus mentions, the rabbis wished to maintain both doctrines despite the tension between them, though they were aware of this tension. Before conception the angel appointed over conception takes a seminal drop and asks God: "What is to become of this drop? Is it to develop into a person strong or weak, wise or foolish, rich or poor?" But no mention is made of its becoming wicked or righteous, because "Everything is in the hands of heaven except the fear of heaven."[59]

The combination of these two doctrines within rabbinic theology may be understood, not so much from the philosophical point of view, but rather from the practical point of view which underlies all rabbinic thinking. On the one hand it is necessary to think of the world as under the complete surveillance and control of heaven, a thought which adds to the confidence and trust of the Jew in God, and on the other hand the individual needs to make his choices and decisions on the assumption that evil and good are both within his grasp. The conceptual integration of these two ideas did not enter rabbinic thought forms. The philosophical problems surrounding God's foreknowledge and man's free will are dealt with in an equally cursory way in the texts. The most striking is the saying of Akiva, "Everything is foreseen, but freedom of choice is given." This has been taken by some commentators—Maimonides, for example—to be a statement of the position that though God has foreknowledge of all our acts, this still does not limit our freedom.[60]

What the sages were primarily concerned with protecting was man's freedom so that he could be judged a moral creature capable of true moral action, while at the same time not denying God's majesty and the related attributes of omnipotence, omniscience, etc. If there were philosophical problems connected with holding both these views so be it—what mattered to the rabbis was religious piety and moral correctness, not philosophical or logical precision.

SIN

The usual rabbinic term for sin is *averah,* from the root *avar* ("to pass over"; i.e., sin is a transgression or a rejection of God's will). The rabbis rarely speak of sin in the abstract and their concern is usually with specific sins. According to the sages there are sins of commission and omission—in the rabbinic terminology, the transgression of negative precepts and the failure to perform positive precepts. Sins of commission are held to be more serious than those of omission and the term *averah* generally refers to the former. In one respect, however, the latter are more severe. If positive precepts have to be carried out at a certain time and that time has passed, the omission cannot be rectified, e.g., the failure to recite the *Shema* on a particular day. To this is applied the verse (Eccles. 1:15): "That which is crooked cannot be made straight, and that which is wanting cannot be numbered." Furthermore, sins involving the transgression of negative precepts are of two kinds—offenses against God and offenses against one's neighbor. The Day of Atonement brings forgiveness for sins committed against

God, i.e., for purely religious offenses. However, it only brings forgiveness for offenses against other human beings if the wrong done to the victim has first been put right. It should also be noted that the intention to sin is not reckoned as sin except in the case of idolatry.[61]

Sins are also divided into light and severe sins. The four most serious sins for the rabbis are murder, idolatry, adultery, and incest. It was eventually ruled that rather than commit these, a man must forfeit his life (Sanh. 74a). A marked tendency to be observed in rabbinic homiletics is to encourage people to take the lighter sins more seriously by treating them as if they were far weightier offenses. Thus, for example, it is said that whoever leaves the Holy Land to reside outside it is as if he had worshipped idols; whoever bears evil tales it is as if he denies the root principle of faith; and whoever shames his neighbor in public it is as if he had shed blood.[62]

Those who cause others to sin were severely castigated by the rabbis. One who causes another to sin is worse than one who slays him, because the murderer only excludes his victim from this life, while the one who causes another to sin excludes him from the life of the world to come (Sif. Deut. 252).

Sin is caused by the evil inclination *(yezer ha-ra),* the force in man which drives him to gratify his instincts and ambitions. Although called the "evil inclination" because it can easily lead man to wrongdoing, it is essential to life in that it provides it with its driving power. Were it not for the *yezer ha-ra,* remarks a rabbinic Midrash, a man would not build a house, or marry, or have children, or engage in commerce. In similar vein is the curious legend that the men of the Great Synagogue wanted to kill the *yezer ha-ra,* who warned them that if they were successful the "world would go down," i.e., would come to an end. They therefore imprisoned him for three days and then searched all the land for a new-laid egg without finding one. Passages such as these, however, must not be construed as suggesting any rabbinic acceptance of the inevitability of sin or of its condonation. The strongest expressions are used of the heinousness of sin and surrender to the *yezer ha-ra.* R. Simeon b. Lakish said "Satan, the *yezer ha-ra,* and the angel of death are one and the same." The *yezer ha-ra* entices people to sin in this world and bears witness against them in the future world. Daily the evil inclination assaults them, endeavoring to slay them, and were God not to support them, they could not resist it; as it is said (Ps. 37:32): "The wicked watcheth the righteous and seeketh to slay him. The Lord will not leave him in his hand." Unless severe control is exercised man becomes the prey of sin. Commenting on II Samuel 12:4, the Talmud notes that the *yezer ha-ra* is at first called a "passerby," then a "guest," and finally "one who occupies the house." When a man sins and repeats the sin, it no longer seems to him as forbidden.[63]

The much discussed question of whether there are any parallels to the Christian doctrine of original sin in rabbinic literature can be disposed of simply by noting that no such parallels exist. The passages which state that "four died through the serpent's machinations" and that "the serpent copulated with Eve and infected her with his filth," quoted in this connection, expressly exclude Israel from the effects of the serpent's machinations and his filth, and in all probability are an intentional polemic against the doctrine of original sin.[64] Nevertheless, while the rabbis do not see sin as hereditary—that man is bound to sin because of Adam's sin—their views are far removed from "liberal" optimism regarding man's inherent goodness, as the doctrine of the *yezer ha-ra* clearly demonstrates.

Counsels are given to man as to how he can rise above sin. He should know that above him there is a seeing eye and a hearing ear and that all his deeds are recorded in a book. He should reflect that he comes from a putrid drop, that he goes to a place of dust, worms, and maggots, and that he is destined to give an account and a reckoning before the King of kings. But the study of the Torah and the practice of the precepts are the best method of avoiding sin. God says: "My children! I created the evil inclination, but I created the Torah as its antidote; if you occupy yourselves with the Torah you will not be delivered into [the inclination's] hand." The school of R. Ishmael taught: "My son, if this repulsive wretch [the *yezer ha-ra*] attacks you, lead him to the house of learning: if he is stone, he will dissolve; if iron, he will sliver into fragments."[65]

REPENTANCE

The rabbis are eloquent in describing the significance of repentance. It is, they teach, one of the things created before the world itself; it reaches to the very Throne of Glory; it prolongs a man's life and brings on the Redemption. God urges Israel to repent and not be ashamed to do so because a son is not ashamed to return to the father who loves him. God says to Israel: My sons, open for Me an aperture of repentance as narrow as the eye of a needle, and I will open for you gates through which wagons and coaches can pass. On public fast-days the elder of the congregation would declare: "Brethren, it is not said of the men of Nineveh: 'And God saw their sackcloth and their fasting' but: 'And God saw their works, that they had turned from their evil way' " (Jonah 3:10).

The rabbis were not unaware of the theological difficulties in the whole concept of repentance. Once the wrong has been done how can it be put right? The general rabbinic answer is that it is a matter of Divine Grace, as in the following passage, in which it is incidentally implied, too, that the concept of *teshuvah* has only reached its full emphasis as a result of a long development from biblical times: "They asked of wisdom: 'What is the punishment of the sinner?' Wisdom replied: 'Evil pursueth sinners' [Prov. 13:21]. They asked of prophecy: 'What is the punishment of the sinner?' Prophecy replied: 'The soul that sinneth it shall die' [Ezek. 18:4]. Then they asked of the Holy One, blessed be He: 'What is the punishment of the sinner?' He replied: 'Let him repent and he will find atonement.' " The third-century Palestinian teachers debate whether the repentant sinner is greater than the wholly righteous man who has not sinned, R. Johanan holding that the man who has not sinned is the greater, R. Abbahu that the repentant sinner is greater. R. Simeon b. Lakish said, according to one version, that when the sinner repents his sins are accounted as if he had commited them unintentionally, but in another version, his sins are accounted as virtues. The talmudic reconciliation of the two versions is that one refers to repentance out of fear, the other to repentance out of love. The Rabbis even held that a man who has been wicked all his days but who repents at the end of his life is pardoned for all his sins. The ideal, however, is for man to spend all his days in repentance, thus when R. Eliezer said: "Repent one day before your death," he explained that since no man can know when he will die he should spend all his days in repentance.[67]

It is taught that the Day of Atonement brings pardon for sin if there is repentance. However, the Day of Atonement is ineffective if a man says: "I will sin and the Day of Atonement will effect atonement." If a man says: "I will sin and repent, and sin again and repent" he will be given no chance to repent. The second-century teacher R. Ishmael is reported as saying: "If a man transgressed a positive precept, and repented, he is forgiven right away. If he has transgressed a negative commandment and repented, then repentance suspends punishment and the Day of Atonement procures atonement. If he has committed a sin to be punished with extirpation *(karet),* or death at the hands of the court, and repented, then repentance and the Day of Atonement suspend the punishment, and suffering cleanses him from the sin. But if he has been guilty of the profanation of the Name, then penitence has no power to suspend punishment, nor the Day of Atonement to procure atonement, nor suffering to finish it, but all of them together suspend the punishment and only death finishes it."[68] This scheme contains all the tensions resulting from the different aspects of atonement mentioned in the Bible.

Repentance involves sincere remorse for having committed the sin. The third-century Babylonian teacher, R. Judah, defined a true penitent as one who twice more encountered the object which caused his original transgression and he kept away from it. R. Judah indicated: "With the same woman, at the same time, in the same place." As part of the act of repentance the penitent sinner must also confess his sins. According to R. Judah b. Bava, a general confession is insufficient: the details of each sin must be stated explicitly. But R. Akiva holds that a general confession is enough. Public confession of sin, however, was frowned upon as displaying a lack of shame except when the transgressions were committed publicly, or, according to others, in the case of offenses against other human beings. But above all, confession without repentance is of no avail. In this connection the ancient parable, as old as Ben Sira (34:25–26), is recounted of a man who immerses himself in purifying waters while still holding in his hand a defiling reptile.[69]

The Rabbis urge that the sinner must be given every encouragement to repent. It is forbidden to say to a penitent: "Remember your former deeds." The rabbis even go so far to facilitate repentance that they change the plain meaning of the biblical text if this will encourage it. Thus, for example they teach (in contradistinction to the literal teaching of the Torah) that if a man stole a beam and built it into his house, he was freed from the obligation of demolishing the house and was allowed to pay for his theft in cash, if this would encourage him to repent. It was even said that if robbers or usurers repent and wish to restore their ill-gotten gains, the spirit of the sages is displeased with the victims, if they accept the restitution, for this may discourage potential penitents from relinquishing their evil way of life.[70]

FORGIVENESS

Divine Forgiveness

The theme of God's forgiveness for man's sins is recurrent in talmudic and midrashic literature and reappears in later rabbinic writings and the synagogue liturgy. Its main theological purport is to counterbalance, and indeed outweigh, the strongly entrenched rabbinic belief in the inevitable punishment of sin. The rabbinic outlook on the subject may be most simply expressed as "God is just"; He rewards the righteous and punishes the wicked. Only the unrepentant sinner incurs His wrath; the sinner who repents is always forgiven. Thus the Talmud states, "He who sins and regrets his act is at once forgiven" and the Midrash states, "Says the Holy One, even if they [your sins] should reach to Heaven, if you repent I will forgive." The Tosefta even gives a statistical figure to the matter, basing itself on Exodus 34:6–7, and says that God's quality of forgiveness is five hundred fold that of His wrath.[71]

The idea is more picturesquely expressed in the talmudic image of God praying to Himself that His mercy should prevail over His anger and that He should deal with His children *"li-fenim mi-shurat ha-din,"* i.e., that He should forgive them even though strict justice would demand their punishment (Ber. 7a). The whole of Jewish thought on the subject stems from the forgiving character of God depicted in the 13 Divine attributes as revealed to Moses (Ex. 34:6–7). The rabbinic mind embroiders the fundamental biblical idea in a homiletic way, thus giving encouragement and hope to the sinner who would turn to God but is troubled by the burden of his past deeds. The liturgy of the Day of Atonement, and indeed its very role, bears eminent testimony to the central role that the idea of God's forgiveness plays within Jewish religious practice.

There are two further general points. Rabbinic literature is more concerned with God's forgiveness for the individual sinner, rather than for Israel as a nation, though the latter notion is certainly treated as of the greater significance (the latter is more characteristic of the prophetic ethos than the rabbinic, for during most of the creative period of rabbinic thought, Israel had ceased to exist as a political-national entity).

Secondly, forgiveness is always and only consequent on repentance and the idea of an arbitrary grace is almost totally absent.

The place of a forgiving God within the rabbinic *weltanschauung* has been of interest in modern times and is discussed by both Jewish and Christian scholars. The immediate causes of this interest were partly a desire to uncover the rabbinic roots of New Testament theology and partly an attempt to rectify the widespread but distorted image of the Jewish conception of God. According to this misconception the Jewish God was seen as legalistic and strict overlord who rewards and punishes according to man's deeds, and the Jew was thus thought to inhabit a somber religious world devoid of Divine compassion. A more thorough acquaintance with the sources shows how wrong such a picture was. Basic to the entire fabric of rabbinic thought is the belief in His love and compassion, which constantly manifests itself in Divine mercy and forgiveness.

Human Forgiveness
For the rabbis God's forgiveness, however extensive, only encompasses those sins which man commits directly against Him, *"bein adam la-Makom."* On the other hand, those in which an injury is caused to one's fellow man, *"bein adam la-ḥavero,"* are not forgiven by God until the injured party has himself forgiven the perpetrator. Hence the custom of seeking forgiveness on the eve of the Day of Atonement from those one may have wronged, without which proper atonement cannot be made. Again, and in like manner, the law regarding physical injury for example, is explicit in that even after the various compensatory payments have been made, the inflicter of the damage must seek the forgiveness of the injured party for the suffering caused.[72]

Moreover, not only must he who sins against his fellow seek forgiveness from him, but the one sinned against is duty bound to forgive. "Man should be pliant as a reed, not hard like the cedar" in granting forgiveness. As the Talmud puts it: "All who act mercifully (i.e., forgivingly) toward their fellow creatures will be treated mercifully by Heaven, and all who do not act mercifully toward their fellow creatures will not be treated mercifully by Heaven." If the injured party refuses to forgive even when the sinner has come before him three times in the presence of others and asked for forgiveness, then he is in turn deemed to have sinned. He is called *akhzari* ("cruel") and said not to be of the seed of Abraham

(Beẓ. 32b), since one of the distinguishing marks of all of Abraham's descendants is that they are forgiving, this quality being one of the gifts God bestowed on Abraham and his heirs.[73]

The rabbis go even further in the ethical demands made upon the injured party, for not only must he be ready to forgive his injurer, he should also pray that God forgive the sinner before he has come to beg forgiveness. This demand is based on the example of Abraham, who prayed that God forgive Abimelech (Gen. 20:17). The reasons for the injured party's readiness to forgive the injurer are mixed. On the one hand is the self-regarding consideration, already mentioned, that forgiveness to one's fellow wins forgiveness from Heaven. As Philo states reflecting rabbinic views: "If you ask pardon for your sins, do you also forgive those who have trespassed against you? For remission is granted for remission." On the other hand there is the purer motive of *imitatio dei*. Just as it is in the nature of God to be merciful to His creatures, so man in attempting to imitate the ways of God should be forgiving toward those who have injured him.[74]

DEATH

Though so complex a subject as death was inevitably not dealt with by the rabbis in an unequivocal way, their discussions on the subject incorporate a series of closely interconnected doctrines. Death itself, though imbued with mystery—contact with the corpse, for instance, meant defilement in the highest degree—was thought of as that moment of transformation from life in this world to that of the beyond. In terms of the mishnaic image, "This world is like a corridor before the world to come" (Avot 4:16), death is the passing of the portal separating the two worlds, giving access to a "world which is wholly good" (Kid. 39b).

At death the soul leaves the body with a cry that reverberates from one end of the world to the other, to pass into a state of existence, the exact nature of which was a matter of considerable dispute amongst the rabbis.[75] Whatever the nature of the world beyond, it was generally accepted that there the dead reap the deserts of the acts they performed while alive. In addition, it was held that the dead were free from Torah and the commandments, and that death served as an atoning process. One confession formula before death, particularly prescribed for the criminal about to be executed, is "May my death be an atonement for all my sins." The atoning value of death received greater emphasis after the destruction of the Temple, with the abolition of sacrificial atonement, so that complete forgiveness for more serious sins was dependent—despite repentance, the Day of Atonement, and suffering—on the final atoning value of death.[76]

Death and birth are viewed as parallel processes: just as man is born with a cry, tears, and a sigh, so he dies. The rabbis considered that there were 903 forms of death, the most severe way of dying being from asthma, or croup, which is compared to a thorn being torn out of a ball of wood, and the lightest is described as "the kiss of death," specially reserved for the righteous, which is like a hair being removed from milk. The way in which a person dies, and the day on which he dies, were thought to be significant as good or bad omens for the deceased. Thus, for example, should he die amid laughter, or on the Sabbath eve, it is a good sign, whereas to die amid weeping, or at the close of the Sabbath, is a bad omen.[77]

Concerning the very necessity of death there was some dispute amongst the rabbis. On the one hand there is the rather extreme view, which did not win general acceptance, that death was the wages of sin: "There is no death without sin," and it is the inevitable fate of man only in that no man is sinless, ". . . there is not a righteous man upon earth, that . . . sinneth not" (Eccles, 7:20). Accordingly, even Moses and Aaron died because they had sinned while the few exceptions, the really righteous such as Elijah, were thought not to have died, or in other cases to have died only as a consequence of the machinations of the serpent in Eden, who caused Adam to sin and thus bring death to the world.[75]

On the other hand an older view, stemming from the tannaitic period, stresses the inevitability of death, its naturalness as part of the very fabric of the world since creation. Thus when God had completed the creation of the world He saw that "it was very good (Gen. 1:31), concerning which R. Meir remarked " 'it was very good,' that is death." The idea behind R. Meir's enigmatic statement would seem to be that death is an integral part of the natural order, making way for new life and continued creation. The naturalness of death is also explicit in the saying that the angel of death was created on the first day of creation.[79] The Mishnah *Avot* (4:22) stresses: "Those who are born will of necessity die . . . for perforce you were created . . . born . . . live, and perforce you will die." According to this view sin only hastens death, but does not cause it in the first place. Lack of sin therefore either enables a man to reach his predetermined span of years, thus saving him from an untimely demise, or helps him to live longer than his allotted span.

These arguments concerning the inevitability of death or its dependence on sin, turn on several factors, among them possible interpretations of the account of Adam's sin in Genesis. According to one view Adam brought death into the world by disobeying God and eating the forbidden fruit. Later the Children of Israel had an opportunity of overcoming the power of death when they received the Torah at Sinai, but they lost this opportunity when they sinned with the golden calf.[80] However, the way Adam's sin was interpreted amongst the *amoraim* may have been influenced by apologetic considerations, particularly the need to negate the Pauline doctrine of original sin as an inheritance from Adam to all mankind (Rom. 5:12).

Finally, that both the wicked and the righteous die was explained as follows. The wicked perish so that they should cease angering God, while the righteous die so that they may have rest from their continual struggle against the evil inclination which has no power over them after death. As noted, the process of dying also may serve the righteous as a means of ridding themselves of their sins and so preparing them for their just rewards in the hereafter. Though mortality affects both wicked and righteous alike, the rabbis were sure that the whole quality of their respective lives, on this earth and in the hereafter, differed greatly. For the wicked are considered as if dead while still alive, and the righteous even in death are called "living."[81]

PART III

GOD AND THE JEW

Judaism

The term Judaism is first found among the Greek-speaking Jews of the first century C.E.[1] Its Hebrew equivalent, *Yahadut,* found only occasionally in medieval literature,[2] but used frequently in modern times, has parallels neither in the Bible[3] nor in the rabbinic literature.[4] The term generally used in the classical sources for the whole body of Jewish teaching is Torah, "doctrine," "teaching." Thus the Talmud (Shab. 31a) tells the story of a heathen who wished to be converted to the Jewish faith but only on the understanding that he would be taught the whole of the Torah while standing on one leg. Hillel accepted him, and in response to his request replied: "That which is hateful unto thee do not do unto thy neighbor. This is the whole of the Torah. The rest is commentary. Go and study." Presumably if the Greek-speaking Jews had told the story they would have made the prospective convert demand to be taught *Judaism* while standing on one leg.

In modern usage the terms "Judaism" and "Torah" are virtually interchangeable, but the former has on the whole a more humanistic nuance while "Torah" calls attention to the divine, revelatory aspects of the tradition. A further difference in nuance, stemming from the first, is that "Torah" refers to the eternal elements in Jewish life and thought while "Judaism" refers to the more historic dynamic elements as manifested in the varied civilizations and cultures of the Jews at the different stages of their development, such as Hellenistic Judaism, rabbinic Judaism, medieval Judaism; and, from the 19th century, Orthodox, Conservative, and Reform Judaism.[5]

It is usually considered to be anachronistic to refer to the biblical religion (the "religion of Israel") as "Judaism" both because there were no Jews (i.e., those belonging to the tribe of Judah) in the formative period of the Bible, and because there are distinctive features which mark off later Judaism from the earlier forms, ideas, and worship. For

135

all that, most Jews would recognize sufficient continuity to reject as unwarranted the description of Judaism as a different religion from the biblical; and moreover they would strongly argue that Judaism is the historic and logical heir and continuator of biblical religion and tradition.

ATTEMPTS TO DEFINE THE ESSENCE OF JUDAISM

The Hebrew writer Ahad Ha-Am[6] observed that if Hillel's convert had come to him demanding to be taught the whole of the Torah while standing on one leg, he would have replied: " 'Thou shalt not make unto thee a graven image, nor any manner of likeness' (Ex. 20:4). This is the whole of the Torah. The rest is commentary," i.e., that the essence of Judaism consists in the elevation of the ideal above all material or physical forms or conceptions.

Ahad Ha-Am's was only one of the latest attempts at trying to discover the essence of Judaism, its main idea or ideas, and its particular viewpoint which sets it off from other religions and philosophies. However, this is an extremely difficult—some would say impossible—task, since the various civilizations, Egyptian, Canaanite, Babylonian, Persian, Greek, Roman, Christian, Muslim, with which Jews came into contact, have made their influence felt on Jews and through them on Judaism itself. It is precarious to think of Judaism in monolithic terms. Developed and adapted to changing circumstances throughout its long history, it naturally contains varying emphases as well as contradictions. Belief in the transmigration of souls, for example, was strongly upheld by some Jewish teachers and vehemently rejected by others. Yet the quest has rarely ceased for certain distinctive viewpoints which make Judaism what it is. In the discussion that follows, we shall examine the major attempts that have been made in this area of concern.

The Bible
In the Bible there are no articles of faith or dogmas in the Christian or Islamic sense of the terms. Although trust in God is regarded as a paramount religious virtue,[7] there is nowhere in Scripture an injunction "to believe." Even a verse like II Chronicles 20:20 "believe *(ha'aminu)* in the Lord your God, and you will be established; believe His prophets, and you will succeed" expresses only King Jehoshaphat's advice to the

people; it is not a religious commandment. Furthermore, the verb *he'emin* ("to believe"), the nound *emunah* ("belief"), and other forms derived from the stem *amn* mean to trust, have confidence; and faithfulness; and in this sense are used both of God and man.[8] It is only in the Middle Ages, when Jewish theologians began to formulate articles of faith, that derivations of the root *amn* came to be used in a dogmatic sense.

The reason for the absence of a catechism in both the Bible and the rabbinic tradition is probably twofold: in Judaism the primary emphasis is not on profession of faith but on conduct; and speculative and systematic thinking is not characteristic of the biblical or the rabbinic genius. Dogmatics entered Judaism as a result of external pressure; contact with alien religious systems, which had formulated theological doctrines, compelled Jewish thinkers to state the basic creeds of their own faith. In a sense, therefore, it can be argued that Jewish dogmatics forms part of the larger category of Jewish apologetics.

No religion, however, is conceivable without fundamental doctrines or axiomatic principles, and Judaism, in its scriptural as well as rabbinic aspects, is no exception. Indeed, the Bible contains certain summary statements that might be considered incipient dogmas. The *Shema,* the proclamation of God's unity in Deut. 6:4; the Ten Commandments (Ex. 20:1 ff.; Deut. 5:6 ff.) providing an epitome of Jewish precepts; the formulation of the divine attributes in Exodus 34:6–7; Micah's sublime summary of human duty (6:18); and the majestic simplicity of the Lord's assurance to Habakkuk "but the righteous shall live by his faith" (2:4) are a few examples culled from many. But valuable as these formulations are, they do not embrace the complete range of fundamental biblical teachings. Only an analysis of scriptural doctrines against the background of the entire complex of biblical thought can yield the essential religious beliefs, moral ideals, and spiritual truths that underlie the faith expounded by the Scriptures.

God's *being* is axiomatic. He is One and incomparable; there are no other gods. He is omnipotent, omnipresent, omniscient, and eternal. Even more important is the doctrine that He is the God of justice and love; and it is His moral nature that makes Him holy. In His might He willed the creation of the universe, and in His love He continues to sustain it. He made the laws of nature; the miracles are exceptions to these cosmic rules, but both the normal and the abnormal conform to the Divine Will.

Correspondingly, mythology, except for idiomatic phrases, is excluded from biblical teaching and magical practices are forbidden; unlike miracles, they do not issue from the will of God, but seek to overrule divinely established laws of nature.[9]

The apex of creation is man, created in the divine image. This "image" is reflected in the moral and spiritual qualities of human nature. In man creation achieves a new dimension—a moral personality endowed with freedom of will. The relationship between God and man has a voluntaristic ethical character. It is an encounter between the Divine Person and His human counterpart, between Father and offspring. Ideally it is a mutual, loving, relation. But man in his freedom may disobey, and as such sin is rebellion which transforms the "nearness" of God into "estrangement."

Man's endowment with human freedom of choice (Deut. 30:15, 19) is the source of man's responsibility, upon which are predicated rewards and penalties, both collective and individual. Divine retribution is a corollary of God's righteousness; but its purpose is primarily not punitive but educative and its primary aim is the restoration of human and divine relation. God is seen not to desire the destruction of the wicked, but rather their return to the path of goodness (Ezek. 18:23, 32); one consequence of this is that one comes to appreciate that Heaven's grace far exceeds the measure of divine punishment.[10] Thus all the predictions of the prophets are held to be conditional[11] while God hopes for His punitive decrees to be nullified. Conceptually there appears to be a contradiction between this understanding of God's omniscience and omnipotence on the one hand, and man's freedom of action on the other. But the Bible harmonizes them in a supreme historic event. Human rebellions will ultimately end in a great reconciliation. In the messianic era Zion's teaching will become a universal heritage.[12] "In the end of days" the divine design of history will be realized as perfectly as His cosmic plan.

Human waywardness was manifest from the beginning of history and man has constantly been tempted to do wrong: "every imagination of the thoughts of his heart was only evil continually" (Gen. 6:5). To aid humanity to persevere along the path of righteousness, divine revelation was necessary. Its purpose was to direct and supplement the basic sense of right and wrong innate in every human being. Certain spiritual geniuses—the patriarchs, the prophets—learned to know the will of God in given situations. But the complete revelation was vouchsafed to the Children of Israel at Sinai. It comprised many elements—legal and ritual, moral and spiritual, individual, national and universal—each component being necessary to its educative and purifying intent. According to the Torah, the precepts given at Sinai were neither to be augmented nor diminished (Deut. 4:2); and the law was binding and immutable for all generations. Instrinsically, according to later Jewish teaching, the prophets did not add to the Torah and their role does not consist in preaching new ideas, but in elucidating the historic covenant and applying its teachings to the circumstances of their time and in calling the people back to faithful observance of Torah. In particular they stressed the moral and spiritual values of the Torah and the universal conception of the consummation of history in the kingdom of God in which Israel plays a central part.

By accepting the Torah, Israel became the "treasured people" of the Lord, a holy nation in the service of the Holy God.[13] They entered into a covenant with Him,[14] calling for unswerving obedience on their part and protective providence on the part of God. The election of Israel was not an act of divine favoritism. On the contrary, it represented a mission involving special responsibility and corresponding retribution. "You only have I known of all the families of the earth; therefore I will visit upon you all your iniquities" (Amos 3:2). Nor was God's providential care limited to Israel; there was a Philistine and Aramean exodus comparable to that of Israel (*ibid.*, 9:7). The covenant with Israel was an integral part of God's universal historic plan of salvation (Isa. 49:6) and hence the Israelites were as indestructible as the cosmos (Jer. 33:25). Their sins would certainly be punished, but just as certainly redemption would succeed every disaster. In this way the national hope of restoration and return to the Land of Israel is indivisibly linked with the redemption of all mankind. Jewish nationalism and universalism are not opposed but complementary biblical ideals.

Since ethics occupies a central position in scriptural theology, theodicy greatly exercised the minds of the prophets and sages of Israel. The thought "shall not the Judge of all the earth do justly?" (Gen. 18:25) is echoed in various forms throughout the Scriptures. It is an essential aspect of the dialogue between man and God. To criticize and challenge God in sincerity is not viewed by Scripture as a sin (witness Abraham, Moses, Jeremiah, Habakkuk, and Job); only pride, hypocrisy and smugness are iniquitous (Job, 42:7). The biblical answers to the problem of the suffering of the righteous are varied; at times it is accounted for by human sin, and at times by the concept of vicarious suffering and "the suffering servant," and at times by the limitations of human knowledge. Man's view is said to be too short but he is assured that however long the process, God's righteousness triumphs in the end (Ps. 92:8) and lastly, in the final analysis it is argued that God's purpose is beyond man's understanding. Therefore, until the ultimate reconciliation at "the end of days," the Incomprehensible God can be apprehended only in faith (Hab. 2:4).[15]

Rabbinic Literature

The next stage of the discussion, and the further development of this biblical outlook are found in the rabbinic material which is marked by a considerable diversity of opinion. Since the sages' method of study was essentially based on argumentation and controversy, it is by no means easy to determine at all times its fundamental ideas. Furthermore, while the rabbis sought to give clear definition to the *halakhah,* the *aggadah* remained vague, unsystematized, and contradictory. Nevertheless in Talmud and Midrash, as in Scripture, it is possible to discern ground patterns of thought and basic concepts that constitute the foundations of the tannaitic and amoraic ideology. It is axiomatic that rabbinic teaching rests firmly on biblical doctrine and precept. Here, as in the Bible, God is the transcendent Creator; the Torah is the unalterable embodiment of His will; providence is motivated by moral principles; there is an intimate relationship between man and God; the election of Israel, linked to the immutable covenant of the Torah, is a paramount idea; and the prophetic promise of Israel's ultimate redemption and the establishment of the kingdom of God upon earth is the national-universal denouement of the drama of history. But rabbinic theology is a superstructure founded on scriptural faith, not a copy of it; there are evolutionary differences in talmudic Judaism that distinguish it from biblical norms and give it its distinctive qualities.

Rabbinic Judaism produced no catechism; but external cultural pressures and internal heresies gave rise to certain formulations of a dogmatic character. Sanhedrin 10:1, for example, in defining those who have no share in the world to come, gives to the belief in resurrection and in the divine origin of the Torah credal status. However it must be noted that this statement is neither couched in the form of a credal affirmation nor is it comprehensive enough to serve as a total expression of Jewish beliefs. However, its insertion into the Mishnah invests it with authority, and it can readily be seen why Maimonides' famous formulation of 13 principles of Judaism (see below) was offered as a kind of elaboration of this particular passage. Similarly Hillel's dictum "That which is hateful to thee do not do unto others" (Shab. 31a) constitutes in its context the principal Jewish dogma. In discussing the precepts of the Torah the rabbis spoke of various biblical figures who reduced the number of precepts (from the traditional 613), ending with Habakkuk who subsumed them all under one fundamental principle, "but the righteous shall live by his faith."[16] But in rabbinic as in scriptural literature, the root-ideas can be reached only by a careful examination of the complete compass of the tradition and a comparative study of its beliefs.

To begin, it can be noted that a new mysticism, emanating from the doctrines of *ma'aseh bereshit* ("work of creation") and *ma'aseh merkavah* ("work of the chariot"), now attaches to the concept of God in which gnostic influence, despite the general opposition of the sages to Gnostic ideas, is discernible. But these esoteric notions were reserved for the few.[17] On the other hand, the broad-based popular approach, found in numerous *aggadot,* inclines toward an anthropopathic presentation of the Deity. According to this presentation, the Holy One of Israel suffers all Israel's tribulations; He too is exiled.[18]

Man, for his part, is conceived as a dualism of body and soul: the latter, being immortal, gives him a place among the angels while his body makes him akin to the beasts (Sif. Deut. 309). However the body is not condemned as a source of evil, nor may the material things of this world be left unenjoyed. They too are the work of God and as such inherently good. Indeed, God is to be served with both lower and higher impulses.[19] As in the Bible, man's freedom of choice is fully recognized, and the sages express this belief in the following way: "All is in the power of heaven except the reverence of heaven" (Ber. 33b), and this despite the fact that the omniscient God foresees all (Avot 3:15). This human freedom is the basis of man's responsibility and the justification of divine retribution. To err is human, but God provides a means of atonement in penitence which is the great shield that protects man. So vital and important was penitence that the sages held that it was created even before the world came into being (Pes. 54a).

The Torah, as the will of God, is immutable, and the sages regarded it as their supreme task to expound and determine its provisions, giving precedence, where needed, to moral principles.[20] To be holy and to walk in the Lord's ways implied in particular the practice of lovingkindness,[21] which was equal to all the precepts put together. The purpose of the commandments is to purify man (Gen. R. 44:1), and the true spirit of observance seeks no reward beyond the service of God (Avot 1:3). But there are two Torahs: the Oral Law (embodied in rabbinic teaching), which was also revealed at Sinai, supplements and elucidates the Written Law (the Hebrew Bible). On the basis of Deuteronomy 17:11 (Ber. 19b), the sages claimed the right to enact laws of their own *(mi-de-rabbanan),* chiefly with a view to their serving as a "fence" (protection) to the biblical ordinances *(mi-de-orayta).* The most daring principle of all originated by the rabbis was their right to interpret the Torah in conformity with their understanding and to decide religious legal matters (by majority vote) accordingly. Thus, for example it was they, not the heavenly court *(pamalia)* that fixed the calendar (TJ, RH 1:3, 57b); and on rare occasions, even if a halakhic ruling ran counter, so to speak, to the view of Heaven, the rabbis still maintained that theirs was the right to decide, for the Torah, having been vouchsafed to mankind, was now subject to human judgment. Nor did this principle favoring human judgment displease the Holy One, Blessed Be He, for He is said to have smiled indulgently when His children outvoted Him (BM 59b). The sages went so far as to declare "the suppression of the Torah may be the foundation thereof" (Men. 99). Thus the rabbis evolved theological machinery for adapting the *halakhah* to historical changes and needs without discarding an iota of the scriptural tradition. Theologically they justified this procedure by the theory that all that the rabbis taught was already inherent in the Sinaitic revelation.[22] Therefore the sages did not innovate but discovered already existing truths.

The rabbinic exaltation of Torah study was a natural concomitant of their attitude to the Scriptures. The Mishnah lists the things whose fruits a man enjoys in this world, while the capital is laid up for him in the world to come, and declares "the study of the Law is equal to them all" (Pe'ah 1:1). The rabbis even (BB 12a) elevate the sage (with his restrained, reflective approach) above the prophet (with his incandescent, intuitive consciousness). And yet the truth that Judaism is life and that learning must lead to deeds was not lost sight of: "Great is the study of the Torah, because it leads to [right] action" (Kid. 40b).

Israel's election is a leading theme in rabbinic thought. It brought comfort and renewed courage to a suffering people who never doubted God's ultimate salvation. Ultimately, the messianic era, despite the preceding tribulation, would bring redemption to Israel and the land. This belief suffuses the entire aggadic literature and inspires every facet of the liturgy. Great emphasis is placed on the importance of Erez Israel in Talmud and Midrash and the prayer book. The rabbis exhaust the language of praise and indulge in unrestrained imagery depicting the future glories of the land. One dictum even avers that "he who dwells outside the Land of Israel is as one who serves idols" (Ket. 110b). This hyperbole was intended not only to encourage Jewish settlement in Erez Israel, but also to strengthen the hope of national restoration. Jewish nationalism did not, however, exclude universalist ideals. Thus the rabbis taught that: "The pious of all nations have a share in the world to come" and that "Whoever repudiates idolatry is called a Jew"; and finally that the greatest Torah principle is enshrined in the verse "This is the book of the generations of Adam," i.e., the proclaimed brotherhood of man.[23]

The idea of this life as a preparation for eternal bliss in the hereafter looms very large in rabbinic thinking, though the value of this life as good in itself is not overshadowed. The second-century teacher, R. Jacob, said: "Better is one hour of repentance and good deeds in this world than the whole life of the world to come; but better is one hour of bliss in the world to come than the whole life of this world." The same teacher said: "This world is like a vestibule that you mayest enter the banqueting hall." In the same vein is the saying that this world is like the eve of Sabbath and the world to come like the Sabbath. Only one who prepares adequately on the eve of the Sabbath can enjoy the delights of the Sabbath.[24] Nor was bliss in the hereafter limited to Jews. The view of R. Joshua, against that of R. Eliezer, was adopted that the righteous of all nations have a share in the world to come (Tosef., Sanh. 13:2).

This talmudic material, which is generally of an intuitive, commonsense and concrete nature, must now be compared to the statement of these themes and their exegeses and analysis in the thought of the medieval Jewish philosophers in whose hands they become more logical, abstract and systematic.

Medieval Jewish Philosophy

The formulation of precise articles of Jewish faith is largely a medieval development, with due acknowledgment to Philo (first century C.E.)

who had spoken of eight essential principles of scriptural religion: (1) the existence of God; (2) His unity; (3) divine providence; (4) creation of the world; (5) unity of the world; (6) the existence of incorporeal ideas; (7) the relevation of the law; and (8) its eternity.[25]

The formulation of articles of faith in the Middle Ages arose in the first instance from theological discussions which had started in Muslim *Kalam,*[26] i.e., the science of *Hadith* or "tradition," and Islamic religious law, and which then had spread to Jewish philosophical and religious circles. Thus it is not surprising that the term *ikkarim* (lit. "roots"), the most widely used Hebrew term denoting the "principles" of Judaism, is a literal translation of the Arabic *uṣul* denoting the "roots" of various disciplines, and that the term *uṣul al-din* ("the roots of religion") is synonymous with *kalam.* In this sense Maimonides refers to the theologians employing the methods of *kalam* as people concerned with *uṣul al-din* (*ikkarei ha-dat; Guide* 3:51).

The most important attempt to formulate Jewish articles of faith was that of Maimonides, but Maimonides' formulation was not without precedent. Earlier, Ḥananel b. Ḥushi'el[27] declared that faith is fourfold and consists in the following beliefs: (1) in God; (2) in the prophets; (3) in the world to come; and (4) in the advent of the Messiah. Likewise, among the Karaites the first enumeration of fundamental Jewish beliefs antedates Maimonides and is found in Judah Hadassi's (mid-12th century) *Eshkol ha-Kofer.* This author lists ten articles (*ishurim*) of faith: (1) God's unity and wisdom; (2) His eternity and unlikeness to any other being; (3) He is the Creator of the world; (4) Moses and the rest of the prophets were sent by God; (5) the Torah which has been given through Moses is true; (6) the Jews are obliged to study the Hebrew language in order to be able to understand the Torah fully; (7) the holy Temple in Jerusalem was chosen by God as the eternal dwelling place of His glory; (8) the dead will be resurrected; (9) there will be a Divine judgment; and (10) God will mete out reward and punishment. It is not clear whether Judah Hadassi offered this statement as an innovation on his part or whether he followed earlier authorities.

Maimonides' classic attempt to formulate a code of essential beliefs for Judaism, his so-called "Thirteen Principles" are set down in his commentary on the Mishnah[28] as introductory to his comments on Sanhedrin 10. Writing in Arabic, Maimonides presents these articles of faith as *uṣul* ("roots") and *qawa'id* ("fundamentals") of Jewish beliefs *(i'tiqadat)* and of the Law *(shari'a)*. The Hebrew versions render *uṣul* by *ikkarim* and *qawa'id* by either *yesodot* or *ikkarim*. Here, the term *uṣul* acquires a new meaning: it no longer denotes the topics of the *Kalam* investigations, but rather the fundamental tenets of faith or the concise abstracts of religion as seen through the eyes of a philosopher. Maimonides undertook such a presentation to teach the rank and file of the community the true spiritual meaning of the belief in the world to come *(ha-olam ha-ba)* and to disabuse their minds of crude, materialistic notions which were inimical to true religion.

Furthermore, since, according to Maimonides' philosophical outlook, the ultimate felicity of the individual depends on the possession of true concepts concerning God, the formulation and brief exposition of true notions in the realm of faith is meant to help the multitude to avoid error and to purify its belief. The "fundamentals" listed by Maimonides are: (1) The existence of God which is perfect and sufficient unto itself and which is the cause of the existence of all other beings. (2) God's unity which is unlike all other kinds of unity. (3) God must not be conceived in bodily terms, and the anthropomorphic expressions applied to God in Scripture have to be understood in a metaphorical sense. (4) God is eternal. (5) God alone is to be worshipped and obeyed. There are no mediating powers able freely to grant man's petitions, and intermediaries must not be invoked. (6) Prophecy. (7) Moses is unsurpassed by any other prophet. (8) The entire Torah was given to Moses. (9) Moses' Torah will not be abrogated or superseded by another divine law nor will anything be added to, or detracted from it. (10) God knows the actions of men. (11) God rewards those who fulfill the commandments of the Torah, and punishes those who transgress them. (12) The coming of the Messiah. (13) The resurrection of the dead.

In a postscript Maimonides distinguishes between the "sinners of Israel" who, while having yielded to their passions, are not thereby excluded from the Jewish community or the world to come, and one who "has denied a root principle" *(kafar be-ikkar)*. Such an individual has excluded himself from the community and is called a heretic *(min)* and Epicurean. Maimonides thus attempted to invest his principles with the character of dogma, by making them criteria of orthodoxy and membership in the community of Israel; but it should be noted that his statement was a personal one and remained open to criticism and revision.

In their creedal form ("I believe with perfect faith that . . .")
Maimonides' "Thirteen Principles" probably appeared for the first time
in the Venice *Haggadah* of 1566. They are found in the Ashkenazi
prayer book as an appendix to the regular morning service. Of the many
poetic versions, the best known is the popular *Yigdal* hymn (c. 1300)
which has been adopted in practically all rites.

Maimonides' "Thirteen Principles" became the prototype of a succession of formulations of the Jewish creed which first merely varied in the
number, order, and the articles of belief selected, but which eventually
(in the 15th century) introduced methodological criteria for determining
whether a certain belief could be regarded as basic. It should be noted
that the discussion was at no time purely academic. It was stimulated by
the controversy over the ellegorical interpretations of traditional beliefs
according to Aristotelian doctrine, and it focussed on such articles of
faith as *creatio ex nuhilo* (creation out of nothing), individual
providence, etc. The formulation of *ikkarim* was designed to accentuate
the vital beliefs of Judaism and to strengthen orthodoxy. On another
level it was also meant to define the position of the Jewish faith vis-à-vis
Christianity, and principles seven and nine are clearly directed against
Christian and Muslim claims[29] made on behalf of the revelations of
Jesus and Mohammed.

In the 13th century David b. Samuel Kochavi and Abba Mari Astruc
b. Moses of Lunel offered fresh formulations of the creed. David
Kochavi in his (unpublished) *Migdal David* uses the term *ikkarim* to
refer to the three elements of Judaism: (1) commandments; (2) beliefs;
and (3) the duty to engage in philosophical speculation in order fully to
understand the Torah.[30] The "beliefs" are outlined in great detail under
seven heads called "pillars" *(ammudim)* of the faith: (1) creation of the
world; (2) freedom of the will; (3) divine providence; (4) divine origin of
the Torah; (5) reward and punishment; (6) the coming of the Redeemer;
and (7) resurrection. The author claims that these articles follow a
logical order. Alternatively, Abba Mari, a defender of orthodoxy in the
Maimonidean controversy (the debate over the "orthodoxy" of
Maimonides' writings), arranged Jewish beliefs under three headings in his
Minhat Kena'ot:[31] (1) God is eternal, incorporeal, and His unity is absolute simplicity (7–11); (2) *creatio ex nihilo* and its corollary, miracles
(11–16); (3) God's individual providence (17–19).

In the 14th century, Shemariah of Negropont (Crete), an Italian philosopher and exegete (d. after 1352), chiefly known for his efforts to reconcile Karaites and Rabbanites, presented five principles of Judaism relating to the existence of God: (1) His incorporeality; (2) absolute unity; (3) creation; (4) creation in time; and (5) creation by divine *fiat*.[32] At the same time, still another philosophical writer of the period, David b. Yom Tov ibn Bilia of Portugal, in a treatise called *Yesodot ha-Maskil*[33] supplemented Maimonides' 13 articles by 13 of his own (making a total of 26 in all). These additional principles include such dogmas as belief in angels, in the superiority of the Torah over philosophy, in the canonicity of the text of the Torah, and in good actions as a reward in themselves. David b. Yom Tov ibn Bilia's additions reflect on orthodox conservative viewpoint and stress the superiority of the Torah over philosophical rationalism. Yet, in spite of this stance they bear a highly intellectual flavor which reflects the medieval philosophical climate of debate and opinion.

The debate continued in the following period with the 15th century and the beginning of the 16th being particularly rich in works on Jewish dogmatics. Some of them are based on strictly methodological considerations, while others stress the purely revelational character of Jewish beliefs. To the first category belong the writings of Hasdai Crescas, Simeon b. Zemah Duran, Joseph Albo, and Elijah del Medigo; to the second, those of Isaac Arama, Joseph Jabez and Isaac Abrabanel.

Hasdai Crescas' *Or Adonai* (completed in 1410)[34] is essentially a treatise on dogmatics, the structure of which is determined by a sharp differentiation between various categories of belief. (1) The existence, (2) unity, and (3) incorporeality of God (1:3) form the three root principles *(shoresh ve-hathalah)* of Judaism. A second group of beliefs comprises the six fundamentals *(yesodot)* or pillars *(ammudim)* of the Jewish faith without whose recognition the concept of Torah loses its meaning (2:1-6): (1) God's knowledge of all beings; (2) His providence; (3) His omnipotence; (4) prophecy; (5) free will; and (6) the purpose of the Torah as instilling in man the love of God and thereby helping him to achieve eternal felicity. The third group represents indisputable beliefs characteristic of Judaism and indispensable for Orthodoxy, yet not fundamental (3:1-8; part 2:1-3). Eight in number, they are: (1) creation of the world; (2) immortality of the soul; (3) reward and punishment; (4) resurrection; (5) immutability of the Torah; (6) supremacy of Moses' prophecy; (7) divine instruction of the high priests by way of the Urim and Thummin; and (8) the coming of the Messiah. There are three additional indisputable beliefs connected with specific commandments: (1) prayers are answered by God; (2) repentance is acceptable to God; and (3) the Day of Atonement and the holy seasons are ordained by God. Finally Crescas lists 13 problems concerning which reason is the arbiter; these include such questions as: will the world last forever; are there more worlds than one; are the celestial spheres animate and rational; do the motions of the celestial bodies influence the affairs of men; are amulets and magic efficacious?

Like Crescas, Simeon b. Ẓemaḥ Duran deals with the problem of dogmatics in his *Ohev Mishpat* (written in 1405) and *Magen Avot.*[35] He arranges Maimonides' 13 articles under the three principles *(ikkarim)*: (1) existence of God (implying His unity, incorporeality, eternity, and His being the only object of rightful worship); (2) revelation (implying prophecy, Moses' supremacy as a prophet, the divine origin of the Torah and its immutability); (3) reward and punishment (implying God's knowledge of things, providence, the coming of the Messiah, resurrection). He finds these three dogmas indicated in the statement of the Mishnah Sanhedrin 10:1 (see above). Duran also mentions earlier attempts to reduce the dogmas to three, and like Maimonides and others distinguishes between basic principles of the Torah and other beliefs, the denial of which do not constitute heresy but mere error.

Joseph Albo's *Sefer ha-Ikkarim,*[36] the most popular work on Jewish dogmatics, is indebted to both Crescas and Duran. Albo criticizes Maimonides' selection of principles, and finds some fault also with Crescas. Like Duran he finds his basic articles in three "root principles" *(ikkarim).* (1) existence of God; (2) divine origin of the Torah; and (3) reward and punishment. From these "root principles" stem derivative "roots" *(shorashim)* which together with the former, constitute the divine Law. Thus, the existence of God implies His unity, incorporeality, independence of time, and freedom from defects. The divine origin of the Torah implies God's knowledge, prophecy, and the authenticity of divine messengers or lawgivers. Reward and punishment implies individual (in addition to general) providence (1:13–15). In addition, of lower rank, although still obligatory, are six beliefs *(emunot)* which ought to be maintained although their denial does not constitute heresy. These six beliefs are: (1) the creation of the world in time and *ex nihilo*: (2) the supremacy of Moses' prophecy; (3) the immutability of

the Torah; (4) the attainment of the bliss of the next world by the fulfillment of a single commandment; (5) resurrection; (6) coming of the Messiah (1:23).

Elijah Delmedigo's *Behinat ha-Dat* (written in 1496)[37] is the last of
the medieval works on Jewish dogmatics with a strong philosophic
orientation. It reflects the doctrine of the "double truth" of the Christian
Averroists. Delmedigo distinguishes between basic dogmas *(shorashim)*
which have to be accepted without interpretation *(perush, be'ur)* by
masses and philosophers alike, and ramifications *(anafim)* which the
masses must accept literally, while the philosophers are required to
search for their deeper meaning. For Delmedigo, Maimonides' 13 articles belong to the category of basic dogmas. Some of them he holds to
be verifiable by reason (existence, unity and incorporeality of God),
while the rest have to be taken on trust. Following Duran, Delmedigo
holds that Maimonides' 13 articles are reducible to three: (1) existence
of God; (2) prophecy; and (3) reward and punishment. Such topics as
the "reasons of the commandments" belong to the category of ramifications as does the whole field of rabbinic *aggadah*. Here, in conservative
fashion, Delmedigo cautions that the philosopher must exercise great
care in publicizing his interpretations in areas where allegorizing may do
harm to the unsophisticated and undermine their faith.

Isaac Arama in his *Akedat Yizhak*[38] criticizes Crescas and Albo, who
saw as the criterion for a "fundamental" of Judaism whether a certain
belief was basic to the general concept of revelation, an approach which
had tacitly equated Torah with revealed religion in a universal rational
sense. According to Arama the Torah reveals principles above and supplementary to reason. Hence a belief in the existence, unity, eternity,
and simplicity of God cannot rank as a principle of the Torah as argued
by Maimonides and his followers, nor can free will and purpose be such
principles as argued by Crescas. The principles *(ikkarim)* of the Torah
cannot be discovered through philosophy but, rather, have to be discovered in the Torah itself. They are embodied in the commandments
(mitzvot), particularly in the laws relating to the Sabbath and the
festivals. Arama counts six "principles of the faith" *(ikkarei ha-
emunah):* (1) the createdness of the world (Sabbath); (2) God's omnipotence (Passover); (3) prophecy and divine revelation (Shavuot); (4)
providence (New Year); (5) repentance (Day of Atonement); (6) the
world to come (Tabernacles; ch. 67; in ch. 55 the Sabbath is described

as implying all the six principles). Arama lays particular stress on the basic principle of creation as the essential dogma of the Torah (ch. 67).

Akin in spirit to Arama are his two contemporaries Joseph Jabeẓ and Isaac Abrabanel, the former being the author of two small treatises on dogmatics, called *Ma'amar ha-Aḥdut* and *Yesod ha-Emunah*.[39] In the first he rejects Maimonides', Crescas', and Albo's formulations of principles, substituting three of his own, all of which are explications of divine unity: (1) God alone is the Creator; (2) God alone is wondrously active in exercising providence; and (3) God alone will be worshipped in the messianic future. In the second he maintains that Maimonides' 13 principles are traceable to these three, but he now formulates them as: (1) createdness of the world *(ḥiddush ha-olam);* (2) providence; and (3) unity of God and, in polemical fashion, the third dogma is taken to imply that God alone will be worshipped in the messianic future. In both treatises the belief in creation is considered the most fundamental principle.

Isaac Abrabanel's *Rosh Amanah*[40] (written from 1499 to 1502) is a closely argued treatise on the "roots and principles" of the Jewish faith. Twenty-two of the work's 24 chapters are devoted to an analysis of Maimonides', Crescas', and Albo's respective positions. Abrabanel raises 28 "doubts" or objections to Maimonides' formulation of the creed, but, resolving these questions, he arrives at a complete vindication of Maimonides' views, while those of Crescas and Albo are found wanting. Abrabanel's own attitude, however, is close to Isaac Arama's. The search for "cardinal tenets" has its place only in the human sciences which operate with "fundamental principles" that are either self-evident or borrowed from other, more fundamental, sciences. In the case of the divinely revealed Torah, there is no exterior frame of reference that could furnish the fundamental principles of its laws and beliefs; everything contained therein has to be believed and there is no sense in trying to establish principles of Jewish belief. Were he to single out one principle of the divine Torah, Abrabanel states, he would select that of the createdness of the world (ch. 22).

The medieval Jewish philosophical tradition is still reflected in Spinoza who in his *Tractatus Theologico-Politicus*[41] formulates seven "dogmas of universal faith" or "fundamental principles which Scripture as a whole aims to convey"; (1) God's existence; (2) unity; (3) omnipresence; (4) supreme authority and power; (5) man's worship of Him in obedience; (6) the felicity of the obedient; (7) forgiveness of penitent sinners (ch. 14). Spinoza's scriptural religion stands between the "universal religion" of the philosopher and the "religion of the masses" (Introd.; chs. 4, 7).

The Modern Period

Moses Mendelssohn, the pioneer of the modern phase in Judaism, formulates the following principles of the Jewish religion: (1) God, the author and ruler of all things, is one and simple; (2) God knows all things, rewards the good and punishes evil by natural and, sometimes, supernatural means; (3) God has made known His laws in the Scriptures given through Moses to the children of Israel. Mendelssohn rejects the Christian dogmas of the trinity, original sin, etc., as incompatible with reason, and stresses the harmony between religion and reason within Judaism.[42] The truths to be recognized by the Jew are identical with the eternal verities of reason, and they do not depend on a divine revelation. Only the laws of Judaism are revealed. Hence the Jewish religion does not prescribe belief nor does it lay down dogmas (symbols, articles of faith). The Hebrew term *emunah* means "trust" in the divine promises.

Mendelssohn's distinction between the rational truths of Judaism and the revealed laws of the Torah did not appeal to the reformers of the 19th century, but it pervaded the catechisms and manuals of the Jewish religion written by the disciples of Mendelssohn in the early part of the century. It soon came up against opposition once the impact of Kant's critique of rational theology made itself felt. Moreover, Hegel's speculative interpretation of Christianity as the "absolute religion" was felt as a serious challenge. Solomon Formstecher's *Religion des Geistes* (1841) and Samuel Hirsch's *Religionsphilosophie der Juden* (1842) presented in their turn Judaism as the "absolute religion." In this changed climate of opinion Manuel Joel[43] spoke of dogmas in Judaism as the essential prerequisite of its cult and ritual while Abraham Geiger agreed with the repudiation of Mendelssohn and stressed the wealth of "ideas" with which Judaism entered history. He denied, however, the validity of the term "dogma" as applied to the Jewish religion, since the absence of ultimately fixed formulations of Jewish beliefs rendered the term a misnomer. David Einhorn, on the other hand, had no objection to using the word,[44] and the same view was strongly expressed by Leopold Loew.[45]

The formulations of the Jewish creed by a number of Jewish theologians in the latter part of the 19th century manifest the strongly-felt desire to offer some clear guidance on the essential elements of the Jewish faith in a period of great change and challenge to traditional Judaism from both inside and outside Jewish circles. Among such works are to be counted Samuel Hirsch's *Systematischer Katechismus der israelitischer Religion* (1856); Solomon Formstecher's *Mosaische Religionslehre* (1860) and Joseph Aub's *Grundlage zu einem wissenschaftlichen Unterricht in der mosaischen Religion* (1865). These catechisms are influenced by the new reform, idealist and historical concerns and try to strike a balance between traditional and modern requirements. Alternatively, the traditional orthodox position found its most powerful and influential spokesman in Samson Raphael Hirsch who in his *Choreb Versuche ueber Jissroels Pflichten in der Zerstreuung* (1837)[46] presented an explanation and defence of a traditional heteronomous view of Judaism and Torah. According to Hirsch, man's role is solely to serve God and to this end God revealed the Torah at Sinai. The Jew is obligated to keep the Torah and traditional *halakhah* and Hirsch summed up his view in the phrase: "The catechism of the Jew is his calendar."

In the latter part of the 19th century the discussion found new expression in such studies as Samuel David Luzzatto's Hebrew work *Yesodei Ha-Torah* (1880) and in Michael Friedlander's *The Jewish Religion* (1896). More important and more consequential, however, was Solomon Schechter's justly well-known essay "Dogma in Judaism" (in *Studies in Judaism* I, 1896; repr. 1945), in which he argued that Judaism, while limiting its dogmatic content, does require certain dogmatic commitments in order to remain what it is. However Schechter, who is one of the fathers of the modern "historical school" in Jewish thought, holds that this need for a certain, albeit minimum, dogmatic consensus does not mean that Judaism is not open to new interpretations, growth and development in response to historical necessity. Instead he believes the essence of Judaism to lie in "the collective conscience of Catholic Israel as embodied in the Universal Synagogue" rather than "in any section of the nation or any corporate priesthood or rabbihood." By this Schechter intends that "neither Scripture nor primitive Judaism" should be the unchallenged rule but rather that "the norm as well as the sanction of Judaism is the practice actually in vogue." In this way history, sociology and tradition are tied together to create a flexible, though not rootless, Judaism. Schechter's position has been widely influential and is one of the pillars of American Conservative Judaism.[47]

While in medieval philosophy the description of faith formed an integral part of the theory of knowledge, the rise of modern science and the concomitant decline of the belief in the divine revelation of Scriptures have made faith a matter of trusting in God rather than of the affirmation of certain propositions. Characteristic of this attitude in recent Jewish thought are the views of Franz Rosenzweig,[48] according to whom religious belief arises from the experience of personal revelation, for which man must always strive and be prepared. It has also been argued by Rosenzweig and others that this non-propositional, existentialist position was already anticipated by Hermann Cohen[49] in his theory of correlation. Similarly, Martin Buber[50] and Abraham Heschel[51] see faith as a relationship of trust between man and God, which arises from, and manifests itself in, personal encounters between man and God and man and man, which Buber calls *I-Thou* relationships. In this dialogical situation there are no cognitive preconditions and no definitive norms or objective standards, and certainly no traditional metaphysical or religious "dogmas" are generated as a result of this encounter. Buber is especially adamant on this "content less" view of religious relationship between God and man and the consequences of this relationship.

Another tendency among modern thinkers is to view belief as a psychological state which is valuable insofar as it motivates man to act in an ethical manner. Mordecai Kaplan,[52] a representative of this pragmatic-naturalistic view, implies that faith is a kind of "self-fulfilling prophecy" insofar as it leads to the redemption of human society. Moreover, Kaplan holds a sociological-pragmatic position, which in some ways is distantly related to Schechter's notion of "Catholic Israel." According to this view, the essence of Judaism resides in the wants, needs and goals of the Jewish people at any given time in its history. In this revaluation of Judaism things are held to be valuable not as they relate to God and His revealed will but only as regards their instrumental value to the Jewish people. In earlier periods of human history, men gave authority to their collective habits by seeing them as divine commandments; today this "fiction" is no longer required. Insofar as the Jewish people are part of history their needs and wants change and develop; accordingly there is no essential dogmatic center to Judaism, nor can there be one. According to others who embrace a naturalistic view, faith is held to be valuable in that it infuses meaning and purpose into an otherwise meaningless and cruel existence. This point is taken up strongly by Richard Rubenstein,[53] who has been concerned with the challenge to Jewish faith posed by the Holocaust and its consequent effects on Jewish theology and the "death of God."

The Concept of "Normative Judaism"
In conclusion it should be noted that Jewish thinkers who hold that an essence of Judaism can be perceived tend to speak of "normative Judaism," with the implication that at the heart of the Jewish faith there is a hard, imperishable core, to be externally preserved, together with numerous peripheral ideas, expressed to be sure by great Jewish thinkers in different ages but not really essential to the faith, which could be dismissed if necessary as deviations.

Unfortunately for this line of thinking no criteria are available for distinguishing the essential from the ephemeral, so that a strong element of subjectivity is present in this whole approach. Almost invariably the process ends in a particular thinker's embracing ideas he holds to be true and valuable, discovering these reflected in the tradition and hence belonging to the "normative," while rejecting ideas he holds to be harmful or valueless as peripheral to Judaism, even though they are found in the tradition. Nor is the statistical approach helpful. An idea occurring very frequently in the traditional sources may be rejected by some thinkers on the grounds that it is untrue or irrelevant, while one hardly mentioned in the sources may assume fresh significance in a new situation, to say nothing of the difficulties in deciding which sources are to be considered the more authoritative. The difficulties which can result from the "normative Judaism" approach can be seen when, for example, contemporary thinkers with a dislike for asceticism, who wish at the same time to speak in the name of Judaism, virtually read out of the faith ascetics such as Baḥya ibn Paquda and Moses Ḥayyim Luzzato.[54]

Nonetheless, if due caution is exercised and no exaggerated claims made, the idea of a normative Judaism is not without value in that it calls attention to the undeniable fact that for all the variety of moods in

Judaism's history there does emerge among the faithful a kind of consensus on the main issues. It has always been recognized, for instance, after the rise of Christianity and Islam, that these two religions are incompatible with Judaism and that no Jew can consistently embrace them while remaining an adherent of Judaism. The same applies to the Far Eastern religions. This, of course, is very different from affirming that there are no points of contact between Judaism and other faiths, or no common concerns. Nor has the idea of a Judaism divorced from the peoplehood of Israel ever made much headway, even in circles in which the doctrine of Israel's chosenness is a source of embarrassment. Nor does Jewish history know of a Torah-less Judaism, even though the interpretations of what is meant by Torah differ widely. The most important work of Jewish mysticism, the Zohar, speaks of three grades or stages bound one to the other—God, the Torah, and Israel (Zohar, Lev. 73a–b). Historically considered it is true that Judaism is an amalgam of three ideas—belief in God, God's revelation of the Torah to Israel, and Israel as the people which lives by the Torah in obedience to God.

Covenant

A covenant, called in Hebrew a *berit* (or *brit*),[1] is a general obligation between two parties confirmed either by an oath, a solemn meal, a sacrifice, or by some other dramatic act such as dividing an animal and having the parties to the covenant pass between the portions.[2] In the Bible covenants are established between individuals, between states or their representatives, between kings and their subjects, and also between husbands and wives. We also have instances in which the term is used figuratively for a relation between men and animals and men and death.[3] The variety of obligations covered by the term indicate that a covenant can be entered into either by equal partners sharing mutual obligations and mutual benefits, or by unequal partners in which the power and authority of the covenantal partners is asymmetrical as are the responsibilities, obligations and rewards. Often this latter type of covenant represents a relationship in which a more powerful party makes a pact with an inferior one freely and out of good will. In this case the superior party takes the inferior one under his protection on conditon that the latter remains loyal to him. The covenant of the Israelites with the Gibeonites in Joshua 9 is an example of a pact of this type.

At times, in addition to the ceremony of confirmation, covenants are accompanied by an external sign or token to remind the contracting parties of their obligations.[4] Such signs are especially to be found in the pacts between God and man. The Sabbath, the rainbow, and circumcision are each a "sign" of a great covenant established by God at a critical stage in the history of mankind; the Sabbath is the sign of Creation; the rainbow is a sign of the renewal of mankind after the Flood; and circumcision of the beginning of the Jewish people and the Hebrew nation.[5] Not surprising, the sign of circumcision given to Abraham and made the obligation of all future Jews came to be regarded in the Jewish tradition as the most distinctive indication of the pact and is known as *berit milah*—"the covenant of circumcision."

Of all the covenants in the Bible the central one is that between God and Israel. Scholars, however, have long debated the origin and nature of the biblical covenants between God and humankind and, until recently, generally held this to be a relatively late idea in the development of biblical religious thought. This, however, seems to be a mistaken position both on scholarly and Jewish grounds. The best 20th-century scholarship has revised this view, arguing for an earlier dating. In addition, scholars have advanced several interesting theories about the context in which the notions of covenant arose. S. Mowinckel[6] argued that it reflected an early annual celebration involving a theophany and proclamation of the law. His arguments were based mainly on Psalm 50:5ff. and Psalm 81, where theophany is combined with covenant-making and decalogue formulas. He was followed by A.At.[7] who argued that the so-called apodictic law had been recited at the Feast of Tabernacles at the beginning of the year of release (cf. Deut. 31:10-13) and that this periodical convocation was a solemn undertaking by the congregation which is reflected in the Sinai covenant. G. von Rad[8] inquiring into the significance of the peculiar structure of Deuteronomy—history (ch. 1-11), laws (12:1-26:15), mutual obligations (26:16-19), and blessings and curses (ch. 27-29)—suggested that this structure, and similarly that of the Sinai covenant—history (Ex. 19:4-6), law (20:1-23:19), promises and threats (3:20-23), conclusion of the covenant (24:1-11)—reflects the procedure of a covenant ceremony. This opened with a recital of history, proceeded with the proclamation of the law—accompanied by a sworn obligation—and ended with blessings and curses. Since according to Deuteronomy 27[9] the blessings and curses had to be recited between Mounts Gerizim and Ebal, von Rad identified Shechem as the scene of the periodic covenant renewal in ancient Israel.

Although no real evidence for a covenant festival has been discovered so far, the observation made by von Rad that the literary structure of Deuteronomy and Exodus 19-24 reflects a covenantal procedure has been confirmed by subsequent investigations. It has become clear that the covenant form, as presented in these texts and especially in Deuteronomy, was in use for centuries in the ancient Near East. G. Mendenhall[10] found that the Hittite treaty has a structure similar to that of the biblical covenant. The basic common elements are: titular descriptions; historical introduction, which served as a motivation for the vassal's loyalty; stipulation of the treaty; a list of divine witnesses;

blessings and curses; and recital of the treaty and deposit of its tablets. The Sinai covenant described in Exodus 19–24 has indeed a similar structure, although it is not completely identical. Thus, the divine address in chapter 19 opens with a historical introduction stressing the grace of God toward the people and its election (19:4–6), followed by the law (23:20–33), and finally the ratification of the covenant by means of a cultic ceremony and the recital of the covenant document (24:3–8).

Admittedly the analogy is not complete, since what is found in Exodus 19–24 is not a treaty, as in the Hittite documents, but rather a narrative about the conclusion of a covenant. Nevertheless, it is clear that the narrative is organized and arranged in line with the treaty pattern, which emerges in a much clearer fashion in Deuteronomy. This book, which is considered by its author as one organic literary creation and represents the covenant of the plains of Moab, follows the classical pattern of treaties in the Ancient Near East. Unlike the Sinai covenant in Exodus which has no list of blessings and curses, Deuteronomy (like the treaties and especially those of the first millennium B.C.E.) has an elaborate series of blessings and curses and likewise provides for witnesses to the covenant, "heaven and earth" (4:26; 30:19), which are missing altogether in the first four books of the Pentateuch. Deuteronomy also makes explicit references to the deposit of the tablets of the covenant and the book of the Law in the divine Ark (10:1–5; 31:25–26). The Ark was considered in ancient Israel as the footstool of the Deity (the cherubim constituting the throne), and it was indeed at the feet of the gods that the treaty documents had to be kept according to Hittite legal tradition. As in the Hittite treaties, Deuteronomy commands the periodical recital of the Law before the public (31:9–13) and prescribes that the treaty be read before the king or by him (17:18–19).

THE COVENANT WITH ABRAHAM AND DAVID

Aside from the covenant between God and Israel described in Exodus and Deuteronomy, two covenants of a different type are found in the Bible. These are the covenant with Abraham (Gen. 15, 17) and the covenant with David (II Sam. 7; cf. Ps. 89), which are concerned respectively with the gift of the land and the gift of kingship and dynasty. In contradistinction to the Mosaic covenants, which are of an obligatory type, the Abrahamic-Davidic covenants belong to the promissory type. God swears to Abraham to give the land to his descendants and similarly promises to David to establish his dynasty without imposing any obligations on them. Although their loyalty to God is presupposed, it is not made a condition for God's keeping His promise. On the contrary, the Davidic promise as formulated in the vision of Nathan contains a clause in which the unconditional nature of the gift is explicitly stated (II Sam. 7:13-15). By the same token, the covenant with the Patriarchs is considered as valid forever *('ad 'olam)*. Even when Israel sins and is to be severely punished, God intervenes to help because He "will not break his covenant" (Lev. 26:43).

In the same way as the obligatory covenant in Israel is modeled on the suzerain-vassal type of treaty so the promissory covenant is modeled on the royal grant. The royal grants in the Ancient Near East as well as the covenants with Abraham and David are gifts bestowed upon individuals who distinguished themselves in loyal service to their masters. Abraham is promised the land because he obeyed God and followed His mandate,[12] and similarly David is rewarded with dynastic posterity because he served God with truth, righteousness, and loyalty.[13] The terminology employed in this context is very close to that used in the Assyrian royal grants. The promises to Abraham and David, which were originally unconditional, were understood as conditional only at a later stage of Israelite history. The exile of northern Israel appeared to refute the claim to eternity of the Abrahamic covenant, and therefore it was stressed that the covenant is eternal only if the donee keeps faith with the donor. A similar interpretation is given to the Davidic covenant in the Book of Kings.[14]

Long before the parallel between the Israelite covenant and the Ancient Near Eastern treaty had been brought to light, W. Eichrodt[15] recognized the importance of the covenant idea in the religion of Israel, seeing in the Sinai covenant a point of departure for understanding Israel's religion. Eichrodt explains that basic phenomena like the kingship of God, revelation, the liberation from myth, the personal attitude to God, etc. are to be explained against the background of the covenant. The discovery of the treaty pattern in the Ancient Near East strengthened this hypothesis, new developments in covenant research throwing light on the idea of the kingship of God. It now becomes clear that God as King of Israel is not an idea born during the period of the monarchy, as scholars used to think, but, on the contrary, is one of the most genuine and most ancient doctrines of

Israel. In the period of the judges the tribes resisted kingship because of the prevailing belief that God was the real King of Israel and that the proclamation of an earthly king would constitute a betrayal. This is clearly expressed in Gideon's reply to the people's offer of kingship (Judg. 8: 22–23), but is even more salient in Samuel's denunciation of the request for a king.[16] Earthly kingship in Israel was finally accepted, but this was was the outcome of a compromise: David's kingship was conceived as granted to him by the Great Suzerain (II Sam. 7). The King and the people alike were thus considered as vassals of God, the real Overlord.[17]

It seems that this suzerain-vassal outlook has its roots in the political actuality of the period of the judges. As is well known, Syria-Palestine of the second half of the second millennium B.C.E. was dominated by two great political powers, the Egyptian and the Hittite empires, in turn. Either the king of Egypt or the king of the Hittites was overlord of the petty kingdoms in the area. The lands and the kingdoms of the latter were conceived as feudal grants bestowed on them by the great suzerain, in exchange for the obligation of loyalty to the master. Israel's concept of its relationship with God had a similar basis. The Israelites believed that they owed their land and royal dynasty to their suzerain, God. Furthermore, as the relationship between the suzerain and the vassal has to be based on a written document, i.e., a treaty, so the relationship between God and Israel had to be expressed in written form. It is not surprising, therefore, that the tablets of the covenant played so important a role in the religion of Israel. As already noted, the tablets had to be deposited in the sanctuary at the feet of the deity, a procedure known from the Hittite treaties. Moreover, it appears that, as in the judicial sphere, the written document expresses the validity of the given relationship. When the covenant is no longer in force the document must be destroyed. Thus the worship of the golden calf, which signifies the breaking of the covenant, is followed by the breaking of the tablets by Moses, the mediator of the covenant (Ex. 32). Indeed, the term for canceling a contract in Babylonian legal literature is "to break the tablet" *(tuppam ḫepū)*. Following the judicial pattern, the renewal of the relationship must be effected by writing new tablets, which explains why new ones had to be written after the sin of the golden calf, and why the ritual decalogue was repeated in Exodus 34: 17–26.[18] Renewal of a covenant with a vassal—after a break in the relationship—by means of writing new tablets is an attested fact in Hittite political life.

This new examination of the covenant elucidates basic phenomena in Israel's prophetic literature. The admonitory speeches of the prophets are often formulated in the style of lawsuit.[19] God sues the people of Israel in the presence of witnesses such as heaven and earth, and mountains,[20] witnesses which also appear in the Ancient Near Eastern treaties and in the Deuteronomy covenant. International strife in the Ancient Near East provides parallels to prophetic denunciations; for example, before going out to battle with the Babylonian king Kaštiliaš, the Assyrian king accuses the latter of betrayal and violation of the treaty between them, and as proof he reads the treaty in a loud voice before the god Šamaš. In a similar way the prophetic lawsuit represents God's accusation of Israel before He proceeds to destroy the people for violating the covenant. This is clearly expressed in Amos 4:6–11, where a series of punishments, similar to those enumerated in Leviticus 26, is proclaimed, in the nature of a warning, before the final judgment or encounter (cf. Amos 4:12: "Be ready to meet your God, O Israel").

Yet despite the parallels between biblical covenant formulae and other Ancient Near Eastern covenants the essential point that must be recognized is that the idea of a pact between a deity and a people is unknown from other religions and cultures. It seems that the covenantal idea was a special feature of the religion of Israel, the only one to demand exclusive loyalty and preclude the possibility of dual or multiple loyalties; so the stipulation in political treaties demanding exclusive fealty to one king corresponds strikingly with the religious belief in one single, exclusive deity.

The prophets, especially Hosea, Jeremiah, and Ezekiel, expressed this idea of exclusive loyalty by speaking of the relationship between God and Israel as one of husband and wife, which in itself is also considered covenantal.[21] Although the idea of marital love between God and Israel is not mentioned explicitly in the Pentateuch, it seems to be present in a latent form. Following other gods is threatened by the statement: "For I the Lord your God am a jealous God."[22] The root (*qna*, "jealous") is in fact used in Numbers 5:14 in the technical sense of a husband who is jealous of his wife. Similarly the verb used in the Pentateuch for disloyalty is *zanah 'aharei*, "to whore after." Furthermore, the formula expressing the covenantal relationship between God and Israel, "you will be my people and I will be your God,"[23] is a legal formula taken from the sphere of marriage, as attested in various legal documents from the

Ancient Near East (cf. Hos. 2:4). The relationship of the vassal to his suzerain or of the wife to her husband leaves no place for double loyalty, and they are therefore perfect metaphors for loyalty in a monotheistic religion.

The concept of the kingship of God in Israel also seems to have contributed to the conception of Israel as the vassal of God. It is true that the idea of the kingship of God (or gods) was prevalent throughout the Ancient Near East; nevertheless, there is an important difference between the Israelite notion of divine suzerainty and the corresponding belief of other nations. Israel adopted the idea long before establishing the human institution of monarchy. Consequently, for hundreds of years the only kingship recognized and institutionalized in Israel was the rulership of God. During the period of the judges YHWH was actually the King of Israel[24] and was not, as in other religions of the Ancient Near East, the image of the earthly king.

This discussion of covenant has primarily focussed on historical and structural elements of biblical covenants, purposely leaving aside their broader theological associations, to which we now turn under the related rubric of the "Chosen People."

The Chosen People

Inseparable from the notion of covenant has been the doctrine of Israel as God's "Chosen People," a common designation for the people of Israel throughout its history. This concept most fundamentally expresses the idea that the people of Israel stand in a special and unique relationship to the universal deity, and has been central to the history of Jewish thought. It is deeply rooted in the Bible and has been developed in talmudic, philosophic, mystical, and contemporary Judaism.

IN THE BIBLE

Narrowly viewed, one Hebrew root, *bḥr* ("to choose"), expresses with unmistakable intent the nature and manner in which the people of Israel is understood to be the people of God. This term, in addition to its ordinary, lay meaning, is used to indicate the choice of persons by God for a particular role or office, such as a priest: "For the Lord your God has chosen him and his descendants to come out of all your tribes, to be in attendance for service in the name of the Lord, forever"; or as a king, when David says to Michal, Saul's daughter, "Before the Lord, who chose me above thy father, and above all his house, to appoint me prince over the people of the Lord over Israel."[1]

This root is also used to indicate the setting aside of a particular place for the site of the sanctuary, "But look only to the site that the Lord your God will choose amidst all your tribes as His habitation . . . there you are to go."[2] Just as in these usages the verb *bḥr* indicates a role for the persons or place that have been chosen by God, so in the Deuteronomic writings (those writings attributed to the 7th-6th century editor of Deuteronomy) it has a particular theological meaning relating to the people of Israel: "For you are a people consecrated to the Lord your God: of all the peoples on earth the Lord your God chose you to be His treasured people."[3]

163

The idea of election was already widespread when the Deuteronomist introduced the technical theological term "chosen" to express it. It is the essence of the covenant, which signifies the fundamental relationship between God and Israel and is referred to throughout the entire Hebrew Bible. However contemporary critical scholarship may define that covenant, there is general agreement that the biblical authors viewed such a relationship as essential. Yet the relationship between God and Israel is broader than that indicated by the term "to choose." In Amos 3:2, for example, the verb *yada'* ("to know intimately") in "I have known only you of all the peoples of the earth; therefore I will visit upon you all your iniquities" points to this special relationship. The second half of this verse is one of the classic passages which emphasizes that the doctrine of election does not imply the conferment of special privileges, but rather imposes extra obligations and responsibility.

The Deuteronomic writers offered a further theological interpretation of the pact aspect, i.e., the status of Israel as the people of God. It was founded upon an act of divine choice motivated by love: "It is not because you are the most numerous of peoples that the Lord set His heart on you and chose you—indeed, you are the smallest of peoples; but it was because the Lord loved you ... " (Deut. 7:7–8). Thus God, who chose Israel, could have chosen any other nation as well. Accordingly, the Deuteronomic writers and Deutero-Isaiah especially emphasized the universal rule of the God of Israel, while at the same time underscoring the particular choice of Israel for special responsibility in the same way that chosen individuals are responsible for certain tasks and are required to assume particular roles. In Genesis 18:19 we read, "For I have singled him out, that he may instruct his children and his posterity, to keep the way of the Lord, by doing what is just and right ... " and in Nehemiah 9:7 as "Thou art the Lord the God, who didst choose *(baharta)* Abram ... " with the obligations spelled out in the earlier verse now present by implication in the verb "choose." The divine choice, therefore, calls for reciprocal human response: "Ye are witnesses against yourselves that ye have chosen you the Lord, to serve Him ... " Josh. 24:22). Israel is obligated by this choice to "keep His statutes, and observe His Laws" (Ps. 105:45).

Unlike the nonentities that the nations of the world worship, God has predicted both the marvelous victories of Cyrus that have already taken place and the miraculous restoration of Israel (led back from Babylonia to their homeland by a verdant, shady, well-watered path across the desert; etc.) that is soon to follow. Israel will convince the nations of the world that there is only one effective God who can do them any good, and so will be the agents of the planting of the true religion and hence success and "light" (i.e., happiness) to the ends of the world. The whole discussion in Isaiah 49 of Israel, God's servant, pivots on the idea of the task to which God has appointed her: that of spreading God's salvation. The passage in Isaiah 49:1ff. has been compared to (even, it is suggested, modeled on) Jeremiah 1:4ff. But whereas Jeremiah is to be a "prophet unto the nations" only in the sense that he will announce future events to them (Jer. 1:10), Israel is to be a prophet to the nations in the sense that it will bring them the light of salvation. This idea of election as imposing a task on the elected, also leads to the doctrine of Israel's vicarious suffering for the nations, a role known as that of the "suffering servant."[4]

Further, although the people of Israel may not presume that God will always consider them favorably, regardless of their acts, the thought of absolute rejection appears unimaginable: "Yet even then, when they are in the land of their enemies, I will not reject them or spurn them so as to destroy them, annulling my covenant with them: for I the Lord am their God." (Lev. 26:44). Indeed, an important element of prophetic writings is the concern to explain why the formally deserved rejection was not effected. The fundamental motive of the choice, love, is seen as ultimately overriding the legal requirement of rejection, although not that of punishment.

IN RABBINIC THOUGHT

After the close of the biblical period the relationship between God and Israel described in Scripture, remained a focal point of religious contemplation and theological speculation not only for the Pharisaic-rabbinic tradition, but in other movements within the community both in Palestine and the Diaspora.[5]

The rabbis themselves, while strongly upholding the doctrine of the Chosen People, insist that the election of Israel is based upon their voluntary acceptance of the Torah at Sinai. This idea, already expressed in Exodus 19:5, "If ye will hearken unto My voice, indeed, and keep My covenant, then ye shall be Mine own treasure from among all the peoples," is developed by the rabbis who state that the Torah was freely offered first to the other nations of the world. All of them, however, rejected it because of its restrictive ordinances which conflicted with their wicked way of life, and only Israel accepted it.[6] The sages also give great prominence to the enthusiastic acceptance of the Torah by Israel, even before they acquainted themselves with its contents: *na'aseh ve-nishma*–"we will do and listen",[7] Israel replies, a fact for which the heathens are made to sneer at them as an "unstable people" (Ket. 112a).

On the other hand, a special relationship of love is said to exist between the children of Israel and God, which is made the basis of rabbinic allegorical interpretations of the Song of Songs, and is expressed in a saying such as, "How beloved is Israel before the Holy One, blessed be He; for wherever they were exiled the *Shekhinah* (Divine Presence) was with them" (Meg. 29a).

Rabbinic literature evinces a concern to explain this election and special relationship as something other than arbitrary and to find in the character or behavior of Israel (or of the Patriarchs) some motive for the divine choice, such as exceptional holiness, humility, loyalty, or obedience. So for example, the Talmud has it that the qualities of mercy and forgiveness are characteristic of Abraham and his seed and are a distinguishing mark of the true Jew[8] and it is for this reason that they are chosen. Yet, as Solomon Schechter has noted, "even those rabbis who tried to establish Israel's special claim on their exceptional merits, were not altogether unconscious of the insufficiency of the reason of works in this respect, and therefore had also recourse to the love of God, which is not given as a reward, but is offered freely."[9]

The rabbinic conception of the election of Israel finds dogmatic expression in the orthodox liturgy. "Thou hast chosen us from all peoples; thou has loved us and taken pleasure in us, and hast exalted us above all tongues; thou has hallowed us by the commandments, and brought us near unto thy service." Likewise, the connection between the election of Israel and her role as guardian of God's Torah is expressed in the liturgy in the blessing recited on being called up to the reading of the Torah, "Blessed art thou, O Lord our God, King of the Universe, who has chosen us from all peoples, and hast given us Thy Torah."[10]

With the rise of Christianity, the doctrine of Israel as the Chosen People acquired an added polemical edge against the background of the claim of the Church to be the "true Israel" and God's chosen people. In times of persecution and despair the doctrine, which was axiomatic in Jewish consciousness, was a source of great strength and forbearance. Similarly the talmudic explanation, that the willingness of Israel to accept and obey the Torah was the reason for their election, helped maintain loyalty to tradition and to *halakhah* in periods of stress and forced conversion to other religions,[11] and provided the Jew with a rationale for survival.

IN MEDIEVAL JEWISH PHILOSOPHY

In medieval Jewish philosophy the notion of the special status of the Jewish people found the most articulate and most radical expression in Judah Halevi's *Kuzari*. The entire Jewish people, according to Halevi, was endowed with a special religious faculty, first given to Adam, and then bequeathed, through a line of chosen representatives, to all of Israel (1:95). As a result of the divine influence thus inherited, the Jewish people was uniquely able to enter into communion with God (1:47). Moreover, according to this view, because of this divine influence, Israel's election implies dependence on a special supernatural providence which maintains the people of Israel, while the rest of humanity is subject to the workings of the general laws of nature (1:109) and providence.

While the notion of Israel as a Chosen People occupies a central position in Judah Halevi's thought, it plays only an incidental role in the writings of other Jewish philosophers. Saadiah mentions in passing God's promise that the Jewish nation will exist as long as the heavens and the earth (*Beliefs and Opinions,* 3:7), and holds that only Israel is assured of redemption, and will be included in the resurrection of the dead (*ibid.,* 7:3). Abraham ibn Daud echoes Halevi's notion that Israel alone is privileged to receive prophecy, while Judah Halevi's theory of a special, supernatural providence which is exercised on behalf of Israel alone is repeated by Ḥasdai Crescas and Isaac Abrabanel. Alternatively, in the view of Maimonides, though Judaism is held to be the one true revealed religion which will never be superseded by another revelation (*Guide,* 2:39), the doctrine of Jewish election does not play a very central role.

It would seem that the more extreme, and exclusive, interpretations of the doctrine of election, among Jewish thinkers, were partly the result of reaction to oppression by the non-Jewish world. The more the Jew was forced to close in on himself, to withdraw into the imposed confines of the ghetto, the more he tended to emphasize Israel's difference from the cruel gentile world without. Only thus did his suffering become intelligible and bearable. This type of interpretation reaches its height in the kabbalistic idea that while the souls of Israel stem ultimately from God, the souls of the gentiles are merely the base material (*kelippot,* "shells"). Accordingly, when the Jew was eventually allowed to find his place in a gentile world, the less exclusivist aspect of the doctrine reasserted itself, most especially in the modern period.

IN THE MODERN PERIOD

The Enlightenment of the 18th century, and the gradual political emancipation of the Jews of Western Europe, challenged and undermined the notion of Jewish uniqueness both directly and indirectly. The earliest of the "modern" Jews, Moses Mendelssohn, considered the metaphysical content of Judaism to be identical with the "religion of reason" whose teachings coincide with philosophy and thus Jew and non-Jew have equal claims on God's love and salvation. In reply to the question, "Why should one remain a Jew?" Mendelssohn stated that the Jews had been singled out in history by the revelation at Sinai, and thus had the obligation to remain the bearers of that revelation[12] though he gained no advantage thereby.

To a large extent this ecumenical position, variously interpreted, has remained the implicit or explicit stance of a major portion of the Jewish community. In addition, the biblical concept of the Jewish mission which stressed the educational role of the Jews was developed and adapted to the new circumstances, especially in Reform circles. It was now stressed that Israel's uniqueness lay only in its possession of divine and moral instruction, which Israel would in turn pass on to the nations of the world, and in this mission to the nations lay her chosenness.

Such a position, however, has been the object of criticism, misinterpretation, and attack from within and without. The anti-Semite has seized upon it as an unveiled claim to Jewish superiority, and caricatured it by maintaining that it is the basis of a program of Jewish world domination. It is this calumny which helped to give such virulently anti-Jewish documents as the notorious forgery "The Protocols of the

Elders of Zion" a semblance of credibility. The misunderstanding, and nonplussed reaction, of certain sections of the non-Jewish world with regard to the Jews' conception of themselves as the Chosen People, is summed up in Hilaire Belloc's jingle "How odd of God to choose the Jews" (to which the retort was penned "It was not odd—the Jews chose God").[13]

It should also be noted that almost from its inception the Church has maintained that by their rejection of Jesus the Jews had forfeited their favored position which had been inherited by the Church, and this claim has been a powerful force in the treatment of Jews in Christian society throughout the centuries. Certain modern liberal Christian theologians have however denied the annulment of the election of Israel. An eloquent contemporary Jewish attempt to come to terms with the criticism while maintaining the concept of election is found in Leo Baeck's *This People Israel* which argues, in its concluding paragraphs: "Every people can be chosen for a history, for a share in the history of humanity . . . . But more history has been assigned to this people than other people."[14]

In the modern world criticism of the concept of election derives in the main from universalist and humanist tendencies: Jews are men among men, and Israel is a nation among the others. In the face of such criticism the defense of the traditional concept is ultimately a philosophical and theological task which will have to sort out the meaning of chosenness while eschewing the notion "superior". Modern Jewish thought is still grappling with the problem of redefining the traditional concept, in a way that does justice both to the universalist values of Judaism on the one hand, and to the specific character of Jewish historical and spiritual experience on the other.[15]

Revelation

IN THE BIBLE

Revelation is the act whereby the hidden, unknown God shows Himself to man. The ancient Hebrews expressed this idea in different ways. Infrequently, the passive form, *nif'al,* of the verb *galah* ("to uncover, reveal"), is used to denote the divine revelation.[1] More generally, however, revelation does not consist in the disclosing of a secret or a mystery but in the manifestation of the invisible God, unknowable to man on his own. This view of revelation is expressed in the widespread use of the *nif'al* of the verbs *ra'ah* ("to see") and *yada* ("to know").

The verb *nir'ah* (the *nif'al* of *ra'ah*), "he let himself be seen, showed himself," which also occurs in the vocabulary of revelation, referred originally to a visionary manifestation of God in a holy place. It occurs principally in narrative passages whose aim was to explain the origin of such a place. In fact, holy places are often regarded as sites where theophanies took place and the accounts of such divine appearances belong to the genre of etiological tales. According to Genesis 12:6–7, for instance, Abraham passed through the land to the holy site of Shechem, i.e., to the terebinth of Moreh (cf. Judg. 9:37). There the Lord "showed Himself" to Abraham, and there Abraham built an altar to the Lord. The particular holiness of the altar marking the sacred spot is explained by its origin, namely, the appearance of the Lord to the patriarch. It should be noted, however, that no attempt is made to describe the apparition, and only what words were uttered and what promise was made are recorded. These words are an essential element, for revelation as an event generally needs further explanation and it is only after the Lord has spoken that His manifestation can be understood and acquires importance for human life. These characteristics are common to most divine revelations in the Bible when marked by the use of the *nif'al* form: *nir'ah.*

170

There is, however, the belief, which originated in ancient times, that it is a mortal danger for man to see the Deity (Ex. 33:20). Dreams and the mediation of angels have no mitigating effect, since the dream gives a stronger vision and the *mal'akh YHWH* ("angel of the Lord") is the epiphanic (apparitional) medium of the Lord, even "the Lord Himself in self-manifestation or in other words, a personification of the theophany."[2] It is, therefore, only rarely and to special persons that YHWH makes Himself visible and communicates His purposes and intentions to humankind. He does so to Abraham, Isaac, Jacob, Moses and Solomon. Nevertheless, He may show Himself to the whole of the people at the Tent of Meeting, which is "a kind of permanent image of the revelation on Mount Sinai."[3] What the people see, however, is the *kavod,* the "Presence of the Lord" (Lev. 9:6, 23), or the *ammud heanan,* the "pillar of cloud" (Deut. 31:15). The latter indicates the Lord's Presence, but, at the same time, veils him from sight. Likewise, the *kavod,* whose original conception goes back to early times,[4] signifies a veiled appearance of God, an appearance in a manner in which no precise form can be discerned. It probably alludes to a manifestation by fire, light, and smoke, connected initially with the circumstances in which the cult operated.

Other texts use the verb *noda,* "he made himself known," which avoids the anthropomorphic connotations of the root meaning "to see." The author of the Priestly document of the Pentateuch, however, uses both verbs, but opposes *noda* to *nir'ah* in Exodus 6:3, the latter denoting the Deity's self-identification by name. In all these texts the verb *noda* is frequently connected with the formula: *ani YHWH* ("I am the Lord"). These texts may be compared with similar expressions known from Mesopotamia: "I am Nigirsu," "I am Ishtar of Arbela," "I am the god Nabu," etc. The difference between these oriental self-revelation formulas and the biblical one consists in the fact that the Tetragrammaton (YHWH) is usually followed by the statement that the Lord is the God Who brought Israel out of Egypt, and Who guides them through history. The God of Israel thus reveals Himself as acting in historical events. It may reasonably be inferred, therefore, that, according to the Bible, history is the milieu of God's revelation.

It has been objected that God's acting in history plays no real role in the biblical Wisdom literature. This has, in fact, been a very awkward point for those who assert that revelation in history is central to Hebrew thought. The difficulty, however, seems to have originated in a confusion between revelation as understood by ancient Israelites, and as viewed by modern scholars who are aware of a systematic biblical theology.

In the Pentateuch and the Former and Latter Prophets, God reveals Himself, His plans or His will through words or events. The other books of the Bible are generally thought not to contain revelations of this kind. In relation to modern theology, it must be emphasized that both revelation and wisdom phenomenologically proceed from experiences of life. Wisdom characteristically classifies the elementary experiences of daily life, whereas revelation results from "prophetic" interpretations of exceptional events in the life of the people or even of the "prophet" himself.

IN TALMUDIC AND MIDRASHIC LITERATURE

The manifestation of God in acts or appearances which overawe man *(gillui Shekhinah)* is the theme of many rabbinic passages and discussions. However, the main concern of talmudic thought is not so much with God's revelation of Himself or of His attributes (although this too is an important topic), but rather with God's revelation of His word to man *(devar Adonai)*. Much is said regarding the revelation of God's word to the forefathers Abraham, Isaac, and Jacob, as well as to other biblical characters and especially to the prophets, and a vast number of talmudic sources deal with the revelation of God's word par excellence, the Torah. Favorite topics of the Midrashim are the giving of the Torah *(mattan Torah)*, the importance of the Torah for the world and for the people of Israel, the nature of the Torah, its permanence, and the like.

Much less attention is devoted to the nature of the act of revelation itself. What is said regarding the process in which God's world is revealed to the Jewish people and to the prophets is not nearly so systematic as the treatment of these topics in medieval philosophy and in patristic (church) literature. Talmudic sources assume a hierarchy of different forms of revelation, varying from inspiration by the Holy Spirit *(Ru'ah ha-Kodesh)* which is the lowest form, to prophecy itself. Of prophecy there are different degrees, with that of Moses representing the highest. However, this gradational scheme is meant especially to demarcate the Torah, which represents the prophecy of Moses, from the works of the prophets, and these again from the other books in the Bible which are inspired by the Holy Spirit. It is bound up, therefore, with the sanctity and authority to be assigned to the different holy writings. Similar remarks apply to the talmudic sources regarding the psychological aspects of revelation. Sometimes the divine manifestation takes place in a vision or in a dream or through the mediation of an angel; but Moses speaks to God face to face whenever he wishes. He beholds God as in a translucent mirror, whereas the other prophets see Him as in a dark glass.[5] The stature of Moses as a prophet thus guarantees the sanctity and authority of *Torat Moshe*—the Pentateuch. In all this however, there is no sustained account of the mechanics of revelation.

The Torah is identified with the wisdom which preexists the creation of the world,[6] and is regarded as the instrument with which the world was created.[7] In this way the concept of Torah is broadened to include not only God's commandments, the admonitions to observe the commandments, and stories of the forefathers, but also the admonition of all the other prophets and the ethical maxims of the other books of the Bible. Thus there occurs the notion that all the prophecies of all the prophets were included in the revelation on Sinai.[8]

The idea of the sanctity of the Torah as based on its being the word of God is, therefore, the core of the talmudic teaching regarding revelation, and forms the theme of several passages which are especially important as representing the sources for the doctrines concerning revelation, which came to be formulated in medieval Jewish philosophy.

One such passage is the Mishnah (Sanh. 10 [11]:1) which tells that among the Israelites who have no portion in the world to come are those who deny that the Torah is from Heaven *(Torah min ha-Shamayim)*. An expansion of this theme is afforded by the Sifrei[9] which says that also he who admits that the Torah is the word of God, but maintains that one particular matter was said by Moses of his own accord is to be regarded as "a despiser of the word of God" (Num. 15:31). The *baraita* parallel to this is quoted in the talmudic discussion as an explanation of the Mishnah in Sanhedrin 99a. It differs from the Sifrei only in emphasizing in more detail that even he who maintains that a particular verse, a particular point, a particular *a fortiori* argument, or a specific inference by analogy was pronounced by Moses of his own accord, is to be regarded as a despiser of the word of God.

Hence, the concept of *Torah min ha-Shamayim* is associated primarily with the notion that every syllable of the Bible has the verity and

God and the Jew

authorship of the word of God. The contents of the sacred books are to be regarded throughout as conscientious and homogeneous, with not only no contradiction in them, but also no real differences. This concept of the underlying unity of the Scriptures, and especially of the Pentateuch, is linked to the notion of layers of deeper meanings beneath the words of the Written Torah of which the plain, literal meaning is only the surface. An approach of this sort not only leads to the mystic notion of the oneness of the Torah, which is hinted at in several talmudic passages and comes to be expressed in particularly striking form by the medieval mystics (particularly Nahmanides); it also forms the basis for the explication of the traditional distinction between the Written and the Oral Law, the latter providing the real significance and true interpretation of the words of the written text.

Scholars such as M. Joel, Kaufman Kohler, Boaz Cohen, and A.J. Heschel[10] have argued, on the other hand, that Abbaye's statement (Meg. 31b) that the curses in Deuteronomy were said by Moses "of his own accord" *(mi-pi aẓmo),* and other statements in similar vein, reflect the dissenting view that there are parts of the Torah that are not literally inspired. However, this may be an error based on the ambiguous meaning of the expression "of his own accord."[11]

The concept of the literal inspiration of the Torah is an important premise of the hermeneutics of the Oral Law (*Torah she-be-Al Peh*), which sometimes treats the written text as little more than a series of mnemonic signs. Such an attitude is especially characteristic of the hermeneutics of R. Akiva and his school. Though even R. Ishmael and his school, although they maintained that the Written Torah speaks the "language of men," nonetheless regarded each word as divinely inspired.[12]

The chief revelation of God to Moses and to His people took place at Mount Sinai. It is not explicitly stated either in the Pentateuch or in talmudic literature that this was a case of mass prophecy, and differing views concerning this are expressed in medieval Jewish philosophy. However, the revelation of the Torah to Moses is naturally interpreted as a prophetic phenomenon. That the revelation at Mount Sinai consisted of the giving to Moses of the whole Torah (including the Oral Law), and not merely the Ten Commandments, is stated in many talmudic and midrashic sources. This would seem to imply that the whole of the Torah was revealed to Moses, detail by detail, during his 40 days on Sinai in such a way that when he came down there was nothing left to be revealed.

However, other commandments are said to have been given in the Tabernacle and at Arboth Moab and talmudic sources offer different opinions to reconcile these statements. Differing views are also expressed regarding the actual writing of the Torah. The Mishnah in Avot 1, which is one of the primary talmudic sources associating the Torah with Sinai, seems to be referring particularly to the Oral Law. Some sources, however,[13] mention a scroll which was given at the same time. Other opinions maintain that the Torah was written piecemeal (scroll by scroll) during the 40 years of wanderings in the desert, or that it was written down all at once at the end of those 40 years (Git. 60a). There are also sources which speak of the existence of scrolls before Sinai.[14]

The attribution of the Written Torah to Moses is affirmed by a tannaitic source[15] which relates that Moses wrote his own book, the portion of Balaam and Job, while Joshua wrote the book which bears his name and the last eight verses of the Pentateuch. In the discussion arising out of this passage a dissenting opinion is quoted, which ascribes even the last eight verses of the Torah (describing his own death) to Moses. The authorship referred to in this passage is ostensibly comparable to Joshua's authorship of the book bearing his name. However, such a straightforward conception of literary authorship will be modified by the claim that the Torah is literally inspired and is the revealed word of God to Moses. Nevertheless, that the Torah is written by Moses, is everywhere assumed in talmudic and midrashic literature, and the Torah is frequently described as *Torat Moshe*—the "Torah of Moses."

It has been argued[16] that of the two traditional notions, the heavenly origin of the Torah *(Torah min ha-Shamayim)* and Mosaic authorship, the former is dogmatic in character in talmudic thought, whereas the latter is more in the nature of an accepted truth about literary authorship. The two notions are at any rate disparate in importance.

In receiving the Torah, Moses acted as a scribe writing from dictation, as was the case with Baruch and the prophet Jeremiah (BB 15a). This is the passage that has been dominant in subsequent attempts to describe the nature of the Mosaic revelation in medieval Jewish philosophy. But there are midrashic sources which would seem to support a less mechanical and more instrumentalist conception of revelation. Thus the Midrash (Ex. R. 47–end) relates that the angels, jealous of the role entrusted to Moses in bringing the Torah to mankind, voice suspicions that Moses might write his own ideas into the Torah. God replies that Moses would not do so; but even if he did he could be trusted to represent reliably the divine will. There is, however, no attempt in the Talmud to provide the sort of instrumentalist analogies of revelation which are offered in patristic thought—the inspired writer as a vessel which the Holy Spirit proceeds to fill, etc. On the other hand, revelation, like prophecy, comes to each individual in accordance with his capacities. When the voice went forth at Sinai, God addressed each person with a voice he could endure (Ex. R. 5:9).

The voice from Sinai (*kol mi-Sinai*) is a characteristic talmudic theme. This voice already included all the words of the prophets, and indeed the Rabbis of later ages received what they themselves taught at Sinai.[17] This may be interpreted[18] as a rabbinic attempt to restrict revelation so far as possible to a onetime act in order to emphasize the lack of any need for, and the irrelevance of, new revelations in matters of *halakhah*. On the other hand, there are alternative sources which argue that the voice from Sinai has not yet stopped; so that even though the Holy Spirit has departed from Israel with the cessation of prophecy, and subsequent revelations are confined to a Heaven-inspired echo (*bat kol)*, this heavenly echo still goes forth each day from Sinai to announce that woe will befall all those who slight the Torah (Avot 6:2).

IN MEDIEVAL JEWISH PHILOSOPHY

As compared to the rabbinic literature, understanding the nature and process of prophetic revelation and especially its relation to reason, constitutes one of the major areas of interest in Jewish philosophy. The question of the authority of the Mosaic revelation appears in its purest form in the works of Philo, who wrote before the rise of Christianity and Islam. In later periods, the differing claims of the other two monotheistic religions had to be taken into account: Islam, primarily in the Judeo-Arabic phase of medieval Jewish philosophy, and Christianity, in the Hebrew phase from the 13th through the 16th centuries in Spain, Southern France, and Italy.

The Mosaic revelation is central for Philo. In his view, statements in the Pentateuch on this issue can be divided into three categories: the ones treating of the direct revelation of God Himself by means of a created voice which Moses heard; those which came about as a result of the questions of Moses; and those which are the result of divine inspiration (Mos. 2:188). Moses himself is viewed as a philosopher-king, in accordance with Plato's *Republic*, as well as a legislator, high priest, and prophet. "Moses necessarily obtained prophecy also, in order that through the providence of God he might discover what by reasoning he could not grasp" (*ibid.*, 2:6). The allegorical method of interpreting revelation is the tool by means of which the conflict between the demands of philosophy and the apparent meaning of revelation can be reconciled. The use of allegorical interpretation is mandatory in respect to anthropomorphic expressions about God which must not be taken literally. Following upon his Platonic model, Philo sees the purpose of the revealed law as serving as the constitution of the ideal state, caring for both the spiritual and material welfare of mankind.

In the age of Saadiah Gaon the claim of the Mosaic revelation to authority had to be justified against the Christian and Islamic assertions that it had been abrogated (*Beliefs and Opinions*, 3). According to Saadiah, confirmation of the prophet's mission lies in the miracles performed by him, whilst the confirmation of the truth of revelation for those living after the time of its promulgation lies in tradition which, for Saadiah, is the fourth source of authentic knowledge in addition to sense perception, the first principles of reason, and logical inference.

The commandments themselves fall into two major divisions: the rational and the nonrational or "obediental." Saadiah supposes that even the rational commandments of the Torah needed to have been revealed in order to fix the details of their performance. Furthermore, he is of the opinion that revelation is necessary with regard to the rational commandments in order to assist those who would take a long time in arriving or who would never arrive at the truth by unaided reason. Saadiah also allows for allegorical interpretation of the Torah but it plays a much more restricted role in his thinking than it does in the case of Philo.

It is interesting to note that the chief exponent of the neoplatonic trend in medieval Jewish thought, Solomon ibn Gabirol, does not even consider the problem of the relation of reason to revelation, nor does he quote Scripture in his *Mekor Hayyim*. His neoplatonic predecessor, Isaac Israeli, however, does deal with the problem of the prophet and prophecy in passing. According to Israeli, the prophet and the sage on the highest level, i.e., he who has achieved union with the Divine, are to be identified with each other. But the prophet expresses himself in imaginative language in order to teach and guide the vulgar masses. Israeli argues that one of the functions of the imaginative faculty of the prophet is to express in figurative symbols and sensible images material derived from reason. This view is related to that held by the great Arabic philosopher al-Farabi and will later be repeated by Maimonides in his discussion of prophecy in the *Guide*.

With Judah Halevi, the autonomous character of revelation and its superiority to reason come to the fore. In Judah Halevi's thought, the "divine command" (*al-amr al-ilāhī*), which is the link between God and man, clings to the prophet chosen by God to reveal His will to man. The prophet is superior to the philosopher by the very fact that his knowledge is derived directly from God, whereas the science of the philosopher is subject to doubt and error. Judah Halevi's concept is based on the neoplatonic concept of nature being ordered hierarchically in a great chain of being, that is, an upward progression from ordinary man to philosopher to Israel and the prophets and then the Divine. Contrary to his predecessor, Judah Halevi considers the unique quality of revelation to lie in its nonrational character. The ritual command- ments are the true link between the people of Israel and God because it is precisely these commandments which Israel would not know without revelation. In the first treatise of his *Kuzari*, the claims of Christianity and Islam to have supplanted the Mosaic revelation are dismissed on the grounds that the beliefs of Christianity are inherently improbable and the Muslim claims lack supporting evidence, while at the same time that the divine origin of the Mosaic revelation is conceded by Christians and Muslims as well as Jews.

As opposed to Judah Halevi, Maimonides returns to a more Aristotelian concept of revelation in which he follows in the footsteps of his Islamic predecessors al-Farabi and Avicenna. Essentially Maimonides treats prophecy as a natural phenomenon: "Know that the true reality and quiddity of prophecy consists in it being an overflowing from God . . . through the intermediation of the Active Intellect, toward the rational faculty in the first place and thereafter toward the imaginative faculty" (*Guide*, 2:36). If the rational faculty alone comes into play, the individual is a philosopher, and if only the imaginative faculty is brought into play, the individual belongs to the class of statesmen. Therefore, essentially the prophet is a philosopher statesman in accordance with the Platonic tradition of the "philosopher-king" as found in the *Republic*. Thus Maimonides takes a position similar to that of Philo mentioned above. The position of Moses in this scheme is problematic since, according to Maimonides in both his *Guide* and his *Mishneh Torah*, the imaginative faculty did not play any role in his prophecy and he prophesied whenever necessary. In a famous passage Maimonides states that "the law as a whole aims at two things: the welfare of the soul and the welfare of the body" (*Guide,* 3:27).

For the masses, belief has a political role to play, for they cannot achieve the heights of metaphysical speculation which alone insure true happiness and the immortality of the intellect. For the philosopher, the Law insures his political well-being and allows him the necessary leisure to indulge in the delights of the mind. Therefore, the function of revelation may be defined as essentially political in nature rather than as a means to individual salvation. In order to reconcile any conflicts between philosophy and the apparent meaning of revelation, Maimonides adopts the allegorical method of interpretation.

Maimonides' view of prophecy exercised great influence on the development of Jewish philosophy by way of both support and criticism. Among Maimonides greatest critics, Hasdai Crescas, writing in 14th-century Christian Spain, and pressed by the attacks of the Catholic Church and its inroads on the Jewish community, argued against Maimonides that the happiness of man lies essentially in the love of God and in the service of God through the observance of the commandments of the Torah and not in intellectual perfection. Here revealed religion is given intrinsic value contrary to the view of Maimonides and the Aristotelians.

Crescas' disciple Joseph Albo tries to steer a middle course between the conservative position of Judah Halevi and the more rational position of Maimonides. He begins his *Sefer ha-Ikkarim* by stating that "human reason is not capable of comprehending things as they are in reality . . . There must therefore be something higher than the human intellect by means of which the good can be defined and the truth comprehended in a manner leaving no doubt at all. This can only be done by means of divine guidance . . . " (*Book of Principles*, 5). For Albo, as it was for Crescas, intellectual perfection is not the ultimate goal, but rather "belief in God and His Torah brings man to eternal happiness and causes his soul to cleave to the spiritual substance" (*ibid.*, 1, ch. 21). His definition of prophecy is worded very much like that of Maimonides (*ibid.*, 3:8, p. 71), but emphasis is laid on the intervention of the divine will which interferes with the natural process more drastically than in the case of Maimonides. Besides philosophical objectives, it would seem that Albo's limitation of the rationalistic approach of Maimonides is due to the pressure of Christian polemics.

IN MODERN JEWISH PHILOSOPHY

In modern Jewish philosophy the term "revelation" embraces a wide variety of meanings, ranging from the supernatural communication of divine truth and instruction to the apprehension of God's will and attributes through the exercise of man's spiritual or rational faculties.

In conformity with deistic doctrines concerning "natural religion," Moses Mendelssohn maintained that the "universal religion of reason" contains all the doctrinal elements and moral perceptions needed for salvation. The supernatural revelation received by Israel at Sinai does not impinge upon the domain of the "universal religion of reason," for Judaism is not a revealed religion but revealed legislation, providing specific laws for the regulation of conduct but not concepts.[18]

Idealistic thinkers reformulated the concept of revelation as a gradual process. Divine truth is revealed to man through his intellectual faculties in an educational process of "continuous" or "progressive" revelation. Naḥman Krochmal, whose views were influenced to a large extent by Hegelian categories of thought, considered revelation the process of ever-increasing consciousness of one immanent Divine Spirit. Similarly, Solomon Formstecher and Samuel Hirsch maintained that revelation constitutes the recognition of the Divine Spirit manifesting itself in man, not the communication received from a transcendent sphere. The last vestiges of opposition between reason and revelation are overcome in the neo-Kantian system of Hermann Cohen. God reveals His will by creating man as a rational creature who through his reason is capable of apprehending the laws of logic and ethics. Thus, revelation no longer refers to any historic event nor even any special mode of cognition; it characterizes a trait of man, who through the possession of his rational faculties becomes the bearer of divine revelation.[19]

In radical opposition to all idealistic trends, Solomon Ludwig Steinheim emphasized the inadequacy of speculative reason in the realm of religious truth. Objecting also to Mendelssohn's position, he stressed the primacy of the doctrinal, rather than legislative, elements in the content of revelation, arguing that only through revelation can belief in a freely creating God arise.[20]

Although Steinheim did not regard revelation as a process, but as a particular event in which the word of God is communicated to man, he was not committed to the doctrine of the verbal inspiration of the Scripture. This latter doctrine, however, is the basis of Samson Raphael Hirsch's neo-orthodox system, which stresses the beliefs in the divine origin of both the Oral and the Written Law[21] and its completely heteronomous character.

Existentialists opposed the theories that consider revelation primarily as the transmission of content consisting either of metaphysical principles or moral and ritual laws. Most outspoken among the Jewish existentialist thinkers in his defense of this view of revelation was Martin Buber, who advocated a conception of revelation involving a dialogic relationship between man and God in which no data or objective content passed between them. Revelation is the encounter of the Presence of God, not the communication of ideas or instructions. Revelation constitutes a wordless address, which in turn stimulates a human response.[22] This response, according to Buber, never gives rise to a general objective law, but only to a unique, subjective deed or commitment.

Although Franz Rosenzweig subscribed to the existentialist premise that revelation represents the manifestation of a relationship in the form of a dialogue, he emphasized that it depends upon the will of God, Who chooses to reveal Himself at specific times to different individuals. Through revelation a covenental relationship is established between man and God. As a responsible partner in this dialogue, man is expected to respond to God's demand, embodied in the revelational event, by concrete action. Thus, the commandments arise through man's response to God's revelation.[23]

According to Abraham J. Heschel, who combines neo-orthodox and existentialist concerns, revelation represents an event in which God communicates His teachings and concern for man. The act of revelation is a unique, mysterious event that cannot be reduced to the categories of mystical experience or psychophysical processes. In this act of revelation both God and man are involved and the recipient plays an active role in casting the content of the revelation into the mold of his own personality, but he must not be considered merely an inspired visionary: he is a witness to a specific act of "God's turning towards man."[24]

Alternatively, naturalist thinkers such as Ahad Ha-Am and Mordecai Kaplan do not see in revelation anything more than a purely human social or subjective experience. Opposed to them, Orthodox thinkers are committed to the traditional view of revelation as the disclosing of God's will to man in the form of specific commandments. They view the process of the development of the Oral Law as an extension of the original revelation at Sinai, which continually provides new insights into God's will for man. Yet, revelation as a process is not necessarily limited to the elucidation or development of the content of the Sinaitic revelation; thus, drawing upon kabbalistic categories of thought, Abraham Isaac Kook maintained that revelation is the ever-increasing apprehension of reality in the light of the *Shekhinah* or "Divine Presence," resulting in the perception of the underlying unity of all existence.[25] It would be fair to conclude by noting that the problem of how to interpret and understand revelation is by no means agreed, and presents one of the most pressing challenges to contemporary Jewish thinkers.

Torah

The term *Torah* is derived from the root *yrh* which in the *hifil* conjugation means "to teach." The basic meaning of the term therefore is "teaching," "doctrine" or "instruction." The commonly accepted translation of Torah as "Law" is incorrect and gives a mistaken impression. This erroneous usage derives from the Greek mistranslation of "Torah" as *Nomos* and its later mistranslation as *Lex*, still later to be rendered in English as "Law." The Hebrew term is used in a variety of ways but the underlying idea common to them all is that of "teaching" or "instruction."

In the Pentateuch the word is used generally in two senses. Firstly, it is employed to refer to the body of instruction referring to a specific subject, e.g., "the *torah* of the meal offering" (Lev. 6:7), of the guilt offering (7:1), and of the Nazirite (Num. 6:21). It is used especially as the summation of all the separate *torot* ("teachings").[1] The second usage occurs in verses such as Deuteronomy 4:44—"This is the Torah which Moses set before the Children of Israel"—and the other verses which make reference to "the Torah of Moses."[2] Here the reference is to the Pentateuch as a whole (to the exclusion of the later parts of the Bible).

In later literature the Bible in its entirety was referred to as *Tanakh,* the initial letters of *Torah* (Pentateuch), *Nevi'im* (Prophets), and *Ketuvim* (Hagiographia), a meaning it retained in halakhic literature to differentiate between the laws which are of biblical origin (in its Aramaic form, *de-Oraita* "from the Torah") and those of rabbinic provenance *(de-rabbanan).* The word "Torah" is, however, also used loosely to designate the Bible as a whole.

A further extension of the term came with the distinction made between the Written Torah (Torah *she-bi-khetav*) and the Oral Torah (Torah *she be-al peh*). The use of the plural *Torot* (e.g., Gen. 26:5) was taken to refer to those two branches of divine revelation which were traditionally regarded as having been given to Moses on Mount Sinai. Justification was found in the verse of Exodus 34:27, which can be translated literally as "Write thou these words for by the mouth of these words I have made a covenant." The word "write" *(ketav)* was regarded as the authority for the Written Law (hence Torah *she-bi-khetav*), while "by the mouth" *(al pi)* was taken to refer to the Torah *she-be-al peh* (cf. Git. 60b.). Lastly, the word is also used for the whole corpus of Jewish traditional law from the Bible to the latest development of the *halakhah*.

Broadly speaking there have been three related topics which have been important elements in the historic discussions of the Torah. The first two are the Torah's origin and pre-existence, while the third relates to its eternity and immutability. Each of these topics illuminates the central role the Torah has played in Judaism and the way Jews have come to understand this precious gift.[3]

ORIGIN AND PREEXISTENCE

Avot (1:1) reminds us that "Moses received the Torah from Sinai." Yet there is an ancient tradition found in a variety of sources that the Torah existed in heaven not only before God revealed it to Moses, but even before the world was created. The apocryphal book of The Wisdom of Ben Sira identified the Torah with preexistent personified wisdom[4] while in rabbinic literature it was taught that the Torah was one of the six or seven things created prior to the creation of the world.[5] Of these preexistent things, it was said that only the Torah and the throne of glory were actually created, while the others were only conceived, and that the Torah preceded the throne of glory.

According to Eliezer ben Yose the Galilean, for 974 generations before the creation of the world, the Torah lay in God's bosom and joined the ministering angels in song[6] and Simeon ben Lakish taught that the Torah preceded the world by 2,000 years and was written in black fire upon white fire.[7] Akiva called the Torah, "the precious instrument by which the world was created" (Avot 3:14) and Rav Hoshaiah, explicitly identifying the Torah with the preexistent wisdom of Proverbs, said that God created the world by looking into the Torah as an architect builds a palace by looking into blueprints. He also took the first word of Genesis not in the sense of "In the beginning," but in that of "By means of the beginning," and he taught that "beginning" (probably in the philosophic sense of the Greek *arche*) designates Torah, since it is written of wisdom (= Torah) in Proverbs that "The Lord made me the beginning of His way" (Gen. R. 1:1).

The concept of the preexistence of the Torah is perhaps also implicit in the philosophy of Philo, who spoke of the preexistence and role in creation of the Word of God *(logos),*[8] while identifying the word with the Torah.[9]

In the medieval period Saadiah Gaon rejected the literal belief in preexistent things on the grounds that it contradicts the principle of creation *ex nihilo.* In his view, Proverbs 8:22, the verse cited by Rav Hoshaiah, means no more than that God created the world in a wise manner (*Beliefs and Opinions* 1:3).[10] To a similar end Judah b. Barzilai of Barcelona raised the problem of place in connection with the Torah's preexistence. Where could God have kept a preexistent Torah? While allowing that God could conceivably have provided an ante-mundane place for a corporeal Torah, he preferred the interpretation that the Torah preexisted only as a thought in the divine mind. Ultimately, however, he expressed the opinion that the Torah's preexistence is a rabbinic metaphor, spoken out of love for the Torah and those who study it, and teaching that the Torah is worthy to have been created before the world.[11]

Comparable to Judah b. Barzilai's concern with space, Abraham Ibn Ezra raised the problem of time. He wrote that it is impossible for the Torah to have preceded the world by 2,000 years or even by one moment, since time is an accident of motion, and there was no motion before God created the celestial spheres; rather, he concluded, as had Judah b. Barzilai, that the teaching about the Torah's preexistence must be a metaphoric riddle.[12]

In a very different and highly interesting comment Judah Halevi explained that the Torah precedes the world in terms of teleology; God created the world for the purpose of revealing the Torah; therefore, since as the philosophers say, "the first of thought [Torah] is the end of the work," the Torah is said to have existed before the world (*Kuzari* 3:73).

The problem also interested Maimonides, who discussed the origin of the Torah from the standpoint of the epistemology of the unique prophecy of Moses.[13] The tradition of the preexistence of the Torah was not discussed in the *Guide of the Perplexed,* but the closely related tradition of the preexistence of the throne of glory was (2:26, 30). However, Maimonides' discussions of Moses' prophecy and of the throne of glory are esoteric and controversial, and each reader will interpret them according to his own views, and possibly infer from these discussions, Maimonides' position concerning the origin of the Torah.

Within the framework of his neoplatonic ontology, Isaac ibn Latif in his *Sh'ar ha-Shamayim,* suggested that the Torah precedes the world not in time, but in rank. He cited the aggadic statements that the Torah and the throne of glory preceded the world, and that the Torah preceded the throne of glory; he further intimated that the Torah is the upper world (wisdom or intellect) which ontologically precedes the middle world (the celestial spheres, the throne of glory) which, in turn, ontologically precedes the lower world (our world of changing elements).

While the tradition of the preexistence of the Torah was being ignored or explained away by most philosophers, it became fundamental in the Kabbalah. Like Ibn Latif, the kabbalists of Spain held that the Torah precedes the created world in an ontological sense and some kabbalists identified the primordial Torah with *Hokhmah* (God's wisdom), the second of the ten *Sefirot* in emanation. Others identified the Written Torah with the sixth *Sefirah, Tiferet,* and the Oral Torah with the tenth *Sefirah, Malkhut.* According to the metaphysics of the Zoharic system, the order in which items come into being indicates their creative power; and it was with the Torah that God created the angels and the worlds, and with the Torah He sustains all (Zohar 3:152a).

Hasdai Crescas, who in the course of his revolutionary critique of Aristotelian physics had rejected the dependence of time on motion, was able to take preexistence literally as chronological. He interpreted the proposition about the preexistence of the Torah as a metonymy, referring actually to the purpose of the Torah. Since, according to him, the purpose of the Torah and the purpose of the world are the same, namely, the establishment of the rule of love, and since the purpose or final cause of an object chronologically precedes it, it follows that the purpose of the Torah (i.e., love) chronologically preceded the world. As its final cause, love (= the purpose of the Torah) is a necessary condition of the world; and this is the meaning of the talmudic statement that, were it not for the Torah (i.e., the purpose of the Torah, or love), heaven and earth would not have come into existence.[14]

Joseph Albo also interpreted the preexistence of the Torah in terms of final causality, but his position was essentially that of Judah Halevi, and not that of his teacher, Crescas. He reasoned that man exists for the sake of the Torah; everything in the world of generation and corruption exists for the sake of man; therefore, the Torah preceded the world, in the Aristotelian sense that the final cause in (the mind) of the agent necessarily precedes the other three causes outlined by Aristotles' metaphysics.[15]

In modern Jewish philosophical literature, Nachman Krochmal analyzed the interpretation of the author of *Sha'ar ha-Shamayim* (who was Ibn Latif and not, as Krochmal supposed, Ibn Ezra) regarding the Torah's preexistence, and his analysis bears implications for his own idealistic concept of the metaphysical and epistemological precedence of the spiritual.[16] Alternatively, Franz Rosenzweig, in his existentialist reaction to the intellectualist interpretation of the Torah by German rabbis, appealed to the *aggadah* of the preexistence of the Torah in an attempt to show the absurdity of trying to base the claim of the Torah merely on a juridical or historical reason: "No doubt the Torah, both Written and Oral, was given Moses on Sinai, but was it not created before the creation of the world? Written against a background of shining fire in letters of somber flame? And was not the world created for its sake?"[17]

NATURE AND PURPOSE

In the Bible, the Torah is referred to as the Torah of the Lord and of Moses, and said to be given as an inheritance to the congregation of Jacob. Its purpose is to make Israel "a kingdom of priests and a holy nation" and it is said that "the commandment is a lamp and the Torah is light." The Torah is called "perfect," its ordinances "sweeter than honey and the flow of honeycombs."[18] Psalm 119, containing 176 verses, is a song of love for the Torah whose precepts are said to give peace and understanding.

In the apocryphal book Ecclesiasticus (Wisdom of Ben Sira), the Torah is identified with wisdom. In another apocryphal work, the laws of the Torah are said to be drawn up "with a view to truth and the indication of right reason" (Arist. 161). The Septuagint rendered the Hebrew *torah* by the Greek *nomos* ("law"), probably in the sense of a living network of traditions and customs of a people. As mentioned, the designation of the Torah by *nomos,* and by its Latin successor *lex* (whence, "the law"), has historically given rise to the sad misunderstanding that Torah means legalism.

It was one of the very few real dogmas of rabbinic theology that the Torah is from heaven (Heb. *Torah min hashamayim*),[19] i.e., the Torah in its entirety was revealed by God. According to the *aggadah*, Moses ascended into heaven to capture the Torah from the angels (Shab. 89a, et al.). In one of the oldest mishnaic statements, Simeon the Just taught that (the study of the) Torah is one of the three things by which the world is sustained (Avot 1:2) and Eleazar ben Shammua said: "Were it not for the Torah, heaven and earth would not continue to exist."[20] God Himself was said to study the Torah daily (Av. Zar. 3b, et al.).

The Sages compared the Torah to fire, water, wine, oil, milk, honey, drugs, manna, the tree of life, and many other things; it was considered the source of freedom, goodness, and life and it was identified both with wisdom and with love.[21] In this latter respect Hillel summarized the entire Torah in one sentence: "What is hateful to you, do not to your fellow" (Shab. 31a) while Akiva taught: "The fundamental principle of the Torah is the commandment 'Love thy neighbor as thyself'" (Lev. 19:18). Intending to teach the same principle, Akiva's disciple Simeon ben Azzar said that the Torah's fundamental principle is found in the verse (Gen. 5:1) which teaches that all human beings are descended from the same man, and created by God in His image.[22]

Often the Torah was personified. Not only did God take council with the Torah before He created the world, but according to one interpretation, the plural in "Let us make man" (Gen. 1:26) refers to God and the Torah (Tanh. Pekudei, 3). In another aggadic statement the Torah appears as the daughter of God and the bride of Israel (PR 20; 95a, while on still other occasions, the Torah is obliged to plead the case of Israel before God (e.g., Ex. R. 29:4).

Though given to Israel, the message of the Torah is for all mankind. Before giving the Torah to Israel, God offered it to the other nations, but they refused it; and when He did give the Torah to Israel, He revealed it in the extraterritorial desert and simultaneously in all the 70 languages, so that men of all nations would have a right to it.[23] Alongside this universalism, the Rabbis taught the inseparability of Israel and the Torah. One rabbi held that the concept of Israel existed in God's mind even before He created the Torah (Gen. R. 1:4), though a contrary view did exist that were it not for its accepting the Torah, Israel would not be "chosen," nor would it be different from all the idolatrous nations.[24]

In the Hellenistic literature contemporaneous with the early rabbinic teachings, Philo considered the Torah the ideal law of the philosophers, and Moses the perfect lawgiver and prophet, the paradigm of the philosopher-ruler of Plato's *Republic* (II Mos. 2). His concept of the relationship of the Torah to nature and man was Stoic: "The world is in harmony with the Torah and the Torah with the world, and the man who observes the Torah is constituted thereby a loyal citizen of the world" (Op. 3). He agreed that the laws of the Torah are "stamped with the seals of nature," and are "the most perfect picture of the cosmic polity" (II Mos. 14, 51). Likewise, Josephus, in his *Against Apion,* discoursed on the moral and universalistic nature of the Torah, emphasizing that it promotes piety, friendship, humanity toward the world at large, justice, charity, and endurance under persecution. Both Philo and Josephus held that principles of the Torah, e.g., the Sabbath, have been imitated by all nations.

In the medieval period, Saadiah Gaon expounded a rationalist theory according to which the ethical and religious-intellectual beliefs imparted by the Torah are all attainable by human reason. He held that the Torah is divisible into (1) commandments which, in addition to being revealed, are demanded by reason (e.g., prohibitions of murder, fornication, theft, lying); and (2) commandments whose authority is revelation alone (e.g., Sabbath and dietary laws), but which generally are understandable in terms of some personal or social benefit attained by their performance. Revelation of the Torah was needed because while reason makes general demands, it does not dictate particular laws; and while the matters of religious belief revealed in the Torah are attainable by philosophy, they are only attained by it after some time or, in the case of many, not at all. He taught that the purpose of the Torah is the bestowal of eternal bliss *(Beliefs and Opinions,* introd. 6, ch. 3), and that Israel is a nation only by virtue of the Torah.

In the period between Saadiah and Maimonides, most Jewish writers who speculated on the nature of the Torah continued in the rationalist tradition established by Saadiah. These included Baḥya ibn Paquda, Joseph ibn Ẓaddik, Abraham ibn Ezra, and Abraham ibn Daud. Judah Halevi, however, opposed the rationalist interpretation. He allowed that the Torah contains rational and political laws, but considered them preliminary to the specifically divine laws and teachings which cannot be comprehended by reason, e.g., the laws of the Sabbath which teach the omnipotence of God and the creation of the world *(Kuzari* 2:48, 50). The Torah makes it possible to approach God by awe, love, and joy (2:50). It is the essence of wisdom, and the outcome of the will of God to reveal His kingdom on earth as it is in heaven (3:17). While Judah Halevi held that Israel was created to fulfill the Torah, he argued that there would be no Torah were there no Israel (2:56; 3:73).

Maimonides emphasized that the Torah is the product of the unique prophecy of Moses. He maintained that the Torah has two purposes; first, the welfare of the body and ultimately, the welfare of the soul (intellect). The first purpose, which is a prerequisite of the ultimate purpose, is political, and "consists in the governance of the city and the well-being of the state of all its people according to their capacity." The ultimate purpose consists in the true perfection of man, his acquisition of immortality through intellection of the highest things. The Torah is similar to other laws in its concern for the welfare of the soul *(Guide* 3:27). Maimonides saw the Torah as a rationalizing force, warring against superstition, imagination, appetite, and idolatry. He cited the rabbinic dictum, "Everyone who disbelieves in idolatry professes the Torah in its entirety,"[25] and taught that the foundation of the Torah and the pivot around which it turns consists in the effacement of idolatry. He held that the Torah must be interpreted in the light of reason.

Of the Jewish philosophers who flourished in the 13th and early 14th centuries, most endorsed Maimonides' position that the Torah has as its purpose both political and spiritual welfare. Some, like Samuel ibn Tibbon and Isaac Albalag, argued that its purpose consists only or chiefly in political welfare. Others emphasized its spiritual purpose, like Levi b. Gershom, who taught that the purpose of the Torah is to guide man—the masses as as well as the intellectual elite—toward human perfection, that is, the acquisition of true knowledge and, thereby, an immortal intellect. This practical rationalistic tendency is, however, at considerable variance from the kabbalistic views we shall consider separately below.

The first Jewish philosopher to construct a metaphysics in which the Torah plays an integral role was Ḥasdai Crescas, who, notwithstanding his distinguished work in natural science, was more sympathetic to the Kabbalah than to Aristotle. He taught that the purpose of the Torah is to effect the purpose of the universe. By guiding man toward corporeal happiness, moral and intellectual excellence, and felicity of soul, the

Torah leads him to the love of neighbor and, finally, the eternal love of God (*devekut*), which is the purpose of all creation (*Or Adonai*, 2:6). Like Judah Halevi, he took an ultimately anti-intellectualist position, and maintained, in opposition to the Maimonideans, that the very definition of the Torah as the communication of God to man implies beliefs about the nature of God and His relation to man which cannot, and need not, be proved by philosophy.

Joseph Albo, developing some Maimonidean ideas, taught that the Torah, as divine law, is superior to natural law and conventional-positive law in that it not only promotes political security and good behavior, but also guides man toward eternal spiritual happiness (*Ikkarim*, 1:7).

In the writings of late medieval thinkers, the conflicting approaches to the Torah of Maimonideanism and the Kabbalah converged to give expression to the theme, already adumbrated in Philo, that the Torah exists in the mind of God as the plan and order of the universe.[26] In Italy, Judah b. Jehiel (Messer Leon), influenced by the Renaissance emphasis on the art of rhetoric, composed the *Nofet Ẓufim*, in which he analyzed the language of the Bible and, in effect, presented the first aesthetic interpretation of the Torah.[27]

Influenced by Maimonides, Baruch Spinoza adopted the position taken by some early Maimonideans that the Torah is an exclusively political law. However, he broke radically with those Maimonideans and with all rabbinic tradition by denying its divine nature, by making it an object of historical-critical investigation, and by maintaining that it was not written by Moses alone but by various authors living at different times. Moreover, he considered the Torah primitive, unscientific, and particularistic, and thus subversive to progress, reason, and universal morality. By portraying the Torah as a product of the Jewish people, he reversed the traditional opinion[28] according to which the Jewish people are a product of the Torah.

Like Spinoza, Moses Mendelssohn considered the Torah a political law, but he affirmed its divine nature. Taking a position similar to Saadiah's, he explained that the Torah does not intend to reveal new ideas about deism and morality, but rather, through its laws and institutions, to arouse men to be mindful of the true ideas attainable by all men through reason. By identifying the beliefs of the Torah with the truths of reason, Mendelssohn affirmed both its scientific respectability and its universalistic nature. By defining the Torah as a political law given to Israel by God, he preserved the traditional view that Israel is a product of the Torah and not, as Spinoza claimed, vice versa.

With the rise of the science of Judaism *(Wissenschaft des Judentums)* in the 19th century, and the advance of the historical-critical approach to the Torah, many Jewish intellectuals, including ideologists of Reform like Abraham Geiger, followed Spinoza in seeing the Torah, at least in part, as a product of the primitive history of the Jewish nation.

Adopting this position, Reformers made a distinction between those parts of the Bible which they took to be archaic legislative and ritual taboos and which represented early stages of religious consciousness, and other portions, primarily ethical in character, which were claimed to be the essential elements of the Torah. In this way Judaism and Torah were translated into the ethical concerns of the 19th century and redesigned to meet these interests which, it should be noted, stemmed primarily from Kantian and post-Kantian thought. The classic expression of this Reform perspective is given in the "Pittsburgh Platform" which affirmed that: "We recognize in the Mosaic legislation a system of training the Jewish people for its mission during its national life in Palestine, and today we accept as binding only its moral laws, and maintain only such ceremonies as elevate and sanctify our lives . . . "[29]

In a radically different spirit Nachman Krochmal, in his rationalist-idealist philosophy, attempted to synthesize the historical-critical thesis that the Torah is a product of Jewish history, with the traditional thesis that the entire Torah is divinely revealed. He maintained that, from the days of Abraham and Isaac, the Hebrew nation has contained the Absolute Spiritual, and this Absolute Spiritual was the source of the laws given to Moses on Mt. Sinai, whose purpose is to perfect the individual and the group, and to prevent the nation's extinction. The Oral Torah, which is, in effect, the history of the evolution of the Jewish spirit, is inseparable from the Written Torah, and is its clarification and conceptual refinement; which is to say, the true science of the Torah, which is the vocation of the Jewish spirit, is the conceptualization of the Absolute Spiritual.[30]

The increasing intellectualization of the Torah in the modern period was opposed by Samuel David Luzzatto and Salomon Ludwig Steinheim, two men who had little in common but their fideism. They contended—as Crescas had against the Maimonideans—that the belief that God revealed the Torah is the starting point of Judaism, and that this belief, with its momentous implications concerning the nature of God and His relation to man, cannot be attained by philosophy. Luzzatto held that the foundation of the whole Torah is compassion. Steinheim, profoundly opposing Mendelssohn, held that the Torah comes to reveal truths about God and His work.

While Spinoza and Mendelssohn had emphasized the political nature of the Torah, many rationalists of the late 19th and early 20th centuries emphasized its moral nature. Moritz Lazarus identified the Torah with the moral law, and interpreted the rabbinical statement, "Were it not for the Torah, heaven and earth would not continue to exist" as corresponding to the Kantian teaching that it is the moral law that gives value to existence. Hermann Cohen condemned Spinoza as a willful falsifier and a traitor to the Jewish people for his claim that the Torah is subversive to universalistic morality. He held that the Torah, with its monotheistic ethics, far from being subversive to universalism, prepares a Jew to participate fully and excellently in general culture (in this connection, he opposed Zionism and developed his controversial theory of "Germanism and Judaism"). He maintained that in its promulgation of commandments affecting all realms of human action, the Torah moves toward overcoming the distinction between holy and profane through teaching all men to become holy by always performing holy actions, i.e., by always acting in accordance with the moral law.[31]

In their German translation of the Bible, Martin Buber and Franz Rosenzweig translated *torah* as *Weisung* or *Unterweisung* ("Instruction") and not as *Gesetz* ("Law"). In general, they agreed on the purpose of the Torah: to convert the universe and God from It to Thou. Yet they differed on several points concerning its nature. Buber saw the Torah as the past dialogue between Israel and God, and the present dialogue between the individual reader, the I, and God, the Thou. He concluded that while one must open himself to the entire teaching of the Torah, he need only accept a particular law of the Torah if he feels that it is being spoken now to him. Rosenzweig objected to this personalist and antinomian position of Buber's. Taking an existentialist position, he maintained that the laws of the Torah are commandments to do, and as such become comprehensible only in the experience of doing, and, therefore, a Jew must not, as Buber did, reject a law of the Torah that "does not speak to me," but must always open himself to the new experience which may make it comprehensible. Like Cohen—and also like

The Ḥasidim—he marveled that the law of the Torah is universal in range. He contended that it erases the barrier between this world and the world to come by encompassing, vitalizing, and thereby redeeming everything in this world.[32]

The secular Zionism of the late 19th and early 20th centuries gave religious thinkers new cause to define the relationship between the Torah and the Jewish nation. Some defined the Torah in terms of the nation. Thus, Mordecai Kaplan translated Aḥad Ha-Am's sociological theory of the evolution of Jewish civilization into a religious, though naturalistic, theory of the Torah as the "religious civilization of the Jews."[33] Others, like Buber and Rosenzweig, considering secular nationalism dangerous, tried to "interdefine" the Torah and the nation. Whereas Buber saw the Torah as the product of a dialogue between the nation and God, he held that the spirit of the nation was transfigured by that dialogue. Rosenzweig, whose position here resembles Judah Halevi's, stated both that the nation's chosenness is prior to the Torah, and that the acceptance of the Torah is an experiential precondition of its chosenness. Other thinkers defined the nation in terms of the Torah. Thus, Abraham Isaac Kook, whose thought was influenced by the Kabbalah, taught that the purpose of the Torah is to reveal the living light of the universe, the suprarational spiritual, to Israel and, through Israel, to all mankind. While the Written Torah, which reveals the light in the highest channel of our soul, is the product of God alone, the Oral Torah, which is inseparable from the Written Torah, and which reveals the light in a second channel of our soul, proximate to the life of deeds, derives its personality from the spirit of the nation. The Oral Torah can live in its fullness only when Israel lives in its fullness—in peace and independence in the Land of Israel. Thus, according to Kook, modern Zionism, whatever the intent of its secular ideologists, has universalistic religious significance, for it is acting in service of the Torah.[34]

In the State of Israel, most writers and educators have maintained the secularist position of the early Zionists, namely, that the Torah was not revealed by God, in the traditional sense, but is the product of the national life of ancient Israel. Those who have discussed the Torah and its relation to the state from a religious point of view have mostly followed Kook or Buber and Rosenzweig. However, a radically rationalist approach to the nature of the Torah has been taught by Yeshayahu Leibowitz who, in the Maimonidean tradition, emphasizes that the

Torah is a law for the worship of God and for the consequent obliteration of the worship of men and things; in this connection, he condemns the subordination of the Torah to nationalism or to religious sentimentalism or to any ideology or institution. Outside the State of Israel, a similarly iconoclastic position has been taken by the French phenomenologist Emmanuel Levinas, who has gone further and written that the love for the Torah should take precedence even over the love for God Himself, for only through the Torah—that knowledge of the Other which is the condition of all ethics—can man relate to a personal God against Whom he can rebel and for Whom he can die.

ETERNITY (OR NON-ABROGABILITY)

In the Bible there is no text unanimously understood to affirm explicitly the eternity or non-abrogability of the Torah; however, many laws of the Torah are accompanied by phrases such as, "an everlasting injunction through your generations" (Lev. 3:17, et al.).

The doctrine that the Torah is eternal appears several times in the pre-tannaitic apocryphal literature; e.g., Ben Sira 24:9 ("the memorial of me shall never cease") and Jubilees 33:16 ("an everlasting law for everlasting generations").

Whereas the rabbis understood the preexistence of the Torah in terms of its pre-revelation existence in heaven, they understood the eternity or non-abrogability of the Torah in terms of its post-revelation existence not in heaven; i.e., the whole Torah was given to Moses and no part of it remained in heaven (Deut. 8:6, et al.). When Eliezer ben Hyrcanus and Joshua ben Hananiah were debating a point of Torah and a voice from heaven dramatically announced that Eliezer's position was correct, Joshua refused to recognize its testimony, for the Torah "is not in heaven" (Deut. 30:12), and must be interpreted by men, unaided by the supernatural (BM 59b). It was a principle that "A prophet is henceforth not permitted to innovate a thing.[35] The rabbis taught that the Torah would continue to exist in the world to come,[36] although some of them were of the opinion that innovations would be made in the messianic era.[37]

Philo saw the eternity of the Torah as a metaphysical principle, following from the Torah's accord with nature. He believed that the laws and enactments of the Torah "will remain for all future ages as though immortal, so long as the sun and the moon and the whole heaven and universe exist." The belief in the eternity of the Torah appears also in the later apocryphal works and in Josephus.[38]

With the rise to political power of Christianity and Islam, two religions which sought to convert Jews and which argued that particular injunctions of the Torah had been abrogated, the question of the eternity or "non-abrogatability" of the Torah became urgent.[39]

Saadiah Gaon stated that the children of Israel have a clear tradition from the prophets that the laws of the Torah are not subject to abrogation. Presenting scriptural corroboration for this tradition, he appealed to phrases appended to certain commandments, e.g., "throughout their generations, for a perpetual covenant" (Ex. 31:16). According to one novel argument of his: the Jewish nation is a nation only by virtue of its laws, namely, the Torah; God has stated that the Jewish nation will endure as long as the heaven and earth (Jer. 31:35–36); therefore, the Torah will last as long as heaven and earth. Accordingly, he interpreted the verses "Remember ye the Torah of Moses . . . Behold, I will send you Elijah . . ." (Mal. 3:22–23), as teaching that the Torah will hold valid until the prophet Elijah returns to herald the resurrection (*Beliefs and Opinions,* 3:7).

Maimonides listed the belief in the eternity of the Torah as the ninth of his 13 principles of Judaism, and connected it with the belief that no prophet will surpass Moses, the only man to give people laws through prophecy. He contended that the eternity of the Torah is stated clearly in the Bible, particularly in Deuteronomy 13:1 ("thou shalt not add thereto, nor diminish from it") and Deuteronomy 29:28 ("the things that are revealed unto us and to our children for ever, that we may do all the words of this Torah"). He also cited the rabbinic principle: "a prophet is henceforth not permitted to innovate a thing." In addition, he offered the following explanation of the Torah's eternity, based on its perfection and on the theory of the mean: "The Torah of the Lord is perfect" (Ps. 19:8) in that its statutes are just, i.e., that they are equibalanced between the burdensome and the indulgent; and "when a thing is as perfect as it is possible to be within its species, it is impossible that within that species there should be found another thing that does not fall short of the perfection either because of excess or deficiency." Likewise, he argued that the prophesied eternity of the name of Israel ("For as the new heavens and the new earth, which I will make, shall remain before Me . . . so shall your seed and your name"; Isa. 66:22) entails the eternity of the Torah. He also held that there will be no change in the Torah after the coming of the Messiah.[40]

Ḥasdai Crescas listed the eternity of the Torah as a nonfundamental true belief, i.e., required by Judaism, but not essential to the concept of Torah. Unlike Saadiah and Maimonides he did not try to found this belief directly on a biblical text[41] but solely on the rabbinic dictum: "A prophet is henceforth not permitted to innovate a thing." He elucidated the belief from the speculative aspect, arguing on the premise of the perfection of the Torah, a contention which differed markedly from its Maimonidean precursor. His argument proceeds as follows: The Torah is perfect for it perfectly guides men toward the ultimate human happiness, love. If God were to abrogate the Torah, He would surely replace it, for it is impossible that He would forsake His purpose of maximizing love. Since the Torah is perfect, it could be replaced only by an equal or an inferior; but if inferior, God would not be achieving his purpose of maximizing love; and if equal, He would be acting futilely. Therefore, He will not abrogate the Torah. Against the thesis that replacement of the Torah by an equal but different law would make sense if there was an appreciable change—for better or worse—in the people who received it, he retorted characteristically that the Torah is the excellent guide for all, including both the intellectuals and the backward (*Or Adonai,* 3, pt. 1, 5:1–2).

Joseph Albo criticized Maimonides for listing the belief in the eternity of the Torah as an independent fundamental belief of Judaism. In a long discussion, which in many places constitutes an elaboration of arguments found in Crescas, he contended that non-abrogation is not a fundamental principle of the Torah, and that moreover, no text can be found in the Bible to establish it. Ironically, his ultimate position turned out to be closer to Maimonides' than to Crescas'; for he concluded that the belief in the non-abrogation of the Torah is a branch of the doctrine that no prophet will surpass the excellence of Moses (*Ikkarim,* 3:13–23).

After Albo, the question of the eternity of the Torah became routine in Jewish philosophical literature,[42] but never so in the Kabbalah. In the 13th-century *Sefer ha-Temunah,* a doctrine of cosmic cycles or *shemittot* was expounded according to which creation is renewed every 7,000 years, at which times the letters of the Torah reassemble, and the Torah enters the new cycle bearing different words and meanings. Thus, while eternal in its unrevealed state, the Torah, in its manifestation in creation, is destined to be abrogated. This doctrine became popular in later kabbalistic and ḥasidic literature, and was exploited by the heretic Shabbetai Zevi and his followers, who claimed that a new cycle had begun, and in consequence he was able to teach that, "the abrogation of the Torah is its fulfillment!"

Like his contemporary Shabbetai Zevi, but for much different reasons, Spinoza committed the heresy of advocating the abrogation of the Torah. Subsequently, in the 19th century, Reform ideologists held that the abrogation of parts of the traditional Torah was not a heresy at all but was necessary for the progress of the Jewish religion. Similarly, many intellectuals and nationalists held that it was necessary for the progress of the Jewish nation. Aḥad Ha-Am called for the Torah of the Heart to replace the Torah of Moses and of the rabbis, which having been written down, had, in his opinion, become rigid and ossified in the process of time.

Jewish philosophers of modern times have not concentrated on the question of the eternity or non-abrogability of the Torah. Nevertheless, it is not entirely untenable that the main distinction between Orthodox and non-Orthodox Judaism is that the latter rejects the literal interpretation of the ninth principle of Maimonides' Creed that there will be no change in the Torah. Again, it is the case that modern Jewish thinkers who eschew the labels of orthodox or non-orthodox, are also to be centrally evaluated and understood vis-a-vis their views on the nature of the text of the Torah. Those like Cohen, Rosenzweig and Buber who would "interpret" it in existentialist fashion hold to shades of opinion which could be fairly said to favor the view that the Torah as understood in its traditional sense, can and must be abrogated; while those like Rav Joseph Soloveitchik, Y. Leibowitz and in some ways A.J. Heschel, would argue a contrary position.

TORAH IN KABBALAH

The kabbalistic understanding of Torah is both complex and diverse. On the most general level the kabbalistic attitude is similar to the traditional halakhic one in seeing in the Torah a divinely revealed way of life for the individual Jew and for Israel as a whole. Secondly, in consonance with the general kabbalistic metaphysical schema, the Torah is seen as the means by which the individual Jew and Israel act out their cosmic roles, not only to overcome the inherent problematic element in earthly life but also, and far more importantly, to help overcome the cosmic and transcendental problematic of the mystic exile of the *Shekhinah* and the divisiveness in the upper worlds of which Israel's historic exile is only a symbol. The principal instrument for repairing the primal fault is engagement in the Torah and this activity restores the world in its outward aspects. Each human action has an effect of which man is not always aware. The actions of the man who is conscious of their significance, however, have the greatest effect and help speed the ultimate *tikkun* ("redemption" or "completion"). Because the world became material as a result of the first sin, the great majority of the commandments in the Torah acquired a material meaning, because every instrument must be adjusted to the end it is meant to serve. Yet this does not detract from the inward spiritual dimension that each commandment possesses, whose collective purpose is the restoration and perfection of the true stature of man in all 613 of the limbs of his soul. The same Torah which prescribes a practical way of life for human beings in the light of revelation simultaneously provides an esoteric guide for the mystic in his struggle to commune with God. Evident in such an approach is the conservative character of the Kabbalah as a factor working to defend and deepen Jewish values. Observance of the Torah was sanctified as the way to abolish division in the world, and every man was called upon to play his part in this task in accordance with the rank of his soul and the role that was allotted him. The spiritual light that shines in every commandment connects the individual with the root of his soul and with the supernal lights in general. Thus, a mission was entrusted to the collective body of the souls of Israel which could not easily be carried out and involved many descents and reascents before all obstacles could be overcome, but which in the final analysis had a clear and urgent purpose: the *tikkun* and final redemption of the world.

In addition to these two aspects, the mystics also see the Torah in further cosmic and universal terms and this broader kabbalistic attitude to the Pentateuch, and in a somewhat lesser degree to the Bible as a whole, was a natural corollary of the overall kabbalistic belief in the symbolic character of all earthly phenomena. There was literally nothing, the kabbalists held, which in addition to its exterior aspect did not also possess an interior aspect in which there existed a hidden, inner reality on various levels. The kabbalists applied this view of the "transparency" of all things to the Torah as well, but inasmuch as the latter was the unique product of divine revelation, they also considered it the one object which could be apprehended by man in its absolute state in a world where all other things were relative. Regarded from this point of view in its quality as the direct word of God and thus unparalleled by any other book in the world, the Torah became for the kabbalists the object of an original mystical way of meditation. This is not to say that they sought to deny the concrete, historical events on which it was based, but simply that what interested them most was something quite different, namely, the conducting of a profound inquiry into its absolute nature and character. Only rarely did they discuss the relationship among the three parts of the Bible, the Pentateuch, the Prophets, and the Hagiographa, and for the most part their attention was concentrated almost exclusively on the Torah in its strict sense of the Five Books of Moses.[43]

The classic formulations of this approach appear as early as the 13th century, nor do later and bolder restatements of them, even in the Lurianic school, add anything fundamentally new. A large part of the literature of the Kabbalah consists of commentaries on the Pentateuch, the Five Scrolls, and the Book of Psalms, and the Zohar itself was largely written as a commentary on the Pentateuch, Ruth, and the Song of Songs. Books such as the commentaries on the Pentateuch by Menahem Recanati, Baḥya b. Asher, Menahem Ziyyoni, and Abraham Sabba became classic kabbalistic texts. The only known kabbalistic commentary ever to have been composed on the entire Bible is the 16th-century *Minḥat Yehudah,* written in Morocco by an unknown author, large sections of which have been preserved in various manuscripts. Outside the Pentateuch, the Song of Songs alone was made the subject of a large number of kabbalistic commentaries, beginning with Ezra of Gerona's and continuing down to several written in recent generations.

The main basis of the kabbalistic attitude toward the Torah is the fundamental kabbalistic belief in the correspondence between creation and revelation. The divine emanation can be described both in terms of symbols drawn from the doctrine of *Sefirot* and of the emanated, supernal lights, and of symbols drawn from the sphere of language and composed of letters and names. In the latter case, the process of creation can be symbolized as the word of God, the development of the fundamentals of divine speech, and as such it is not essentially different from the divine processes articulated in the Torah, the inwardness of which reveals the same supreme laws that determine the hierarchy of creation. In essence, the Torah contains in a concentrated form all that was allowed to develop more expansively in the creation itself. Strictly speaking, the Torah does not so much mean anything specific, though it in fact means many different things on many different levels, as it articulates a universe of being. God reveals Himself in it as Himself rather than as a medium of communication in the limited human sense. This limited, human meaning of the Torah is only its most external aspect. The true essence of the Torah, on the other hand, is defined in the Kabbalah according to three basic principles: the Torah is the complete mystical name of God; the Torah is a living organism; and the divine speech is infinitely significant, and no finite human speech can ever exhaust it.

TORAH AS THE MYSTICAL NAME OF GOD

Underlying this principle is an originally magic belief which was transformed into a mystical one. Such a magical belief in the structure of the Torah can already be found in the *Midrash Tehillim* (on Ps. 3): "Had the chapters of the Torah been given in their correct order, anyone who read them would have been enabled to raise the dead and work miracles; therefore, the Torah's [true] order has been hidden and is known [only] to God." Far from having to do with historical narrations and commandments, the Torah thus read is solely concerned with concentrations of the divine power in various combinations of the letters of God's Holy Names. From the magical belief that the Torah was composed of God's Holy Names, it was but a short step to the mystical belief that the entire Torah was in fact nothing else than the Great Name of God Himself. In it God expressed His own being insofar as this being pertained to creation and insofar as it was able to manifest itself through creation. Thus, the divine energy chose to articulate itself in the form of the letters of the Torah as they express themselves in God's Name. On the one hand this Name comprises the divine potency;

on the other hand it comprehends within it the totality of the concealed laws of·creation. Obviously, such an assumption about the Torah did not refer to the physical text written on parchment but rather to the Torah in its pre-existential state in which it served as an instrument of the creation.[44] In this sense, the creation of the Torah itself was simply a recapitulation of the process by which the *Sefirot* and the individual aspects of the Divine Names were emanated from the substance of *Ein-Sof* (God as He is in Himself). Nor is the Torah separate from this substance, for it represents the inner life of God. In its earliest and most hidden existence it is called "the primordial Torah," *Torah Keduman*, which is occasionally identified with the *Sefirah Hokhmah*.

THE TORAH AS A LIVING ORGANISM

The association of the Torah with the Ineffable name suggested to the Kabbalists the analogy that the Torah is a living texture, a live body in the formulation of both Azriel of Gerona and the Zohar. The Torah "is like an entire building; just as one man has many organs with different functions, so among the different chapters of the Torah some seem important in their outward appearance and some unimportant," yet in actual fact all are bound together in a single organic pattern. Just as man's unified nature is divided up among the various organs of his body, so the living cell of God's Name, which is *the* subject of revelation, grows into the earthly Torah that men possess. Down to the last, seemingly insignificant detail of the masoretic text, the Torah has been passed on with the understanding that it is a living structure from which not even one letter can be excised without seriously harming the entire body. The Torah is like a human body that has a head, torso, heart, mouth, and so forth, or else it can be compared to the Tree of Life, which has a root, trunk, branches, leaves, bark, and pith, though none is distinct from another in essence and all form a single great unity.

INFINITE SIGNIFICANCE OF THE DIVINE SPEECH

A direct consequence of this belief in the different manifestations of Torah was the principle that the content of the Torah possessed infinite meaning, which revealed itself differently at different levels and according to the capacity of its contemplator. The unfathomable profundity of the divine speech could not possibly be exhausted at any one level alone, an axiom that applied as well to the concrete, historical Torah revealed by God in the theophany at Mount Sinai. From the outset this Torah possessed the two aspects mentioned above, a literal reading formed by its letters that combined to make words of the Hebrew language, and a mystical reading composed of the divine Names of God. But this was not all. "Many lights shine forth from each word and each letter," a view that was summed up in the well-known statement that "the Torah has 70 faces." The conventional four categories by which the Torah was said to be interpretable, the literal (*peshat*), the allegorical (*remez*), the hermeneutical or homiletical (*derash*), and the mystical (*sod*), served only as a general framework for a multiplicity of individual readings, a thesis which from the 16th century on was expressed in the widespread belief that the number of possible readings of the Torah was equal to the number of the 600,000 children of Israel who were present at Mount Sinai—in other words, that each single Jew approached the Torah by a path that he alone could follow. These four categories were first collectively given the acronym *pardes* (literally, "garden") by Moses de Leon. Basically, this "garden of the Torah" was understood as follows. The *peshat* or literal meaning did not embrace only the historical and factual content of the Torah but also the authoritative Oral Law of rabbinic tradition. The *derash* or hermeneutical meaning was the path of ethical and aggadic commentary. The *remez* or allegorical meaning comprised the body of philosophical truths that the Torah contained. The *sod* or mystical meaning was the totality of possible kabbalistic commentaries which interpreted the words of the Torah as references to events in the world of the *Sefirot* or to the relationship to this world of the biblical heroes. The *peshat*, therefore, which was taken to include the corpus of talmudic law as well, was only the Torah's outermost aspect, the "husk" that first met the eye of the reader. The other layers revealed themselves only to that more penetrating and latitudinous power of insight which was able to discover in the Torah general truths that were in no way dependent on their immediate literal context. Only on the level of *sod* did the Torah become a body of mystical symbols which unveiled the hidden life-processes of the Godhead and their connections with human life. Explication on the level of *sod*, of course, had limitless possibilities, a classic illustration of which is Nathan Spira's *Megalleh Amukkot* (1637), in which Moses' prayer to God in Deuteronomy 3:23ff. is explained in 252 different ways. In the main corpus of the Zohar, where use of the term "Kabbalah" is studiously avoided, such mystical interpretations are referred to as "mysteries of the faith" (*raza de-meheimnuta*), that is, exegesis based on esoteric beliefs. The author of the Zohar, whose belief in the primacy of kabbalistic interpretation was extreme, actually expressed the opinion (3:152a) that had the Torah simply been intended as a series of literal narratives, he and his contemporaries would have been able to compose a better book! Occasionally kabbalistic interpretations would deliberately choose to stress certain words or verses that seemed insignificant on the surface and to attribute to them profound symbolic importance, as can be seen in the Zohar's commentary on the list of the kings of Edom in Genesis 36 or on the deeds of Benaiah the son of Jehoiada related in II Samuel 23.

Since the Torah was considered to be essentially composed of letters that were nothing less than configurations of the divine light, and since it was agreed that it assumed different forms in the celestial and terrestial worlds, the question arose of how it would appear in paradise or in a future age. Certainly its present reading had been affected by the corporealization of its letters that took place at the time of Adam's sin. The answer given to this conundrum by the kabbalists of Safed was that the Torah contained the same letters prior to Adam's sin but that in a different sequence that corresponded to the condition of the worlds at that time. Thus, it did not include the same prohibitions or laws that we read in it now, for it was adjusted in its entirety to Adam's state before his fall. Similarly, in future ages the Torah will cast off its garments and will again appear in a purely spiritual form whose letters will assume new spiritual meanings. In its primordial existence, the Torah already contained all the combinational possibilities that might manifest themselves in it in accordance with men's deeds and the needs of the world. Had it not been for Adam's sin, its letters would have combined to form a completely different narrative. In messianic times to come, therefore, God will reveal new combinations of letters that will yield an entirely new content. Indeed, this is the "new Torah" alluded to in the Midrash in its commentary on Isaiah 51:4, "For Torah shall go forth from Me." Such beliefs continued to be widespread in later mystical and hasidic literature.

Mitzvot

Inseparably connected to Torah is the Jewish understanding of the holy deed, the *mitzvah*. The term has several related senses: "commandment," "precept," "religious obligation," but most generally it has come to mean a "good deed." The term is derived from the Hebrew root *ẓvh* which means "to command" or "to ordain."

IN RABBINIC THOUGHT

Already in the Talmud, this word was used for a meritorious act as distinct from a positive commandment. The rabbis for instance declared "a *mitzvah* to hearken to the words of the sages."[1] Moreover, although many different terms such as *ḥukkah* ("statute"), *mishpat* ("ordinance"), *edut* ("testimony"), *mishmeret* ("observance"), and *torah* ("teaching"),[2] are mentioned in the Pentateuch to indicate laws, only the word *mitzvah* is generally used to include all its commandments.

There are traditionally said to be 613 biblical commandments which are divided into 248 positive mandates and 365 prohibitions. The number 613 (usually known by the Hebrew mnemonic TaRYaG (ת= 400, ר= 200, י= 10, ג= 3), is found as early as tannaitic times in sayings of Simeon b. Eleazer, Simeon b. Azzai, and Eleazer b. Yose the Galilean and is apparently based upon an ancient tradition which crystallized in the school of R. Akiva.[3]

With the increased ritual obligations imposed by the rabbis, the *mitzvot* were also separated into two main categories: *mitzvot de-oraita*, the biblical commandments, and *mitzvot de-rabbanan*, the rabbinic commandments. There are also instances when the *mitzvot* were classified as *mitzvot kallot*, less important precepts, and *mitzvot ḥamurot*, more important *mitzvot*.[4] Nevertheless, the rabbis exhorted the people to be mindful of all the *mitzvot*, both light and grave, since the reward for the

205

fulfillment of each is not known to man (Avot 2:1). The *mitzvot* were further divided in the medieval period into *mitzvot sikhliyyot* (rational commandments) and *mitzvot shimiyyot* (revealed commandments). This is an important distinction which will be discussed fully below. Other distinctions have also been made, such as: commandments performed with the external limbs of the body, and those by the heart; commandments regulating conduct between the individual and his Maker and between man and his fellows; and commandments applicable only to Erez Israel and those not dependent upon Erez Israel.

Responsibility for the *mitzvot* is formally assumed by boys at the age of 13 plus one day, and by girls at 12 plus one day (i.e., *Bat mitzvah*, though traditionally no public ceremony marked a girl's religious maturity as was the case in a boy's *Bar Mitzvah*). Women are generally exempt from all affirmative precepts contingent upon a particular time or season, although the Talmud specifically makes those of the Sabbath, Hanukkah, Purim, and Passover obligatory on them. Alternatively, all negative precepts, whether limited to a certain time or not, are binding upon both men and women (Kid. 1:7). It should also be noted that the performance of most *mitzvot* is preceded by a benediction which is usually worded "Who has sanctified us by His commandments and commanded us to . . ." The omission of the benediction, however, does not invalidate the performance of the *mitzvah*.

One of the most significant elements in the discussion of the *mitzvot* is, quite naturally, the attempt to explain and justify them to Jews and non-Jews alike. In addition to valuing them as God's revealed will, and thereby requiring human obedience, one seeks to understand them as more than arbitrary dictates of God, possessing some inherent merit and intrinsic value. This search for "reasons" for the *mitzvot* has had a long and continuous history from biblical days to our own. Thus we find that the Pentateuch itself offers reasons for some commandments and emphasizes the "wisdom" of the Law.[5] In addition it also differentiates between *mishpatim* ("ordinances") and *ḥukkim* ("statutes") without, however, offering any clear principle of division.

Classical rabbinic literature contains a more formal discussion of the problem. The *mishpatim* are said to represent laws that would have been valid even without having been "written" in the Torah, such as the prohibitions against robbery, idolatry, incest, and murder, while the *ḥukkim,* such as the prohibition of swine's flesh and the wearing of garments made of both wool and flax, are "decrees" of God. It is to the latter class that "the evil inclination" and the gentiles object and which are the unique distinction of Israel.[6] This instructional and rather ambiguous approach gave way however from the second century onward, in response to Christian attacks on "the Law." The attacks provoked many Jewish replies stressing the importance of the *mitzvot*. For example, the Rabbis argued that: the commandments were given for the sole purpose of purifying man; they strengthen man's holiness; they enable Israel to acquire merit.[7] Furthermore, R. Simeon b. Yohai is known to have favored the exposition of the reasons of Scripture (*doresh ta'amei dikera*), but he did not go beyond offering exegetical observations. On the other hand there were Rabbis who held that the *ta'amei ha-mitzvot* ("reasons for the commandments") are not revealed and should not be revealed,[8] and that the yoke of the commandments "is to be cherished without probing its reasons." This difference of opinion points up the fact that in the final event no detailed rationalization of the commandments is to be found in the rabbinic sources which is definitive.

It is significant to note that the need for a rational explanation of the Mosaic law was expressed, for the first time, in Hellenistic literature; it was motivated by a desire to present the Jewish religion to the pagan world as a legislation designed to produce a people of the highest virtue. The *Letter of Aristeas* describes the dietary laws and other commandments, e.g., those concerning sacrifices, wearing of *ziẓit*, the *mezuzah*, and *tefillin*, as divinely ordained means for awakening holy thoughts and forming character, while in Maccabees (5:23–24) divine law is identified with reason and held to be the chief aid to a virtuous life.

Developing this earlier Hellenistic tendency, Jewish Hellenism's greatest representative, Philo, offered the first systematic exposition of the reasons for the commandments. He presented the law of Moses as the ideal law envisaged by the philosophers, that is, the law that leads men to live according to virtue.[9] According to Philo, the laws of Moses are divided into positive and negative laws and into those relating to man and those relating to God, and they are all subsumed under the Ten Commandments. Aside from these classifications, the laws of Moses also fall into the following four categories: (1) beliefs; (2) virtuous emotions; (3) actions symbolizing beliefs; and (4) actions symbolizing virtues. However, under the influence of Judaism this fourfold classification of philosophic virtues is expanded to include such

religious virtues as faith, piety, prayer, and repentance. Unlike the
natural law, the Mosaic law is revealed by God; nevertheless, it is in accord with human nature and every law in it has a rational purpose.[10] In
the explanation of some laws, particularly those involving the sacrifices
and festivals, Philo used the allegorical method to overcome any difficulties that might seem present in the literal meaning of the text.
Elsewhere he tried to present the Mosaic legislation as a form of government that combines the best features of the three types of rule described
as good by Plato and Aristotle, namely, monarchy, aristocracy, and
democracy (38ff.).

MEDIEVAL PHILOSOPHY

The medieval discussion of the *mitzvot* begins with Saadiah Gaon, who
was the first Jewish thinker to divide the commandments into those
obligatory because they are required by reason (*sikhliyyot*) and those
given through revelation (*shimiyyot*). In making this distinction he followed the parallel teachings of the Mu'tazilite Kalam, but also added a
Platonic account. According to the Mu'tazilite exposition, the rational
laws are divided into three kinds: gratitude, reverence, and social conduct; and from these three categories he derived many special laws. In
his Platonic exposition he showed the rational character of certain laws
by pointing out the damaging effects of the acts prohibited: theft and
robbery, for example, undermine the economic basis of society, and un-
truthfulness destroys the harmony of the soul. Discussing the
revelational laws, Saadiah holds that while they are primarily an expression of God's will, they have some rational aspects or "usefulness,"
although he repeatedly reminds himself that God's wisdom is superior
to man's. Accordingly he argues, for example, that the holy seasons
enable man to pursue spiritual matters and human fellowship; the
priesthood guides and helps people in time of stress; and dietary laws
combat animal worship.[11]

The next important medieval contributor to the discussion was Baḥya
ibn Pakuda. Baḥya combined Saadiah's division of the commandments
with another classification, also derived from Mu'tazilite sources, that
of "duties of the members (of the body)" (*ḥovot ha-evarim*) and "duties
of the hearts" (*ḥovot ha-levavot*). The "duties of the members" are of
two kinds: duties obligatory by virtue of reason, and duties neither en-

joined nor rejected by reason, e.g., the prohibition of eating milk and meat together. The "duties of the hearts," on the other hand, are of an intellectual and attitudinal kind, such as belief in God, trust in Him, and fear and love of Him.[12] Of the two types of "duties" Bahya emphasized the "duties of the hearts" (3:3). In conjunction with this he asserted that it is only on account of the weakness of the intellect that the revelational commandments are necessary. Unlike Saadiah, however, he does not try to explain the revelational laws in terms of usefulness for specific ends; they are seen simply as expressions of piety and, thereby, effective aids to the attainment of the perfect life of attachment to God which is man's ultimate goal.

As a next stage, drawing upon and developing earlier analysis, Judah Halevi classified the commandments under three headings: (1) rational laws (*sikhliyyot*), also termed psychic laws (*nafshiyyot*), such as those having to do with belief in God, justice, and gratitude; (2) governmental laws (*minhagiyyot*), which are concerned with the functioning and well-being of society and (3) revelational laws (*shimiyyot*), or divine laws (*elohiyyot*), whose main function is to elevate a Jew to communion with God and whose highest manifestation is prophecy.[13]

In accordance with his general opposition to philosophy and his supra-rational approach to Judaism, Judah Halevi argued that God alone is capable of determining the revelational laws, which in themselves are neither demanded nor rejected by reason, and therefore the revelational laws are supreme and the rational and governmental laws are only a "preamble."[14]

Judah Halevi's contemporary Abraham Ibn Ezra dealt with the subject of the *mitzvot* in his commentaries on the Torah and in his small treatise *Yesod Mora*. He distinguished between laws which are implanted in the human heart prior to revelation (*pikkudim*), and laws which prescribe symbolic acts reminding us of such matters as creation, e.g., observance of the Sabbath, and the exodus from Egypt, e.g., the observance of Passover.[15] In addition he speaks of "obscure commandments" (*mitzvot ne'elamot*), which have no clear-cut reason. Certain of these commandments he tried to explain as prohibitions of acts contrary to nature, e.g., seething a kid in its mother's milk, and others, as serving utilitarian purposes, e.g., the separation of the leper as a sanitary measure (Lev. 13:45–46) and the dietary laws in order to prevent injurious influences to body and soul.[16]

As compared to Saadiah, Baḥya, Judah Halevi, Abraham Ibn Ezra, and his other predecessors, Abraham Ibn Daud, who initiated the Aristotelian trend in medieval Jewish philosophy, abandoned the Kalam terms "rational" and "revelational" and replaced them with "generally known"[17] and "traditional." This change of terminology reflects the Aristotelian view that good and evil are not a matter of demonstrative knowledge but of practical opinion. Having adopted this view, Ibn Daud then equated the majority of commandments of the Torah with the "generally known" truths held by all men. He also assumed that these "generally known" laws, i.e., the laws of social conduct, are identical in all religions. Consequently, the formation of states composed of different religious communities is possible, no matter how contrary their religions may be. As opposed to this, and given their source in less precise and non-demonstrative "practical opinion," the "traditional" commandments vary from religion to religion, and though less important than the "generally known" (primarily ethical) commandments, this set of ordinances has the value of allowing man to show his allegiance and unswerving obedience to God.[18]

The classic presentation of the Aristotelian position is to be found in Maimonides, who like Ibn Daud, discarded as illegitimate the distinction between "rational" and "revelational" laws. In his view, all laws set forth in the Torah have a "cause" (*illah*), that is, a "useful purpose" (*takhlit mo'ilah*), and follow from God's wisdom, not from an arbitrary act of His will. In some cases, such as the prohibitions against killing and stealing, their utility is clear, while in others, such as the prohibition against sowing with diverse seeds, it is not. Maimonides identified the former commandments with the biblical laws known as *mishpatim* ("ordinances") and the latter, with those known as *ḥukkim* ("statutes"). Although general laws, e.g., the institution of sacrifices, have a reason, particular laws, e.g., the number of animals for a particular sacrifice, do not. According to Maimonides there are two overall purposes of the Torah: the welfare of the soul, in which man finds his ultimate perfection in this world and the next, and welfare of the body, which is a means to the welfare of the soul. For the welfare of the soul the law promotes correct opinions, and for the welfare of the body it sets down norms for the guidance of society and the individual. To promote correct opinions, the law fosters two kinds of beliefs: absolutely true beliefs, such as the existence and unity of God, and beliefs necessary for the well-being of the state, such as God's anger in punishing evildoers.[19]

Introducing a new method of interpretation of Jewish law, Maimonides regarded many *ḥukkim* of the Torah as directed toward the abolition of the idolatrous practices of the ancient pagans, as described in a tenth-century book by Ibn Wahshiyya, known as the *Nabatean Agriculture*. He even maintained that it is the first intention of the law to put an end to idolatry *(Guide, 3:29)*. Another method that Maimonides used to explain certain laws is described by the term "gracious ruse" *(ormah)*, which is borrowed from the Greek philosopher Alexander of Aphrodisia.[20] Thus, for example, God graciously tolerated the customary mode of worship through animal sacrifice, but transformed it from idols to His own name and through this "ruse" effaced idolatry (3:22). However, to obtain a complete picture of Maimonides' view it should also be noted that in marked contrast to the utilitarian treatments of the commandments in his *Guide of the Perplexed* is the deeply religious approach of his *Mishneh Torah*. The *ḥukkim*, including the sacrifices, appear in the latter work as important vehicles of the spiritual life.[21]

Following Maimonides, the next great Jewish Aristotelian, Levi b. Gershom, also set forth explanations of the commandments in terms of their utility. In his commentary on the Torah he largely follows Maimonides' *Guide* in this respect, though in some respects he goes even further.

In reaction against the views of Maimonides and the widespread rationalism of his day, Ḥasdai Crescas offers an approach of an entirely different nature. Crescas rejected the notion, implicit in the views of his predecessors, e.g., Maimonides, that the Torah had to adapt itself to the low level of religion prevalent at the time of its revelation, an assumption which tended to render part of the commandments obsolete. He was also the first to introduce theological instead of moral or metaphysical concepts for the interpretation of the commandments. In this context it is important to recall that Crescas was concerned with refuting Christian theological notions and the charge of the apostate Abner of Burgos that Judaism had succumbed to philosophy. In his polemic with Christianity, Crescas accepted the notion of original sin but argued that all *mitzvot* are means of redemption from the "poison" injected into Eve by the serpent. Unlike the Aristotelians who saw intellectual perfection as the final goal of the Torah, Crescas maintained that its ultimate purpose is to instill the love of God in man.[22]

Crescas' pupil Joseph Albo continued his master's polemics against

Christian attacks on the Mosaic law, arguing that it is more perfect than any other law and that the Gospels are really no law at all. Distinguishing three kinds of laws, Albo held that natural law (*ha-dat ha-tivit*) contains those rules that are indispensable for the merest association of men; that conventional law (*ha-dat ha-nimusit*) promotes virtues according to human opinion, or the "generally known" (*ha-mefursam*); and that divine law, the Torah (*ha-dat ha-Elohit*) guides man to true happiness, which is the bliss of the soul and eternal life.[23]

A similar treatment is found in the work of Albo's predecessor, Simon b. Zemah Duran, *Keshet u-Magen* (12b). On the other hand, Shem Tov ibn Shem Tov, in his work *Kevod Elohim* (1556), completely discarded the philosophical approach. He considered it wrong even to investigate reasons for the commandments, since the divine in principle cannot be explained by natural reasons (21b ff.). Only in a secondary sense can the commandments be called "rational"; primarily they are "decreed" based on the will of God, who must be presumed to have a purpose, but whose purpose we cannot know. This attitude became increasingly popular in the last phase of medieval Jewish philosophy and persisted until the dawn of the modern age.

IN THE KABBALAH

In Kabbalah the reasons for the commandments are integrated in the general system in relation to two basic principles: a symbolic view according to which everything in this world and all human acts, especially religious acts, are a reflection of divine processes and particularly those of the divine emanation; and the notion of reciprocal influence between the upper and lower worlds, which are not separated from each other but affect each other in all matters. Thus is appears that the commandments both reflect a mystical reality and the relations between heavenly forces, and also themselves influence this heavenly reality. On the other hand, a person who fulfills a commandment integrates himself into the divine system and into the harmony of the divine processes and thus confirms the order of the true universe as it should be. On the other hand, the actual performance of a commandment radiates backwards, strengthening the supernal system. Therefore there is a natural connection between the symbolic and the magical significance of every act; i.e., a direct connection between all planes of existence and the action of each plane on the others. While the symbolic evaluation gave rise to no particular doubts or vacillations and was also in tune with other religious and philosophical views in Judaism, the magical perception of reciprocal influence was bound to create problems. A major difficulty was how to define that divine world upon which the fulfilling of commandments acts. Because the kabbalists saw that world as the world of divine emanation (*Azilut*) which is divine, unique, and united by the ten *Sefirot* and by the other manifestations of the divine creative power, the question arose as to how anyone could presume to speak of the influence of human action on the divine world itself. The kabbalists found themselves in a dilemma on this issue: they believed in the existence of such a magical-theosophical link between God and man—a link which is the soul of religious activity—yet they shrank from an explicit and unequivocal formulation of this relationship, justifying it by weak explanations designed to soften the magical interpretation and make it seem as if it were only allegorical.

At first only a few commandments were kabbalistically interpreted in terms of the activity of certain *sefirot*. Thus the *Sefer ha-Bahir* interprets the commandments involving acts *(mitzvot ma'asiyyot)* such as *tefillin, zizit,* the *lulav* of Sukkot and *terumah* ("the offering") as indications of the last *Sefirah* and its relations with the other *Sefirot,* especially of *Binah* and *Tiferet* (here called *Emet*) and the *Yesod.* The early kabbalists in Spain also interpreted according to these principles only those commandments that have no rational explanations (*hukkim,* or, according to theological terminology, *mitzvot shimiyyot*), e.g., sacrifices and worship in the Temple in general, and the major prayers. Moral and rational commandments were not yet included. Ezra b. Solomon of Gerona, in his commentary on the Song of Songs, was the first to explain the reasons for these commandments in a kabbalistic framework. He was succeeded by his colleagues, Jacob b. Sheshet Gerondi and Nahmanides. From the late 13th century on, the reasons for the commandments became more widely discussed in the Kabbalah. Even those commandments whose principles seem manifest to reason, such as love of God, fear of God, and *yihud* ("the unity of God"), were interpreted in terms of man's relation to the world of the divine *Sefirot.* The reasons behind the commandments on the Sabbath, festivals, sacrifices, prayers and many others are discussed in the main part of the Zohar, according to the general rule that spiritual awakening on earth causes a divine awakening. The author of the Zohar saw in many commandments the act which symbolizes the union of the *Sefirah* of *Malkhut* with the *Sefirah* of *Yesod* or *Tiferet*. The details of the commandments were explained as reflecting the processes of the supernal emanation, and a man who fulfills the commandment integrates within the process of *shefa* ("emanation"), strengthening the divine life which pulsates in every creature.

Fulfilling the commandments also strengthens divine harmony in the universe; the *yihud* (unity) is not merely a declaration of faith in the One God but also an increase in the oneness of the living God through man's acts in the world and man's intention *(kavvanah)* during the performance of such activity. The disunited world becomes reunited by the performance of commandments.[24] Moses de Leon's *Sefer ha-Rimmon* (written in 1287), which deals solely with the reasons for the commandments, included interpretations for over 100 positive and negative commandments. In the same era two anonymous kabbalists also composed comprehensive and detailed works (one of which was improperly attributed to Isaac ibn Farhi of Salonika 250 years later), on the reasons behind the commandments; these have survived in manuscript. Around 1300 the *Ra'aya Meheimna,* a later layer of the Zohar which was highly influential, offered a lengthy exposition according to which all 613 commandments may be interpreted mystically. Two classic works on this subject were written in the 14th century: Menahem Recanati's *Ta'amei ha-Mitzvot,*[25] and *Sefer Kanah* by an anonymous Spanish kabbalist who interpreted most of the commandments in detail and argued radically that the only correct interpretation of the statutes of the Oral Law, and not only those of the Torah (Written Law), is through Kabbalah. In Safed in 1556 David b. Solomon ibn Abi Zimra wrote *Mezudat David,* summarizing previous literature.

With the development of Lurianic Kabbalah the commandments were interpreted according to its special theses: i.e., the doctrine of *tik-kun* ("restitution") and the divine *parzufim* ("countenances"). Many comprehensive works were devoted to this subject, beginning with Hayyim Vital's *Sha'ar ha-Mitzvot.* Noteworthy also are *Mekor Hayyim, Tur Bareket,* and *Tur Piteda* on the reasons for the laws in the *Shulhan Arukh* by Hayyim ha-Kohen of Aleppo, Vital's disciple; *Ez Hayyim* by Judah ibn Hanin of Morocco (late 17th century); *Devar ha-Melekh* by Abraham b. Israel of Brody; and *Yalkut Yizhak* by Isaac Zaler, an important anthology on the reasons for the commandments.

ḤASIDISM

In Ḥasidism the understanding of *mitzvot* took a new form. A ḥasidic tale relates that the Ba'al Shem Tov was unable to enter a certain synagogue because it was full of lifeless prayers, which, lacking the wings of love and fear, were unable to ascend to God. As observant Jews the *Ḥasidim* did not seek to deny the value of the *mitzvot* but they taught repeatedly that the *mitzvot* could only be elevated when carried out in a spirit of devotion. R. Ḥayyim of Czernowitz writes: "There is a man whose love for his God is so strong and faithful that he carries out each *mitzvah* with superlative excellence, strength and marvelous power, waiting in longing to perform the *mitzvah,* his soul expiring in yearning. For, in accordance with his spiritual rank, his heart and soul know the gracious value of the *mitzvot* and the splendor of their tremendous glory and beauty, infinitely higher than all values. And how much more so the dread and fear, the terror and trembling, which fall on such a man when he performs a *mitzvah,* knowing as he does with certainty that he stands before the name of the Holy One, blessed be He, the great and terrible King, before Whom 'all the inhabitants of the earth are reputed as nothing; and He doeth according to His will in the host of heaven' [Dan. 4:32], who stands over him always, seeing his deeds, for His glory fills the earth. Such a man is always in a state of shame and lowliness so intense that the world cannot contain it, especially when he carries out the *mitzvot.* Such a man's *mitzvot* are those which fly ever upward in joy and satisfaction to draw down from there every kind of blessing and flow of grace to all worlds."

This idea was applied to all man's deeds, not only to his religious obligations. In all things there are "holy sparks" *(niẓoẓot)* waiting to be redeemed and rescued for sanctity through man using his appetites to serve God. The very taste of food is a pale reflection of the spiritual force which brings the food into being. Man should be led on by it to contemplate the divine vitality in the food and so to God Himself. In the words of the highly charged mythology of the Lurianic Kabbalah, the "holy sparks" released by man provide the *Shekhinah* with her "Female Waters" which, in turn, cause the flow of the "Male Waters" and so assist "the unification of the Holy One, blessed be He, and His *Shekhinah*" to produce cosmic harmony. Because of the importance of man's role for the sacred marriage and its importance in the ḥasidic scheme, the *Ḥasidim* adopted from the kabbalists the formula: "For the sake of the unification of the Holy One, blessed be He, and His

Shekhinah" *(le-shem yiḥud)* before the performance of every good deed.[21]

IN MODERN AND CONTEMPORARY JEWISH THOUGHT

Modern Jewish thought, marked by a deep crisis of traditional beliefs and halakhic authority, dealt with the subject of reasons for divine commandments on various levels.

The first major modern Jewish philosopher, Moses Mendelssohn, distinguished three layers within the body of Jewish teachings: (1) religion par excellence, consisting of eternal truths that all enlightened men hold in common; (2) historical truths, concerning the origin of the Jewish nation, which faith accepts on authority; and (3) laws, precepts, commandments, and rules of life revealed by God through words and Scripture as well as oral tradition.[28] Revealed legislation prescribed only actions, not faith nor the acceptance of eternal truths. The actions prescribed by the revealed law are the "ceremonies," and the specific element of Judaism, therefore, is the ceremonial laws.

In opposition to Spinoza, who considered the Mosaic legislation a state law designed only to promote the temporal happiness of the Jewish nation, Mendelssohn contended that Mosaic laws transcend state law, because of their twofold goal: actions leading to temporal happiness, and meditation on eternal and historical truths leading to eternal happiness. Every ceremony has a specific meaning and a precise relation to the speculative aspect of religion and morality. Since the Mosaic law is more than a state law, those of its parts which apply to the individual remain valid even after the destruction of the Jewish state and should be steadfastly observed. Moreover, it retains its important function as a bond between Jews everywhere, which is essential as long as polytheism, anthropomorphism, and religious usurpation continue to rule the earth.[29]

In the nineteenth century Jewish philosophers continued to take up the issue. Isaac Noah Manheimer and Michael Sachs wrote against the alarming neglect of observance of the ceremonial law in the period of Emancipation. They reemphasized the significance of ceremonial law in terms borrowed partly from Mendelssohn and partly from Kant's vindication of the cultus as a means of furthering morality. Of great moment was Leopold Zunz's forthright stand on behalf of the rite of circumcision, which occasioned his study of the ceremonial law as a whole.[30] Alternatively, Abraham Geiger, one of the major leaders of 19th-century Reform, recognized only the validity of those ceremonies which proved capable of promoting religious and moral feelings.[31] Still other Reformers and more liberal Jewish thinkers under the influence of the German philologist Friedrich Cruezer and Hegel, began to view the rituals prescribed in the Torah, especially the sacrificial cult, as merely symbolic expressions of ideas, as, for example, in D. Einhorn's *Das Prinzip des Mosaismus* (1854). In contrast, opposing all reform and defending an orthodox position, Samson Raphael Hirsch evolved a system of symbolism based chiefly on ethical values in order to give fresh meaning to the totality of *Halakhah* while requiring strict observance of all its teachings.[32]

The increasing secularity and historicism of modern life have presented considerable objections to traditional accounts and justifications of the *mitzvot* and have forced modern philosophers to rethink these issues. The consequences of this re-evaluation are clearly evident in Hermann Cohen's systematic re-interpretation of Judaism. Cohen understood the *mitzvot* in neo-Kantian terms. That is to say, he argued that their primary purpose was ethical and that they were made to appear as Divine Commandments in order to give them sufficient authority to obligate men to do what is ethically required. Man shows himself to be righteous in carrying out the requirements of the law, i.e., moral action. Thus, in Cohen's system, the *mitzvot* are understood as norms which help man achieve his ethical ambitions and so reach the highest goal, which is ethical perfection. The seemingly non-ethical *mitzvot* also serve the purpose of morally educating men through the channels of obedience and holiness.[33]

Cohen's student and disciple, Leo Baeck, developed the ethical neo-Kantian interpretation his master had given Judaism, while at the same time trying to transcend the limitations placed on Judaism by Cohen's attempt to comprehend it primarily in ethical categories. Baeck understands Judaism as a religion which actively works to bring about the messianic perfection of history. The *mitzvot* are the instruments of progress towards this goal. They have their source in God who is, for Baeck, ultimately mysterious, yet who sanctions and commands man through primarily ethical commandments, to be an active partner in the world's redemption. Through the commandments God, though mysterious, makes Himself eternally present; conversely, in response to God's will as made known in the commandments, the individual acknowledges his Creator and his willingness to co-operate with Him. Because God is mysterious His will, as expressed by Torah and *mitzvot,* are not reducible to any single human category, not even the moral one. As God is more than ethics, so too His will cannot be reduced solely to ethics. Thus we have in the Torah *mitzvot* which are rational and ethical as befit a moral God, and also *mitzvot* which transcend ordinary human reason and morality, reflecting a God who is ultimately mystery. Baeck sees Judaism as having understood this dialectical requirement, and of having produced the perfect religious balance between reason and revelation, mystery and commandments.[34] Though Baeck still stresses the ethical commandments and, despite his own best insights, often seems to be giving little more than a strict neo-Kantian interpretation, his account does represent a new religious sensitivity and awareness of what is important in Judaism in its totality.

Franz Rosenzweig, another great student of Cohen's, took the discussion of Judaism in a very different direction. Rosenzweig, reacting against Idealism in both its Kantian and Hegelian forms, saw *mitzvot* not as ethical imperatives or laws but rather in the strict sense as "commandments," i.e., as the direct, living address of God to each individual man in the concreteness of his own particular life situation. For Rosenzweig, the Jew must confront the Torah and the *mitzvot* not as static, frozen entities from the past, but as living, dynamic speech addressed to every living man. In this way, he argues that the Torah ceases to be *gesetz* ("law") and becomes instead *gebot* ("commandment"). In other words, each man actualizes the *mitzvah* and makes it relevant to his own life.

This distinction cuts across both moral and ritual, rational and nonrational *mitzvot.* God's address takes many forms and manifests itself in the ritual law as well as in the moral law; and both are based on a dialogical love relation between God and man. Julius Guttman has succintly described Rosenzweig's view in the following way: "The commandments are not arbitrary *obiter dicta* of God's will, but requests made by God of those who love Him."[35]

Rosenzweig's friend and collaborator, Martin Buber, also saw Judaism from an existentialist perspective. For him the essence of Judaism lay in the dynamic *"I-Thou"* relation between the Jew and

God. However, unlike Rosenzweig, Buber was unsympathetic to any sort of account of the mitzvot which understands them primarily in legal or other specifiable, particular, forms. According to Buber, "God is not a Lawgiver," and thus there can be no objective and divinely sanctioned *mitzvot* in the traditionally understood sense. Any action can be a holy action, a *mitzvah,* if done with the right intention; conversely, no action can claim preference on the basis of an assertion that it has been divinely revealed—God's revelation never takes such positive forms. Buber asserts that revelation is always solely a revelation of God's "Presence," and never of any data or objective content which can be put forward as religious or moral imperatives for men to follow. In this respect Buber's views are extreme and leave little, if any, reason for traditional Jewish observance and the practice of the *mitzvot* as generally understood.[36]

Standing apart from either the neo-Kantian or existentialist Germanic tradition, Mordecai Kaplan has argued for a pragmatic-naturalistic interpretation of Judaism in which the *mitzvot* are seen as supporting these ends. According to Kaplan all religion, including Judaism, is to be understood sociologically, i.e., as functioning to support and create certain desirable social ends. Thus the essences of religion are not static but change and evolve in response to new social requirements and goals. Judaism has found an effective way of giving expression to its group needs and social requirements by projecting them as the commandments of God, when in fact they are really the wishes of the group will. In this way the goals of the group are given greater sanction and authority and correspondingly, greater motivating power.

The traditional *mitzvot* must be understood in this way. They have no transcendental ground or sanction but are valuable insofar as they further the desires of the Jewish people. However, as the Jewish people evolve, some *mitzvot* will cease to be functional and will therefore become inoperative, while new ones will come into being and become central. Kaplan's view, which stresses anthropological and sociological categories for explaining and understanding the *mitzvot,* rejects the distinction between moral and ritual commandments by recognizing, and indeed encouraging, the fact that social groups such as Judaism require more than ethical prescriptions to have a viable group existence. Kaplan has termed his version of Judaism, not without good reason, Reconstructionism.[37]

A variation on Kaplan's position has also found expression in

Richard Rubenstein's "death of God" theology. Rubenstein, while asserting that the horror of the Nazi holocaust shows that "God is dead," nevertheless makes a strong plea for the retention of Jewish ritual and a personal and communal life of *mitzvot* on sociological and psychological grounds. He argues that now that God is dead men need each other more than ever, and more particularly, Jews need their Judaism and other Jews more than ever for solace, identity and psychological well-being. Thus on the basis of these modern grounds Rubenstein defends much of the traditional Jewish regimen of *mitzvot*.[38]

The period since the Second World War has also seen the forceful presentation of a Neo-orthodox defence of the *mitzvot* which, opposed to the reductionism of Kaplan and Rubenstein, stresses that the source of *mitzvot* is in God's revelation. As such the *mitzvot* transcend human reason, requiring faith and trust and an active service rather than a sceptical or liberal attempt to choose between ritual and ethical commandments, rational and irrational commandments. The most outstanding spokesmen for this view have been Rabbi Joseph Soloveitchik, the Israel thinker Yeshayahu Leibowitz, and in his way, the late Abraham Joshua Heschel.[39]

Piety, Study, Charity and Prayer

We have already discussed in detail the general nature of Torah and *mitzvah* in Judaism. These concepts are the backbone of Jewish life and thought. However, in order to understand fully how these general concepts come to fruition in every-day life, and how the daily existence and the active religiosity of the Jew is affected by them, it is worth examining four related issues: Piety, Study, Charity and Prayer. Piety is a more general term, inseparable in Judaism from Torah and *mitzvot*, while study, charity and prayer may be considered the three elemental Jewish activities—the three essential *mitzvot*.

PIETY AND THE PIOUS

As a consequence of its theocentric orientation, Judaism regards piety as the supreme virtue leading to man's highest good. Moreover, according to the Mishnah, the *zaddik* ("righteous person") is credited with contributing to the preservation of the world (Avot 5:1).

In rabbinic literature a variety of terms is employed to distinguish between different types or degrees of piety, but the emphasis on the service of God and the imitation of His ethical attributes appear to be the constant components of all the different types.[1]

Although obedience to halakhic norms represents a necessary condition of piety, it is far from representing its perfection. Thus it was expected that obedience to the law would inculcate such virtues as the love and fear of God. Hence, R. Johanan, a Palestinian *amora*, attributed the destruction of Jerusalem to the failure of the Jews to observe the moral demands that extend beyond the strict requirements of the law. Likewise, his contemporary, the Babylonian *amora*, Rav, indicated that even in civil litigation one must take into consideration the ethical-religious imperative of Proverbs 2:26, "to walk in the ways of the good and to keep the path of the righteous" (BM 83a). Moreover, abundant references to the special standards of piety, or the "Mishnah of the pious," are found in talmudic literature.² Naḥmanides cites the talmudic statement "Sanctify yourself within the domain of the permissible" as evidence for his contention that even an individual who has not violated any of the specific and detailed rules set forth in the Torah may still be branded a scoundrel.³

Man's total commitment to the service of God, according to Judaism, extends over all areas of life. For example, R. Yose stated that all our actions should be performed for the sake of God (Avot 2:12). Rabbinic Judaism believed that performance of a religious act could be disciplinary, leading to higher religious sensitivity. This idea was manifested in the relatively positive attitude taken towards deeds inspired by impure motives. The individual is encouraged to perform an act even though it may originate in unworthy motives, because, ultimately, these motives may be transformed and the act performed for the sake of God (Pes. 50b).

The aim of all piety is the sanctification of life, not the withdrawal from it. There is relatively little endorsement of asceticism in rabbinic Judaism. A widely prevalent attitude is represented by the statement of the medieval philosopher, Judah Halevi, that "contrition on a fast day does nothing to bring man nearer to God than joy on the Sabbath" (*Kuzari* 2:50). Similarly, Judaism generally recoils from tendencies designed to remove the pious from involvement with the community. Man's confrontation with God is not meant to lead to self-centeredness or a sense of isolation, but to participation in a holy community. This attitude is reflected in Hillel's maxim "Do not separate thyself from the community" (Avot 2:5). Moreover, according to a talmudic comment, the overall objective of the entire Torah was to promote peace and thus contribute to the improvement of society (Git. 59b).

Although rabbinic Judaism produced a number of extraordinary individuals endowed with special capacities for mystical union, apocalyptic visions, and saintliness, these aspects of piety were never recognized as displacing the normative component, which stressed faithful adherence to the Covenant as interpreted by the Oral Law. It was felt that the practice and, especially, the study of the Torah are not merely intrinsically valuable activities, but are also instrumental in refining man's character and lifting him to higher levels of piety.

STUDY

The study of the Torah *(talmud Torah)* as a supreme religious duty is one of the most typical and far-reaching ideas of rabbinic Judaism. Talmudic literature is full of references to the *mitzvah* of Torah study, especially of the difficult halakhic portions which require the fullest application, C.G. Montefiore[4] has correctly observed that: "All these legal discussions, all this 'study of the Law,' all these elaborations and minutiae, were to the Rabbis the breath of their nostrils, their greatest joy and the finest portion of their lives."

An early Mishnah (Peah 1:1), after describing such duties as honoring parents and performing acts of benevolence among the *mitzvot* for which there is reward both in this world and the next, concluded that the study of the Torah is "equal to them all." A tannaitic treatise, *Baraita Kinyan Torah,* devoted to the ideal of Torah study, contains the advice: "This is the way of the Torah: a morsel of bread with salt to eat, water by measure to drink; thou shalt sleep on the ground, and live a life of hardship, while thou toilest in the Torah. If thou doest thus, happy shalt thou be, and it shall be well with thee; happy shalt thou be—in this world, and it shall be well with thee—in the world to come" (Avot 6:4). Quoting the verse, "This is the Law (Torah): when a man dieth in a tent" (Num. 19:14), the third-century teacher Resh Lakish taught: "The words of the Torah become firmly established only for one who kills himself (in study) for it" (Ber. 63b).

Dedicated students, "toiling in the Torah," were found to number in the thousands in the great Palestinian and Babylonian academies during the first five centuries of the present era. Only against such a background of unqualified devotion does the saying of the second-century R. Jacob become intelligible: "If a man was walking by the way and studying and he ceased his study to declare, 'How fine is this tree!' or 'How fine is this plowed field!' Scripture reckons it to him as though he were guilty against his own soul" (Avot 3:7). Of Rava it was said (Shab. 88a) that he was once so engrossed in his studies that he was unaware that his fingers were spurting blood. It was taken for granted that a scholar would be incapable of diverting his mind from Torah study; hence it was ruled that a scholar is forbidden to remain in unclean alleyways where Torah should not be studied (Ber. 24b).

The ideal of Torah study had a twofold aim. First it was believed to lead to the practical observances, since without knowledge of what it is that the Torah enjoins full observance is impossible. "An empty-headed man cannot be a sin-fearing man, nor can an ignorant person be pious" (Avot 2:5). Secondly, Torah study was itself a religious duty of the highest order. This dual function of study is presumably given expression in the discussion said to have taken place in the early part of the second century: "R. Tarfon and the Elders were once reclining in the upper story of Nithza's house in Lydda, when this question was put to them: 'Which is greater, study or practice?' R. Tarfon replied: 'Practice is greater.' R. Akiva replied: 'Study is greater for it leads to practice.' Then they all answered and said: Study is greater, for it leads to practice" (Kid. 40b). Yet study without any intention of carrying out the precepts was seen as having no value. "Whoever says that he has only [an interest] in the study of the Torah, he does not even have [the study of] the Torah" (Yev. 109b).

There is evidence of tension between the scholarly ideal and that of extraordinary piety without learning. The famous scholars were commited to Torah study as the highest pursuit, yet they were compelled to recognize the achievements of men of outstanding piety who were in no way renowned for their learning. The scholars yielded only grudgingly, as in the tale (Ber. 34b) of the miracle-working saint, R. Ḥanina b. Dosa, who prayed successfully for the recovery of R. Johanan b. Zakkai's son, whereas the prayers of R. Johanan would have accomplished nothing. When R. Johanan's wife asked him, "Is Ḥanina greater than you are?" he replied, "No; but he is like a servant of the king who can enter his presence at any time whereas I am like a nobleman who is allowed only to appear at fixed times."

The qualifications for study were carefully mapped out, 48 "excellences" by which the Torah is acquired being listed (perhaps for rehearsal by the prospective student):

"By study, the hearing of the ear, by the ordering of the lips, by the understanding of the heart, by the discernment of the heart, by awe, by reverence, by humility, by cheerfulness; by attendance on the Sages, by consorting with fellow-students, by close argument with disciples; by assiduity, by knowledge of Scripture and Mishnah; by moderation in business, in worldly occupation, pleasure, sleep, conversation, and jesting; by long-suffering, by a good heart, by faith in the Sages, by submission to sorrows; by being one that recognizes his place and that rejoices in his lot and that makes a fence around his words and claims no merit for himself; by being one that is beloved, that loves God, that loves mankind,. that loves well-doing, that loves rectitude, that loves reproof, that shuns honor and boasts not of his learning, and delights not in rendering decisions; that helps his fellow to bear his yoke, and that judges him favorably, and that establishes him in the truth and establishes him in peace; and that occupies himself assiduously in his study; by being one that asks and makes answer, that hearkens and adds thereto; that learns in order to teach and that learns in order to practice; that makes his teacher wiser; that retells exactly what he has heard, and reports a thing in the name of him that said it" (Avot, 6:6).

The demands made on the student were thus both of intellect and of character. The successful student acquired in addition to factual knowledge the capacity for skill in debate and of particularly brilliant scholars it was said that they were able to provide 24 answers to every problem.[5] It was not unusual for teachers to encourage their disciples to cultivate alertness of mind by appearing on occasion to act contrary to the Law, to see whether the error would be spotted. The debators were compared to mighty warriors taking part in the "battles of the Torah." Another comparison was that to competent craftsmen. The "craftsmen and the smiths" (II Kings 24:14) were identified with the scholars and said to possess acute reasoning powers. Of a text presenting severe problems of interpretation it was said that neither a carpenter nor his apprentice could provide the correct solution. In similar vein keen scholars were compared to builders, to pearl divers capable of reaching great depths in pursuit of treasure, and to weavers. The purveyor of the difficult halakhic teachings was compared to a dealer in precious stones for the connoisseur, whereas the more popular but less profound aggadic teacher was compared to the retailer of cheap tinsel goods which all can afford to buy.[6]

While the saying of R. Judah in the name of Rav, that a man should study the Torah even if his motives were not of the purest *(she-lo li-Shemah)*, was generally accepted because the right motive would eventually emerge (Pes. 50b), the rabbinic ideal was that of Torah "for its own sake" *(Torah li-Shemah)*. R. Meir said: "Whoever labors in the Torah for its own sake merits many things; and not only that, but the whole world is indebted to him: he is called a friend, beloved, a lover of the All-present, a lover of mankind; it clothes him in meekness and reverence; it fits him to become just, pious, upright and faithful; it keeps him far from sin, and brings him near to virtue; through him the world enjoys counsel and sound knowledge, understanding and strength" (Avot 6:1). The *Sifrei*[7] remarks: "Suppose you say, I am learning Torah that I may get rich, or that I may be called Rabbi, or that I may gain reward (from God)—the teaching of Scripture is: 'To love the Lord your God' (Deut. 11:13)." "Suppose you say, I will learn Torah in order to be called learned, to have a seat in the academy, to have endless life in the world to come—the teaching is: 'To love the Lord your God.'"

From the rabbinic period and onward great centers of Jewish learning were established. In Palestine there was the academy at the seacoast village of Jabneh, which came into especial prominence after the destruction of the Temple; at Lydda under the guidance of R. Eliezer b. Hyrcanus and R. Tarfon; at Bene-Berak under R. Akiva; at Usha in Galilee; and there were also centers in Sepphoris, Tiberias, and Caesarea. R. Yose b. Kisma said: "I was once walking by the way, when a man met me and greeted me and I returned his greeting. He said to me, 'Rabbi, from where are you?' I said to him, 'I come from a great city of sages and scribes.' He said to me, 'If you are willing to dwell with us in our place, I will give you a thousand golden dinars and precious stones and pearls.' I said, 'If you were to give me all the silver and gold and precious stones in the world, I would not dwell anywhere but in a home of the Torah'" (Avot 6:9).

"Homes of the Torah" rose to a position of importance in third-century C.E. Babylonia. At the beginning of this century two Palestinian-trained scholars, Rav and Samuel, returned to their native Babylonia, the former to found the academy at Sura, the latter to revive the long-established academy at Nehardea. When Nehardea was destroyed during the Roman-Persian wars in the year 259 C.E., Samuel's disciple, R. Judah b. Ezekiel, founded an academy at Pumbedita which existed as a sister and rival institution of Sura for over eight centuries. After the decline of Sura and Pumbedita in the 11th century, new schools sprang up in North Africa and Europe to take their place. The schools of Paris, Troyes, Narbonne, Metz, Worms, Speyer, Altona, Cordoba, Barcelona, and Toledo were renowned in the Middle

Ages. From the 16th century, Poland, with its own academies, emerged as the pre-eminent Jewish intellectual center.

Yet it should not be imagined that the rabbinic ideal of Torah study was for the scholar alone. It was binding on every Jew as a *mitzvah*. R. Johanan said in the name of R. Simeon b. Yoḥai, "Even though a man reads no more than the *Shema* morning and evening he has thereby fulfilled the precept of 'This book of the law shall not depart'" (Josh. 1:8). It is, however, forbidden to say this in the presence of the ignorant (who would draw the consequence that detailed Torah study is not important). But Rava said it is meritorious to say it in the presence of the ignorant (so that they should not despair of having no part in Torah study; Men. 99b). There is no doubt that the rabbinic ideal was devotion to Torah study on the part of every Jew. Maimonides follows his rabbinic mentors in ruling:[8] "Every man in Israel is obliged to study the Torah, whether he is firm of body or a sufferer from ill-health, whether a young man or of advanced age with his strength abated. Even a poor man who is supported by charity and obliged to beg at doors, and even one with wife and children to support, is obliged to set aside a period for Torah study by day and by night, as it is said: Thou shalt meditate therein day and night."

The Laws of Study
Three benedictions are to be recited before studying the Torah.[9] Since the whole of the Jew's waking life is a time for study these benedictions are recited at the beginning of each day and suffice for the whole day's study. It is considered meritorious to set aside a fixed time each day for Torah study, preferably in the company of others. Each community is expected to have a special "house of study" *(bet ha-midrash)*, the sanctity of which is greater than that of a synagogue. As evidence of this it is ruled that while it is not permitted to run from a *bet ha-midrash* to a synagogue it is proper to run from a synagogue to a *bet ha-midrash*. A person unable to study himself should assist in supporting students of the Torah, in whose learning he will then have a share.[10] The Psalmist (Ps. 19:19) speaks of the precepts as "rejoicing the heart." Consequently, it is forbidden to study the Torah during the week of mourning for a close relative or on the Ninth of Av. The rabbis believed in the psychological value of verbal expression and therefore advised that Torah study should not be a purely mental exercise but the words

of the text should be uttered aloud, customarily with a chant. Since the study of the Torah is equal to all the other precepts, a man should not interrupt his studies to do a good deed unless there is no one else to carry it out. At the completion of the study of a whole tractate of the Talmud it is customary to celebrate the occasion with a festive meal.

Scope of Study

"At five years the age is reached for the study of Scripture, at ten for the study of Mishnah, at thirteen for the fulfillment of the commandments, at fifteen for the study of Talmud" (Avot 5:21). This may reflect the actual ages when the young students were gradually introduced to the more complex subjects of study. Elsewhere (Kid. 30a) it is said that a man should divide his study time so that a third is devoted to Scripture, a third to Mishnah, and a third to Talmud. In the Middle Ages, especially in France and Germany, most of the students' efforts were directed to the study of the Babylonian Talmud, in particular to its halakhic portion, with a certain neglect of other topics. Typical is the admission of Rabbenu Tam[11] that the rabbinic schools relied on the fact that the Babylonian Talmud is full of all matters, containing Scripture and Mishnah. This tendency toward a certain narrowing of studies to the virtual exclusion of all except *halakhah* became more and more the norm in Russia and Poland.

The medieval thinkers, however, not only urged the study of their discipline but tended to identify philosophical investigation with the highest type of Torah study. Maimonides[12] identified the esoteric disciplines known as the "Work of Creation" and "Work of the Chariot" with Aristotelian physics and metaphysics, respectively, and ranked them higher in the Jewish scale of studies than talmudic debates. Similarly, the kabbalists zealously regarded their subject—the "soul of the Torah"[13]—as the highest pursuit. The kabbalist Ḥayyim Vital[14] recommended that a man should spend an hour or two each day on halakhic casuistry in order to remove the coarse "shell" which surrounds the "fruit," but should devote the rest of his study time to the true science of the kabbalistic mysteries. In the 16th century R. Moses Isserles[15] summed up the rabbinic attitude as follows: "A man should only study Scripture, Mishnah, and Gemara, and the Codes based on them. In this way he will acquire this world and the next. But he should not study other sciences. However, it is permitted to study other sciences occasionally, provided that this does not involve in the reading of heretical works. This is called by the Sages 'strolling in Paradise.' A man must not 'stroll in Paradise' until he has filled his stomach with meat and wine, namely, the knowledge of that which is forbidden and that which is permitted and the laws of the precepts."

The rise of the ḥasidic movement in the 18th century presented a serious challenge to the ideal of Torah study as the supreme religious duty. The early ḥasidic masters accused the conventional scholars of engaging in Torah study for motives of fame, wealth, and prestige. Prayer, in the traditional scheme inferior to study, was frequently elevated by the *Ḥasidim* above study. In addition, the rabbinic ideal of *Torah li-Shemah* ("for its own sake") was interpreted in early Ḥasidism to mean attachment to God *(devekut),* while studying, especially in the sense of intense concentration on the letters of the text, was believed to reveal on earth the divine forces by means of which God governs the world.[16] The comparatively large number of classical talmudic scholars among the second and third generations of ḥasidic masters prevented, however, any radical departure from the older ideal. In a statement which combines the older ideal with the new ḥasidic emphasis on attachment to God while studying, R. Shneur Zalman of Lyady describes[17] the religious significance of even the legalistic debates:

"Behold, with regard to every kind of intellectual perception, when one understands and grasps an idea in one's mind, the mind seizes the idea and encompasses it in thought so that the idea is held, surrounded, and enclosed in the mind in which it is comprehended. Conversely, the mind is clothed by an idea it has grasped. For instance, when one understands fully a rule in the Mishnah or the Gemara, his mind seizes the rule and encompasses it and, at the same time, his mind is encompassed by the rule. Now, behold, this rule is the wisdom and will of the Holy One, blessed be He, for it rose in His will that, for instance, when A pleads thus and B thus the rule will be thus. And even if, in fact, a case of this kind will never come before the courts, nonetheless, seeing that it rose in the will and wisdom of the Holy One, blessed be He, that this is the rule, it follows that when a man knows and grasps this rule in his mind in accordance with the decision laid down in the Mishnah or the Gemara or the Codes he grasps, seizes hold of, and encompasses in his mind the will and wisdom of the Holy One, blessed be He, of whom no thought can conceive."

A less mystical approach is advocated in the famous broadside fired against the *Ḥasidim* by the disciple of the Gaon of Vilna, R. Ḥayyim of

Volozhin *(Nefesh ha-Ḥayyim)*. R. Ḥayyim reiterates the conventional view that Torah study even out of ulterior motives is not to be despised and that, moreover, Torah for its own sake does not mean that the student should have God in mind when he studies the texts (such an attempt, R. Ḥayyim argues, would interfere with the intense concentration required for the mastery of the difficult halakhic studies he favored above all else). The student should have a few moments of prayer and devout thoughts before his actual studies and then he should immerse himself in the texts. For R. Ḥayyim[18] the Torah student has little need for the moralistic and devotional literature *(Musar)* in order to become God-fearing. The Torah itself possesses the property of inducing the fear of God in the hearts of its diligent students. A work in similar vein, from the same school, singing the praises of traditional Torah study, is *Ma'alot ha-Torah* by Abraham, brother of the Gaon of Vilna. The book expresses the ideal taught in the yeshivah of Volozhin and in the Lithuanian yeshivot influenced by it in the 19th and 20th centuries, in which, however, *Musar* did eventually come to occupy a considerably important place.

In Western Europe, from the beginning of the 19th century, more and more time had to be found for secular studies, frequently to the detriment of Torah study. Samson Raphael Hirsch adapted the rabbinic ideal of "Torah and *Derekh Erez*" ("worldly occupation") so that the latter came to embrace Western learning and culture. Moreover, the critical investigation of the classical sources known as *Juedische Wissenschaft* posed problems of its own for the traditional ideal of Torah study. In a sense the objective, "scientific" scholarship that is the ideal of this school is opposed to that of study as a devotional exercise, if only because it is far more difficult to treat as sacred texts those that are critically examined, and, conversely, acknowledging the sanctity of a text tends to prejudge critical questions regarding its background and authorship. The achievements of *Juedische Wissenschaft* have shed new light on many obscure corners of Jewish thought and history, but critics such as G. Scholem[19] have questioned whether the movement has ever had any real religious significance. There have undoubtedly emerged two vastly different worlds of Jewish studies: the world of the yeshivot indifferent or even hostile to critical scholarship, and the world of modern learning with no formal interest in study as an act of religious worship. To date there has been little meeting between these two worlds.

CHARITY

The obligation to help the poor and the needy and to give them gifts is stated many times in the Bible and was considered by the rabbis of all ages to be one of the cardinal *mitzvot* of Judaism.

The Bible itself legislates several laws which are in effect a tax for the benefit of the poor. Among these are the laws of gleaning as well as the special tithe for the poor. Furthermore, the institution of the sabbatical year was in order "that the poor of thy people may eat" (Ex. 23:11) as well as to cancel debts about which the warning was given "If there be among you a needy man, one of your brethren, within thy gates, in thy land which the Lord thy God giveth thee, thou shalt not harden thy heart nor shut thy hand from thy needy brother; but thou shalt surely open thy hand unto him and shalt surely lend him sufficient for his need in that which he wanteth. Beware that there be not a base thought in thy heart, saying 'The seventh year, the year of release, is at hand'; and thine eye be evil against thy needy brother and thou give him nought; and he say unto the Lord against thee and it be sin in thee. Thou shalt surely give him, and thy heart shall not be grieved when thou givest unto him; because that for this thing the Lord thy God will bless thee in all thy work ..." (Deut. 15:7–10). The Pentateuch also insists that the needy be remembered when the festivals are celebrated, e.g., "And thou shalt rejoice before the Lord thy God, thou, and thy son, and thy daughter, and thy man-servant, and thy maid-servant, and the Levite that is within thy gates, and the stranger, and the fatherless and the widow that are in the midst of thee" (16:11, 14). The Bible expects Israel to be aware of the needs of the poor and the stranger (who is considered to be in an inferior economic position) because Israel itself had experienced this situation in Egypt: "Love ye therefore the stranger; for ye were strangers in the land of Egypt" (10:19) and promises "for this thing the Lord thy God will bless thee in all thy work and in all that thou puttest thy hand unto" (15:10).

So important is charity that it is said to be an attribute of God Himself: "For the Lord your God, He is God of gods, and Lord of lords ... He doth execute justice for the fatherless and widow and loveth the stranger, in giving him food and raiment" (10:17, 18). This theme was developed at considerable length by the psalmist and both Isaiah and Ezekiel[20] considered charity as an indispensable requirement for a life of piety. Indeed, Isaiah proclaims that the "acceptable day to the Lord" is not the fast which only consists of afflicting the soul and wearing sackcloth and ashes but rather the day on which bread is dealt to the hungry, the poor that are cast out are brought into the house and the naked clothed; while Ezekiel attributes the destruction of Sodom to its lack of charity, "neither did she strengthen the hand of the poor and needy." "A woman of valor" is one who "stretcheth out her hand to the poor; Yea, she reacheth forth her hands to the needy" (Prov. 31:20). The author of Proverbs teaches that charity to the poor is equated with "lending to the Lord, and his good deed will He repay unto him" (*ibid.,* 19:17) and the virtue of charity and the fact that it deserves reward from God is stressed over and over in the arguments in the book of Job.[21] Following the precedent in the Pentateuch, the book of Esther (9:12) makes sending gifts to the poor a part of the new festival it inaugurates (Purim), and when Ezra and Neḥemiah taught the people anew the meaning of Rosh Ha-Shanah, they told them, "Go your way, eat the fat, and drink the sweet and send portions unto him for whom nothing is prepared" (Neh. 8:10).

Although the idea of charity and almsgiving is spread thoughout the whole of the Bible, there is no special term for it. The rabbis of the Talmud, however, adopted the word צדקה *(zedakah)* for charity and it is used (but not exclusively so) throughout rabbinic literature in the sense of helping the needy by gifts. The word has since passed into popular usage and is almost exclusively used for charity. The term חסד *(ḥesed,* "loving-kindness"), which is used widely in the Bible, has taken on the meaning of physical aid, or lending without interest.

The word *zedakah* literally means "righteousness" or "justice"; by their very choice of word the rabbis reveal a great deal of their attitude to the subject, for they see charity not as a favor to the poor but something to which they have a right, and the donor, an obligation. In this way they teach "The poor man does more for the householder (in accepting alms) than the householder does for the poor man (by giving him the charity)" (Lev. R. 34:8) for he gives the householder the opportunity to perform a *mitzvah.* This attitude stemmed from the awareness that all men's possessions belong to God and that poverty and riches are in His hand. This view is aptly summed up in *Avot* (3:8): "Give unto Him of what is His, seeing that thou and what thou hast are His" and is further illustrated in a story told of Rava. A poor man came before

Rava who asked him what he usually had for his meal. The man replied, "Fatted chicken and old wine." "But do you not" said Rava "feel worried that you are a burden on the community?" "Do I eat what is theirs?" said the man, "I eat what is God's." At that point Rava's sister brought him a gift of a fatted chicken and some old wine, which Rava understood to be an omen and apologized to the poor man (Ket. 67b).

The importance the rabbis attached to the *mitzvah* of *zedakah* can be understood from R. Assi who stated that "*zedakah* is as important as all the other commandments put together and from R. Eleazar who expounded the verse "To do righteousness *(zedakah)* and justice is more acceptable to the Lord than sacrifice" (Prov. 21:3) to mean that charity is greater than all sacrifices. *Zedakah,* to the rabbis, hastens the redemption, ensures that the doer will have wise, wealthy, and learned sons, and atones for sins. Giving charity is the way in which man can "walk after the Lord your God" and is also said to save from death. Together with Torah and service (i.e., prayer), the practice of charity is one of the pillars on which the world rests. Moreover, giving charity does not impoverish, and not giving is held to be tantamount to idolatry. Charity is an act of devotion and a complement to prayer; as such the wise give charity just before praying as it is written "and I, in righteousness *(zedek)* will see Thy face" (Ps. 17:15).[22]

Since *zedakah* is considered a biblical commandment, the rabbis found it necessary—as in the case of every other *mitzvah*—to define it in minute detail, e.g., who is obligated to give, who is eligible to receive, how much should be given and in what manner. These laws are scattered throughout the Talmud and were codified by Maimonides in his *Mishneh Torah.*[23]

According to the sages, everybody is obliged to give charity; even one who himself is dependent on charity should give to those less fortunate than himself (Git. 7a). The court can even compel one who refuses to give charity—or donates less than his means allow—to give according to the court's assessment. The recalcitrant can even be flogged, and should he still refuse, the court may appropriate his property in the assessed sum for charity.[24]

For the purposes of charity the following rules apply. A poor man is one who has less than 200 zuz. This sum is the criterion if it is static capital (i.e., not being used in business); if, however, it is being used, the

limit is 50 zuz (Ket. 9:13). A man with more than these sums is not entitled to take the poor man's tithe or charity—and he who does will be
reduced to real poverty (*ibid.*, 10:19). Charity should also be dispensed
to the non-Jewish poor in order to preserve good relations; however,
charity should not be accepted from them unless it is entirely unavoidable. Women take precedence over men in receiving alms, and
one's poor relatives come before strangers. The general rule is "the poor
of your own town come before the poor of any other town," but this
rule is lifted for the poor of Erez Israel who take precedence over all.[25]
A traveler in a strange town who is out of funds is considered to be poor
and may take charity even though he has money at home. When he
returns to his home he is not obliged to repay the charity he has taken
(Pe'ah 5:4). A man is not obliged to sell his household goods in order to
maintain himself but is eligible for charity (Pe'ah 8:8); even if he owns
land, houses, or other property, he is not required to sell them at a dis-
advantage if the prices are lower than usual (BK 7a–b). It is permitted
to deceive a poor man who, out of pride, refuses to accept charity, and
to allow him to think that it is a loan; but a miser who refuses to use his
own means is to be ignored (Ket. 67b).

No exact amount of charity to be given was fixed. However, to give a
tenth of one's wealth to charity is considered to be a "middling"
amount, while to give a 20th or less is to be "mean." On the other hand,
in Usha the rabbis enacted that one should not give more than a fifth
lest he become impoverished himself and dependent on charity.[26] The
psychological needs of the poor should be taken into consideration even
though they may appear to be exaggerated. Thus a once wealthy man
asked Hillel for a horse and a runner to go before him, which Hillel supplied; on another occasion, when Hillel could not afford to hire a runner
for him, Hillel acted as one himself (Ket. 67a).

This appreciation of the importance of charity led the rabbis to be especially concerned about the manner in which alms are to be dispensed.
The prime consideration is that nothing be done that might shame the
recipient. "R. Jonah said: It is not written 'Happy is he who gives to the
poor,' but 'Happy is he who considers the poor' (Ps. 41:2); i.e., who
ponders how to fulfill the command to help the poor. How did R. Jonah
act? If he met a man of good family who had become impoverished he
would say, 'I have heard that a legacy has been left to you in such a
place; take this money in advance and pay me back later.' When he

accepted it he then said to him, 'It is a gift.'"[27] When R. Yannai saw somebody giving a zuz to a poor man in public he said, "It were better not to have given rather than to have given him and shamed him" (Hag. 5a). Out of consideration for the sensibilities of the poor the rabbis considered the best form of almsgiving to be that in which neither the donor nor the recipient knew each other. "Which is the *zedakah* which saves from a strange death? That in which the giver does not know to whom he has given nor the recipient from whom he has received" (BB 10a), and R. Eliezer saw the "secret" giver as being greater than Moses (BB 9b). Stories are told throughout the Talmud illustrating this principle and relating how the pious used to devise ingenious methods of giving alms so as to remain anonymous.[28] For the same reason it is important to receive the poor in good humor, and even if one cannot afford to give, one must at least appease the poor with words.[29]

Maimonides[30] lists eight ways of giving *zedakah* which are progressively more virtuous: to give (1) but sadly; (2) less than is fitting, but in good humor; (3) only after having been asked to; (4) before being asked; (5) in such a manner that the donor does not know who the recipient is; (6) in such a manner that the recipient does not know who the donor is; and (7) in such a way that neither the donor nor the recipient knows the identity of the other. The highest form of charity is not to give alms, but to help the poor to rehabilitate themselves by lending them money, taking them into partnership, employing them, or giving them work, for in this way the end is achieved without any loss of self-respect at all.

In order to see that charity is in fact properly dispensed, every Jewish community[31] is under an obligation to set up a communal structure, which will be responsible for it. "In every town where there are Jews they must appoint 'charity wardens' *(gabba'ei zedakah),* men who are well known and honest that they should collect money from the people every Sabbath eve and distribute it to the poor . . . We have never seen or heard of a Jewish community which does not have a charity fund." Because the charity warden was involved in the collection and distribution of public funds, special care was taken to ensure that there should not be even the slightest suspicion of dishonesty. The actual collection had to be made by at least two wardens who were not permitted to leave each other during the course of it. The distribution of the money was to be made by at least three wardens in whose hands lay the decision as to whom to give and how much. Besides money, food and clothing were also distributed. It seems that the poor were registered with the fund and mendicants who went from door to door begging were not to be given any sizable sums (BB 9a); the fund did, however, supply the needs of strangers. Apart from maintaining the poor, the fund was also used for redeeming captives and dowering poor brides, both of which were considered to be among the most virtuous of acts. In addition to the fund *(kuppah)* there were also communal soup kitchens *(tamḥui)* at which any person with less than enough for two meals was entitled to eat.[32]

Collecting and distributing charity is to some extent distasteful work and at times even humiliating. In order to encourage the men to undertake it, the rabbis interpreted several scriptural verses as extolling the wardens who are considered to be "eternal stars" and greater even than the givers (BB 8a, 9a). R. Yose, however, prayed "May my lot be with those who collect charity rather than with those who distribute it" (Shab. 118b), apparently preferring the risk of humiliation to that of misjudgment.

Charity is a form of vow, and a promise to give must be fulfilled immediately.[33] Generally speaking the charity money must be used for the purpose for which it was given and it is forbidden to divert the funds to some other cause.

Finally, the sages stress that the accepting of charity, when necessary, is perfectly legitimate and no shame attaches itself to the poor who are otherwise unable to support themselves. However, one is advised to do everything in one's power to avoid having to take alms: "Make your Sabbath a weekday (by not eating special food or wearing good clothes) rather than be dependent on other people" (Pes. 112a); and, "even a wise and honored man should do menial work (skinning unclean animals) rather than take charity" (Pes. 113a). The greatest of the sages did physical labor in order to support themselves and remain independent.

Over the centuries these teachings regarding charity have been faithfully followed in the Jewish communities throughout the world. Jewish contributions to both Jewish and non-Jewish charities and causes, and in recent years to rebuilding the State of Israel, are a matter of record. This generous philanthropy might be considered one of Judaism's most noble achievements.

PRAYER

In the Bible

The concept of prayer is based on the conviction that God exists, hears, and answers,[34] that He is a personal deity. In a sense it is a corollary of the biblical concept that man was created "in the image of God" (Gen. 1:26–27), which implies, inter alia, fellowship with God. Although prayer has an intellectual base, it is essentially emotional in character. It is an expression of man's quest for the Divine and his longing to unburden his soul before God.[35] Hence prayer takes many forms: petition, expostulation, confession, meditation, recollection (anamnesis), thanksgiving, praise, adoration, and intercession. For the purpose of classification, "praise" is distinguished from "prayer" in the narrower supplicatory sense, and "ejaculatory" from formal, "liturgical" prayer. But the source is the same; in its irresistable outpouring, the human heart merges all categories. Thus prayer and praise may intermingle as in Sam. 2:1–10, and supplication and thanksgiving follow in close succession, as in Psalm 13. Indeed many scriptural passages might be called "para-prayers"—they seem to hover between discourse and entreaty, as in Ex. 3:1–122; meditation and petition as in Jer. 20:7ff.; or expostulation and entreaty, as found throughout Job. It has been estimated that there are 85 prayers in the Bible, apart from 60 complete psalms and 14 parts of psalms that can be so termed; five psalms are specifically called prayer.[36] But such liturgical statistics depend on the definition given to prayer.

The variegated character of biblical prayer has given rise to a rich nomenclature for praying. The rabbis already noted that "prayer is called by ten different expressions" (Sif. Deut. 26), but on closer examination even more can be found. The most common word for prayer is *tefillah* (Isa. 1:15); the corresponding verb is *hitpallel* (I Kings 8:42). The stem, *phl* signifies "to interpose, judge, hope." These meanings are eminently suited to the biblical conception of prayer as intercession and self-scrutiny leading to hope.[37]

Despite its multifaceted character, biblical prayer is essentially a simple human reaction. The rabbis called it "the service in the heart," and the expression has its roots in biblical thought.[38] But the needs of man are so numerous and complex that prayer inevitably came to reflect the vast range of human moods, fears, hopes, feelings, desires, and aspirations. In early times—in the patriarchal age—a simple invocation, a calling upon the name of the Lord,[39] would suffice. The approach to God at this stage was marked by spontaneity, directness, and familiarity—God was near. Yet the future was veiled by mystery; man was often undecided how to act. Hence one finds in the biblical material the request for a sign or oracle addressed directly to God, or indirectly through a priest or prophet [40] and from this rudimentary stratum grew the magnificent prayers for understanding and guidance which are found elsewhere in the text.

But in emergency man does not merely want to know the future; he seeks to determine it by entreating God's help. Thus Jacob (in a votive supplication) prayed for essential material needs; Eliezer for the success of his mission; Abraham for the salvation of Sodom; Moses for erring Israel; Joshua for divine help in the hour of defeat; Hezekiah for deliverance from Sennacherib; the prophets on behalf of their people; Daniel for Israel's restoration; Ezra for the sins of his people; and Nehemiah for the distress of his people. Solomon's noble dedication prayer at the consecration of the Temple includes almost every type of prayer—adoration, thanksgiving, petition, and confession. It also strikes a universal note so often echoed by the prophets. The spectrum of biblical prayer thus ranges from the simplest material needs to the highest spiritual yearnings transcending, like prophecy, the horizon of history and reaching to the realm of eschatology.[41]

There was an early relationship between sacrifice and prayer[42] which persisted until the destruction of the Second Temple. The sacrifice suggested man's submission to the will of God; the prayer often provided a commentary on the offering. But the two are not necessarily linked. It is noteworthy that the sacrificial regulations make no liturgical provisions (except for the Day of Atonement, Lev. 16:21); but actually the offerings were themselves a dramatic form of prayer. In contrast, prayer could replace sacrifice (Ps. 141:2) and indeed, later, in the synagogue, prayer, accompanied by Scripture reading and exposition, entirely took the place of altar offerings.

Examples of prayers of intercession have already been cited. The intercessor, whether prophet, priest, king, or national leader, does not point to the need for an intermediary in worship: "The Lord is near to all who call upon Him in truth" (Ps. 145:18). The intercessor is one who, by his innate spiritual attributes, lends weight to the entreaty. The ultimate criterion still remains not the worthiness of the pleader but of those for whom he is pleading.

Prayer, unlike sacrifice, could be offered up anywhere,[43] but there was a natural tendency to prefer a sacred site (e.g., Shiloh or Gibeon). Eventually the Temple at Jerusalem became the major place of prayer (Isa. 56:7); those who could not be there physically at least turned toward it when worshipping[44] and it was prophesized that in time to come the Temple would be a house of prayer for all nations (Isa. 56:7). The synagogue had its origin during the Babylonian exile; originally a place of assembly, it became in due course a house of prayer and study. The emphasis on congregational prayer began to grow but private prayer was never abolished. The heart and not the hour dictated the occasion for prayer. Day and night the Heavenly Father could be entreated.[45] But the need for regularity brought about a synchronization of the times of prayer and sacrifice; morning worship corresponded to the morning oblation, afternoon orisons to the late afternoon sacrifice.[46] Nightfall provided yet another occasion for worship, so that prayers came to be offered thrice a day,[47] while the seven times mentioned in Psalms 119:164 was understood to mean "often" or "constantly."

In the Bible no particular gestures are prescribed in connection with prayer. But certain postures developed naturally to lend emphasis to the content of the prayer: standing which is normal, kneeling, prostration head bowed; hands stretched out or uplifted, face between knees and even sitting. More important accompaniments of prayer were fasting, mourning, and weeping, but the ultimate criterion remained earnestness of heart.[48]

Originally prayer was undoubtedly spontaneous and personal; but the need to organize religion gave rise to liturgical patterns, and musical renderings and prayer formulas are found already in the Pentateuch.[49] The Psalms provide examples of fuller liturgical development, including choral and instrumental features and the response "Amen" occurs in a number of places.[50]

That prayer is answered is an accepted biblical verity,[51] but Scripture is no less emphatic that not all prayers are answered.[52] Ritual is not enough, while hypocritical worship is an abomination[53] and there are occasions when intercession is forbidden.[54] It is at this point that the biblical concept of prayer is seen in its true inwardness. Paganism regarded worship as a form of magic, whereby the deity could be compelled to fulfill the worshipper's wishes; the moral element was wholly absent. In biblical faith the divine response is essentially linked to ethical and spiritual values. Man, as it were, answers his own prayer, and fundamentally the answer is a significant change of spirit and outlook. Abraham learned the lesson of faith. Moses became his people's deliverer; Isaiah was transformed into a prophet.[55] Prayer and prophecy were probably closely correlated, the former providing spiritual soil in which the revelatory seed took root.[56] In many instances prayer assumes a tempestuous character[57] but the storm always ends in newfound faith and peace. At times, moreover, God answers before He is appealed to[58] for man not only beseeches God, but God also seeks man. The Divine-human relationship is reciprocal.

In sum, the Bible conceives prayer as a spiritual bridge between man and God. It is a great instrument of human regeneration and salvation, worthy even of martyrdom. Rooted in faith and moral integrity, it banishes fear and asks, in its noblest formulations, only the blessing of divine favor (Num. 6:24–26). Clothed in language of simple but matchless beauty, it is imbued with religious love and a sense of sweet fellowship with God.

In Later Thought

On the biblical verse "And serve Him with all your heart" (Deut. 11:13), the rabbis commented "What is service of the heart? This is prayer" (Ta'an 2a). "Service" *(avodah)* in this context is connected with the Temple and its worship, for which prayer is seen as a substitute. On the other hand, the saying of R. Eleazar that prayer is dearer to God than good works and sacrifices (Ber. 32b), though hyperbolic, may nonetheless be intended to express the real superiority of prayer. Possibly, the tension in this matter is to be perceived in the two reasons given for the statutory prayers of the day. According to one opinion, these were ordained by the patriarchs, while another view has it that they correspond to the perpetual offerings in Temple times (Ber. 26b).

The obligation of offering up prayer, though supported by a scriptural verse, is considered to be rabbinic, not biblical. Prayers are to be recited three times a day: morning, afternoon, and night.[59] In addition to the statutory prayers and private prayers of various kinds, public prayers were offered in times of distress; prayers for rain, for instance, in times of drought (Ta'an 2:1–5).

In the rabbinic world-view and hierarchy of values prayer stands so high that even God Himself is pictured as praying (Ber. 6aff.), His prayer being that His mercy might overcome His judgment. Nevertheless, the study of the Torah occupies a higher rung than prayer, and some scholars, whose main occupation was study, seem only to have prayed periodically.[60] Indee in one instance, a rabbi who spent too much time on his prayers was rebuked by his colleague for neglecting eternal life to engage in temporal existence (Shab. 10a). Likewise communal prayer is held to be of greater significance than private prayer[61] and too much reflection on one's prayers in the expectation that these will be answered is to be discouraged (Ber. 32b). In addition prayer should be offered with proper concentration *(kavvanah)* on the words uttered in God's presence. R. Eliezer said: "He that makes his prayer a fixed task, his prayer is not supplication." R. Simeon b. Nethanel said: ". . . and when thou prayest make not the prayer a fixed form, but (a plea for) mercies and supplications before God." One way of avoiding the deadening familiarity of a "fixed form" was to recite a new prayer each day. When R. Eliezer was asked by his disciples to teach them the ways of life that they might learn them and by following them attain the life of the world to come, part of his reply was: "When you pray, know before Whom you stand."[62]

Just as not every prayer is answered, so not every prayer is valid. A prayer for God to change the past, for instance, is a "vain prayer" (Ber. 9:3). The impossibility of God answering every prayer addressed to Him is acknowledged in the account of the prayer of the high priest on the Day of Atonement who used to pray before the rainy season that the prayers of the travelers who required fair weather should not be allowed to enter God's presence (Yoma 53b). So a man should not only pray for himself but should also think of others, using the plural form "grant us" rather than the singular "grant me" (Ber. 29b–30a). Thus, for example, if a man needs something for himself but prays to God to grant that very thing to his neighbor who also needs it, such an unselfish prayer causes God to grant him his wish first (BK 92a). Man should never despair of offering supplication to God "even if a sharp sword rests upon his neck" (Ber. 10a). In praising God, man should be circumspect, using only the standard forms of praise found in Scripture and established for use in prayer. Prayers of thanksgiving, particularly in the form of the benediction *(berakhah),* are repeatedly enjoined by the rabbis, as well as praise of God for His wondrous works and the marvelous beings He has created.[63]

A fundamental belief in Judaism is that prayers are to be addressed directly to God. R. Judah said that if a human being is in trouble and wishes to invoke the aid of his patron he must first stand at the door and call out to a servant or a member of the patron's family and he may or may not be allowed to enter. But it is otherwise with God. God says, "When a man is in trouble, do not cry out to the angel Michael or to the angel Gabriel but to Me and I will answer immediately" (TJ, Ber. 9:1, 13a). In addition, some men were renowned for their capacity to pray and to have their prayers answered, so that even great scholars, less gifted in this direction, would ask these saints to pray on their behalf and a number of miracle tales are told to illustrate the immediacy of God's response to the prayers of such men.[64]

In Medieval Thought and Hasidism

In the medieval period, although Jewish thinkers profoundly considered most major theological problems, there is surprisingly little discussion in their writings of the intellectual difficulties involved in prayer. One of the few discussions as to why prayer should be necessary, since God knows man's needs, is that of Joseph Albo.[65] Albo notes that the act of turning to God in prayer is itself one of the conditions upon which God's help depends, just as it depends on other forms of human effort. Thus prayer is essential.

Maimonides' view is a corollary of his more general position. Thus prayer is an essential element of the divine-human relationship. True to his doctrine of theological negation, he holds that in the standard liturgy one may use only those divine attributes in prayer which have been ordained by the "prophets," and he is therefore opposed to the indiscriminate writing of hymns[66] and additional prayers. Moreover, in spite of the talmudic statement that the obligation to pray is of rabbinic origin *(mi-de-rabbanan),* Maimonides observes that this only applies to the number, form, and times of prayer, and that in fact it is a biblical duty for the Jew to pray daily.[67]

One aspect of prayer that the medievals did devote special attention to was the question of inwardness and intention while praying, indicated by the Hebrew term *kavvanah*. This concern with the need for adequate concentration in prayer *(kavvanah)* is part of the more general tendency prevalent among medieval Jewish thinkers to stress greater inwardness in religious life. Baḥya ibn Paquda,[68] for example, remarks that prayer without concentration is like a body without a soul or a husk without a kernel. Similarly, Maimonides' definition of *kavvanah* reads: "*Kavvanah* means that a man should empty his mind of all other thoughts and regard himself as if he were standing before the Divine **Presence**."[69]

As compared to the concerns of the medieval philosophers, the kabbalists stress the difficulty of petitionary prayer to a God who is unchanging. In keeping with their basic metaphysical position they advance the view that prayer cannot, in fact, be offered to God as He is in Himself *(Ein-Sof)*, but only to God as He is manifested in the ten divine potencies (the *Sefirot*). God Himself is, therefore, not entreated directly to show mercy for example, but prayer is directed to God as He is manifested in the *Sefirah* of loving-kindness. As a result of the power of man's prayer, this divine potency might function on earth. There were serious problems raised by this account and the magical nature of kabbalistic prayer and the dangers of setting up the *Sefirot* as divine intermediaries were the topic of much subsequent debate.[70] One of the major deviations of the kabbalists, in fact, was their substitution for the older doctrine of *kavvanah* a new concept of special intentions *(kavvanot)* i.e., meditations on the realm of *Sefirot*. Instead of concentrating on the plain meaning of the prayers, the kabbalist dwells on the realm of divine potencies and directs his mind, when reciting the words, to the supernal mysteries which govern and are controlled by them.[71]

In Ḥasidism, the kabbalistic type of *kavvanot* yields to a far more emotional involvement and attachment *(devekut)* to God. "The metamorphosis which took place in the meaning of *kavvanot* at the advent of Ḥasidism, and more explicitly after the Great Maggid (Dov Baer of Mezhirech), consists in this—that an originally intellectual effort of meditation and contemplation had become an intensely emotional and highly enthusiastic act."[72] In Ḥasidism, prayer is a mystical encounter with the Divine, the heart leaping in ecstasy to its Source. Violent movements in prayer were not unusual; some of the ḥasidic groups even encouraged their followers to turn somersaults during their prayers.[73]

Prayer is frequently seen in Ḥasidism as man's most important religious activity. R. Shneur Zalman of Lyady, the founder of the intellectual Ḥabad sect in Hasidism, writes: "For although the forms of the

prayers and the duty of praying three times a day are rabbinic, the idea
of prayer is the foundation of the whole Torah. This means that man
knows God, recognizing His greatness and His splendor with a serene
and whole mind, and an understanding heart. Man should reflect on
these ideas until his rational soul is awakened to love God, to cleave to
Him, and to His Torah, and to desire His commandments."[74]

In Ḥabad Ḥasidism, the true meaning of prayer is contemplation on
the kabbalistic scheme whereby God's infinite light proceeds through
the whole chain of being, from the highest to the lowest. Man should
reflect on this until his heart is moved in rapture, but he should not
engage in prayer for the sake of the pleasure such rapture will bring
him; he must take care not to confuse authentic ecstasy with artificial
spiritual titillation.[75] Many ḥasidic groups, otherwise strictly conformist,
disregarded the laws governing prayer at fixed times on the grounds
that these interfere with the need for adequate preparation and with the
spontaneity which is part of the prayer's essence.

In the Modern Period

In the modern period the most prominent features of the discussion
about prayer have been concerned with the reform of the classical
liturgy and its attendant problems. In fact, Reform Judaism, as Jacob
Petuchowski has noted in his valuable work *Prayerbook Reform in
Europe,* "made its first appearance on the stage of Jewish history as a
movement for liturgical reform."[76] The aim of this reform of the liturgy
was part of the wider aim of adapting and modernizing Judaism to the
prevailing conditions of the time. Foremost and most common among
the changes were a shortening of the liturgy, the dropping of most of the
traditional *piyyutim* (liturgical poetical prayers), the use of the vernacular (in most cases this was German in the first instance), and most
radically, the elimination of all references to the sacrificial cult and a
personal Messiah, the ingathering of the exiles, and the rebuilding and
return to Zion—all three being theologically unacceptable to the general
Reform outlook. In addition, it became accepted practice to introduce
an organ, a mixed choir, mixed seating, and a sermon in the vernacular.

These alterations were justified on the grounds that the sacrificial
system represented a more primitive stage of religious development inappropriate to the modern period; that few Jews desired to return to
Israel and most were satisfied to remain in their present lands; that in

any case Judaism and Jews were a religion not a people, and that the belief in a personal Messiah was an unjustified dogma inappropriate for rational men. The specific reforms of the liturgy and use of the vernacular, and other innovations were defended on the grounds that the synagogue service was a human creation and therefore open to change in accordance with changing historical situations.

Since the 19th-century reforms, various events, especially the Holocaust and recreation of the State of Israel, have altered the Reform position generally, and their liturgy specifically, so that today it is an accepted part of the Reform service to include prayers for the State of Israel and to be more positive regarding all the traditional folk elements of the liturgy which had earlier been rejected.

Related to the reform of the liturgy was the dramatic change in the role of women in the synagogue in Reform, and more recently in American Conservative Judaism. It is now accepted in both movements that women can be called to *aliyot* and generally can take a full and equal part in the public synagogue ritual and liturgy.

In addition to the question of reform, modern Jewish thinkers have also been concerned with questions of the nature and efficacy of prayer. Foremost among these is the philosophical question whether petitionary prayer is efficacious, a question which is already well known and much discussed in all the earlier phases and ages of the Jewish tradition.

The majority of modern opinion tries to answer this question by reinterpreting it. That is to say, most modern authors deny the efficacy of petitionary prayer in a direct cause-and-effect manner; they have attempted, instead, to reformulate the understanding of prayer as being not so much a request for favors as an act of existential communication between man and God, and between man and man. Prayer is also regarded as a means of confession, obedience, and an attempt to create a parallelism between the Divine and human will.

This view of prayer has been formulated in a variety of ways by different figures in the 20th century. In 1918 Kaufman Kohler in his *Jewish Theology* argued that prayer was primarily concerned with altering humanity's attitude, not God's: "Self-expression before God in prayer thus has a double effect: it strengthens faith in God's love and kindness, as well as his all-wise and bountiful prescience. But it also chastens the desires and feelings of man, teaching him to banish from his heart all thoughts of self-seeking and sin, and to raise himself toward the purity and freedom of the divine will and demand."[77] More recently, in the same vein, J. Petuchowski has argued: "Petitionary prayer is a human need rather than something required by God ... (through prayer) man was afforded an opportunity of rehearsing his wants and his concerns before God. It was the genius of Judaism to turn man's petitionary prayers into a praise of God."[78]

The existentialists have favored the view that prayer is primarily dialogue and communication between God and humankind and is not petitionary in the traditional sense. The precursor of this fully articulated, dialogical interpretation of prayer is to be found in the final sections of Hermann Cohen's last work, *Die Religion der Vernunft.* Here Cohen speaks of prayer as a longing: "The desire of the prayer for God is a search for God ..." Cohen understands prayer as the act of reconciliation between the individual and God and he calls prayer a "dialogical monologue": "The lyrical confession has to sing the monologue as a dialogue. The soul unites both persons of the dialogue; for the soul is really God-given, therefore it is not exclusively human soul. Thus, it may seek God and talk with him."[79]

Franz Rosenzweig and Martin Buber develop this dialogical notion of prayer to some extent though neither offers any major analysis. It remained for Abraham Joshua Heschel to express this view most forcefully. He first developed it in a paper read to the Rabbinical Assembly of America in 1953 and continued to treat this theme in later related papers, returning to it in a moving presentation to the same rabbinical body in 1969. In this later presentation Heschel expressed the essence of his (and other existentialists') position thus: "Prayer is exceedingly urgent, exceedingly relevant, or inane and useless. Our first task is to learn to comprehend why prayer is an ontological necessity. God is hiding, and. man is defying. Every moment God is creating and self-concealing. Prayer is disclosing, or at least preventing, irreversible concealing. God is ensconced in mystery, hidden in depths. Prayer is pleading with God to come out of the depths. 'Out of the depths have I called Thee, O Lord.' "[80] This dialogical position has been characterized by Louis Jacobs as a "supernaturalistic position." Jacobs "unashamedly adopts the religious supernaturalistic position and believes it to be the only one true to the Jewish attitude."[81]

Alternatively, there has been a more radical reinterpretation of prayer among those aligned with Mordecai Kaplan's reconstructionist position and religious naturalism generally. This group has argued that prayer is not an address to a personal God but rather an attempt to attune oneself to those powers in the universe which make for human fulfillment and a reaching out to those forces in nature which encourage the development of man's own highest potentials. An important version of this naturalistic position was presented by Eugene Kohn to the same 1953 session of the Rabbinical Assembly which heard Heschel's defense of a dialogical account. Kohn defended the naturalistic position as follows: "Many people find prayer difficult because, having rejected the idea that God is a transcendent person, they feel that prayer cannot be addressed to God, that at best it is a form of talking to oneself. But the term 'self' has more than one meaning. It may be used in the sense of the 'ego,' the source of egoism and selfishness, or in the sense of the 'soul,' the transcendent aspect of the Divine Nature. When we seek communion with God, it is not important whether we address God in the second person as Thou, or think of God in the third person. What is important is that we keep our conception of God before us, and that we endeavour to bring our thoughts and our desires into harmony with our idea of God."[82]

Kohn's position, however, has not found wide acceptance. In replying to it Heschel gave expression to the main objection of most Jewish scholars to this naturalistic reinterpretation when he commented: "When you pray know before Whom you stand." "*Before Whom.* To have said before *what* would have contradicted the spirit of Jewish prayer. *What* is the most indefinite pronoun. In asking *what,* one is totally uncommitted, uninitiated, bare of any anticipation of an answer: any answer may be acceptable. But he who is totally uncommitted, who does not even have the inkling of an answer, has not learned the meaning of the ultimate question, and is not ready to engage in prayer. If God is a *what,* a power, the sum total of values, how could one pray to it? An 'I' does not pray to an 'it'. Unless, therefore, God is at least as real as my own self; unless I am sure that God has at least as much life as I do, how could I pray?"[83]

There is no question that many modern men find prayer difficult no matter how one understands this concept. Yet, recently there has been renewed interest in prayer, especially among certain radical Jewish youth groups and *chavorot* who see prayer as both mystical communion and as a way of expressing their humanity and Jewishness.

Kiddush Ha-Shem

The antithetical terms *kiddush ha-Shem* ("sanctification of the [Divine] Name") and *hillul ha-Shem* ("defamation of the [Divine] Name") are opposingly complementary and denote the two aspects of one of the most significant concepts in Judaism. They imply, respectively, the glorification of the God of Israel and the diminution of His honor. The specific terms are rabbinic; the concepts themselves, however, are biblical in origin and are included among the 613 commandments: "Ye shall keep My commandments and do them: I am the Lord. Ye shall not profane My holy Name; but I will be hallowed among the children of Israel; I am the Lord who hallow you" (Lev. 22:31, 32). The entire people was subject to these principles, although the priests were especially cautioned to avoid *hillul ha-Shem*.[1]

Two patterns of thought are discernible in the biblical conception of *kiddush ha-Shem* and *hillul ha-Shem*. One considers God as the primary actor, while Israel remains passive; the other regards the Israelites as the initiators of either the sanctification or the desecration of God's Name. The first is fully crystallized in Ezekiel[2] for whom the sanctification of the Name is essentially an act of the Lord bestowed upon Israel before the onlooking nations of the world. The Name is sanctified when God wondrously redeems Israel and the gentiles behold the vindication of the divine promise and are moved to worship Him. Conversely, if the Lord visits privation or exile upon Israel, or suffers the people to remain in captivity, the nations question God's strength or faithfulness, and the Name is thus defamed. This general understanding holds true for Ezekiel and for most instances of *kiddush ha-Shem* in the Pentateuch.

According to the second view, man is responsible for God's honor in the eyes of the world. Moses and Aaron were punished because of their failure to sanctify God's Name which must be sanctified not only before

248

the gentiles but in the eyes of Israel as well.[3] Jeremiah accuses his countrymen of profaning God's Name when they circumvent the law and emancipate their slaves only to capture and enslave them again (34:16) while Amos condemned extortion from the poor and immorality as *ḥillul ha-Shem* (2:7). The rabbinic tradition laid more emphasis on the personal-ethical than on the national-redemptive significance of the concept. It developed especially the second view of the biblical theme: human initiative, and a wider designation so as to include Jews as well as non-Jews. *Kiddush ha-Shem* could even be performed in private with no one present, as in the case of Joseph who, by restraining himself in the face of temptation, fulfilled the sanctification of God's Name (Sot. 36b). This does not mean that the rabbis entirely ignored *kiddush ha-Shem* and *ḥillul ha-Shem* as divine acts. When God decided to visit destruction indiscriminately on both the righteous and the wicked of Sodom, Abraham protested that this would be *ḥillul ha-Shem*.[4] Similarly, were God to have permitted Absalom to slay his father David, His Name would have been publicly profaned (Sanh. 107a), while the punishment of the righteous for their sins, relative to their own high standards, is divine *kiddush ha-Shem*.[5]

The sanctification of God's Name before gentiles was always a potent element in the folk understanding of the concept. The rabbis, however, for the most part, concerned themselves with the active role of man in the drama of bestowing glory upon, or detracting from, the honor of God. This human initiative in *kiddush ha-Shem* could be consummated in three different ways: martyrdom, exemplary ethical conduct, and prayer.

The readiness to sanctify God's Name has its most dramatic expression in the willingness to die a martyr, and since tannaitic times the term *kiddush ha-Shem* has also denoted martyrdom. When a person willingly suffers death rather than violate one of three specific commandments (idolatry; unchastity; murder) he achieves *kiddush ha-Shem;* if he fails to do so in these cases, or in other instances where the *halakhah* demands martyrdom, he is guilty of *ḥillul ha-Shem*.[6] On the verses, "Ye shall not profane My holy Name, . . . I am the Lord who hallow you, brought you out of the land of Egypt, to be your God: I am the Lord," the rabbis taught: "On this condition did I bring you out of the land of Egypt that you submit yourselves to sanctify My Name, that I be your God even by force; I the Lord am faithful to grant you your reward."[7]

God and the Jew

Since the second century, "to die for the sanctification of the Name" has been the accepted idiom for dying a martyr's death. A martyr was, appropriately, called a *kadosh,* one who is holy, and a child, growing up in the Jewish tradition, was made receptive to the concept of martyrdom as a religious ideal. From his earliest youth he was exposed to stories about martyrs, e.g., Hannah and her seven sons, R. Akiva and the ten martyrs; the latter in the form of a lamentation is part of the synagogue service on the Day of Atonement and on the Ninth of Av. Hananiah, Mishael, and Azariah (Dan. 3) are held up by the rabbis as models of conduct in the sanctification of the Name (Pes. 53b).

The concept of *kiddush ha-Shem* has always been implicit in the Judaic faith and view of life. Its first explicit expression occurred during the confrontation of Judaism with Hellenism, the first pagan culture with "missionary" and synthesizing tendencies. The Book of Daniel tells about the three "Jewish men"—Shadrach, Meshach, and Abed-Nego—who disobeyed a royal command to worship an idol and endangered their lives. Under Antiochus Epiphanes (came to power in 175 B.C.E.) Hellenization employed violent and coercive methods in regard to Jews, causing the Hasmonean rebellion of 167 B.C.E. After the victorious revolt of the Hasmoneans, a Jew in the Hellenistic Diaspora recorded the martyrdom of an old man, little children, and their mother who had died for their faith:

"Eleazar, one of the principal scribes, . . . of a noble countenance, was compelled to eat swine's flesh . . . Now those in charge of that forbidden sacrificial feast took the man aside, for the sake of old acquaintance, and privately urged him to bring some flesh of his own providing, such as he was lawfully allowed to use, and to pretend he was really eating of the sacrifice which the king had ordered, so that in this way he might escape death and be kindly treated for the sake of their old friendship. But he with a high resolve, worthy of his years and of the dignity of his descent . . . and, still more, of the holy laws divinely ordained, spoke his mind accordingly: '. . . It ill becomes our years to dissemble,' said he, 'and thus lead many younger persons to imagine that Eleazar in his ninetieth year has gone over to a heathenish religion . . . for the mere sake of enjoying this brief and momentary life . . . Even were I for the moment to evade the punishment of men, I should not escape the hands of the Almighty in life or in death . . . I will . . . leave behind me a noble example to the young how to die willingly and nobly on behalf of our reverend and holy laws.' With these words he stepped forward at once to the instrument of torture, while those who a moment before had been friendly turned against him, deeming his language to be that of a sheer madman . ... Under the strokes of torture, he groaned out: 'The Lord who has holy knowledge understandeth that, although I might have been freed from death, I endure cruel pains in my body from scourging and suffer this gladly in my soul, because I fear Him."[8]

The basic ideals motivating *kiddush ha-Shem* are thus set out at this early stage: personal nobility and courage, a categorical refusal to employ any form of dissimulation or live an undercover existence, and readiness to undergo bodily and spiritual torture in the full knowledge that this behavior may appear sheer madness to those who inflict it. Hannah, "the mother of the Maccabees" according to Christian tradition, exhorts her seven sons in a similar way not to be afraid of either hangmen or death. These figures became the prototypes for and symbols of martyrdom and martyrs in both Judaism and Christianity. The Fourth Book of Maccabees is almost entirely a philosophical sermon on the meaning and glory of *kiddush ha-Shem* in Hellenistic times.

Whereas in the Christian and Muslim interpretation martyrdom became an act of mainly individuals, the lot of saints chosen by God for their individual path of suffering—and (in Christianity) their participation in the mystery of Crucifixion, the martyred saints following Christ on the cross—in Judaism *kiddush ha-Shem* remained a task set for each and every Jew to fulfill if the appropriate moment came. It found logical expresion in the readiness to die as a son of the Chosen People. In the war against Rome of 66–70/73, whole communities commited suicide as a culmination of their fight against alien power. Thus, in the many trials of revolt and war in which Jews were tested, from the wars of liberation of the Maccabees up to the failure of the revolts against the Romans both in Erez Israel and the Diaspora, *kiddush ha-Shem* acted as a motivating force giving meaning to the struggle of the Jewish warriors, strength of endurance under cruel torture by victors, and offering suicide as a way out of submission and slavery. The famous mass suicide at Masada was inspired more by the conception of *kiddush ha-Shem* as a commandment, and a proud refusal to submit to the Roman enemy, than by the philosophical argumentations that Josephus put in the mouths of the defenders of Masada.

As if referring to an everyday, ordinary incident, one of the *tannaim* describes "those who dwell in the land of Israel and risk their lives for the sake of the commandments: 'Why are you being led out to be decapitated?' 'Because I circumcised my son to be an Israelite.' 'Why are you being led out to be burned?' 'Because I read the Torah.' 'Why are you being led out to be crucified?' 'Because I ate the unleavened bread.' 'Why are you getting a hundred lashes?' 'Because I performed the ceremony of the *lulav*.' These wounds caused me to be beloved of my Father in heaven."[9] They were conscious that this behavior appeared strange to the gentiles who asked the Jews: What is the nature of your God that "you are so ready to die for Him, and so ready to let yourselves be killed for Him ... you are handsome, you are mighty, come and intermingle with us."[10]

At the famous rabbinical council in Lydda (second century), the laws of martyrdom were formulated. *Kiddush ha-Shem* was declared obligatory in the case of three commandments and a person was expected to suffer death rather than violate them. The three nontransgressible cardinal commandments are idolatry, unchastity (*gillui arayot:* including incest, adultery, and, under certain circumstances, any infraction of the moral code), and murder (Sanh. 74a). Alternatively, one should violate all other commandments rather than suffer death. Should a Jew, however, in the presence of ten other Jews, be coerced into transgressing these other laws in order to demonstrate his apostasy, he must sanctify God's Name and choose death. If ten Jews are not present, he should transgress rather than be killed. These rules hold for "normal" times. In times of religious persecution of the entire community, however, one must choose to die for *kiddush ha-Shem* even if no other Israelites are present, and one man must not violate any commandment, including minor customs which are distinctively Jewish.[11]

Martyrdom rather than violation, when transgression is permissible, became a point of discussion; the *halakhah* had to decide between two opposing principles—that of sanctifying God's Name versus that of preserving life ("and he shall live by them" [Lev. 18:5], i.e., the commandments). According to Maimonides, a person who chose *kiddush ha-Shem* where the law decides for life is culpable; others consider such voluntary martyrdom praiseworthy.[12] The Ashkenazi talmudists were instinctual rather than rationalistic in their attitude to martyrdom—an attitude characteristic of most of medieval German Jewry. The tosafists reacted negatively to the problem as it is viewed in the *halakhah*. They recoiled—"Heaven forbid!"—from such formal halakhic reasoning that does not require martyrdom of a person forced to worship an idol in private, and they demanded obligatory *kiddush ha-Shem*.[13]

Among modern halakhic authorities, the question whether an individual should sacrifice his life in order to save the entire community is a point of contention. Rabbi A. I. Kook considered it obligatory as an emergency measure, while others regarded such action as meritorious but not mandatory.[14] The problem arose often during the Holocaust in Europe. In one typical responsum of this period, the question was asked whether (considering the danger to the emissary who might be imprisoned and killed) a particular rabbi should accept his mission of approaching the Lithuanian henchmen of the Nazi authorities in Kovno in 1941 in order to release certain Jews. The answer was that he may not be ordered to accept the mission but he should do so as an act of piety; he did, and subsequently survived.[15]

The sages of the Talmud were divided in their opinions as to whether gentiles are required to sanctify God's Name. Abbaye held that a non-Jew who is forced to violate one of the seven Noachide laws is not obligated to suffer *kiddush ha-Shem;* Rava maintained that he is (Sanh. 74b). The accepted ruling is that non-Jews are not required to sanctify the Name.[16] According to some authorities, however, a gentile must perform *kiddush ha-Shem* rather than be forced to commit murder.

The ideal of man's initiative in sanctifying God's Name beyond the strict requirements of the law was developed by rabbinic tradition in the area of ethical conduct. When Simeon b. Shetaḥ bought an ass from an Arab and his servants were delighted at finding a jewel hanging from his neck, he at once returned the gem to its owner, who cried out, "Blessed be the God of the Jews Who renders His people so scrupulous in their dealings with other men."[17] Joshua kept his oath to the Gibeonites, though they exacted it from him by fraud (Git. 46a). In addition, moral acts such as Joseph's restraint in the face of temptation and Judah's public confession of his relations with Tamar are also considered *kiddush ha-Shem* (Sot. 10b).

The designation of an unethical act as *ḥillul ha-Shem* likewise proved a powerful deterrent. The punishment for such is immediate, even if the sin was unintentional (Shab. 33a); it is the most heinous of all sins for which only death can atone.[18] According to R. Akiva, there is no forgiveness at all for it (ARN 39).

In the Talmud, the concepts of *kiddush ha-Shem* and *ḥillul ha-Shem* are discussed with reference to stealing from a non-Jew (BK 113a–b). According to R. Akiva, the law itself prohibits this, and thus protects all property, whether of a Jew or non-Jew. R. Ishmael, however, holds that biblical law applies formally only to the relation of Jews with fellow Jews. The protection of non-Jews, therefore, requires a supplementary principle, that of *kiddush ha-Shem*. Hence, ethical perfection beyond the minimum standards of the law itself becomes law, that of sanctifying the Name: reflecting honor upon God and the Torah by striving for moral excellence. Although medieval talmudists almost unanimously decided in favor of R. Akiva, they had to use the themes of *kiddush ha-Shem* and *ḥillul ha-Shem* to plug occasional loopholes in the formal law. They often cited the Tosefta (BK 10:15) that stealing from a non-Jew is a worse crime than stealing from a Jew, since the former includes *ḥillul ha-Shem* as well as "ye shall not steal."

Above the normal requirements of the doctrine *kiddush ha-Shem* imposes special standards of conduct on the scholar. He must, for instance, pay his debts promptly, never cause embarrassment to his colleagues, not walk four cubits without *tallit* or *tefillin,* and not overindulge in merrymaking.[19]

While the ethical motive is quite strong in *kiddush ha-Shem,* the latter should not be interpreted exclusively as moral didacticism toward others. *Kiddush ha-Shem* includes martyrdom for any of a number of reasons: refusing to worship an idol, under certain conditions circumcising one's son or studying Torah or abiding by the dietary laws. In all these cases, it is not necessarily a question of performance in the presence of non-Jews. The *halakhah* considers any consciously rebellious act against God as *ḥillul ha-Shem.*[20] The principal motif of *kiddush ha-Shem* is religious and this includes the ethical dimension; the aim of the latter is not so much to teach the world morality as to increase the respect of the world for the morality of Judaism.[21] Principally, *kiddush ha-Shem* seeks to demonstrate to Jew and non-Jew alike the power of the Jewish commitment to God and to Torah.

Kiddush ha-Shem also found expression in prayer; this took two forms. One was in a liturgical declaration of readiness to accept martyrdom if necessary: "'Nay, but for Thy sake are we killed all the day; we are accounted as sheep for the slaughter' (Ps. 44:23). Is it then possible to be 'killed all the day?' When one takes upon himself to sanctify His great Name every day, he is accounted as 'sheep for the slaughter'" (Sif. Deut. 6:5). Similarly, when reciting the *Shema* a person must spiritually have the intention of offering himself for *kiddush ha-Shem*.[22] Second, the recital of the prayer is itself regarded as an act of sanctification of God's Name. A number of such liturgical expressions of *kiddush ha-Shem* have been found in the Talmudic mystical Merkabah literature.[23]

Two formal prayers stand out in this respect: the *Kedushah* and the *Kaddish*. The *Kedushah* is based on the Song of the Seraphs in Isaiah 6:1–3. The more esoteric *Kedushah*, recited before the *Shema*, refers to the praise of God by the angels, while the *Kedushah* of the *Amidah* (the Eighteen Benedictions) prayer speaks of Israel sanctifying God's Name. The latter is parallel to and perhaps surpasses the *Kedushah* of the angels, adding a cosmic element to the theme of *kiddush ha-Shem*. The Zohar (Lev. 93a) considers the key verse "I will be hallowed among the children of Israel" (Lev. 22:32) as the source and warrant for the *Kedushah*.

In the *Kaddish*, the key parts refer quite literally to the "sanctification" of the "Name." At a comparatively early period, the *Kaddish* was already ascribed to the biblical source of *kiddush ha-Shem*.[24] The absence of any specific Divine Name in this prayer, and the emphasis on the "Name" as such, has been thought by some scholars to have been deliberate, in order to emphasize its idiomatic affinity to the biblical *"kiddush ha-Shem."* It has been suggested that the *Kaddish* was originally recited by martyrs who, at the threshold of death, declared the sanctification of God's Name and consoled the bereaved onlookers by speaking of the redemption and the Messiah "in your lifetime and in your days."[25]

PART IV

NOTES

Notes to Part I

¹ This conception of God is built up from the following sources, presented in the order of the ideas in our discussion. We begin with God's unity as discussed in Deut. 6:4; Isa. 45:21, 46:9; Ex. 20:3–5; Isa. 45:2; Ezek. 28:2ff; Gen. 14:18–22; Num. 25:2–3; Isa. 40:18; Ex. 20:4; Deut. 4:35; Isa. 40:13; Zech. 4:6.

² This conception of God is built up from the following biblical sources, presented in the order of the ideas in our discussion. We begin with the theophanies that accompanied God's revelation and presence in Ex. 19:18, 20:15; Hab. 3:4ff; Job 42:2, 41:2, 28:23ff; Isa. 43:9; Ps. 36:10; Ex. 28:3; Ps. 139:7–12; Jer. 33:25; Isa. 40:6–8, 44:6; Ps. 90:2; Isa. 41:4; Mal. 3:6; II Sam. 22:32. For more details on these biblical themes see Y. Kaufmann's *Toledot ha-Emunah ha-Yisre'elit,* 4 vols. (1937–1957); a one-volume English summary is available: *The Religion of Israel* (1960). See also U. Cassuto's *Commentary on Genesis* (1964).

³ See Y. Kaufmann, *Religion of Israel* (1960), 68.

⁴ See Y. Kaufmann, *Toledot ha-Emunah ha-Yisre'elit* (1937), vol. 1.

⁵ Cf. also N. H. Tur-Sinai, in *EM,* 3 (1958), 593.

⁶ Theories trying to relate the Jewish Sabbath to Assyro-Babylonian *sabbattu* or *sapattu* are discussed in U. Cassuto, *From Adam to Noah* (1961), 65–9, and in R. De Vaux, *Ancient Israel* (1965), 475–483; also see bibliography.

⁷ These aspects of the divine governance of history are presented in the Bible in the order in which the ideas are raised in our discussion, beginning with governance of the world in righteousness stated in Ps. 96:13; Ps. 33:16; Ps. 76:10; Isa. 57:15; Gen. 15:16; Num. 14:34; Dan. 9:24; Ps. 68:2. Cf. also M. D. Cassuto in: *Tarbiz* 12 (1941), 1–27 (in Hebrew).

⁸ See the essay on "Covenant" in the section "God and the Jew" in this volume. See also the works listed in the bibliography on "Covenant."

⁹ On the universality of the prohibition against murder, etc., see Gen. 6:12–13; 9:5; 20:3; 39:9; Amos 1:3ff.

¹⁰ These anti-Halakhic sentiments quoted are from Isa. 1:11–15; Jer. 7:22; 7:4; Ps. 50:8–13; Micah 6:8; Hosea 2:21–22; Amos 5:14; Isa. 1:17.

¹¹ The Law vs. Morality interpretation of the Torah, and especially of the

259

Prophets, is essentially a Christian exegetical procedure based on Christian and christological necessities. For a thoroughly Jewish perspective, see A. J. Heschel, *The Prophets* (1962). See also the articles on "Prophets and Prophecy" in the *Encyclopaedia Judaica,* 13 (1971), 1150–1181.

[12] These four human protests against the Divine are from Gen. 18:25; Ex. 5:22; Jer. 12:1; Ps. 22:2.

[13] "It is certain because it is impossible," Tertullian, *De Carne Christi,* 5. This decidedly anti-rationalistic stance has a sustained and outstanding lineage in Christian thought. Elements in Paul, Tertullian, Augustine, Luther, Kierkegaard and twentieth-century Christian existentialists express this perspective. In Jewish thought there is no comparable anti-rationalist tradition. One might reasonably speculate that this difference can be traced back to the demands made by an Incarnational and Trinitarian theology, which by the Church's own tradition is necessarily and inescapably paradoxical and "mysterious."

[14] For more on this question of Pharaoh, see J. H. Hertz, *Commentary on the Pentateuch; Exodus.* See also L. Ginzberg, *Legends of the Jews,* 7 (1938), 368–70, s.v. index.

[15] See Sotah 35A for a similar view. Cf. also Ps. 50:12. For a different explanation see Kimḥi on II Samuel 6:6.

[16] For more on this essential issue in biblical, philosophical and theological language about God, see the separate discussion of "anthropomorphism" below. For the relation of God and man, see the discussion below on "Man in the Bible" and "Judaism," among others.

[17] For the use of these analogies in rabbinic literature see, for example, Sif. Deut. 341; Gen. R. 12:12; Mid. Ps. 23 to 24:1; Gen. R. 39:1.

[18] For the use of these analogies in rabbinic literature, see, for example, Mid. Ps. to 103; Lev. R. 4:3.

[19] See, for example, the rightfully famous story of "Akhnai's stove" recorded in Baba Meẓia 59 a–b.

[20] For a detailed account of medieval Jewish philosophy the reader is referred to S. Katz (ed.), *Jewish Philosophers* (1975). The reader should also consult the relevant sections of the histories of Jewish philosophy listed in the bibliography. Specifically for the "proofs for the existence of God" see H. A. Wolfson, in: *HUCA,* 1 (1924), 575–596.

[21] See Saadiah Gaon, *Sefer Emunot ve-Deot* (Book of Beliefs and Opinions), English translation (1948), Ch. 146, *Sha'ar Yiḥud.*

[22] See Baḥya Ibn Pakuda, *Ḥovot Ha-Levavot* (Duties of the Heart), English translation (1974), Ch. 6.

[23] See Levi ben Gershom, *Milḥamot Adonai* (ed. 1866), Bk. V Pt. 3, Chs. 4–6, 247–268.

[24] See Saadiah Gaon, *Sefer Emunot ve-Deot,* Treatise 1, ch. 2, p. 46f.

[25] See Maimonides, *Guide* (English translation by S. Pines, 1963), Pt. II, Ch. 1.

[26] See Abraham Ibn Daud, *Emunah Ramah* (ed. S. Weil, 1852).

[27] Maimonides, *Guide,* Pt. II, Ch. 1.

[28] Ḥasdai Crescas, *Or Adonai,* Bk. II, Pt. III, Ch. 2, 40b–41a.

[29] This was perhaps the most popular of all specifically Jewish arguments for the existence of God, for it not only "proved" God's existence, but even more importantly in the face of medieval inter-religious polemics, it "proved" the trustworthiness and authenticity of Judaism.

[30] For a clear analysis of this "negative" approach to the attributes of God, see Zvi Diesendruck's paper on the employment of this approach by Maimonides, in: *PAAJR,* IV (1934). For a general treatment of the problem of Divine attributes in medieval Jewish philosophy see the discussion "Attributes of God" in this section.

[31] On this view of positive Divine attributes see Crescas' *Or Adonai,* 1:3; Levi ben Gershom, *Milḥamot Adonai* 3:3; J. Albo, *Sefer ha-Ikkarim* II:22.

[32] See M. Cordovero, *Tomer Devorah* (The Palm Tree of Deborah), English translation (1960); *Pardes Rimmonim* (1592); *Elimah Rabbati* (1881). On Ḥabad, see Shneur Zalman of Liady, *Tanya* (English translation, 1964–66). For more details see G. Scholem, *Major Trends* (1961).

[33] See Abraham ben Isaac of Granada, *Berit Menuḥah,* Amsterdam, 1648. This edition however is very poor.

[34] See Menaḥem Azariah da Fano (1548–1620), *Asarah Ma'amarot* (Venice, 1597).

[35] There is an inadequate English translation of the *Zohar* (it is not complete) by H. Sperling and M. Simon (1931–34).

[36] For a more detailed account of Jewish mystical doctrines, see G. Sholem's books cited in the Bibliography at the end of this book.

[37] Mendelssohn's view is most clearly stated in his *Jerusalem* (English translation by A. Jospe, 1969) and in his *Morgenstunden.* Readers are referred to A. Altmann's biography, *Moses Mendelssohn: A Biographical Study* (1973). Discussions of Mendelssohn's views will also be found in Katz, *Jewish Philosophers* and J. Guttman, *Philosophies of Judaism* (English translation, 1966).

[38] Formstecher presented his views in his *Die Religion des Geistes* (1841). This work has not been translated. Readers can consult the summaries of his views presented by N. Rotenstreich, *Modern Philosophies of Judaism* (1968) and J. Guttman, *Philosophies of Judaism* (1966).

[39] Samuel Hirsch's major work *Die Religionsphilosophie der Juden* (1842) has not been translated. Readers are referred to E. Fackenheim, "Samuel Hirsch and Hegel" in A. Altmann (ed.), *Studies in Nineteenth-Century Jewish*

Intellectual History (1964); M. Meyer, *The Origins of the Modern Jew* (1967) and the standard histories of Jewish philosophy.

[40] Steinheim's work, *Die Offenbarung nach dem Lehrbegriff der Synagoge* (1835–1865) has not been translated.

[41] N. Krochmal's work has not been translated. Readers should consult S. Schechter, *Studies in Judaism* (1896), 46–72; J. Guttman in *Knesset*, 6 (1941), 259–286; I. Schorsch in *Judaism*, 10 (1961), 237–245; J. Taubes in *Judaism* 12 (1963), 150–164. Readers should also consult the standard histories of Jewish philosophy.

[42] H. Cohen's great work on Jewish philosophy, *Die Religion der Vernunft aus den Quellen des Judentums* (1919, 2nd ed. 1929) has been translated into English by Simon Kaplan as *The Religion of Reason out of the Sources of Judaism* (1972). Readers should also see M. Kaplan, *The Purpose and Meaning of Jewish Existence* (1969); S. H. Bergmann, *Faith and Reason* (1963); H. Leibeschuetz, in *YLBI*, 13 (1968), 3–33; and the standard histories.

[43] F. Rosenzweig's great work *Der Stern der Erlosung* (2nd ed., 1930), is available in English translation by W. Hallo as *The Star of Redemption* (1971). Readers should also see N. N. Glatzer, *Franz Rosenzweig* (1953); S. Schwarzschild, *Franz Rosenzweig: Guide for Revisioners* (1960); and the standard histories of Jewish philosophy.

[44] Almost all Buber's work is available in English. For complete details the reader is referred to the bibliographies of S. Katz, *Jewish Philosophers;* M. Friedman, *Martin Buber: The Life of Dialogue* (1960); A. Schilpp and M. Friedman (eds.), *The Philosophy of Martin Buber* (1967).

[45] M. Kaplan's very productive output is generally available. The reader is referred for bibliographical details to the bibliographies in C. Liebman, in *AJYB*, 71 (1970), 3–71 and I. Eisenstein and E. Kohn (eds.), in *M. Kaplan: An Evaluation* (1952).

[46] Louis Jacobs, *A Jewish Theology* (1973), 52.

[47] For more details on all the figures and issues mentioned here see S. Katz's essay "Jewish Thought Since 1945" in S. Katz (ed.) *Jewish Philosophies*.

[48] Readers should consult a biblical concordance for the complete listing of the use and context of every name of God in the Bible.

[49] See Gen: 31:42, 53; 49:24; Isa. 49:26.

[50] The term *el elyon* is found in pre-Israelite Canaanite literature, e.g., in the Tell-el-Amarna Letters of the 15th and 14th centuries B.C.E. The form is also found in the Aramaic *Sefire* Inscriptions of the 8th century B.C.E. For details of these usages see M. Pope, *EL in the Ugaritic Texts* (1955), pp. 54ff.

[51] See for this rabbinic exegesis, Hag., 12a.

[52] See Gen. 17:1; 28:3; 35:11; 43:14; 48:3.

[53] *Elohim* also occasionally refers to something godlike, preternatural or extraordinarily great, e.g., the ghost of Samuel in I Sam. 28:13; cf. also Isa. 18:19; Zech. 12:8; Ps. 68:16; Gen. 30:8.

[54] The Lachish letters are an important collection of inscribed ostraca shards discovered at Lachish (in central Israel) dating from the 1st Temple (7th century B.C.E.) period.

[55] Another possible reason for the substitution of *Ha-Shem* for YHWH is given in the discussion of "the Names of God In the Talmud" in this section.

[56] The correct translation of *Ehyeh Asher Ehyeh* is very controversial. Its grammatical form properly suggests a future-active rendering rather than the static one usually given to it, especially in the medieval tradition when it was interpreted in the light of Aristotle's static-ontological conception of Being.

[57] It is disputed whether the term "King" was used for YHWH before the monarchical period in Israel. The rare use of this title for YHWH in the Pentateuch (Ex. 15:18; Num. 23:21; Deut. 33:5) may be due to later editing of additions made in these older books. However, even Gideon, in refusing to "rule over" Israel, does not speak of YHWH as the king of Israel but says, "It is YHWH who is to rule over you" (Jdg. 8:22–23). The term "King" is not mentioned in this passage. Certainly, at least in Israel's nomadic period, the idea of kingship, even as attributed to YHWH, was foreign to Israelite thought. The phrase "Ancient of days," which is employed as an epithet of God in modern times, is biblical in origin, but its use as a divine epithet is not.

[58] See Mishnah Sota 6:2 for the service of the High Priest on *Yom Kippur* and Sota 7:6 on the Priestly blessing. See also H. Albeck (ed.), Seder Nashim (1954), 387.

[59] Shev. 35a–b. See also Allon, *Meḥkarim* I (1957), 194ff; Saul Lieberman, *Tosefta ki feshutah (Mo'ed),* 4 (1962), 755.

[60] See for example, Ned. 3:11; Sot. 5:5; Avot 3:2, 5:4. See on this and the other names of God and for a detailed discussion of the talmudic "Names," A. Marmorstein, *The Old Rabbinic Doctrine of God: The Names and Attributes of God* (reprinted 1968), 17–145; and Louis Jacobs, *A Jewish Theology,* ch. 10, which contains a discussion of this theme and also a great deal of useful bibliography.

[61] For examples of these names in talmudic literature see Av. Zar. 40b; Nid. 49b; Ber. 16b; Git. 17a; Ket. 45a; Ber. 16b; Yoma 8:9; Shab. 10b; Suk. 53a.

[62] Maimonides' view is presented in the *Guide* 1:61–64; Albo's position is stated in *Sefer ha-Ikkarim* 2:28. For more on this and related material see the section, "Attributes of God in medieval Jewish philosophy," below which is integrally related to this discussion.

[63] For more on Buber and Rosenzweig's view, see the discussion of the principles used in their Bible translation in their *Die Schrift und ihrer Verdeutschung* (1936). For the view of others see, for example, Louis Jacobs, *A Jewish Theology* (1973), 52–55. For details of Kaplan's, Olan's and Gittelsohn's views and the criticism of Berkovits and Fackenheim, see the discussion of "Reconstructionism" in Katz, *Jewish Philosophers,* 245–247. For Katz's critical view of Kaplan see *SH'MA* (Nov. 1974).

[64] See C. Siegfried, *Philo* (1875), 203–4; H. A. Wolfson, *Philo* 2 (1947), 86–90 and 119–126.

[65] H. A. Wolfson, *Philo* 1 (1947), 86–87.

[66] *Ibid.*, 97–110.

[67] See A. Altmann and S. M. Stern, *Isaac Israeli* (1958), 151–158.

[68] Ibn Gabirol's *Mekor Ḥayyim ("Fountain of Life")* was partially translated into English by J. Bluwstein (1926). His poem *Keter Malkhut* is also available in English as *The Kingly Crown* (translated by B. Lewis, 1961).

[69] See Wolfson in *Homenaje a Millas-Vallicrosa*, 2 (1956), 545–571. A. M. Goichon (translator), *Ibn Sina, Livre des Directives et Remarques* (1951), 366–9, note 2.

[70] Ed., S. Weil (1852), 48–57.

[71] See H.A. Wolfson in *JQR* 7 (1916/17), 1–44, 175–225.

[72] H. Cohen's *Religion der Vernunft*, 51–54, 70 (2nd ed. 1929); for Cohen's view of God as creator, *ibid.*, 73–77. For Cohen's interpretation of Maimonides' theory of negative attributes, see his *Juedische Schriften*, 3 (1924), 252, 257, and his *Religion*, 72–73.

[73] See A. Altmann's essay on Hermann Cohen's "Begriff der Korrelation" in *In Zwei Welten* (1962), 377–399. See also Cohen's *Religion*, 109ff, 252, 313, 475, 480, etc.

[74] For a logical criticism of this view see S. Katz, "Dialogue and Revelation in the Thought of Martin Buber," in *Religious Studies* (March 1977).

[75] See A. J. Heschel, *Man is not Alone*, 100–109; *Between God and Man*, 118ff. For a more detailed account of Heschel's views see the discussion by F. Rothschild, *Between God and Man;* and by S. Katz in *Jewish Philosophers*, and again in an article by the same author on "A. J. Heschel and Hasidism" in *Jewish Social Studies* (1977). A full bibliography of Heschel's writings is also given in *Jewish Philosophers*.

[76] For more details see the sources already cited in note 63 above.

[77] This is equivalent to the Greek $\theta\acute{\epsilon}\mu\iota\zeta$ or $\mu o\widehat{\iota}\rho a$, the Egyptian *Ma'at* and the Iranian-Persian *Artha* ("Truth").

[78] See, for example, the doctrinal introduction in Judges 2:11–23; 3:1–8; 6:7–10; 6:13–17; 10:6–15; II Kings 14:26–27; 17:7ff.

[79] For example, in II Macc. 3, Heliodorus, who goes to desecrate the Temple, falls into a faint due to the intervention of angels. Also in II Macc. 10:29–30 angels are seen hastening to the aid of Judah Maccabee. And yet again in II Macc. 11:13, Lysias realizes the Jews are invincible because God assists them in various ways.

[80] See Joesphus, *Ant.* 13:171–3, 18:11f. and *Wars* 2:119f.

[81] For this talmudic image of a long-suffering God and loving providence see T.J. Kid. 1:10, 61d; Shab. 32a; Sanh. 39b; Tanh. Beshallaḥ 10; Sot. 9a; Av. Zar. 3a, among many such passages.

⁸² The Hebrew term *hashgaḥah* itself was apparently first coined by Samuel ibn Tibbon. In his *Guide of the Perplexed* Maimonides uses the latter synonymously with *tadbīr*, the Hebrew equivalent of which is *hanhagah* (i.e., governance of the world). In most Hebrew philosophical works, however, *hanhagah* designates the universal providence which determines the natural order of the world as a whole, while *hashgaḥah* is generally individual providence. For the latter, Judah al-Ḥarizi also used the Hebrew term *shemirah* ("safekeeping"), and it should be noted that originally Ibn Tibbon, too, preferred this, as is shown in a manuscript copy of a letter to Maimonides. The letter of Ibn Tibbon to Maimonides was published by Z. Diesendruck in *HUCA*, 11 (1936), 341–366.

⁸³ Ed., S. Weil (1852), 93ff.

⁸⁴ In his letter to Maimonides, see n. 82, Samuel ibn Tibbon calls attention to a contradiction between Maimonides' treatment of providence in *Guide*, 3:17ff., and his discussion at the end of the *Guide* in chapter 51, where, departing from the philosophical approach that providence is relevant only to the welfare of the soul, Maimonides expresses the conviction that the devout man will never be allowed to suffer any harm. Shem Tov ibn Falaquera (*Moreh ha-Moreh*, 145–8), Moses ibn Tibbon, in a note to his father's letter (ed., Diesendruck, *op. cit.*), Moses of Narbonne, in his commentary on the *Guide* (3:51), and Efodi (Profiat Duran) in his commentary on the same chapter, all dwell on this point. Shem Tov b. Joseph Ibn Shem Tov, in his book *Emunot* (Ferrara, 1556, 8b–10a), and Isaac Arama in his *Akedat Yiẓḥak*, take Maimonides to task for having made the degree of providence exercised over man dependent on perfection of the intellect rather than on performance of the commandmants.

⁸⁵ See G. Scholem, *Shabbetai Ẓevi*, p. 784.

⁸⁶ Vienna, 1891.

⁸⁷ See *Peer Li-Yesharim*, No. 38.

⁸⁸ R. Ḥayyim of Sanz, *Divre Ḥayyim* to *Mikketz*. For more on the Hasidic attitude towards Providence, see *Shomer Emunim*, ed., I. Stern (1965), pp. 31–33.

⁸⁹ Gen. 18–25; Ps. 9:5; Ps. 119:137–44; Deut. 13:5; Sotah 14a; Maimonides, *Guide* 1:54, 3:54; Isa 11:5ff; Deut. R. 5:7; Ex. R. 30:19.

⁹⁰ Sanh. 90b–92a; Joseph Albo, *Sefer Ha-Ikkarim*, 1:15.

⁹¹ PR 5:11, 40:2; Maimonides, *Guide* 3:53.

⁹² See G. F. Moore, *Judaism*, 1, 386–400.

⁹³ See A. Marmorstein. *The Old Rabbinic Doctrine of God*, 1, 43–53, 181–208.

⁹⁴ Saadiah, *Emunot ve-Deot*, ch. 9, 172.

⁹⁵ G. Scholem, *Major Trends*, 237; see also the original zoharic discussion, *Zohar I*, 17a–18a; 146:148a; 161b.

[96] For some of the rabbinic discussion on this issue see *Tosef. Yad.* 2:14; Song R. 1:1, no. 5.

[97] On the unequal gift of the spirit, see Lev. R. 15:2.

[98] The reference of the *Ru'aḥ ha-Kodesh* and its presence among the sages at Jericho is found in TJ Hor. 3:7; 48c. The gift of the Spirit to teachers is mentioned in Song R. 1:1, no. 8, and to those who study from pure motive in *Seder Eliyahu Zuta* 1; and to those who perform just one *mitzvah* in pure faith in Mekh. Be-Shallaḥ 2:6. The question cited from the Midrash is from Tanh. Vayeḥi 13. And finally the teaching of Phineas b. Jair is found in Sot. 9:15 end. On this see also Av. Zar. 20b and T.J. Shab. 1:3, 3c for different versions of this teaching.

[99] D. Flusser, *Scripta Hierosolymitana* (1958), 252ff.

[100] A. J. Heschel, *Ru'aḥ Ha-Kodesh in the Middle Ages* (Hebrew) in *Alexander Marx Jubilee Volume* (1950), 175–208.

[101] See H. Cohen, *Die Religion der Vernunft*, 116–30.

[102] See Kaufman Kohler, *Jewish Theology* (1918), 200ff.

[103] For an example of this careful use of the term indicated by the rabbinic phrase *'kivyakhol'* ("as if it were possible"), see Mekhilta Pisḥa 12; see also S. Schechter, *Some Aspects of Rabbinic Theology* (1909), 40, note 1; E. E. Urbach, *Ḥazal* (in Hebrew, 1969), 33, note 15 and page 50.

[104] J. Abelson, *The Immanence of God in Rabbinical Literature* (1912). For a critical discussion and disagreement with his views see Urbach, *Ḥazal*, 32, 35. For a detailed discussion of anthropomorphism see the last essay of this section "Anthropormorphism."

[105] For a more detailed discussion of "Anthropormorphism," see below.

[106] For these roles of the *Shekhinah* see Shab. 12b; Sot. 17a; BB. 10a; Ber. 43b; Hag. 16a; Shab. 30b; Sot. 42a. See also Sanh. 7a; Shab. 31a; Ser. 6:29.

[107] See Saadiah's interpretation of Ezek. 1:26; I Kings 22:19, and Dan. 7:9 in his *Emunot ve-Deot* 2:10.

[108] For more details of this complicated zoharic doctrine and related issues see I. Tishby, *Mishnat ha-Zohar* 1 (1949), 219ff. and passim; and G. Scholem, *Major Trends* (1961), ch. 6, and his *Kabbalah* (1974).

[109] This three-fold biblical use of the notion of the *devar Adonai* can be found in Gen. 15:1; I Sam. 3:21; Isa. 55:10–11; Ezek. and Zech. passim; Ps. 33:6; 107:20; 47:18.

[110] Aristobolus' view is recorded in Eusebius, *Praeparatio Evangelica* 13:12. For further details of Philo's view and the sources of his views, see Wolfson, *Philo* 1, 200–282.

[111] Philo's remarks in I *Som.* 228f. are not evidence for the earlier existence of the Johannine view.

[112] For a more detailed discussion of the *Logos* doctrine, see Wolfson, *Philo* 1, 200–282; and idem, *The Philosophy of the Church Fathers* (1956). Also, for

a discussion of the implications and relations of the notions of *Memra*, *Shekhinah* and *Logos* in rabbinic Judaism and the New Testament, see S. Katz. *"A Jewish View of Christology"* in the *Scottish Journal of Theology*, 24 (May 1971), 184–200.

¹¹³ These anthropomorphic expressions can be found, in the order they are mentioned, in Ex. 24:10–12; Num. 12:8; Ps. 8:4; Ex. 31:18; Gen. 3:8; Gen. 11:5; 18:21; Ex. 19:18; 34:5; Gen. 17:22; 35:13; Ex. 12:12–13; Isa. 6:1; Num. 7:89; Ps. 132:13; 135:21; Dan. 7:9; Ex. 33:23; Ex. 15; II Sam. 22; Ps. 18.

¹¹⁴ For such expressions see, for example, Ex. 24:16–17; Lev. 9:23; Num. 14:10; Deut. 12:5; 16:2.

¹¹⁵ For Onkelos' substitution of *Shekhinah* for the divine names YHWH and *Elohim* see above.

¹¹⁶ Symmachus was a Greek (Jew?) who translated the Bible into Greek in the late 2nd/early 3rd century.

¹¹⁷ Aristobolus of Paneas (1st half of 2nd century B.C.E.), Jewish Hellenistic philosopher and one of the earliest allegorical interpreters of the Bible.

¹¹⁸ The sages refer to this notion by the use of the phrase *bilshon bnei adam*, i.e., "Scripture is written in the language of man." See Maimonides, *Guide*, 1:47.

¹¹⁹ For full details of the medieval philosophical debate, see discussion of "Attributes" above.

¹²⁰ Abraham ben David of Posquieres' gloss to Maimonides, *Yad, Teshuvah* 3:7. For more details, see I. Twersky, *Rabad of Posquieres* (1962).

¹²¹ For details of *Shi'ur Komah*, see G. Scholem, *Jewish Gnosticism, Merkabah Mysticism, Talmudic Tradition* (1960).

¹²² *Teshuvot Rambam*, ed., Freimann, nos. 373, 694.

¹²³ See Saul Liebermann's appendix to G. Scholem's *Jewish Gnosticism*.

¹²⁴ To avoid repetition, readers are referred to the discussion of "the Attributes of God in modern Jewish thought," to gain some idea of modern and contemporary views not only on the issue of Divine attributes, but also on the necessarily related issue of "anthropomorphism," which we are discussing here.

Notes to Part II

[1] For the use of these terms, see Gen. 6:7; 2:23–24; 13:16; 34:30; 41:33; I Sam. 23:3, 12; Isa. 51:7, 12; 56:2; Jer. 20:10; Ps. 90:3; Job 28:4; Ex. 10:11; Josh. 7:14; Deut. 2:34; 4:27.

[2] On these psychological terms, see Gen. 2:7; 2:23–24; 9:4; 46:26; Ex. 21:23; Lev. 17:11; I Sam. 1:26; Job 16:4; Gen. 6:17; Ex. 35:21; 28:3; Isa. 11:2; 31:3; 40:6; Judg. 3:10; Prov. 20:27.

[3] These connections can be seen in Ps. 7:10; 45:2; 51:10; I Sam. 24:6; Job 27:6; Deut. 2:7, 24; 6:5; 13:18; 19:6; 32:36; Isa. 16:11; 30:29; 63:15; Lev. 19:17; Jer. 12:2; 48:4; Gen. 6:5; Lam. 2:11.

[4] For a suggested discussion between these two terms, see I. Epstein, *The Faith of Judaism* (1954), 224.

[5] The rabbis refer to man as *shuttaf*, i.e., God's co-partner. See Gen. R. 73 (ed.) H. Albeck (1940); cf., Shab. 10a.

[6] These legal views can be found, in the order mentioned, in Gen. 24:5, 8; Deut. 21:10–14; Ex. 21:28–31; Ex. 21:22–25; Lev. 20:10, 11, 17–18; Lev. 11; Ex. 20:12; Deut. 5:16.

[7] These legal views can be found, in the order mentioned, in Deut. 17:2, 5; 29:17; Num. 5:6–7; Ex. 23:17; 34:23; Deut. 16:16; I Sam. 1–2; Deut. 31:10–13; Num. 6:2ff; Num. 30:4–16.

[8] On these acts see, in the order mentioned, Ex. 35:22–29; 38:8; II Sam. 6:19; Ps. 68:26; Neh. 12:43; Ex. 22:17; I Sam. 28:3ff; Ezek. 8:14; I Sam. 21:4–5.

[9] An analytic study of these three terms has been undertaken by R. Knierim (in *VT*, 16 (1966), 366–85). He has shown that the three terms are often found together, even in poetic parallelism, and concludes that there cannot be an appreciable difference between them, though they are certainly not simple synonyms. For the relevant biblical passages, see Ex. 34:7; Lev. 16:21; Num. 14:18; Isa. 59:12; Jer. 33:8; Ezek. 21:29; Micah 7:18–19; Ps. 32:1, 5; 51:3–7; 59:4–5; Job 7:20–21; 13:23; Dan. 9:24; cf. Isa. 1:2, 4; Ezek. 33:10, 12.

[10] See Gen. 31:39; Lev. 5:15–16; Num. 14:40; Judges 20:16; Ps. 25:8; Prov. 8:36, etc.

¹¹ These biblical citations can be found, in the order mentioned, in Gen. 31:36; II Sam. 20:1; I Sam. 24:12; Gen. 40:1, 41:9; Ex. 5:16; Gen. 42:22; Judges 11:27; II Kings 18:14.

¹² See, for example, Isa. 58:1ff; 59:2ff; Jer. 2:35; 5:25; Ezek. 14:13; 16:51; 33:14; Hos. 12:9; Amos 5:12; Micah 3:8, 6:13.

¹³ For this use of the term see, for example, Gen. 31:36; 50:17; Ex. 22:8; I Sam. 24:11; Kings 8:20; Amos 1–2; Micah 3:8; Prov. 28:24; I Kings 12:19; II Kings 1:1; 3:5; 8:20, 22; Hos. 8:1; Gen. 31:36; Ex. 22:8; Prov. 28:24; I Kings 8:50; Ps. 25:7; 51:3.

¹⁴ See, for example, Num. 18:22; 27:3; Deut. 21:22; 22:26; II Kings 14:6; Ezek. 3:20; 18:4; Amos 9:10; II Chron. 25:4.

¹⁵ Ex. 32:33; Lev. 20:20; 22:9; 24:15–17; Num. 9:13; 16:26; 17:3; 18:22; I Sam. 15:18; I Kings 13:34; 14:11–18; 15:29–30; 16:12–13, 18–19; Isa. 13:9; 38:17; 43:27–28; 64:4–5; Jer. 8:14; Ezek. 3:20; 18:24; Amos 9:8, 10; Ps. 104:34.

¹⁶ *ḥt'*: Num. 27:3; Deut. 24:16; II Kings 14:6; *avon*: Josh. 22:20; Ezek. 4:17; Gen. 4:13; Ex. 28:43; Lev. 5:1, 17; 7:18; 19:8, 17; 20:17, 19, 20; 22:9; 24:15; Num. 5:31; 9:13; 14:34; 18:22, 23, 32; Ezek. 14:10; 44:10, 12.

¹⁷ Gen. 50:17; Ex. 10:17; 32:32; I Sam. 15:25; Hos. 14:3; Ps. 25:18; Ex. 34:7; Num. 14:18; Micah 7:18; Ps. 32:1; 85:3; 32:5; Josh. 24:19; Isa. 53:12.

¹⁸ Num. 18:1; Ex. 28:38; Num. 30:16; Ezek. 4:4–6; Lev. 22:16; Lev. 16:22; Lev. 10:17.

¹⁹ I Kings 8:30, 34, 36, 50; Ps. 51:4; 79:9; Gen. 20:7; Ex. 9:27–29; 10:17; 32:30–33; Num. 21:7; Deut. 9:18–20; I Sam. 7:5; 12:19; Jer. 14:11; 15:1.

²⁰ Gen. 39:9; Ex. 9:27; 10:16; Num. 22:34; Josh. 7:20; I Sam. 15:24, 30; II Sam. 12:13; 24:10, 17; Jer. 2:35; Micah 7:9; Ps. 41:5; 51:6; I Chron. 21:8, 17; cf. Job 7:20; 10:14; 33:27; Gen. 20:9; 43:9; 44:32; Judg. 11:27; I Sam. 24:11; 26:21; II Sam. 19:21; II Kings 18:14; Jer. 37:18.

²¹ The individual confession of sins is also expressed by the words *pesha'ai* (Ps. 25:7; 32:5; 39:9; 51:3–5) and *'awonatai* (Ps. 38:5; 40:13); by the singular *pishi* (Micah 6:7; Job 7:21; 14:17) and *'awoni* (Gen. 4:13; Ps. 32:5; 38:19); or else by various locutions, using one of these words (Gen. 44:16; I Sam. 25:24; II Sam. 14:9).

²² For the use of *ḥatanu*, see Num. 21:7; Deut. 1:41; Judg. 10:10; 15:1; Kings 8:47; Isa. 42:24; Jer. 3:25; 8:14; 14:7, 20; 16:10; Ps. 106:6; Lam. 5:16; Dan. 9:5, 8, 11, 15; Neh. 1:6 (twice); II Chron. 6:37. For the use of *pesha'enu*, see Isa. 53:5; 59:12; Ezek. 33:10; Ps. 65:4; 103:12; Lam. 1:14, 22. As far as these texts can be dated, they all were composed in the 6th century B.C.E. The term *awoneno* also occurs with that meaning, namely in Isa. 53:5–6; 64:5; Ps. 90:8; Dan. 9:13; Ezra 9:6, 13.

²³ Cf. E. Lipinski, *La liturgie pénitentielle dans la Bible* (1969), 35–41.

²⁴ See Micah 7:18; Ps. 32:1, 5; 85:3; Prov. 10:12; 17:9; 19:11; 28:13; Job 31:33; Isa. 64:8; Ps. 25:7; Ex. 32:32; 34:7; Num. 14:18; Josh. 24:19; Hos. 14:3; Micah 7:18; Ps. 25:18; 32:1.

²⁵ For example, *tiher* ("purify"; Jer. 33:8); *mahah* ("wipe"; Isa. 43:25); *kibbes, rahaz* ("wash"; Isa. 1:16; Ps. 51:4, 9); *kipper* ("purge"; Ezek. 16:63; Ps. 78:38.).

²⁶ For example, Ex. 34:7; Num. 14:18; Hos. 14:3; Micah 7:18; Ps. 32:5.

²⁷ See Num. 15:30–31; Sam. 3:14. For other non-sacrificial means of expiation, see Ex. 23:21; Josh. 24:19. On the need for inner contrition, see Lev. 5:5–6; 16:21; Num. 5:6–7; Joel 2:12–14; I Sam. 7:5–6.

²⁸ For example, David in II Sam. 12:13 ff; Ahab in I Kings 21:27–29. See also, Ps. 32:5; 38:19; 41:5; Lam. 3:40ff.

²⁹ See Isa. 1:10ff; 29:13; Hos. 7:14; Joel 2:3.

³⁰ See Isa. 33:15; Ps. 15; 24:4; Isa. 1:17; 58:5 ff; Jer. 7:3; 26:13; Amos 5:14–15; Ps. 34:15–16; 37:27.

³¹ See, e.g., II Sam. 24:14, 17; cf. Ps. 25:10; 80; 103:17–18; 106:45.

³² Num. 14:18–20; Ex. 32:11 ff; 34:6ff.

³³ Ex. 4:22; Num. 11:12; Deut. 32:6, 19; Isa. 64:7; Jer. 3:19; 31:19; Hos. 11:1ff; Deut. 8:5; Prov. 3:12.

³⁴ For example, Ex. 9:27ff; 10:16ff; 34:8–9; Num. 12:11ff; 21:7ff; Deut. 9:16; 10:10; Jer. 15:1.

³⁵ See Ex. 2:24; 3:6; 4:5; 6:3–5; Lev. 26:42; Deut. 4:31, 37; 7:8, 12; 8:18; 9:5, 27; 13:18; 29:12; Josh. 18:3; 21:44; I Kings 18:36ff; II Kings 13:23; Isa. 41:8; 51:2; Micah 7:20; Ps. 105:9; Neh. 9:7; II Chron. 30:6.

³⁶ See Ex. 32:12; Num. 14:13–16; Josh. 7:9; Ps. 74:10, 18; 83:3, 19; 92:9–10; 109:27; 143:11–12; Ps. 79:6; 102:16; 115:1; 138:3–5; Isa. 48:9–11; Ezek. 36:22ff.

³⁷ Gen. 2:7; 3:19; see also Job 10:9.

³⁸ Isa. 14:9–12; Ezek. 32:17–32.

³⁹ On these expressions, see in the order mentioned I Sam. 28:13; Jonah 2:7; Job 10:21–22; Ps. 88:12; Isa. 26:6, 19; cf. Gen. 3:19; Isa. 14:15; 38:18; Prov. 28:17; cf. Akkadian *buru;* Ps. 7:16; cf. Akkadian *suttu;* Job 28:22; II Sam. 22:5, 6; Ezek. 31:14; Lam. 3:55; Job 10:21.

⁴⁰ Gen. 47:29–30; 49:29; 50:25; II Sam. 21:12–14.

⁴¹ Cf. I Kings 14:11.

⁴² For more on these themes see the relevant discussions, indexed by subject, in *Encyclopedia Judaica* (1972).

⁴³ Ber. 10a; Nid. 31a; Lev. R. 14:3, 4; 15:2, 3; 34:3.

⁴⁴ Kid. 30; Nid. 31a; T.J. Kid. 8:3, 31c; Eccl. R. 5:10, 2.

⁴⁵ Mss. *Midrash ha-Hefez.*

⁴⁶ For more on the theme of man as a microcosm see the discussion on this theme in *Encyclopedia Judaica* (1972).

[47] *Mid. Tadshe* in *Beit ha-Midrash*, ed. A. Jellinek, vol. 3, 175f.; cf. the New Testament denomination of the human body as a tabernacle, II Cor. 5:1, 4; II Pet. 1:13, 14.

[48] Gen. R. 28:3; Eccl. R. 12:5. This bone is called the "*luz* of the spine."

[49] For a detailed discussion of the individual's two *yezer's* (inclinations), see G. F. Moore, *Judaism*, 2 (1927); S. Schechter, *Some Aspects of Rabbinic Theology* (1909) ch. 15 and 16.

[50] On this question of moral character and possessions, see, in the order mentioned, the following talmudic discussions: Avot 5:10; Shab. 117b; 153a; Gen. R. 19:6; Ket. 105b; Tosef Sot. 3:6; Ber. 32a; Sanh. 108a; Gen. R. 26:5; 28:6; Tanh. Naso 28; Shev. 40b; BM 3a.

[51] The biblical sources for this idea are found in Lev. 19:2; Deut. 10:12; 10:18–19; 11:22; 26:17; Ex. 20:10–11. For more on this point, see D. Shapiro in *Judaism*, 12 (1963), 57–77.

[52] For these talmudic sources see, in the order cited, Mekh. Shirah 3; Sifra 19:2; Sota 14a; D. Shapiro, in *Judaism*, 12 (1963), 57–77; H. A. Wolfson, *Philo* I (1947), 194ff.

[53] For these views see Tanh. Pekudei 3, and Tanh. Toledot 12.

[54] These talmudic views are expressed in Ber. 61a–b; Eccl. R. 5. The debate on man's creation between Hillel and Shammai is found in Er. 13b. For the attempt of later commentators to explain it away see, for example, Maharsha to Mak. 23b and E. Urbach's discussion of this in his *Hazal*, 224ff.

[55] On this more general optimistic point of view, see the rabbinic discussions in Gen. R. 8:3–9; 19:6; Alphabet of R. Akiva 59; Avot de R. Natan 31; Avot 3:15; Num. R. 19:3; Gen. R. 21:5; Tanh. B. Gen. 28.

[56] For these rabbinic views, in the order mentioned, see Yev. 62b; Kid. 31b; Sot. 11b; BM 59a; Sif. Num. 133; Nid. 45b; Meg. 14b; Yev. 63b; Ex. R. 41:5.

[57] Josephus, *Wars*, 2:162ff.; *Ant.* 13:171; 18:12f. See G. F. Moore, *Judaism*, 3 (1930), 139; and Urbach, *Hazal*, 227.

[58] These seemingly deterministic views can be found, in order cited, in Yoma 38b; Hul. 7b; Eccles. R. 10:1; Ket. 30a; Sot. 2a.

[59] See Deut. 30:15–19; Sif. Deut. 53–54; Nid. 16b.

[60] Maimonides, *Commentary to the Mishnah, Avot* 3:15.

[61] These views on sin are found, in order mentioned, in Yoma 8:8; Yoma 85–86a; Ber. 26a; Yoma 8:9; Kid. 39b.

[62] These three examples are taken from Sifra, Be-Harb; Ar. 15b; BM 58b.

[63] These rabbinic views, in order cited, are found in Gen. R. 9:7; Yoma 69b; BB 16a; Suk. 52b; Yoma 86b.

[64] These passages are found in Shab. 55b, 146a.

[65] These views, in order cited, are found in Avot 2:1, 3:1; Sot. 21a; Kid. 30b.

[66] These praises of repentance *(Teshuvah)* are found, in order cited, in Pes. 54a; Yoma 86a, 86b; Deut. R. 2:24; Song R. 5:2, no. 2; Ta'an. 2:1.

[67] These views are found, in order cited, in T.J. Mak. 2:7, 31d; Ber. 34b; Yoma 86b; Kid. 40b; Shab. 153a.

[68] These views on the efficacy of the Day of Atonement *(Yom Kippur)* are found in Yoma 8:8, 9; and 86a.

[69] These views are cited, in order mentioned, in Yoma 86a, b; Ta'an. 16a.

[70] These views are cited, in order mentioned, in BM 4:10; Git. 5:5; Bk 94b.

[71] These views, in order cited, are found in Ḥag. 5a; Ber. 12b; Pes. Rab. 44:185a; Tosef. Sot. 4:1.

[72] On this important rabbinic teaching, Yoma 8:9, basing itself on Lev. 16:30. See on this also Maimonides, *Yad,* loc. cit., 2:9; *Sh. Ar., OH* 605:1; see also RH 17b; Sifra, Aḥarei Mot, ch. 8. On physical damage, see BK 92a; Maimonides, *Yad, Ḥovel-u-Mazzik* 5:9; *Sh. Ar.* HM 422.

[73] See, in order cited, Ta'an. 20a; Shab. 151b; see also RH 17a and Meg. 28a. On the injured party who refuses to forgive, see Tanḥ. Ḥukkat 19; Bez. 32b; Yev. 79a; Num. R. 8:4; Maimonides, *Yad, Teshuvah* 2:10.

[74] See Maimonides, *Yad, Teshuvah* 2:10; Tosef., BK 9:29; *Sefer Ḥasidim,* R. Margalioth (1957), 267 no. 360. Shab. 133b; see also: Lev. R. 19:2.

[75] Yoma 20b; see also Shab. 152–153a; Ber. 186–19a; Maimonides, *Yad, Teshuvah* 8:2; and the critical remarks of Abraham b. David of Posquieres (Rabad) on Maimonides' position.

[76] These rabbinic views are expressed, in order mentioned, in Shab. 30b; Sif. Num. 112; Sanh. 6b. See also Urbach, *Hazal,* 380–3.

[77] On these views of death see, in order cited, Eccles. R. 5:14; Ber. 8a; BB 17a; Ket. 103b.

[78] See on this view of death, in order cited, Shab. 55a; Shab. 55b; Lev. R. 27:4; Eccl. R. 3:15; Deut. R. 9:8; Shab. 55a; in the Talmud this view is ascribed to those who maintain that death is not dependent on sin, but the impact of the original passage is unclear; see also Urbach, *Hazal* (1969), 376–7.

[79] R. Meir's statement is found in Gen. R. 9:5; see Maimonides comment on this passage in *Guide,* 3:10. The creation of the angel of death on the first day of creation is mentioned in Tanḥ. Va-Yeshev 4; see also *BB* 10a, where death is described as the strongest thing in the world.

[80] Mekh. Be-Ḥodesh 9; Ex. R. 32:1; cf. also Num. R. 9:45.

[81] See on these views, Gen. R. 9:5; Tosef. Yoma 5(4):6; Ber. 18a, b; Tanḥ. Ber. 7.

Notes to Part III

JUDAISM

[1] The Greek term was *Judaismos,* see II Macc. 2:21; 8:1; 14:38; Galatians 1:13–14.

[2] See, for example, Ibn Ezra to Deut. 21:13.

[3] But see Esther 8:17, where we find the phrase *mityahadim,* "become Jews."

[4] The term *dat Yehudit,* found in Ket. 7:6, means no more than Jewish law, custom or practice in a particular instance, e.g., that a married woman should not spin or have her head uncovered in the street.

[5] The term *Yiddishkeit* is the Yiddish equivalent of "Judaism," but has a less universalistic connotation and refers more specifically to the practical and folk elements of the faith.

[6] Ahad Ha-Am, *Al Parashat Derakhim,* 4 (Berlin, 1924), 42.

[7] See Gen. 15:6; Isa. 7:9; cf. Job 2:9.

[8] See Gen. 15:6; Deut. 32:4; Prov. 20:6; Job 4:18.

[9] These Attributes of God, in the order mentioned, are found in Deut. 6:4; Isa. 40:18; Deut. 4:39; Job 42:2; Ps. 137:7, 12; Job 28:23ff; Isa. 40:6–8; 44:6; Ex. 34:6–7; Isa. 5:16; Gen. 1; Ps. 104; 145:14f; Deut. 18:10.

[10] See, for example, Ex. 20:5–6; Deut. 5:9–10.

[11] An outstanding example is found in the Book of Jonah.

[12] See, for example, Isa. 2:2ff; Mic. 4:1ff.

[13] See Ex. 19:5; Lev. 19:2. See also the chapters on "God" and "Covenant" in this volume.

[14] See Ex. 24:7; Deut. 29:11–12. See also the chapter on "Covenant" in this volume.

[15] See Isa. 55:8; Job 42:3; cf. here the chapter on "God" in this volume for a further discussion of these issues.

[16] Hab. 2:4; cf. the talmudic discussion in Mak. 24a.

[17] Hag. 2:1. For a detailed discussion of these mystical and gnostical speculations in the talmudic period see G. Scholem, *Jewish Gnosticism, Merkabah Mysticism and Talmudic Tradition* (1960).

[18] Sif. Num. 84; Ber. 9b; cf. the remarks on the *"Shekhinah"* in the section on "God" in this volume.

[19] See, for example, TJ, Kid. 4:12, 66d; see also on serving God with both impulses, Sif. Deut. 32; Ber. 54a.

[20] See, for example, TJ, BM 2:5, 8c.

[21] See Sifra 19:1; Sif. Deut. 49; TJ, Pe'ah 1:1, 15b.

[22] See Lev. R. 22:1; TJ, Pe'ah 2:6, 17a.

[23] These important rabbinic doctrines about non-Jews are taught, in the order mentioned, in Tosef. Sanh. 13:10; Meg. 13a; TJ, Ned. 9:4, 41c.

[24] These views on the relation of this world to the next one are found in Avot 4:16; 4:17; Av. Zar. 3a.

[25] H. A. Wolfson, *Philo* I (1947), 164ff.

[26] For a detailed discussion of *Kalam* and all subsequent medieval thinkers, see S. Katz, *Jewish Philosophers,* and J. Guttman, *Philosophies of Judaism.* The great system of Jewish *Kalam* philosophy is that of Saadiah, *Emunot ve-Deot* (*The Book of Beliefs and Opinions,* translated by S. Rosenblatt [1948]). The most sustained and unparalleled discussion of *Kalam* is found in H. A. Wolfson, *The Philosophy of Kalam* (1976).

[27] Hananel ben Hushi'el (d. 1055/56), *Commentary on the Talmud.*

[28] Maimonides, *Commentary on the Mishnah.*

[29] For a discussion of Maimonides' *"Thirteen Principles,"* see S. Schechter, *Studies in Judaism* (1896, repr. 1945), 147–181. See also Louis Jacobs, *The Principles of Judaism* (1964), which is a modern reformulation and modification of Maimonides' creed in light of modern philosophy and biblical criticism and theology.

[30] M. Steinschneider, *Hebr. Bibliographie,* 8 (1865), 63, 100–103.

[31] Abba Mari Astruc, *Minhat Kena'ot,* ed., M. Bisliches (1838). For details of the Maimonidean controversy, see the discussion and bibliography in S. Katz ed., *Jewish Philosophers.*

[32] M. Steinschneider, *Catalogue... Muenchen,* No. 210.

[33] David ben Yom Tov ibn Bilia's *Yesodot ha-Maskil* was published in E. Ashkenazi's *Divrei Hakhamim* (1849), No. 8.

[34] Hasdai Crescas, *Or Adonai* (completed in 1410); first published in Ferrara in 1555, then in Vienna (1859–60), and Johannesburg (1961). Two sections are available in English in H. A. Wolfson, *Crescas' Critique of Aristotle* (1929).

[35] *Ohev Mishpat,* was published in Venice (1589); his *Magen Avot* was published in three parts in Leghorn (1758).

[36] Joseph Albo's *Sefer ha-Ikkarim* was translated into English as *The Book of Principles* by I. Husik (1946).

[37] Ed., I. S. Reggio (1833).

[38] Isaac Arama (c. 1420–1494) *Akedat Yizhak.* First published in Salonika

(1522) and many times subsequently. For more details see S. Heller-Wilensky, *Rabbi Yizhak Arama u-Mishnato ha-Filosofit* (1956); I. Bettan, *Studies in Jewish Preaching* (1939), 130–191; and Chaim Pearl, *The Medieval Jewish Mind: The Religious Philosophy of Isaac Arama (1971).*

[39] Joseph Jabez, *Ma'amar ha-Aḥdut* and *Or ha-Ḥayyim* were published together in Ferrara (1554). For more on Jabez, see H. H. Ben-Sasson, in *Zion* 26 (1960/61), 23–64.

[40] Published in 1505. For more details, see B. Netanyahu, *Don Isaac Abrabanel* (1968); A. J. Heschel, *Don Jizchak Abrabanel* (1937); J. B. Trend and H. Loewe (eds.) *Isaac Abrabanel: Six Lectures* (1937).

[41] First published in 1670. An English translation is available.

[42] M. Mendelssohn, *Betrachtungen ueber Bonnets Palingenesie,* in *Gesammelte Schriften,* 3 (1843), 159–66. For details of Mendelssohn's views, see A. Altmann, *Moses Mendelssohn: A Biographical Study* (1973).

[43] *Zur Orentierung in der Cultusfrage* (1869).

[44] *Das Prinzip des Mosaismus* (1854), 11–13.

[45] *Juedische Dogmen* (1871), 138–49. See also Loew's *Gesammelte Schriften,* 1 (1889), 31–52; 133–176.

[46] Samson Raphael Hirsch's *Choreb* (1837), was translated into English as *Horeb: Philosophy of Jewish Law and Observances* (1962).

[47] All of this material is taken from S. Schechter, "Dogma in Judaism."

[48] See *The Star of Redemption,* translated by W. Hallo (1971), and *On Jewish Learning,* N. N. Glatzer, ed. (1955).

[49] See first part of n. 42 in Part I.

[50] See his *Ich und Du,* which has been translated into English twice under the title *I and Thou;* the first translation was by R. G. Smith (1958), and the second by W. Kaufman (1970).

[51] See his *God in Search of Man* (1956) and *Man is not Alone* (1951).

[52] See his *Judaism as a Civilization* (1934); also his "Creeds and Wants" in *Judaism in Transition* (1941), 206–238, and his *The Purpose and Meaning of Jewish Existence* (1964).

[53] See his *After Auschwitz* (1966); also his *Eros and Morality* (1970) and *The Religious Imagination* (1968). For a full account of Rubinstein's views see the discussion of his thought by S. Katz in *Jewish Philosopers,* pt. IV.

[54] See, for instance, Abba Hillel Silver, *Where Judaism Differed* (1957), 182–223.

COVENANT

[1] The etymology of the Hebrew word *berit* is uncertain. Most probably it was used in the sense of binding (cf. Akkadian *birītu,* "fetter"), since the terms for covenant in Akkadian *(riksus)* and in Hittite *(ishiul)* also signify binding.

Hebrew has two additional terms for covenant, *edut* and *alah*. These also have
their counterparts in the cognate languages: *'dy'* in old Aramaic *(Sefire)* and
ade in Akkadian on the one hand, and *'lt* in Phoenician, *māmitu* in Akkadian,
and *lingai* in Hittite on the other. The term *alah* and corresponding usages in
Akkadian and Hittite connote an oath which actually underlies the covenantal
deed. The terms *berit* and *alah* often occur together (Gen. 26:28; Deut. 29:11,
13, 20; Ezek. 16:59; 17:18) rendering the idea of a binding oath, as does the
Akkadian *hendiadys adê māmīt* or *adê u māmīte*. For concluding a covenant
the Bible uses the expression "cut *(karat)* a covenant." The same idiom is used
in Aramaic treaties in connection with *'dy'* (cf. *gzr'dy'* in the *Sefire* treaties) and
in a Phoenician document in connection with *'lt* (cf. the incantation from
Arslan Tash). It is quite possible that this idiom derives from the ceremony ac-
companying the covenant, viz., cutting an animal. The expression *hekim berit*
and *natan berit* should not be considered synonyms of *karat berit,* used by different sources. The first term means "to fulfill a covenant (already made)"; the
second signifies "the voluntary granting of special privileges."

2 Covenants confirmed by an oath are found in Gen. 21:22ff; 26:26ff; Deut.
29:9ff; Josh. 9:15–20; II Kings 11:4; Ezek. 16:8; 17:33ff; by a solemn meal
in Gen. 26:30; 31:54; Ex. 24:11; II Sam. 2:20; by a sacrifice in Ex. 24:4ff;
Ps. 50:5; or by an act such as the division of an animal in Gen. 15:9ff; Jer.
34:18ff.

3 Covenants between individuals are found in Gen. 21:22ff.; 31:44ff. I Sam.
18:3; 23:18; between states in II Sam. 3:13, 3:21; I Kings 5:26; 15:19;
20:34; between kings and their subjects in II Sam. 5:3; II Kings 11:4; 11:17;
between husband and wife in Ezek. 16:8; Mal. 2:14; Prov. 2:17; between man
and animals in Job 5:23; 40:28; cf. Hos. 2:20; and with death in Isa. 28:15;
28:18.

4 Compare, Gen. 21:30; 31:44–45; 31:52; Josh. 24:27, etc.

5 On the Sabbath see Gen. 1:1–2:3; and cf. Ex. 31:16–17; on the rainbow
see Gen. 9:1–17; on circumcision see Gen. 17:7ff.

6 *Le Decalogue* (1927).

7 *Kleinere Schriften,* 1 (1953), 278 ff.

8 *The Problem of the Hexateuch and Other Essays* (1966).

9 Cf. Josh. 8:30–35.

10 In: *BA,* 17 (1954), 50ff.

11 For full details of the comparison of Hittite treaties and the biblical covenants see *Encyclopaedia Judaica,* 5:1015–17.

12 Gen. 26:5; cf. Gen. 22:16–18.

13 See I Kings 3:6; 9:4; 11:4; 11:6; 14:8; 15:3.

14 See I Kings 2:4; 8:25; 9:4–5.

15 *Theology of the Old Testament,* 1 (1964).

16 See I Sam. 8:6–7; 10:18ff; 12:17.

[17] See I Sam. 12:14; 12:24–25; II Kings 11:17.
[18] Cf. Ex. 23:10–19.
[19] Isa. 1:2ff; Jer. 2:4ff; Hos. 4:1ff; Micah 6:1ff.
[20] Isa. 1:2; Micah 6:1–2.
[21] Cf. above and especially Ezek. 16:8.
[22] Ex. 20:5; Deut. 5:9; cf. Ex. 34:14; Josh. 24:19.
[23] Lev. 26:12; Deut. 29:12, etc.
[24] Cf. Judges 8:23; I Sam. 8:7; 10:19.

THE CHOSEN PEOPLE

[1] For its secular meaning, see, e.g., Gen. 13:11. With regard to the special function of the priests, see Deut. 18:5; see also I Sam. 2:28. With regard to the choice of a King, see II Sam. 6:21 and Kings 8:16.

[2] Deut. 17:5; 12:14; 12:18; 12:21; 12:26.

[3] Deut. 7:6; cf. Deut. 14:2.

[4] For this view of Israel as God's agent among the nations, see Isa. 42:3ff; Isa. 49; and on the relation of this role to that of the "Suffering Servant," see Isa. 52:13; 53:12.

[5] See, for example, Jub. 2:19; 15:30–31; 16:8; Philo, Abr. 98. One must also pay close attention to the treatment of this theme in the Dead Sea (Qumran) literature. See F. C. Cross, *The Ancient Library of Qumran and Modern Biblical Studies* (1958); see also W. H. Brownlee, *Meaning of the Qumran Scrolls for the Bible* (1964). On the theme of "Chosenness" and "Covenant" in early Christianity, see K. Stendahl (ed.), *The Scrolls and the New Testament* (1958); H. H. Rowley, *The Biblical Doctrine of Election* (1950).

[6] This famous rabbinic teaching is found in Av. Zar. 2b–3a; Num. R. 14:10; Sif. Deut. 343.

[7] See Ex. 24:7, and the rabbinic discussion in Shab. 88a.

[8] See Beẓah 32b; Yev. 79a; cf. Maimonides, *Yad, Teshuvah* 2:10.

[9] S. Schechter, *Some Aspects of Rabbinic Theology* (1909), 61.

[10] Festivals, *Amidah,* in J. H. Hertz, *Siddur* (Prayer Book) (1961), 819; cf. *Kiddush* for festivals, ibid, 809; *Alenu* prayer, ibid, 209; Blessing on being called to Torah, 191.

[11] J. Katz, *Exclusiveness and Tolerance* (1961), 13–14.

[12] On Mendelssohn see, Leo Baeck, *Von Mendelssohn zu Franz Rosenzweig,* p. 23. (This was translated into English in *Judaism* vol. 11, Nos. 1 and 2.) See also A. Altmann, *Moses Mendelssohn: A Biographical Study* (1973), and M. Meyer, *The Origin of the Modern Jew* (1967).

[13] Certain modern intellectuals have found the doctrine of Israel's "election" objectionable. The most notorious example is Arnold Toynbee's remark in his

Study of History, 4 (1961), 262; "The most notorious historical example of idolization of an ephemeral self is the error of the Jews...They persuaded themselves that Israel's discovery of the One True God had revealed Israel itself to be God's Chosen People." From the Jewish side, consider the view of the Hebrew writer J.H. Brenner who declared: "...I would blot out from the prayer book of the Jews of our day the 'Thou hast chosen us' in every shape and form." (Quoted by S. Spiegel in, *Hebrew Reborn* (1930), 375–89.) Brenner's wish has become reality in the Prayer Book of the Jewish Reconstructionist movement which states in its Introduction: "Modern-minded Jews can no longer believe...that the Jews constitute a divinely chosen people." *Sabbath Prayer Book,* The Jewish Reconstructionist Foundation (1954), xxiv.

[14] Leo Baeck, *This People Israel* (1964), 402.

[15] For the modern discussions of election see W. G. Plaut, *The Case for the Chosen People* (1966) and his bibliography. See also Emil Fackenheim's *Quest for Past and Future* (1968).

REVELATION

[1] See Gen. 35:7; I Sam. 2:27; 3:21.

[2] J. Skinner, *Genesis* (1910), 286.

[3] These direct revelations of God to various individuals and then to the entire people at Sinai are found in the Bible, in the order mentioned, in Gen. 12:6–7; 17:1–2; 26:24; 35:9–10; 48:3–4 (cf. Ex. 6:3); Ex. 3:2ff; 3:16–17; Judg. 13:21–22; I Kings 3:5ff; 9:2ff; Lev. 9:4; 9:6; 9:23; Deut. 31:15; (cf. Deut. 31:11); and on the Theophany at Mt. Sinai see also, M. Haran, in *JSS*, 5 (1960), 50–65, especially p. 58.

[4] I Sam. 4:21; I Kings 8:11; Ps. 24:7–10.

[5] See Lev. R. 1:14; Yev. 49b. This is also the source of the N.T. expression "Through a glass darkly."

[6] Sif. Ekev 37; Gen. R. 1:4.

[7] Sif. Devarim 48; Avot 3:14.

[8] Ex. R. 29:6; Tanh. Yitro 11.

[9] Sif. Shelah, ed. Horowitz, p. 121.

[10] See on this question the following works: M. Joel, *Blicke in die Religionsgeschichte,* 2 (1883), 176f; K. Kohler, in: *Jewish Encyclopedia,* "Inspiration"; B. Cohen, *Law and Tradition in Judaism* (1959), 7–17; A. J. Heschel, *Torah min ha-Shamayim,* 2 (1965), chs. 7 and 9.

[11] For traditional sources concerning this, see M. M. Kasher, *Torah Shelemah,* 19 (1959), 332–42. This work is now being translated into English as *The Encyclopedia of Biblical Interpretation* (1953ff.).

[12] The contrary has been argued by Heschel, who asserts that Akiva and Ishmael held basically different conceptions of the Torah and the nature of

revelation. See, on this, Heschel, *Torah min ha-Shamayim,* 1 (1962), 16; and 2 (1965), Chs. 6 and 7.

   [13] TJ, Shek. 6:49d and Sot. 8:22d; Song. R. 5:11, Deut. R. 3:12, etc.
   [14] See Kasher, *Torah Shelemah,* 19, 356–62 for these traditional sources.
   [15] Quoted in BB 14b and TJ Sot. 5:6-end.
   [16] By J. J. Petuchowski in: *Hibbert Journal,* 57 (1958/59), 356–60. See also his *Ever Since Sinai: A Modern View of Torah* (1961).
   [17] Ex. R. 28:6; Tanḥ. Yitro 11, etc.
   [18] E. Urbach, *Ḥazal,* p. 270.
   [19] H. Cohen, *Die Religion der Vernunft aus den Quellen des Judentums* (1919), 82–92.
   [20] See Steinheim's *Die Offenbarung nach dem Lehrbegriffe der Synagoge,* 1 (1835), 318.
   [21] See S. R. Hirsch's *Horeb* (English translation, 1962) and *Judaism Eternal* (English translation, 1956).
   [22] See M. Buber, *Ich und Du,* Part III. See also Buber's *Eclipse of God* (1952), 135, and his correspondence with F. Rosenzweig, available in English in *On Jewish Education* (1965), ed. and trans., N. Glatzer.
   [23] See N. Glatzer (ed.), *On Jewish Learning* (1965), 109–24. See also *The Star of Redemption* (English translation, 1971), Pt. II, "Revelation."
   [24] A. J. Heschel, *God in Search of Man* (1956), 198.
   [25] See A. I. Kook, *Orot ha-Kodesh,* Pt. I (1963), 73.

TORAH

   [1] Cf. Lev. 7:37–38; 14:54–56.
   [2] Cf. Josh. 1:7; Ezra 3:2; 7:6; 8:1; 8:8; Mal. 3:22.
   [3] To avoid repetition, the reader is referred to the discussion of "Revelation" above, which, of course, shares much common ground with the discussion of Torah, as Torah, for Jews, is God's supreme, perfect, and complete revelation.
   [4] Ben Sira 1:1–5; 1:26; 15:1; 24:1ff; 34:8. cf. Prov. 8:22–31.
   [5] Gen. R. 1:4;*Pes.* 54a, et al.
   [6] ARN 31, p. 91; cf. Gen. R. 28:4, et al.
   [7] Lev. R. 19:1 et al.; and TJ Shek. 6:1, 49d et al.
   [8] Philo, *Op.* 20, 25, 36; *Cher.* 127. See also the remarks in Pt. I, "Names of God" in this volume.
   [9] Philo, *Mig.* 130; cf. *Op.* and II *Mos.* See also the remarks on Philo and Logos above, Pt. I.
   [10] Cf. Saadiah's, *Commentary on Proverbs,* ad loc.
   [11] Judah ben Barzillai of Barcelona, *Commentary on Sefer Yeẓirah,* pp. 88–89; cf. Solomon ben Abraham Adret, *Perushei Aggadot.*
   [12] Abraham ibn Ezra, *Commentary on the Torah,* "Introduction," 'The

fourth method'; cf. also Judah Hadassi, *Eshkol ha-Kofer,* 25b–26a; and cf. Abraham Shalom, *Neveh Shalom,* 10:8.

[13] See *Guide* 2:35; 3:51; et al.; cf. *Yad,* Introduction.

[14] See Pes. 68b; Hasdai Crescas, *Or Adonai,* 2:6; cf. Nissim ben Reuben Gerondi, *Commentary on Ned.* 39b.

[15] Joseph Albo, *Sefer ha-Ikkarim,* 3:12; cf. Jacob ben Solomon ibn Habib, *Ein Ya'akov,* "Introduction"; cf. also Joseph Solomon Delmedigo, *Novelot Hokhmah.*

[16] N. Krochmal, *Moreh Nevukhei ha-Zeman,* 17; cf. 12, 16 (2nd revised edition 1961).

[17] F. Rosenzweig, "The Builders" in N. Glatzer (ed.) *On Jewish Learning* (1955), 78.

[18] These aspects and attributes of the Torah, in the order mentioned in our text, are found in Ex. 13:9; Josh. 8:31 et al.: Deut. 33:4; Ex. 19:6; Prov. 6:23; Ps. 19:8; cf. Ps. 119:103; Prov. 16:24.

[19] Sanh. 10:1, et al.; cf. Ex. 20:22; Deut. 4:36.

[20] Pes. 68b; Ned. 32a; cf. Crescas' interpretation discussed above.

[21] On these comparisons see, for example, Avot 6:2, 3, 7; and for the Torah's identification with wisdom and love see, for example, Mid. Ps. to 1–18.

[22] See Sifra, Kedoshim 4:12; TJ Ned. 9:3, 41c; Gen. R. 24:7.

[23] See Mekh., Yitro, 5; Sif. Deut. 343; Shab. 88b; Ex. R. 5:9; 27:9; cf. Av. Zar. 3a: "a pagan who studies the Torah is like a high priest."

[24] See Num. 14:10; Ex. R. 47:3, et al.

[25] Sifre, Num. 110: See Maimonides, *Guide* 3:29; *Yad, Ovedei Kokhavim,* 2:4.

[26] See I. Arama, *Akedat Yizhak;* I. Abrabanel, *Mifalot Elohim,* 1:2; M. Alshekh, *Torat Moshe* to Genesis 1:1; Judah Loew, *Netivot Olam,* 1:1; *Tiferet Yisroel,* 25.

[27] Cf. Judah Abrabanel (Leone Hebreo), *Dialoghi di Amore,* ed. C. Gebhardt (1929). An English translation, *The Philosophy of Love,* was published by F. Friederburg (1937).

[28] But compare the view of Judah Halevi disccused above.

[29] G. Plaut, *The Growth of Reform Judaism,* p. 34.

[30] N. Krochmal, *Moreh Nevukhei ha-Zeman,* especially 6–8, 13.

[31] For the works of these modern authors see bibliography.

[32] See N. Glatzer (ed.) "The Builders" in *On Jewish Learning* (1955), for the discussion of Torah by Rosenzweig and Buber.

[33] See, among Kaplan's many works, his greatest, *Judaism as a Civilization* (1934).

[34] See especially A. I. Kook, *Orot ha-Torah* (1961).

[35] Sifra, Be-Hukkotai 13:7; Tem. 16a; but a prophet was permitted to suspend a law temporarily. On this point see Sif. Deut. 175.

³⁶ See, e.g., Eccles. R. 2:1.

³⁷ See, e.g., Gen. R. 98:9; Lev. R. 9:7.

³⁸ For Philo's views see: II *Mos.* 14; cf. Jer. 31:32–35. For the apocryphal material see, e.g., I Bar. 4:1; Ps. of Sol. 10:5. For Josephus' position see: *Contra Apion* 2:277.

³⁹ For a detailed discussion of this issue in terms of Judaism and Christianity, see W. D. Davies, *The Torah in the Messianic Age or the Age to Come* (1952).

⁴⁰ Maimonides, *Commentary on the Mishnah*, Sanh. 10; *Yad, Yesodei ha-Torah*, 9; cf. his *Sefer ha-Mitzvot; Guide* 2:29; 2:39. Compare Maimonides' views to those in Abraham ibn Daud's *Emunah Ramah.*

⁴¹ However, cf. Ḥasdai Crescas' anti-Christian polemic, *Bittul Ikkarei ha-Noẓerim*, 9.

⁴² See, e.g., Abraham Shalom, *Neveh Shalom* 10:3–4; Isaac Abrabanel, *Rosh Amanah* 13.

⁴³ Joseph Gikatilla, *Ginnat Egoz* (1612) 34dff.

⁴⁴ On the pre-existence of the Torah, see above.

MITZVOT

¹ Hul. 106a; cf. Git. 15a.

² For these terms see, for example, Ex. 27:21; Deut. 4:5; 4:45; Lev. 8:35; Ex. 16:28.

³ The reference to 613 commandments by Simeon ben Eleazar is found in Mekh., Yitro, Ba-Ḥodesh, 5, only in the edition of J. H. Weiss (1865), 74, (75a); the saying of Simeon b. Azzai is found in Sif., Deut. 76, where 365 prohibitions are mentioned; the view of Eleazar b. Yose is given in Mid. Hag. to Gen. 15:1. The still more ancient tradition which stands behind these views can be found in Tanh. B., Deut. 17; Ex. R. 33:7; Num. R. 13:15–16; 18:21; Yev. 47b. On R. Akiva's role and views, see A. H. Rabinowitz, *Taryag*, 38–39.

⁴ For example, Hul. 12:5; Yev. 47b; Av. Zar. 3a.

⁵ See, for example, Ex. 22:26; 23:9; Deut. 11:19; 17:16–17; 23:4–5. On the 'wisdom' of the Law, see Deut. 4:6–8.

⁶ Sifra, Lev. 18:4, para. 140.

⁷ On these rabbinic "reasons," see Gen. R. 41:1; Mekh. 89a; Mak. 3:16.

⁸ Pes. 119a; cf. Sanh. 21b.

⁹ See Wolfson, *Philo* 2 (1947), 200ff.

¹⁰ *Ibid.*, 305–6.

¹¹ On Saadiah's exposition of the "revealed" *mitzvot*, see *Beliefs and Opinions*, 3:5, 1–3.

¹² See Bahya's 'Introduction' to his *Ḥovot ha-Levavot*.

[13] This three-fold division is developed in Judah Halevi, *Kuzari* 2:48; 3:11.

[14] See *ibid.,* 1:98, 2:23; 2:48; 3:53.

[15] *Yesod Mora,* ch. 5; *Commentary to Gen.* 26:5; *Short Commentary to Ex.* 15:26.

[16] *Commentary to Lev.* 19:23; 11:43.

[17] The term "generally known" is a translation of the Arabic *mashhūrāt* and the Hebrew *mefursamot,* both of which are themselves substitutes for the Greek *endoxa.* The term "traditional" is translated in Arabic as *maqbūlāt* and in Hebrew as *mekubbalot.* This dichotomy is stated by Aristotle in his *Topics* 1:1, and is discussed by Maimonides in his *Millot ha-Higgayon* ch. 8, and his *Guide* 1:2.

[18] Ibn Daud, *Sefer ha-Emunah ha-Ramah* (1852), 5:2, 75.

[19] For Maimonides' discussion of these issues, see *Guide,* ch. 3.

[20] See S. Pines' "Introduction" to his translation of the *Guide* (1963), LXXIIff.

[21] Compare, *Yad, Me'ilah,* end; *Temurah,* end; *Mikva'ot,* end. An English edition of the *Mishneh Torah* is being produced by Yale University Press. Eleven of the fourteen volumes have already appeared.

[22] On these views, see Ḥasdai Crescas, *Or Adonai* 2:2, 6; 2:6, 2.

[23] Joseph Albo, *Sefer ha-Ikkarim,* 1:7 and passim. See also, I. Husik in *HUCA,* 2 (1925), 381ff; R. Lerner in *Ancients and Moderns,* ed. J. Cropsey (1964).

[24] See the discussion of "Torah" in Kabbalah above.

[25] Recanati's *Ta'amei ha-Mitzvot* was first published in Constantinople in 1544. A new complete edition was published in London (1963). *Sefer ha-Kanah* was published in Cracow (1894).

[26] R. Ḥayyim of Czernowitz, *Sha'ar ha-Tefillah* (1813), 7b.

[27] This ḥasidic practice was vehemently attacked by R. Ezekiel Landau in his *Noda bi-Yehuda,* YD, No. 93.

[28] M. Mendelssohn, *Jerusalem* (1783), 113–115.

[29] This view is stated in *Jerusalem,* 127–9; see also Mendelssohn's letter to Herz Homberg in *Gesammelte Schriften,* 5 (1844), 669. Mendelssohn's polemic against Spinoza was also taken up in the late 19th–early 20th century by H. Cohen. See Cohen's *Juedische Schriften,* ed. B. Strauss (1924), 290–372.

[30] L. Zunz, *Gutachten ueber die Beschneidung* in his *Gessammelte Schriften,* 2 (1876), pp. 190–203.

[31] Geiger's views can be found in his *Nachgelassene Schriften,* ed. L. Geiger, 1 (1875), 254ff., 324–5, 486–8.

[32] Compare S.R. Hirsch, *Nineteen Letters,* sections "Edoth" and "Horeb," and his major work *Horeb* (English edition, 108).

[33] H. Cohen, *Die Religion der Vernunft* p. 399ff.

[34] For Baeck's views, see his *Essence of Judaism,* and more especially his essay "Mystery and Commandment" in *Judaism and Christianity,* ed. and trans. by W. Kaufman (1958), 171–184.

[35] Julius Guttmann, *Philosophies of Judaism,* trans. by D. W. Silverman (1966), 433. See also Rosenzweig's *Der Stern der Erlosung* (Star of Redemption) II, p. 115.

[36] For Buber's views, see *I and Thou* part III, and his famous discussion with Rosenzweig in *On Jewish Learning,* ed. by N. Glatzer (1955). For critical evaluation, see Steven Katz, "Dialogue and Revelation in the Thought of Martin Buber" in *Religious Studies* (1971); A. Cohen, "Revelation and Law: Reflections on Martin Buber's View of *Halachah"* in *Judaism,* vol. I, no. 3 (July 1952).

[37] See M. Kaplan, *Judaism as a Civilization* (1934), for his classic account of Reconstructionist Judaism.

[38] For a full discussion of Rubenstein's position, see S. Katz's discussion in *Jewish Philosophers,* pt. IV, 223–228. See also Rubenstein's most important book, *After Auschwitz* (1966).

[39] For details of their views and a bibliography of their work, see S. Katz's essay in *Jewish Philosophers,* pt. IV (1975). See also for a critical evaluation of their views, S. Katz, "Philosophical reflections on the Holocaust" in *Religious Studies,* forthcoming.

PIETY, STUDY, CHARITY AND PRAYER

[1] There is, however, no uniform system of ranking such terms as *yere ḥet* ("sin-fearing"), *yere shamayim* ("God-fearing"), *ẓaddik* ("righteous"), and *ḥasid* ("pious"). For example, Maimonides, explicating the term *ḥasid,* asserts that it carries overtones of excess or extremism not found in other terms describing piety, but in fact this is not always so. There are many instances when the term describes what elsewhere would be called *ẓaddik* or *yere ḥet.* See Maimonides, *Commentary to Avot* 5:7; *Guide* 3:53.

[2] See, for example, BM 52B; Hul. 130b; Ter. 8:10.

[3] Nahmanides, *Commentary on Leviticus,* 19:1.

[4] C. G. Montefiore, *A Rabbinic Anthology* (1938), Introduction, 17.

[5] Shab. 33b; BM 84a.

[6] These views can be found, in the order mentioned, in Ber. 33b; Hul. 43b; Nid. 4b; Sanh. 111b; Sifre, Deut. 321; Av. Zar. 50b; Ber. 64a; BK. 91a: Ber. 24a; Sot. 40a.

[7] *Sifrei, Deut.* 41 and 48.

[8] Maimonides, *Yad, Talmud Torah* 1:8.

[9] See Singer, *Prayer Book,* 5.

[10] See *Shulḥan Arukh,* YD, 246:1.

[11] Tos. Kid. 30.

[12] Maimonides, *Yad, Yesodei ha-Torah* 4:13.

[13] *Zohar* III 152a.

[14] Ḥayyim Vital, *Sha'ar ha-Hakdamot,* "Introduction."

[15] R. Moses Isserles, *Shulḥan Arukh,* YD, 246:4.

[16] See J. G. Weiss, in *Essays presented to . . . I. Brodie* (1966), Hebrew Section, 151–169.

[17] R. Shneur Zalman of Lyady, *Tanya* ch. 5, *Likkutei Amarim* (1912), 17–19.

[18] R. Ḥayyim of Volozhin, *Nefesh ha-Ḥayyim* (1874), 4:9, 40a.

[19] G. Scholem in: *Perakim be-Yahadut,* ed. by E. Spicehandler and J. Petuchowski (N.D.), 312–327.

[20] On this theme in the Psalms, see Ps. 145:15–16; 132:15; for Isaiah see Isa. 58:5–7; and for Ezekiel see Ez. 16:49.

[21] Job 22:5–9; 29:12–13.

[22] For the talmudic sources of the views cited in our text, in the order mentioned, see BB 9a; Suk. 49b; BB 10a; BB 19b; BB 9a; Avot 1:2; Ket. 68a.

[23] The laws of charity are also collected and codified in Jacob ben Asher's *Arba'ah Turim,* and in *Shulḥan Arukh,* YD, 247–59.

[24] See Ket. 49b; and Maimonides, *Yad, Mattenot Aniyyim* 7:10.

[25] *Shulḥan Arukh,* YD, 251:3.

[26] Ket. 50a; Maimonides, *Yad, Mattenot Aniyyim* 7:5.

[27] TJ, Pe'ah 8:9, 21b.

[28] See, for example, Ket. 67b; Ta'an. 21b–22a.

[29] Lev. R. 34:15; see also Maimonides, *Yad, Mattenot Aniyyim,* 10:5.

[30] Maimonides, *Yad, Mattenot Aniyyim,* 10:7–12.

[31] Maimonides, *Yad, Mattenot Aniyyim,* 9:1–3.

[32] Maimonides, *Yad, Mattenot Aniyyim,* 9:13.

[33] Maimonides, *Yad, Mattenot Aniyyim,* 8:1.

[34] Ps. 65:3; cf. Ps. 115:3–7.

[35] Ps. 42:2–3; 62:9.

[36] Ps. 17, 86, 90, 102, 142.

[37] Other terms for prayer are: *qara* ("to call" on the name of the Deity, i.e., worship—Gen. 4:26); *za'aq* ("to cry out" for redress of wrongs—Judg. 3:9); *shiwwa'* ("to cry aloud" for help—Ps. 72:12); *rinnah* ("ringing cry" of joy or sorrow—Ps. 17:1); *darash* ("to seek" God—Amos 5:4); *biqqesh penei* ("to seek the face of" God—Hos. 5:15); *sha'al* ("to inquire"—Ps. 105:40); *nasa* ("to lift up"—Jer. 7:16); *paga* ("to encounter," i.e., to appease, gain favor—Jer. 7:16); *hithannen* ("to seek favor," i.e., beseech—Deut. 3:23); *shafakh lev* ("to pour out [one's] heart"—Ps. 62:9[8]); and *si'aḥ* ("complaint"—Ps. 142:3[2]).

[38] The rabbinical view is stated in Ta'an. 2a; for the biblical sources, see Hos. 7:14; Ps. 108:2; 111:1.

[39] Gen. 12:8; 21:33.

[40] The request for a sign addressed to God is found in Gen. 24:12-14; through a priest, in I Sam. 14:36; through a prophet, in II Kings 19:2ff. For later prayers see, for example, Num. 6:24-26; I Kings 3:6ff; Ps. 119:33ff.

[41] For the sources of these biblical prayers, in order mentioned, see Gen. 28:20ff; 24:12-14; 18:23-33; Ex. 32:31-32; Josh. 7:6-9; II Kings 19:15-19; Jer. 14:1ff; 15:1ff; Amos 7:2ff; Dan. 9:3-19; Ezra 9:6-15; Neh. 1:4-11; I Kings 8:12-53; 8:41ff; Ps. 51:1ff; 119:1ff; Isa. 66:22-23.

[42] See Gen. 13:4; 26:25.

[43] See Gen. 24:26; Dan. 6:11; Ezra 9:5ff.

[44] Dan. 6:11; cf. Ps. 5:8.

[45] See, for example, I Sam. 15:11; Ps. 86:3; 88:2.

[46] On the times of prayer, see, Ps. 5:4; I Kings 18:36; Ezra 9:5.

[47] Ps. 55:18; Dan. 6:11; though twice in I Chron. 23:20.

[48] For these prayer postures, in order mentioned, see I Sam. 1:26; I Kings 8:22; Dan. 6:11; Ezra 9:5; Josh. 7:6; Gen. 24:26; Neh. 8:6; I Kings 8:22; Ps. 28:2; I Kings 18:42; II Sam. 7:18; Isa. 58:2-5; Joel 2:12; Joel 2:13.

[49] On these liturgical patterns and prayer formulas, see Ezra 2:65; I Chron. 16; Deut. 21:7ff; 26:5-15.

[50] The response "Amen" is found in Num. 5:2; Ps. 41:14, etc.; Neh. 8:6; 9:5, 32; 9:6-10:1.

[51] See, for example, Gen. 19:17-23; Num. 12:9ff.

[52] Gen. 18:17ff; Isa. 29:13ff.

[53] Isa. 1:15; Amos 4:4ff.

[54] Jer. 7:16; 1:14.

[55] For these biblical events, see Gen. 4:7; Gen. 15:1-6; Ex. 3:2-4; 18; Isa. 6:5-8.

[56] Jer. 1:6ff; Hab. 1:13; 2:3.

[57] Jer. 12; Ps. 22; Job, passim (cf. 16:17).

[58] Isa. 65:24; cf. Dan. 9:20ff; Isa. 50:2; 65:12.

[59] On the rabbinic inauguration of prayer, see Ber. 21a; and on the obligation to pray 3 times daily, Ber. 4:1.

[60] Shab. 11a; RH 35a.

[61] Ber. 8a; Deut. R. 2:12.

[62] These talmudic views on the necessity of praying with *kavvanah*, and of the need to avoid falling into mechanical prayer, are found, in order mentioned, in Ber. 31a; Ber. 4:4; Avot 2:13; TJ, Ber. 4:3; 8a; Ber. 28b.

[63] On use of the established prayer formulae, and on the use of the berakhah and praise of God, see, for example, Ber. 33b; Ber. 6:1-3; Ber. 9:1-2; 58b.

[64] See, for example, Ber. 34b; Ta'an. 3:8; Ta'an. 23a-b.

[65] See Joseph Albo, *Sefer ha-Ikkarim* 4:18.

[66] Maimonides, *Guide,* 1:59; cf. Ibn Ezra, *Commentary on Eccles.* 5:1.

[67] Maimonides, *Yad Tefillah,* 1:1.

[68] Bahya, *Hovot Ha-Levavot,* 8:3, 9.

[69] Maimonides, *Yad Tefillah,* 4:16; cf. H. G. Enelow, "Kawwanah" in: *Studies in Jewish Literature, Issued in Honor of Prof. Kaufman Kohler* (1913), 82–107.

[70] See, for example, Ribash (Isaac ben Sheshet Perfet), *Resp.* No. 157.

[71] See I. Tishby, *Mishnat ha-Zohar,* 2 (1961), 247–306.

[72] See J. G. Weiss, in *JSS,* 9 (1958), 163–92.

[73] S. Dubnow, *Toledoth ha-Hasidut,* I (1930–32) 112–15.

[74] Cited by M. Teitelbaum, *Ha-Rav mi-Ladi u-Mifleget Habad,* 2 (1914), 219.

[75] See Dov Baer of Lubavich, *Kunteres ha-Hitpa'alut.*

[76] J. Petuchowski, *Prayerbook Reform in Europe* (1968) XI.

[77] K. Kohler, *Jewish Theology* (1918), 275.

[78] J. Petuchowski (ed.), *Understanding Jewish Prayer* (1972), 42. See also the other essays in this volume.

[79] H. Cohen, *Die Religion der Vernunft,* p. 457. It is a complex problem in the interpretation of Cohen's thought just how far prayer is a dialogue with God or merely a monologue with a philosophical God-idea. For more detailed expositions of Cohen's views, see E. Berkovitz, *Major Themes in Modern Jewish Philosophies of Judaism* (1974), 35–36; N. Rotenstreich, *Jewish Philosophy in Modern Times* (1968), 100.

[80] This paper by Heschel was published in *Conservative Judaism* XXV, 1 (Fall, 1970). The earlier paper by Heschel was published in the *Proceedings of the Rabbinical Assembly of America,* XVII (1953).

[81] L. Jacobs, *A Jewish Theology,* (1974) 193. See his entire discussion of prayer in ch. 13.

[82] Eugene Kohn, *Proceedings of the Rabbinical Assembly of America,* vol. XVII 1953.

[83] Heschel, *op cit.;* for details see note 80 above.

KIDDUSH HA-SHEM

[1] See Lev. 21:6; 22:2.

[2] Ezekiel, chs. 20, 36, 39.

[3] Num. 20:12; Deut. 32:51; Num. 20:12; Deut. 32:51; Lev. 22:32.

[4] On this rabbinic tradition, see Gen. R. 49:9.

[5] See Sifra to Shemini 45d; Zev. 115b.

[6] This view is formulated in Av. Zar. 27b; Sanh. 74a–b.

[7] Lev. 22:32, 33, Sifra, Emor, *perek* 9.

[8] II Macc. 6:18–30.

[9] Mekh. Ba-Hodesh, 6.

[10] Mekh. Shirata, 3.

[11] Maimonides, *Yad, Yesodei ha-Torah*, 5:3.

[12] Maimonides, *Yad, Yesodei ha-Torah*, 5:1; for alternative views see, for example, Tos. Av. Zar. 27b.

[13] See, for example, Tos. Av. Zar. 54a.

[14] A. I. Kook, *Mishpat Kohen* (1966), No. 143; in contradistinction to Kook see, for example, J. J. Weinberg, *Seridei Esh*, 1 (1961), 303–16.

[15] E. Oshry, *Mi-Ma'amakim*, 2 (1963) Resp. No. 1. For more on *"Kiddush ha-Shem"* in the Nazi period, see *Kiddush Hashem: Keta'im Mimei Hashoah Mitokh Hagenazim shel Arkion Ringelblum Begetto Warsha*, ed. by N. Blumenthal and J. Karmish (1969). See also P. Schindler, in *Tradition*, 13, No. 4 (1973), 88–104.

[16] For these differing views, see TJ, Shev. 4:3, 35b; Maimonides, *Yad, Melakhim*, 10:2; *Mishneh le-Melekh* to *Yad, Melakhim*, 10:2.

[17] TJ, BM. 2:5, 8c.

[18] TJ, Ned. 3:14, 38b; Yoma, 86a.

[19] Yoma 86a; Av. Zar. 28a; Maimonides, *Yad, Yesodei ha-Torah*, 5:11.

[20] Maimonides, *Yad, Yesodei ha-Torah*, 5:10.

[21] See, H. G. Friedman in: *HUCA* (1904), 193–214.

[22] *Zohar*, 3:195b.

[23] See G. Scholem, *Jewish Gnosticism, Merkabah Mysticism and Talmudic Tradition* (1960), Appendix C.

[24] See Zedekiah ben Abraham ha-Rofe, *Shibbolei ha-Leket*, ed. S. K. Mirsky (1966), 149–50.

[25] J. Kaufman, *Midreshei Ge'ullah* (1954), 58, n. 12, quoting H. N. Bialik.

Glossary

ADONAI — (Heb.) "Lord."

AGGADAH — (Heb.) Non-legal parts of the Talmud, i.e., homiletics, ethical teachings, parables, biographical details.

AHARIT HA-YAMIM — (Heb.) "the end of days," i.e., the end of time and history.

AHAVAT HA-SHEM — (Heb.) "Love of God."

AKEDAH — (Heb.) Literally "binding"; used most commonly to refer to the binding of Isaac, i.e., the sacrifice of Isaac (Gen. 22:1–19).

AMIDAH — (Heb.) "standing"; the "Eighteen Benedictions"; the principal Jewish prayer. In Hebrew it is also called the *Shemoneh Esreh*.

AMORAIM — (Heb.) Title given to the talmudic Sages of the Gemara, i.e., those who appear in the later discussions of the Talmud after the close of the Mishnah (200 C.E. approx.).

AMUDIM — (Heb.) "pillars" (of the faith).

AM SEGULLAH — (Heb.) A treasured people, i.e., "Chosen People".

ANAFIM — (Heb.) "branches," i.e., derivative principles (of the faith).

ASHKENAZIM — (Heb.) The name given to Jews living in or descended from Eastern Europe, Germany and Northern Europe.

AV BET DIN — (Heb.) Head of the Court, i.e., the chief justice of a Jewish religious court.

AVODAH ZARAH — (Heb.) Idolatry.

AVODAT HA-ELOHIM — (Heb.) Divine worship.

AZILUT — (Heb.) Emanation.

BARAITA — (Aramaic) Literally, "external"; more generally means tannaitic sayings (pre 200 C.E.) not included in the Mishnah but recorded in later rabbinic sources.

BET DIN — (Heb.) Literally "House of Law," i.e., a Jewish court of law.

BITTAHON — (Heb.) Trust (in God).

BNEI YISRAEL — (Heb.) Literally "children of Israel," i.e., the people of Israel.

CREATIO EX NIHILO — (Lat.) "creation from nothing," i.e., created solely by God without any existent material.

289

DAT ELOHIT – (Heb.) Divine law, i.e., laws revealed by God.

DAT NIMUSIT – (Heb.) Conventional law, i.e., laws created by man in society.

DAT TIVIT – (Heb.) Natural law, i.e., the regulation and order found in the workings of nature.

DAYAN – (Heb.) Judge.

DE'OT – (Heb.) Beliefs.

DEVEKUT – (Heb.) "clinging or adhesion to God." A term used to express an extreme closeness to God; used especially by Jewish mystics to describe the mystical relation of man and God.

EIN-SOF – (Heb.) Literally "without end." Term used by the Kabbalists for God as. He exists in his unknowable and inexpressible self-perfection and transcendence.

ELOHIM – (Heb.) God.

EMUNAH – (Heb.) trust, belief, in God.

EMUNOT – (Heb.) dogmas.

EPICUREAN (APIKOROS) – A follower of the Greek philosopher Epicurus, more generally used in Jewish thought as a term of reproach and disapproval for one who denies the existence or Kingship of God; also to those who seek pleasure as an end in itself.

GALUT – (Heb.) Exile; the term applied to Jewish life outside of the land of Israel.

GAN EDEN – (Heb.) Garden of Eden; paradise.

GAON (pl. GEONIM) – (Heb.) Formal title of the heads of the talmudic academies of Babylonia between the 7th and 11th centuries. The Geonim were recognized by the Jews as the highest authority in religious matters and were considered to be the successors of the talmudic Sages.

GEHENNA, GEHINNOM – (Heb.) Hell.

GEMARA – (Heb.) Traditions, discussions and rulings of the Amoraim (200–500 C.E.) commentating on and supplementing the Mishnah; part of the Talmud.

GENIZAH – (Heb.) Literally "hiding"; more generally the name given to the synagogue store room for old and unusable Torah Scrolls and sacred books.

GEULAH – (Heb.) "redemption."

GEZERAH – (Heb.) "a decree," a technical term for a rabbinical prohibition.

GILGUL – (Heb.) Transmigration of souls or Reincarnation; a doctrine of Jewish mystics.

GOLEM – (Heb.) "shapeless mass"—(used once in the Bible: Ps. 139:16). In medieval Hebrew it means "formless matter." Later it came more generally to mean a robot or Frankenstein-type monster; often associated in legend with R. Judah Loew of Prague who is said to have created one.

HALAKHAH — (Heb.) A legal enactment; more generally the term applied to the whole biblical-rabbinic legal tradition whose pronouncements on legal matters are considered binding on every Jew.

HA-MAKOM — (Heb.) "The Place." A rabbinic reference for God.

HASHGAHAH — (Heb.) Providence.

HASID (pl. HASIDIM) — (Heb.) "a pious one"; generally used for pious Jews; more technically refers to a follower of the Hasidic movement (18th century).

HASIDEI ASHKENAZ — (Heb.) "the Hasidim (pietists) of Germany"; a mystical-pietistic movement of 13th- and 14th-century Germany.

HASIDISM — (Heb.) The 18th-century religious-mystical movement founded by Israel ben Eliezer (the Baal Shem Tov). It began in southern Poland and the Ukraine and soon spread throughout East European Jewry. Today it is found in many parts of the Jewish world.

HASKALAH — (Heb.) Jewish "Enlightenment" movement begun in the late 18th century to bring modern culture and secular learning to the Jewish people.

HEIKHALOT — (Heb.) "palaces." More generally, the ancient mystical tradition which centered on the soul's mystical ascent through the upper worlds and palaces.

HEREM — (Heb.) Ban of excommunication.

HESED — (Heb.) "mercy."

HOKHMAH YEVANIT — (Heb.) Literally "Greek wisdom"; more generally, Greek philosophy.

HOMER — (Heb.) Matter.

HOVOT HA-LEVAVOT — (Heb.) "duties of the heart"; more specifically, title of Bahya ibn Paquda's famous 11th-century pietistic work.

IKKARIM — (Heb.) "principles" (literally "roots"). It is used to refer to the basic premises of a philosophical or theological system.

ISHURIM — (Heb.) Articles (of faith).

KABBALAH — (Heb.) Literally "tradition"; more generally used to describe the Jewish mystical tradition.

KALAM — (Arabic) Literally "speech" or "word"; more generally, the term for Islamic theology.

KARAITES — (Heb.) 8th-century Jewish sect founded by Anan ben David. This sect rejected the rabbinic Oral Law, insisting that only the Written Law (Torah) was authoritative. The sect continued to exert considerable influence until the late 12th and early 13th century.

KAVVANAH — (Heb.) "Intent," "Intention." More generally, the inner intensity and intent of a religious act.

KEHILLAH (pl. KEHILLOT) — (Heb.) Literally "community," i.e., the Jewish community.

KIDDUSH HA-SHEM — (Heb.) Literally "sanctification of the name"; more generally, the doctrine that Jews must act so as not to blemish or discredit their God. The most extreme and well-known case is martyrdom in the face of conversionary pressures, i.e., dying rather than discredit Judaism.

KINOT — (Heb.) A religious poem of lament composed for personal or national tragedies.

MA'AMARIM — (Heb.) "treatises."

MA'ASEH BERESHIT — (Heb.) "the mysteries of Creation," the name given to the esoteric mystical theories regarding the world's creation.

MA'ASEH MERKAVAH — (Heb.) "the mysteries of the chariot," the name given to the esoteric mystical doctrines connected with Ezekiel's chariot (Ezek. 1–3).

MALKHUT SHAMAYIM — (Heb.) Kingdom of Heaven.

MASORAH — (Heb.) The "authorized" Hebrew version of the Bible used by Jews.

MEMRA — (Aramaic) "word" (of God).

MIDDAH (pl. MIDDOT) — (Heb.) Conduct, ethical behavior or virtue; also used for "quality" or dimension.

MIDRASH — (Heb.) from the Hebrew root "to inquire." It is the process whereby one claims to discover meanings in biblical texts which are not apparent or based on a literal reading of the text. The sages drew both legal meanings from the biblical text (Midrash Halakhah) and non-legal meanings (Midrash Aggadah) in this way.

MIN (pl. MINIM) — (Heb.) Heretic(s).

MINHAGIM — (Heb.) Customs.

MISHNAH — (Heb.) earliest codification of Jewish Oral Law, edited and codified c. 200 by R. Judah the Prince in Palestine.

MISHPAT — (Heb.) Justice.

MITZVOT SHIMIYYOT — (Heb.) *mitzvot* (religious norms), which do not seem to have their basis in human reason.

MITZVOT SIKHLIYYOT — (Heb.) *mitzvot* which have their basis in reason, i.e., which appear rational to man.

MUSAR — (Heb.) Ethical instruction.

MUTAZILITES — (Arabic) Members of the Islamic theological school of Mutazilah. This was the most influential early Islamic theological school, which was later superseded.

NESHAMAH — (Heb.) "Soul."

NAVI — (Heb.) "Prophet."

OLAM HA-BA — (Heb.) Literally, "the world to come"; more generally, reference to the world beyond the grave.

PARDES — (Heb.) Literally "garden" (Song of Songs 4:3; Ecc. 2:15). More generally in Jewish thought, a term which is used by Jewish mystics to refer to the four levels of biblical interpretation to paradise.

PERUSH — (Heb.) "interpretation."

PERISHUT — (Heb.) Asceticism.

PESHAT — (Heb.) Literal meaning of a text; more specifically applied to the literal exegesis of the Bible.

PILPUL — (Heb.) The process of dialectical reasoning applied to the Oral Law. Sometimes used pejoratively to refer to extreme casuistic-type reasoning.

PIYYUT (pl. PIYYUTIM) — (Heb.) Synagogue poetry which became standard elements of Jewish liturgy.

RAHAMIM — (Heb.) "mercy."

RAZON — (Heb.) "will."

RUAH HA-KODESH — (Heb.) Holy Spirit.

SAVORAIM — (Heb.) 6th-century sages who were responsible for the final editing of the Talmud, and thus the first post-talmudic group of sages.

SEFER HA-BAHIR — (Heb.) literally "Book of Brilliance." One of the most ancient Jewish mystical texts. Ascribed by tradition to a 1st-century sage, it was probably produced in the early medieval period (8th to 10th century C.E.).

SEFER YEZIRAH — (Heb.) "Book of Creation." An ancient Jewish mystical text (3rd to 6th century C.E.) which gives an esoteric account of creation.

SEFIRA (pl. SEFIROT) — (Heb.) Literally "numbers"; more generally the kabbalistic term for God's emanations, manifestations and attributes.

SEPHARDI (Sefaradi; pl. SEPHARDIM, Sefaradim) — (Heb.) The name given to Jews of the Iberian peninsula and their descendants. More generally used to cover the Jews of North Africa and the Middle East who were influenced by Spanish Jewry in their religious practices and liturgy.

SEPTUAGINT — (Latin) "The Seventy." The earliest translation of the Bible into Greek in the 3rd century B.C.E.

SHEKHINAH — (Heb.) Literally (the) "Dwelling," i.e., God's Presence. The term was sometimes used interchangeably with the word God.

SHEMA — (Heb.) At the very heart of Judaism lies the *Shema*, the fervent declaration of the Unity or Oneness of God. This is the Jewish prayer most often recited, an affirmation most insistently made by the pious from childhood until death.

SHE'OL — (Heb.) Netherworld; the regions of the dead.

SHORASHIM — (Heb.) Secondary derivative principles.

SUFISM — (Arabic; Suf = a garment worn by Moslem ascetics.) Islamic mysticism which aimed at mystical union with Allah.

TAKKANAH (pl. TAKKANOT) — (Heb.) Positive rabbinic enactments which supplement the written Torah; usually promulgated to aid the public welfare or to strengthen the religious and moral life of the community.

TALLIT — (Heb.) Prayer shawl worn by adult males.

TALMID ḤAKHAM (Ḥakham) — (Heb.) Torah scholar.

TANNAIM — (Heb.) Earliest strata (group) of talmudic sages; the title given to the sages of the Mishnah (approx. 200 B.C.E. to 200 C.E.).

TARGUM — (Aramaic) Literally "interpretation" or "translation"; more commonly it is the name given to the Aramaic translation of the Bible.

TARGUM ONKELOS — (Aramaic) Aramaic translation of the Bible, attributed to Onkelos the proselyte, 2nd century C.E.

TARGUM YERUSHALMI (also known as TARGUM JONATHAN) — Aramaic translation of the Bible composed in Galilee (date uncertain) no later than 7th–8th century C.E.

TE'ARIM — (Heb.) Attributes or predicates (of God).

TEFILLAH — (Heb.) Prayer.

TEFILLIN — (Aramaic) Literally "attachment"; more generally, the head and arm phylacteries worn during daily prayer by Jewish adult males.

TEḤIYYAT HA-METIM — (Heb.) Resurrection of the dead.

TESHUVAH — (Heb.) Repentance.

TETRAGRAMMATON — (Engl.) The most sacred name of God in the Bible and made up of four letters: YHWH. It is incorrectly vocalized as *JEHOVAH*.

TIKKUN — (Heb.) "completion" or "restitution." More specifically, the mystical doctrine of the unification of reality.

TORAH SHE-BE-AL PEH — (Heb.) "the oral Torah," i.e., post-Biblical; the rabbinic writings such as the Mishnah, Gemara and Midrashim.

TORAH SHE-BIKHTAV — (Heb.) Literally "the written Torah," i.e., the five books of Moses, or the Pentateuch.

TOSAFOT — (Heb.) Literally "additions"; more generally, the name given to the talmudic interpretations and explanatory notes by French and German scholars of the 12th to 14th centuries.

TZURAH — (Heb.) form.

WISSENSCHAFT DES JUDENTUMS — (German) "Science of Judaism." Primarily a 19th-century movement which attempted to apply modern scientific methods to all branches of Jewish scholarship. Intended to help with the emancipation and integration of the Jew into modern society.

UNIO MYSTICA — (Latin) "mystical union"; the state of most intimate attachment to the Divine sought by mystics.

YESOD (pl. YESODOT) — (Heb.) "fundamental"; foundation or fundamental elements.

YEẒER HA-RA — (Heb.) "evil inclination."

YEẒER HA-TOV — (Heb.) "good inclination."

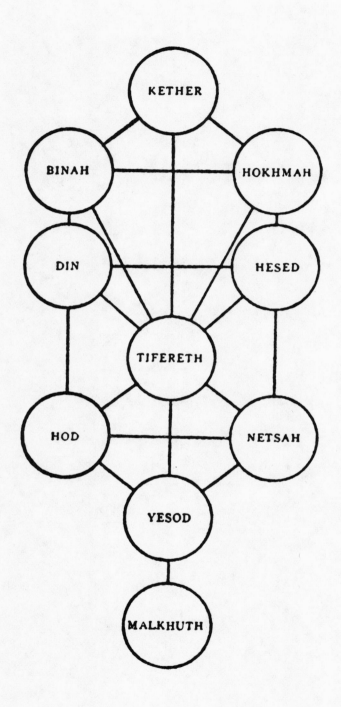

1. *Kether Elyon,*   the "supreme crown" of God;

2. *Hokhmah,*   the "wisdom" or primordial idea of God;

3. *Binah,*   the "intelligence" of God;

4. *Hesed,*   the "love" or mercy of God;

5. *Gevurah* or *Din,*   the "power" of God, chiefly manifested as the power of stern judgment and punishment;

6. *Rahamim,*   the "compassion" of God, to which falls the task of mediating between the two preceding Sefiroth; the name *Tifereth* "beauty", is used only rarely.

7. *Netsah,*   the "lasting endurance" of God;

8. *Hod,*   the "majesty" of God;

9. *Yesod,*   the "basis" or "foundation" of all active forces in God;

10 *Malkhuth,*   the "kingdom" of God, usually described in the Zohar as the *Keneseth Israel,* the mystical archetype of Israel's community, or as the Shekhinah.

Biographical Index

Aaron ben Elijah (c. 1330–1369)—The major Karaite thinker. Lived mostly in Constantinople.

*Abelard (Abaelard), Peter (1079–1142)—French Christian philospher and theologian.

Abner of Burgos (1270–1340)—Physician and philosopher. Apostate to Christianity.

Abrabanel, Isaac ben Judah (1437–1508)—statesman, philosopher and biblical exegete. Born in Lisbon.

Abrabanel, Judah (called Leone Ebreo or Leo Hebraeus; c. 1460–after 1523)—Italian poet, physician, and one of the foremost philosophers of the Renaissance.

Abraham bar Hiyya (Hayya; d. c. 1136)—Spanish philosopher, mathematician, astronomer and translator.

Abraham ben Moses ben Maimon (1186–1237)—leader *(nagid)* of the Egyptian Jewish community and religious philosopher; only son of Maimonides.

Abulafia, Abraham ben Samuel (1240–d. after 1291)—Spanish mystic.

Abulafia, Meir (1170?–1244)—talmudic commentator, thinker, and poet; the most renowned Spanish rabbi of the first half of the 13th century.

Adret, Solomon ben Abraham (known from his initials as RaShBA; c. 1235–c. 1310)—Spanish rabbi and one of the foremost Jewish scholars of his day.

Agus, Jacob Bernard (1911–   )—American rabbi and historian of Jewish philosophy.

Ahad Ha'am (Asher Hirsch Ginsberg; 1856–1927)—Hebrew essayist, thinker and leader of the Hibbat Zion movement; he wrote under the name of Ahad Ha'am ("One of the People").

Albalag, Isaac (13th century)—translator and philospher.

Albo, Joseph (d. 1444)—Spanish philosopher and preacher; author of *Sefer ha-Ikkarim* ("Book of Principles"), a famous treatise on Jewish articles of faith which he completed in Soria (Castile) in 1425.

**Al-Farabi, Abu Nasr Muhammad (c. 870–c. 950)—one of the greatest Islamic

299

philosophers of the medieval Islamic world; had considerable influence on Jewish philosophers, particularly Maimonides.

**Al-Ghazali, Abu Hamid Muhammad Ibn Muhammad Al-Tusi (1058–1111) – Persian Muslim theologian, jurist, mystic and religious reformer; wrote mainly in Arabic.

Altmann, Alexander (1906–   ) – rabbi and historian of Jewish philosophy; born in Germany; now holds chair at Brandeis Univ. in U.S.

*Anselm of Canterbury (1033–1109) – abbot of Bec (Normandy) and from 1093 archbishop of Canterbury; theologian and philosopher; canonized by the Catholic Church. Originator of the ontological argument for the existence of God.

*Aquinas, Thomas (1225–1274) – most important of the Christian medieval philosophers; the author of the *Summa Theologica;* canonized by the Church.

Arama, Isaac ben Moses (c. 1420–1494) – Spanish rabbi, philosopher, and preacher.

Aristobulus of Paneas (first half of the 2nd century B.C.E.) – Jewish Hellenistic philosopher; one of the earliest allegorical interpreters of the Bible.

***Aristotle (4th century B.C.E.) – greatest Greek philosopher and founder of the peripatetic school; the most influential philosopher in the late medieval period (12th century onward).

Asher ben Jehiel (also known as Asheri and Rosh; c. 1250–1327) – **talmudist.**

*Augustine (354–430) – bishop of Hippo (North Africa) and most important Church Father of early Western Christianity.

Avempace (Abu Bakr Muhammad ibn Yahya ibn Bajja, called **Ibn Al-Sa'igh; d. 1138) – Muslim philosopher, born in Saragossa; lived in Seville, Granada, and Fez. He was a celebrated philosopher, mathematician, musician, poet, and served as vizier.

**Averroes (Abu Al-Walid Muhammad Ibn Rushd; 1126–1198) – one of the greatest Islamic philosophers and a noted physician; primarily known as commentator on Aristotle's works; lived in Spain.

**Avicenna (Abu Ali Al-Hussein ibn Abu Abdallah ibn Sina; 980–1037) – physician, scientist, man of affairs, and one of the greatest Muslim philosophers.

Baal Shem Tov – see Israel ben Eliezer.

Baeck, Leo (1873–1956) – German rabbi and religious thinker; leader of Progressive Judaism.

Bahya (Baḥye) **ben Joseph Ibn Paquda** (2nd half of the 11th century) – Jewish moral philosopher and author of the most important Jewish ethical work of the medieval period, *Duties of the Hearts.*

Baron, Salo W. (1895–)—Jewish historian; author of *A Social and Religious History of the Jews*.

Bergman, S. H. (1883–)—Israel historian of philosophy; Professor at Hebrew University, Jerusalem.

Berkovits, Eliezer (1908–)—American Orthodox rabbi and theologian.

*Bernard of Clairvaux (1090–1153)—French Cistercian, homilist, and theologian.

Borowitz, Eugene Bernard (1924–)—American Reform rabbi and existentialist theologian.

Buber, Martin (1878–1965)—philosopher and theologian; Zionist thinker and leader; born in Germany; Professor at Hebrew University, Jerusalem.

*Buridan, Jean (c. 1295–c. 1358)—medieval logician and thinker; taught at the University of Paris.

Caspi, Joseph (1297–1340)—Provençal philosopher, exegete, and grammarian.

Cohen, Arthur A. (1928–)—American author and theologian.

Cohen, Hermann (1842–1918)—German idealist philosopher and Jewish thinker.

Cohen, Morris Raphael (1880–1947)—American philosopher.

Cordovero, Moses (known as the Remak: 1522–1570)—Kabbalist of the 16th century Safed school; disciple of Joseph Karo.

Crescas, Hasdai (d. 1412?)—Spanish philosopher, theologian, and statesman; most important Jewish critic of medieval Aristotelianism.

Da Costa (Acosta), Uriel (1585–1640)—Dutch Jewish philosopher and free thinker; older contemporary of and influence on Spinoza.

Delmedigo, Elijah ben Moses Abba (c. 1460–1497)—philosopher and talmudist; born in Candia (Crete); also known as Elijah Cretensis.

Delmedigo, Joseph Solomon (1591–1655)—rabbi, philosopher, mathematician and astronomer; also known as Joseph Solomon Rofe (acronym YaSHaR) of Candia (Crete).

Dubnow, Simon (1860–1941)—Polish Jewish historian.

*Duns Scotus, John (1266–1308)—Catholic theologian and philosopher; opposed many of the views of Thomas Aquinas.

Duran, Profiat (Profayt; d. c. 1414)—scholar and physician; one of the outstanding anti-Christian polemicists of Spanish Jewry.

Duran, Simeon ben Zemah (RaSHBaZ, Hebrew acronym of Rabbi SHimon Ben Zemah; 1361–1444)—rabbinic authority, philosopher, and scientist.

*Eckhart, Meister (c. 1260–c. 1327)—theologian and one of the great Christian mystics.

Efros, Israel Isaac (1891–   )—Hebrew educator, scholar, and historian of Jewish philosophy.

Eleazar of Worms (ben Judah Kalonymous; 1165–1236)—Kabbalist and talmudist; important figure in Ashkenazi Ḥasidism.

Elijah ben Solomon Zalman (the "Vilna Gaon" or "Elijah Gaon"; acronym Ha-GRA = Ha-Gaon Rabbi Eliyahu; 1720–1797)—one of the greatest spiritual and intellectual leaders of Jewry in modern times. He was the leading opponent of Ḥasidism, the followers of which he excommunicated.

Fackenheim, Emil Ludwig (1916–   )—Canadian rabbi and existentialist theologian; born in Halle (Germany).

Falaquera (Ibn Falaquera, Palquera), **Shem Tov ben Joseph** (c. 1225–1295) medieval Spanish philosophical author and translator.

***Fichte, Johann Gottlieb** (1762–1814)—German idealist philosopher.

Formstecher, Solomon (1808–1889)—German Jewish idealist philosopher and rabbi.

Friedlaender, David (1750–1834)—communal leader and author in Berlin; a pioneer of the practice and ideology of assimilation and a forerunner of Reform Judaism.

****Galen** (Galenus) **Claudius** (131 C.E.–201 C.E.)—prominent physician in antiquity and author of important works.

Gans, David ben Solomon (1541–1613)—chronicler, astronomer, and mathematician.

Geiger, Abraham (1810–1874)—one of the leaders of the Reform movement in Judaism and an outstanding scholar of the "Wissenschaft des Judentums" (Science of Judaism),

Gerondi, Jonah ben Abraham (c. 1200–1263)—Spanish rabbi, author, and moralist.

Gordon, Aharon David (1856–1922)—Hebrew writer and spiritual mentor of the Zionist labor movement which emphasized self-realization through settlement on the land (ḥalutziut); born in Troyanov (Russia).

Gracian, Zerahiah ben Isaac ben Shealtiel (13th century)—physician, philosopher, and translator.

Graetz, Heinrich (1817–1891)—Jewish historian and Bible scholar; author of the well-known *History of the Jews.*

Guttmann, Julius (Yiẓḥak; 1880–1950)—German philosopher and historian of Jewish philosophy.

Hegel, Georg Wilhelm Friedrich (1770–1831)—German idealist philosopher whose work dominated 19th-century thought.

Heller, Yom-Tov Lipmann ben Nathan Ha-Levi (Yom-Tov Heller; 1579–1654) —Moravian rabbi; commentator on the Mishnah.

Herberg, Will (1906–   )—American theologian and sociologist.

Herder, Johann Gottfried (1744–1803)—German philosopher, author, critic, and translator.

Heschel, Abraham Joshua (1907–1972)—European-born American scholar and philosopher.

Ḥibat Allah, Abu Al-Barakat (11th–12th century)—philosopher, physician, and biblical commentator.

Hillel ben Samuel (c. 1220–c. 1295)—physician, talmudic scholar, and Aristotelian philosopher.

Hirsch, Samson (ben) Raphael (1808–1888)—rabbi and theologian; leader and foremost exponent of Orthodoxy in Germany in the 19th century; critic of the Reform movement.

Ḥiwi Al-Balkhi (2nd half of 9th century)—from Khorasan, Persia (now Afghanistan); freethinker and radical Bible critic.

Husik, Isaac (1876–1939)—American historian of medieval Jewish philosophy.

Ibn Alfakhar, Judah (d. 1235)—physician at the court of Ferdinand III of Castile; opponent of Maimonides.

Ibn Daud, Abraham ben David HaLevi (known as Rabad; c. 1110–1180)— Spanish historian, physician, and astronomer; first Jewish Aristotelian of the medieval period.

Ibn Ezra, Abraham (1089–1164)—poet, grammarian, biblical commentator, philosopher, astronomer, and physician.

Ibn Ezra, Moses ben Jacob (also known as Abu Harun; c. 1055–after 1135)— Spanish Hebrew poet and philosopher.

Ibn Gabirol, Solomon ben Judah (c. 1020–c. 1057)—in Arabic: Abu Ayyub Sulayman ibn Yahya ibn Gabirol; in Latin: Avicebron; Spanish poet and Neoplatonic philosopher; influenced medieval Christian thought.

Ibn Migash, Joseph ben Meir Ha-Levi (1077–1141)—Spanish talmudic scholar.

Ibn Tibbon, Samuel ben Judah (c. 1160–c. 1230)—French philosopher; disciple and translator of Maimonides' *Guide* into Hebrew; a member of the famous Tibbonide family which comprised at least four generations of translators and scholars.

Ibn Ẓaddik, Joseph ben Jacob (d. 1149)—philosopher and poet.

Isaac ben Sheshet Perfet (known as RIBaSH from the initials of Rabbi Isaac Ben SHeshet; 1326–1408)—Spanish rabbi and halakhic authority.

Israel ben Eliezer Ba'al Shem Tov (known by the initials BESHT—Ba'al SHem Tov; c. 1700–1760)—charismatic founder and first leader of the Hasidic movement.

Israeli, Isaac ben Solomon (c. 855–c. 955)—physician and Neoplatonic philosopher; North African.

Jabez, Joseph ben Hayyim (d. 1507)—Hebrew homilist and exegete.

Jacobs, Louis (1920–)—English rabbi and theologian; translator of Hasidic texts.

Joseph ben Abraham Ha-Basir (11th century)—Persian Karaite philosopher.

Judah ben Barzillai of Barcelona (11th–12th century)—Spanish talmudist and halakhic codifier.

Judah ben Samuel He-Hasid (d. 1217)—German author of *Sefer ha-Hasid;* mystic and talmudist; leader of German Ashkenazi Hasidism.

Judah Halevi (before 1075–1141)—great Spanish Hebrew poet and philosopher; one of the most important figures in the medieval period.

Judah Loew (Liwa, Loeb) **ben Bezalel** (known as Der Hohe Rabbi Loew and MaHaRaL mi-Prag; c. 1525–1609)—rabbi, talmudist, moralist and mathematician.

*Kant, Immanuel (1724–1804)—German philosopher; the most important of all modern philosophers who exerted a major influence on Jewish thought in the 19th and 20th centuries.

Kaplan, Mordecai Menahem (1881–)—U.S. rabbi, theologian, and founder of the Reconstructionist movement.

Karo, Joseph (1488–1575)—great halakhist and codifier of the *Shulhan Arukh,* one of the most important of all halakhic works.

Kimhi David (known as RADAK from the acronym of Rabbi David Kimhi; Maistre Petit; (1160?–1235?)—grammarian and Bible exegete of Narbonne, Provence.

Kohler, Kaufmann (1843–1926)—American Reform rabbi and president of Hebrew Union College; author of works on Jewish theology.

Kook (Kuk), Abraham Isaac (1865–1935)—rabbinical authority and mystical thinker; first Ashkenazi Chief Rabbi of modern Israel.

Krochmal, Nachman (1785–1840)—philosopher and historian; one of the founders of the "science of Judaism" ("Wissenschaft des Judentums"); a leader of the Haskalah movement in Eastern Europe.

Landauer, Gustav (1870–1919)—German philosopher and writer.

*Lavater, John Casper (1741–1801)—Swiss theologian who engaged in a famous debate with Moses Mendelssohn.

Lazarus, Moritz (1824–1903)—German philosopher and psychologist; author of important work on Jewish ethics written from a Kantian perspective.

*Leibnitz, Gottfried** (1646–1716)—major German rationalist philosopher and mathematician.

*Lessing, Gotthold Ephraim** (1729–1781)—German dramatist, philosopher and critic; one of the outstanding representatives of the Enlightenment in Germany; devoted to the principles of toleration; a close friend of Moses Mendelssohn.

Levi ben Gershom (acronym: RaLBaG; also called Maestre Leo de Bagnols, Magister Leo Hebraeus, Gersonides; 1288–1344)—mathematician, astronomer, Aristotelian philosopher and biblical commentator; born probably at Bagnols-sur-Creze (France).

Loanz, Elijah ben Moses (1564–1636)—German kabbalist.

*Locke, John** (1632–1704)—probably the most important 17th-century empiricist philosopher; an important figure in the spread of political toleration and parliamentary democracy.

Luria, Isaac ben Solomon (referred to as Ha-Ari; 1534–1572)—Kabbalist; one of the most important figures in the Jewish mystical tradition; led the mystical community in Safed in Erez Israel.

Luria, Solomon ben Jehiel (known as *Rashal* or *Maharshal*—Morenu Ha-Rav Shelomo Luria; c. 1510–1574). Rabbinic authority and Talmudic commentator.

Luzzatto, Moses Ḥayyim (Ramḥal; 1707–1746)—Italian Kabbalist and moralist.

Luzzatto, Samuel David (SHaDaL or SHeDaL; 1800–1865)—Italian scholar, philosopher, Bible commentator, and translator.

*Magnus, Albertus** (c. 1206–1280)—Christian theologian.

Maimonides—see Moses ben Maimon.

Malbim, Meir Loeb (1809–1879)—rabbi, preacher, and biblical exegete.

Meiri, Menahem ben Solomon (1249–1316)—Provençal scholar and commentator on the Talmud.

Mendelssohn, Moses (Moses ben Menahem, acronym RaMbeMaN or Moses of Dessau; 1729–1786)—philosopher of the German Enlightenment in the pre-Kantian period and spiritual leader of German Jewry. First major modern Jewish philosopher.

*Moore, George Foot** (1851–1931)—American scholar; expert on Talmudic Judaism.

Moses ben Joshua of Narbonne (Narboni; d. 1362)—French Aristotelian philosopher and physician.

Moses ben Maimon (Maimonides; known in rabbinical literature as "Rambam" from the acronym Rabbi Moses Ben Maimon; 1135–1204)— rabbinic authority, codifier, Aristotelian philosopher, and physician. The greatest single figure in medieval Judaism in both philosophical and halakhic scholarship.

Moses ben Naḥman (Naḥmanides; also known as Naḥamani and RaMBaN— Rabbi Moses Ben Naḥman; 1194–1270)—Spanish rabbi and scholar; philosopher, Kabbalist, biblical exegete, poet, and physician; one of the leading authors of talmudic literature in the Middle Ages.

Naḥman (ben Simḥah) of Bratslav (1772–1811)—grandson of the Baal Shem Tov; ḥasidic *ẓaddik* in Podolia and the Ukraine and the center of a theological and social storm throughout most of his life.

Nissim of Gerondi (Nissim ben Reuben Gerondi; known from the acronym of Rabbenu Nissim as the RaN; c. 1310–c. 1375)—Spanish talmudist.

Petuchowski, Jacob (1925–   )—American Reform rabbi; Professor of Rabbinics at Hebrew Union College; Reform thinker.

Philo Judaeus (Philo of Alexandria; c. 20 B.C.E.–50 C.E.)—Hellenistic Jewish philosopher; credited by some with being the founder of the medieval philosophical movement though he lived hundreds of years earlier.

*Pico della Mirandola, Giovanni (1463–1494)—one of the most remarkable figures of the Italian Renaissance.

***Plato (427–347 B.C.E.)—major Greek philosopher who exerted enormous influence on all later thinkers, especially in the early medieval period.

***Plotinus (205–270 C.E.)—the most important neo-Platonic philosopher in the Hellenistic period; author of the *Enneads*.

Pollegar, Isaac (early 14th century)—Spanish talmudist and philosopher.

***Proclus (410–485 C.E.)—Neoplatonist thinker; his commentaries on Greek thought were links in the transmission of Greek learning to later ages.

Rashi (Solomon ben Isaac; 1040–1105)—leading commentator on the Bible and Talmud.

Rosenstock-Huessy, Eugen (1888–1973)—German philosopher and theologian; convert from Judaism to Christianity; important influence on Franz Rosenzweig.

Rosenzweig, Franz (1886–1929)—German Jewish theologian; influential modern Jewish thinker.

Rossi, Azariah (Bonaiuto) **ben Moses Dei** (c. 1511–c. 1578)—scholar of Hebrew letters during the Italian Renaissance.

Rotenstreich, Nathan (1914–   )—Israeli phenomenologist and philosopher;

Professor at Hebrew University, Jerusalem; historian of philosophy.

Roth, Leon (1896–1963)—English philosopher and historian of philosophy.

Rubenstein, Richard Lowell (1924–)—American Conservative rabbi; proponent of a Jewish "death of God" theology.

Saadiah (ben Joseph) Gaon (882–942)—scholar and author of the geonic period; leader of Babylonian Jewry. The first medieval Jewish philosopher.

Samuel ben Hophni (d. 1013)—gaon of Sura (Babylonia); halakhist and translator of the Bible into Arabic.

*Schelling, Friedrich Wilhelm Joseph (1775–1854)—German idealist philosopher.

Scholem, Gershom Gerhard (1897–)—Jewish scholar; pioneer and leading authority in the field of Kabbalah and Jewish mysticism.

Shneur Zalman of Lyady (1745–1813)—founder of Ḥabad Ḥasidism.

Simon, Ernst (1899–)—Israeli thinker; Professor at Hebrew University, Jerusalem.

Solomon ben Abraham of Montpellier (13th century)—French talmudic scholar; initiator of the Maimonidean controversy that took place in the third decade of the 13th century.

Soloveitchik, Joseph Dov (1903–)—American talmudist and theologian; the leader of American Orthodoxy.

Spinoza, Baruch (Benedict) **de** (1632–1677)—Dutch philosopher; one of the greatest philosophers of all time; critic of normative Judaism and expounder of a pantheistic system.

Steinberg, Milton (1903–1950)—American Conservative rabbi; disciple and popularizer of Mordecai Kaplan's thought.

Steinheim, Salomon Ludwig (1789–1866)—German poet and religious philosopher.

Steinschneider, Moritz (1816–1907)—father of modern Jewish bibliography; one of the founders of modern Jewish scholarship.

**Tabrizi, Mahomet Abu-Bekr-At-Ben Mahomet (probably 2nd half of the 13th century)—Persian Muslim commentator on the 25 propositions appearing at the beginning of the second part of Moses Maimonides' *Guide of the Perplexed.*

Vajda, Georges (1908–)—French Arabist and Hebraist; historian of medieval Jewish philosophy.

Wiesel, Elie (Eliezer; 1928–)—novelist and witness to the Holocaust; the author of works on the Holocaust, Soviet Jewry and Hasidism.

*William of Ockham (c. 1285– 1349)— English medieval logician and philosopher of major significance.

Wolfson, Harry Austryn (1887– 1974)— American historian of philosophy, author of works on Philo, the Church Fathers, and Spinoza.

Zacuto, Abraham (c. 1450–1510)—Spanish thinker and astronomer.

Zerahiah ben Isaac Ha-Levi (known as Ferrarius Saladi; 14th– 15th century)— rabbi of Saragossa and of all the communities of Aragon.

Zunz, Leopold (Yom Tov Lippmann; 1794– 1886)— historian; among the founders of the Wissenschaft des Judentums ("Science of Judaism") in Germany in the early 1820s. Subsequently he produced important pioneer studies on the liturgy of the synagogue and on Jewish religious literature and cultural history.

*Christian thinker
**Muslim thinker
***Greek (or non-Christian) thinker

Bibliography

PART I: GENERAL HISTORIES OF JUDAISM AND OTHER STANDARD WORKS

So as not to repeat these standard works under each topic they are listed here. Readers should consult the "indices" of these works for specific topics

General

S. Baron, *–Social and Religious History of the Jews* (1952–) 16 vols. completed; more in progress.

——, *Jewish Community* (1948), 3 vols.

H. Graetz, *History of the Jews* (1891–98), 6 vols.

S. Dubnow, *World History of the Jewish People* (Eng. trans. 1967–74), 5 vols.

——, *History of the Jews in Russia and Poland* (1946²), 3 vols.

H.H. Ben Sasson, *History of the Jewish People* (1976).

G. Scholem, *Kabbalah* (1974).

——, *Major Trends in Jewish Mysticism* (1961³).

——, *On the Kabbalah and its Symbolism* (1965).

L. Finkelstein, *The Jews* (1960), 2 vols.

S. Schechter, *Studies in Judaism* (1896–1919), 3 vols.

Louis Jacobs, *Principles of the Jewish Faith* (1964).

——, *A Jewish Theology* (1974).

K. Kohler, *Jewish Theology* (1968 reprint).

Encyclopedia Judaica (1972), 16 vols.

Jewish Encyclopedia (1901–06), 10 vols.

Biblical Period

Y. Kaufman, *Toledoth Emunah ha Yisroelit* (1937–57), 8 vols. Abridged 1 vol. English Trans., *The Religion of Israel* (1960).

J. Pederson, *Israel, Its Life and Culture* (1940), 4 vols.

J. Bright, *The Religion of Israel* (1960).

U. Cassutto, *Commentary on Genesis* (Engl. trans. 1961–64), 2 vols.

——, *Commentary on Exodus* (Engl. trans. 1968).

309

O. Eissfeldt, *The Old Testament; An Introduction* (1965).
S. Sandmel, *The Hebrew Scriptures* (1963).

Rabbinic Period
S. Schechter, *Some Aspects of Rabbinic Theology* (1923).
E. Urbach, *The Sages* (1975).
J. Neusner, *History of the Jews in Babylonia* (1965–71), 5 vols.
G. Scholem, *Jewish Gnosticism, Merkabah Mysticism and Talmudic Tradition* (1965²).
L. Finkelstein, *The Pharisees* (1962), 2 vols.
V. Tcherikover, *Hellenistic Civilization and the Jews* (1959).
G.F. Moore, *Judaism in the First Centuries of the Christian Era* (1927–30), 3 vols.
E.R. Goodenough, *Graeco-Roman Symbols in Jewish Palestine* (1953–68), 13 vols.
L. Ginzberg, *The Legends of the Jews* (1942–47), 7 vols.
R. Blackman (ed.), *Mishnayoth* (Engl. trans. 1965), 6 vols.
C.G. Montefiore and H. Loewe, *A Rabbinic Anthology* (1938).
J. Klausner, *The Messianic Idea in Israel* (1955).
A. Cohen, *Everyman's Talmud* (1949).
Soncino *Talmud* (Engl. trans. 1935–48), 34 vols.

Medieval Period
I. Tishby, *Mishnat ha-Zohar* (1957²), 2 vols.
F. Baer, *History of the Jews in Christian Spain,* (1961–66), 2 vols.
I. Abrahams, *Jewish Life in the Middle Ages* (1932).

Modern Period
S. Dubnow, *Toledoth ha-Hasiduth* (1930–32), 2 vols.
H.M. Sachar, *The Course of Modern Jewish History* (1958).

For further bibliographical assistance readers are referred to the two volumes of *Bibliographical Essays on Judaism* published by Ktav (vol. 1, 1972; vol. 2, 1976).

PART II: TOPICAL BIBLIOGRAPHY

God
A. Marmorstein, *The Old Rabbinic Doctrine of God* (1968 reprint).
D. Kaufman, *Attributenlehre in der jüdischen Religionsphilosophie* (1877).
S. Cohen, in *HUCA* 23 (1950–51), pp. 579–604.

G. Vadja, *L'Amour de Dieu dans la theologie juive du Moyen Age* (1957).

M. Kaplan, *The Meaning of God in Modern Jewish Religion* (1937).

M. Buber, *I and Thou* (English translation 1970).

H. Cohen, *Religion within the Bounds of Reason* (Engl. trans. 1971).

R.E. Clements, *God and Temple* (1965).

J. Abelson *Immanence of God in Rabbinic Literature* (1912).

A. Marmorstein, *Studies in Jewish Theology* (1950).

A.J. Heschel, *The Prophets* (1962).

—, *God in Search of Man (1956).*

—, *Torah min ha-Shamayim* (1962–65), 2 vols.

H. Wolfson, *Studies in the History of Philosophy and Religion* (ed. I. Twersky) Vol. I (1973); Vol. II (1977). Contains a number of important articles on various aspects of the philosophical discussion of the nature and attributes of God in Jewish thought.

Man

I. Epstein, *The Faith of Judaism* (1954).

R. Gordis, *The Book of God and Man* (1968).

J. Petuchowski, "The Concept of Teshuvah in the Bible and Talmud" in *Judaism* 17 (1968), pp. 175–85.

A.J. Heschel, *God in Search of Man* (1956).

—, *Man is Not Alone* (1951).

U. Cassuto, *Commentary on Genesis* (1975).

L. Kohler, *Old Testament Theology* (1957).

D. Daube, *Sin, Ignorance and Forgiveness in the Bible* (1960).

A. Buechler, *Studies in Sin and Atonement* (1928).

J. Neusner, *The Idea of Purity in Judaism* (1975).

C.R. Smith, *The Biblical Doctrine of Sin* (1953).

M. Buber, *Between Man and Man* (1948).

—, *I and Thou* (Engl. trans. 1970).

F. Sutcliffe, *Providence and Suffering in the Old and New Testaments* (1955).

A. Kook, *Rabbi Kook's Philosophy of Repentance* (Engl. trans. 1968).

J. Soloveitchik, *Teshuvah* (1976).

—, "The Lonely Man of Faith" in *Tradition* (Summer, 1965), pp. 5–67.

H. Rabinowicz, *A Guide to Life* (1964).

H.H. Rowley, *The Faith of Israel* (1956).

A. Marmorstein, *The Doctrine of Merits in Old Rabbinical Literature* (1920).

Judaism, Covenant and Chosen People

W. Eichrodt, *Theology of the Old Testament* (1964), 2 vols.

D.J. McCarthy, *Treaty and Covenant* (1963).

G. Mendenhall, in *Biblical Archeologist,* 17 (1954).
M. Weinfeld, *Deuteronomy and the Deuteronomic School* (1971).
W.G. Plaut, *The Case for the Chosen People* (1966).
H.H. Rowley *The Biblical Doctrine of Election* (1950).
M. Kaplan, *The Religion of Ethical Nationhood* (1970).
D.R. Hillers, *Covenant, the History of a Biblical Idea* (1969).

Revelation, Mitzvot and Torah
J. Heinemann, *Ta'amei ha-Mitzvot b-Sifrut Yisroel* (1954).
A. Chill, *The Mitzvot* (1974).
Maimonides, *The Commandments* (Engl. trans., C. Chavel, 1967), 2 vols.
J.M. Guttman, *Behinat ha-Mitzvot* (1928).
A. Marmorstein, *Studies in Jewish Theology* (1950).
S.R. Hirsch, *Horeb* (1962), 2 vols.
A.J. Heschel, *Torah min ha-Shamayim ba-Aspaklaryah shel ha-Dorot* (1965),
  2 vols.
J. Mann, *The Bible as Read and Preached in the Old Synagogue* (1940).
B. Cohen, *Law and Tradition in Judaism* (1959).
S.H. Hooke, *Alpha and Omega: A Study in the Pattern of Revelation* (1961).
J.J. Petuchowski, *Ever Since Sinai* (1961).
H.A. Wolfson in *Jewish Quarterly Review* 32 (1942) pp. 345–70; 33 (1942)
  pp. 49–82.
S. Pines, "Spinoza, Maimonides and Kant" in *Scripta Hierosolymitana* 20
  (1968), p. 3–54.

Piety, Study, Charity, Prayer
A. Buechler, *Types of Jewish Palestinian Piety* (1968).
L. Jacobs, *Jewish Values* (1960).
S. Belkin, *In His Image* (1960).
A.Z. Idelsohn, *Jewish Liturgy* (1967).
K. Kohler, *The Psalms and their Place in the Liturgy* (1897).
M. Kadushin, *Worship and Ethics* (1964).
E. Munk, *World of Prayer* (1963), 2 vols.
A. Milgrom, *Jewish Worship* (1975).
J.J. Petuchowki, *Prayerbook Reform in Europe* (1968).
B. Bogen, *Jewish Philanthropy* (1917).
J. Bergman, *Ha-Zedakah be-Yisroel* (1944).
M. Kadushin, *Worship and Ethics* (1964).

Kiddush Ha-Shem
J. Katz, *Exclusiveness and Tolerance* (1961).

H.G. Friedman, in *Hebrew Union College Annual* (1904), pp. 193–214.

A. Holz, in *Judaism* 10 (1961), pp. 360–67.

S. Spiegel, *The Last Trial* (1974).

Ha-Hevrah ha-Historit ha-Yisroelit, *Milḥemet Kodesh u-Martyrologyah* (1968).

III. GENERAL, GREEK, CHRISTIAN, AND ISLAMIC THOUGHT

Readers are advised to consult the bibliography found in F. C. Copleston's *History of Philosophy* (8 volumes; N.Y., 1946, 1950, 1953) for much bibliographic information on every aspect of western philosophical thought: Copleston's *History of Medieval Philosophy* (London, 1972) provides a fine specialized bibliography of the medieval period.

For works on Greek philosophy readers are referred to W. K. C. Guthrie's *History of Greek Philosophy* (in progress, 4 volumes have already appeared; Cambridge University Press). For the Hellenistic and early Christian period, *The Cambridge History of Later Greek and Early Medieval Philosophy*, ed. A. H. Armstrong (Cambridge, 1966), is valuable. For all aspects of Islamic thought and bibliographical assistance, *The Cambridge History of Islam* (Cambridge, 1970) is recommended.

IV. HISTORIES OF JEWISH PHILOSOPHY

There are a number of standard histories of Jewish philosophy. Some cover the whole history of the subject while others concentrate on a specific period, i.e., medieval or modern. In order to avoid repetition in the individual bibliographies, these works are listed here. In addition, where there is no individual listing of a particular thinker in this bibliography, readers can consult the relevant bibliographies in the works listed below, especially the English translation of J. Guttmann's *Philosophies of Judaism*.

Agus, J., *The Evolution of Jewish Thought: From Biblical Times to the Opening of the Modern Era* (New York, 1959).

——, *Modern Philosophies of Judaism: A Study of Recent Jewish Philosophies of Religion* (New York, 1941; paperback 1970). A reasonable account of 19th and 20th-century Jewish thought.

Bergman, S. H., *Faith and Reason: An Introduction to Modern Jewish Thought*. Translated and edited by Alfred Jospe (Washington, 1961; New

York, paperback 1963). Six excellent introductory essays on 20th-century thinkers: Cohen, Kook, Buber, Rosenzweig, Magnes, and A. D. Gordon.

Blau, J. L., *The Story of Jewish Philosophy* (New York, 1962). A light, general treatment for the non-specialist.

Cohen, A. A., *The Natural and the Supernatural Jew: An Historical and Theological Introduction* (New York 1962, paperback, 1964). An uneven though helpful study of modern Jewish thought since Mendelssohn.

Guttmann, Julius, *Philosophies of Judaism: The History of Jewish Philosophy from Biblical Times to Franz Rosenzweig.* Translated by David W. Silverman (New York, 1964; paperback 1966). The classic work in the field, covering the whole of Jewish history until Rosenzweig; for serious students of the subject.

Husik, I., *A History of Medieval Jewish Philosophy* (New York, 1930). The standard history of medieval Jewish thought written in English.

Kaplan, M. M., *The Greater Judaism in the Making: A Study of the Modern Evolution of Judaism* (New York, 1960). Standard work for the medieval and early modern period with a valuable discussion of the modern period.

Katz, Steven, *Jewish Philosophers* (New York and Jerusalem, 1975). The only general history covering the whole history of the subject, including the post 1945 period.

Rotenstreich, N., *Jewish Philosophy in Modern Times: From Mendelssohn to Rosenzweig* (New York, 1968; translated from the Hebrew original, Tel Aviv, 1950).

Steinschneider, M., *Die hebraeischen Uebersetzungen des Mittelalters* (Berlin 1893). Standard work on Jewish philosophy for the medieval and early modern period.

Vadja, G., *Introduction à la pensée juive du moyen age* (Paris, 1947). An excellent introduction to medieval Jewish philosophy.

V. INDIVIDUAL PHILOSOPHERS

Original works, for the most part, are cited here. For the enormous secondary literature, see the Bibliographies in J. Guttmann, *Philosophies of Judaism* and S. Katz, *Jewish Philosophers,* described in Part IV above.

Philo

An edition of Philo's writings in the original Greek with English translation has been published in the *Loeb Classical Library Series* (F. H. Colson and G. H. Whitaker, translators), 10 vols. (1929–62), with two supplementary volumes containing English translations of the writings preserved in Armenian (R. Marcus, trans.; 1953). Each volume contains an introduction. An English translation by H. Lewy of selections of Philo's writings is to be found in *Three*

Jewish Philosophers (New York, 1960). For literature on Philo prior to 1937 an exhaustive list is given by H. L. Goodhart and E. R. Goodenough, "A general bibliography of Philo" in E. R. Goodenough, *The Politics of Philo Judaeus* (New Haven, 1938). For literature 1937–1962, see L. H. Feldman, *Scholarship on Philo and Josephus* (New York, 1963).

Saadiah (Ben Joseph) Gaon
Saadiah Gaon, *The Book of Beliefs and Opinions.* Transl. by S. Rosenblatt (New Haven, 1948).
——, *Sifrei R. Saadia Gaon.* Edited by J. Derenbourg and M. Lambert, (5 vols.; Paris, 1849–1893).

Issac Israeli
Isaac Israeli, For the English translation of Israeli's work see A. Altmann and S. Stern, *Isaac Israeli, a neo-Platonic Philosopher* (Oxford, 1958).

Ibn Gabirol
Ibn Gabirol, S., *The Fountain of Life.* A partial translation by H. E. Wedneck with an introduction by E. James (New York, 1962).
——, *The Improvement of the Moral Qualities.* Translated by S. S. Wise, and includes the Hebrew text (New York, 1902).
——, *Selected Religious Poems.* Translated by I. Zangwill. Edited and with an introduction by I. Davidson (Philadelphia, 1930).
Marx, A., *HUCA,* 4 (1927) pgs. 433–448.
Rosin, D., "The Ethics of Solomon Ibn Gabirol", in *JQR* n.s. (1891) pgs. 159–181.

Bahya Ibn Paquda
Bahya ibn Paquda, *Sefer Torat Ḥovot ha-Levavot.* Edited by A. Zifroni (Jerusalem, 1928).
——, *Duties of the Heart.* English translation of *Ḥovot ha-Levavot.* Text and translation by M. Hyamson (Philadelphia, 1925). New translation by M. Mansoor (London, 1973).

Abraham Bar Ḥiyya
Bar Ḥiyya, A., *Hegyon ha-Nefesh ha-Aẓuvah.* Edited by Y. I. Freimann (Leipzig, 1860). English translation by G. Wigoder, *Meditation of the Sad Soul* (London, 1969).

Judah Halevi
Judah Halevi, *Shirei Rabbi Yehudah Halevi.* Edited by S. Bernstein (New York, 1945). Popular edition with notes and an explanation.

——, *Selected poems of Jehudah Halevi.* Translated by N. Salaman (Philadelphia, 1924).

——, *Judah Halevi's Kitab al Khuzari.* English translation of *Sefer ha-Kuzari* by H. Hirschfeld (1905–6, 1931; repr. 1945; reprinted with an introduction by H. Slonimsky, 1964).

Baron, S., in *JSOS,* 3 (1941) pgs. 243–272.

Druck, D., *Yehuda Halevy: His Life and Works.* Translated by M. Z. R. Frank (New York, 1941).

Neumark, D., "Jehuda Halevi's Philosophy in its Principles," in Hebrew Union College Catalogue (Cincinnati, 1908) pgs. 1–91.

Strauss, L., "The Law of Reason in the Kuzari", in *PAAJR,* XIII (1943) pgs. 47–96.

Wolfson, H. A., "Halevi and Maimonides on Prophecy", in *JQR* n.s., XXXII (1942) pgs. 345–370: *JQR,* XXXIII (1942) pgs. 49–82.

Ibn Daud

Ibn Daud, A., *Sefer Ha-Qabbalah* ("Book of Tradition"). Edited with English translation by G. D. Cohen (London, 1967).

——, *Sefer ha-Emunah ha-Ramah* ("The Exalted Faith"). Edited with German translation by Samson Weill (Frankfurt a. M., 1852; Hebrew text reprinted 1967).

Moses ben Maimon (Maimonides)

Maimonides, Moses, *The Guide of the Perplexed.* Translated with introduction and notes by S. Pines (Chicago, 1963). Also contains introduction by L. Strauss.

——, *Le Guide des Egares.* Edited by S. Munk (3 vols.: Paris, 1856–1866). Contains the Arabic text and a French translation.

——, *Moreh Nebukhim,* with vowel points and a commentary by Judah Even Shemuel (3 vols.; Tel-Aviv, 1935–60).

——, *Iggeret Teman: Epistle to Yemen.* Edited with introduction and notes by Abraham Halkin. English translation by Boaz Cohen (New York: American Academy for Jewish Research, 1952).

——, *Sefer ha-Mitzvot.* New Hebrew translation from the original Arabic published by Y. Kafaḥ (Jerusalem, 1958). An English version based on this translation was published by C. B. Chavel as *The Commandments: Sefer ha-Mitzvoth of Maimonides,* 2 vols. (London, 1967).

——, *Mishneh Torah, The Code of Maimonides.* An English translation of the entire *Code* started to appear in 1949 in the Yale Judaica Series; by 1973 eleven volumes had appeared.

——, *Shemonah Perakim.* Translated into English by J. L. Gorfinkle under the title, *The Eight Chapters of Maimonides on Ethics* (New York, 1912).

Baron, S. Ed., *Essays on Maimonides: An Octocentennial Volume* (New York, 1941).

Epstein, I. Ed., *Moses Maimonides: 1135–1204* (London, 1935). Contains essays by (among others) W. M. Feldman, S. Rawidowicz, E. Rosenthal, and includes a bibliography prepared by J. L. Gorfinkle.

Heschel, A. J., *Maimonides, Eine Biographie* (Berlin, 1935).

Twersky, I., *A Maimonides Reader* (New York, 1972). Contains a helpful introductory bibliography.

The following are important essays by H. A. Wolfson on Maimonides:

Wolfson, H. A. in *JQR*, 1 (1911–12) pgs. 297–339; *JQR*, 25 (1934/35) pgs. 441–467; *JQR*, 26 (1935/36) pgs. 369–377; *JQR*, 32 (1941/42) pgs. 345–370; *JQR*, 33 (1942/43) pgs. 40–82; *PAAJR*, 11 (1941) pgs. 105–163; *Mordecai M. Kaplan Jubilee Volume* (New York, 1953) pgs. 515–530; "The Amphibolous Terms in Aristotle, Arabic Philosophy and Maimonides," in *Harvard Theological Review*, XXXI (1938); "The Aristotelian Predicables and Maimonides' Division of the Attributes" in *Essays and Studies in Memory of Linda R. Miller* (New York, 1938) pgs. 201–234; "Maimonides on Negative Attributes" in *Louis Ginzberg Jubilee Volume* (New York, 1945) pgs. 411–446.

Maimonidean Controversy

Sarachek, I., *Faith and Reason. The Conflict over the Rationalism of Maimonides* (Williamsport, 1935).

Silver, D. J., *Maimonidean Criticism and the Maimonidean Controversy, 1180–1240* (Leiden, 1965) Bibliography pgs. 199–210.

Levi ben Gershom (Gersonides)

Levi ben Gershom, *Sefer Milḥamot Adonai* (Leipzig, 1866; reprint of the 1560 edition).

——, *Die Kampfe Gottes von Lewi ben Gerson,* 2 vols. (Berlin, 1914–16), A German translation of Parts 1–4 of *Sefer Milḥamot Adonai* by B. Kellerman, with notes.

Husik, I., "Studies in Gersonides", in *JQR* n.s. 8 (1917–18), pgs. 113–156; 231–268.

Wolfson, H. A., in *M. M. Kaplan Jubilee Volume* (New York, 1953) pgs. 515–530.

Crescas

Crescas, Ḥasdai, *Or Adonai* (Ferrara, 1555; Vienna 1859–60; Johannisburg, 1861). Two sections have been translated, one into English in H. A. Wolfson: *Crescas' Critique of Aristotle* (Cambridge, Mass., 1929); and the other into German by P. Bloch: *Die Willensfreidheit von Chasdai Crescas* (Munich, 1879).

Waxman, M., *The Philosophy of Don Hasdai Crescas* (New York, 1920).

Wolfson, H. A., *Crescas' Critique of Aristotle* (Cambridge, Mass., 1929). Includes bibliography.

Joseph Albo

Albo, Joseph, *Sefer ha-Ikkarim.* Edited with an English translation and introduction by I. Husik (Jewish Publication Society: Philadelphia, 1946).

Isaac Abrabanel

Abrabanel, I., *Perush le-Moreh Nebukhim* (Vilna, 1904).

Netanyahu, B., *Don Isaac Abravanel* (Philadelphia, 1953).

Reines, A., *Maimonides and Abrabanel on Prophecy* (Cincinnati, 1970).

Trend, J. B., and Loewe, H. M., Eds., *Isaac Abravanel: Six Lectures* (London, 1937). Collection of important articles.

Spinoza

Spinoza, *Opera.* Edited by C. Gebhardt (4 vols.; Heidelberg, 1924). This is the standard edition in the original Latin.

——, *The Chief Works of Spinoza.* Translated by R. H. M. Elwes (2 vols.; New York, 1955; paperback, New York, 1956).

All Spinoza's works have been translated into English in various editions and translations although no complete and uniform edition of his works in English translation exists. For the enormous literature on Spinoza, see Copleston's *History of Philosophy,* vol. 4.

Moses Mendelssohn

Mendelssohn, M., *Gesammelte Schriften.* 7 vols. New edition by I. Elbogen, E. Mittwoch and F. Bamberger (Berlin, 1938–1939). Uncompleted: work has again begun on this edition by A. Altmann.

——, *Jerusalem and other Jewish Writings.* Translated by A. Jospe (New York, 1969).

Altmann, A., *Mendelssohn: A Biographical Study* (Alabama Univ. Press, 1973).

Barzilay, I. E., "Moses Mendelssohn: A Study in Ideas and Attitudes", in *JQR,* 52 (1961), pgs. 69–93 and 175–186.

Meyer, M. A., *The Origins of the Modern Jew* (Detroit, 1967), pgs. 11–56.

Nachman Krochmal

Krochmal, Nachman, *Moreh Nevukhei* ha-Zeman. Critical edition by S. Rawidowicz (Berlin, 1924; revised edition, 1961).

Schechter, S., *Studies in Judaism* (Philadelphia, 1896) pgs. 46–72.

Samson Raphael Hirsch

Hirsch, S. R., *Horeb: A Philosophy of Jewish Laws and Observances.* Translated by Isidor Gruenfeld (London: Soncino, 1962).

——, *Judaism Eternal: Selected Essays from the Writings of Samson Raphael Hirsch.* Translated by Isidor Gruenfeld (London: Soncino, 1956).

——, *The Nineteen Letters of Ben Uziel: Being a Spiritual Presentation of the Principles of Judaism.* Translated by Bernard Drachman (New York, 1899; reissued New York, 1969).

Gruenfeld, I., *Three Generations: The Influence of Samson Raphael Hirsch on Jewish Life and Thought* (London, 1958). Includes extensive bibliography.

Heinemann, I., *Ta'amei ha-Mitzvot be-Sifrut Yisrael,* 2 (Jerusalem, 1956) pgs. 91–161.

Samuel Hirsch

Hirsch, S., *Die Religionsphilosophie der Juden* (Leipzig, 1842).

Fackenheim, Emil, "Samuel Hirsch and Hegel: A Study of Hirsch's *Religionsphilosophie der Juden* (1842)," in A. Altmann, Ed., *Studies in Nineteenth-Century Jewish Intellectual History* (Cambridge Mass., 1964) pgs. 171–201.

Samuel David Luzzatto

Luzzatto, S. D., *The Foundations of the Torah.* Printed in English translation in Noah H. Rosenbloom, *Luzzatto's Ethico-Psychological Interpretation of Judaism* (New York, 1965).

Moritz Lazarus

Lazarus, M., *Ethik des Judentums.* Translated into English by Henrietta Szold as *Ethics of Judaism* (2 vols.; New York, 1900–1901).

Hermann Cohen

Cohen, H., *Judische Schriften* ("Writings on Judaism"). Edited by Bruno Strauss with an introduction by Franz Rosenzweig (3 vols.; Berlin, 1924).

———, *Religion of Reason from the Sources of Judaism.* English translation of *Religion der Vernunft* (New York, 1971).

Altmann, A., "Hermann Cohens Begriff der Korrelation", in *In zwei Welten: Siegfried Moses zum 75. Geburtstag.,* edited by Hans Tramer (Tel Aviv, 1962) pgs. 377–399.

Kaplan, M., *The Purpose and Meaning of Jewish Existence* (New York, 1964), pgs. 42–252.

Melber, J., *Hermann Cohen's Philosophy of Judaism* (New York, 1968).

Leo Baeck

Baeck, Leo, *The Essence of Judaism.* English translation by V. Grubenwieser and L. Pearl of *Das Wesen des Judentums,* the primary source for Baeck's view of Judaism (Revised edition, New York, 1948; paperback, 1961).

——, *Judaism and Christianity.* Translated with an introduction by Walter Kaufmann (Philadelphia, 1964).

——, *This People Israel.* English translation of *Dieses Volk* (New York, 1965).

Friedlander, A. H., *Leo Baeck: Teacher of Theresienstadt* (New York, 1959).

Abraham Isaac Kook

Kook, A. I., *Rabbi Kook's Philosophy of Repentance.* English translation of *Orot ha-Teshuvah* (New York, 1968).

Agus, J. B., *Banner of Jerusalem* (New York, 1948).

Epstein, I., *Abraham Yitzhak Hacohen Kook: His Life and Times* (London, 1951).

Franz Rosenzweig

Rosenzweig, F., *Judaism Despite Christianity.* Edited by E. Rosenstock-Huessy with essays by A. Altmann and D. M. Emmett. Contains Rosenzweig's correspondence with Eugen Rosenstock-Hussy (New York, 1969).

——, *Understanding the Sick and the Healthy: A View of World, Man and God.* Edited and with an introduction by Nahum N. Glatzer. This is the English translation from the manuscript of *Das Buchlein vom gesunden und kranken Menschenverstand* (New York, 1953).

——, *On Jewish Learning,* edited by Nahum N. Glatzer. English translation of the three epistles: "Zeit ists", "Bildung und kein Ende", "Die Bauleute", and additional material (New York, 1955; paperback, 1965).

——, *The Star of Redemption.* English translation of *Der Stern der Erlosung;* translated by William Hallo from the second (1930) edition (New York, 1971).

Glatzer, N. N., *Franz Rosenzweig, His Life and Thought* (New York, 1953; paperback, 1961). Includes bibliography.

Schwarzschild, S., *Franz Rosenzweig: Guide for Reversioners* (London, 1960).

Martin Buber

Buber, Martin, *At The Turning; Three Addresses on Judaism* (New York, 1952).

——, *Between Man and Man.* Translated by Ronald Gregor Smith (New York, 1948; paperback edition, 1965).

——, *Eclipse of God: Studies in the Relation between Religion and Philosophy* (New York, 1952; paperback edition, 1957).

——, *Hasidism and Modern Man.* Translated and edited by Maurice Friedman (New York, 1958); second volume of set is *Origin and Meaning of Hasidism.*

——, *I and Thou.* Translated by Walter Kaufmann (New York, 1970).

——, *Tales of the Hasidim.* Translated by Olga Marx (2 vols.: New York, 1947–48, paperback edition, 1961).

For a complete bibliography of Buber's writings see the bibliography in the *Philosophy of Martin Buber,* ed. by P. Schilpp and M. Friedman (details below).

Friedman, M., *Martin Buber: The Life of Dialogue* (Chicago, 1955; New York, 1960).

Schilpp, P. and M. Friedman, Eds., *The Philosophy of Martin Buber,* The Library of Living Philosophers, Vol. 12 (Illinois, 1967). Contains contributions by thirty authors and Buber's replies.

The volumes listed above are the most important secondary sources on Buber in English. There is, however, a very extensive bibliography of secondary literature on Martin Buber's thought and the reader should consult the Friedman and Schilpp volumes listed above for further details of these studies.

Mordecai Kaplan

Kaplan, M., *The Greater Judaism in the Making: A Study of the Modern Evolution of Judaism* (New York, 1960).

——, *Judaism as a Civilization: Toward a Reconstruction of American-Jewish Life* (New York: Schocken, 1967).

——, *The Meaning of God in Modern Jewish Religion* (New York, 1937).

——, *The Religion of Ethical Nationhood* (New York, 1970).

Berkovits, E., *Reconstructionist Theology: A Critical Evaluation* (New York, 1959). Reprinted from *Tradition,* vol. 2 (1959).

Eisenstein, I. and E. Kohn, Eds., *Mordecai M. Kaplan: An Evaluation* (New York, 1957).

Post-1945 Jewish Thought

Berkovits, Eliezer, *Faith After the Holocaust* (New York, KTAV, 1973).

——, *God, Man & History* (New York, Jonathan David, 1959).

Borowitz, Eugene, *A New Jewish Theology in the Making* (Philadelphia: Westminster Press, 1968).

——, *How Can a Jew Speak of Faith Today?* (Philadelphia: Westminster Press, 1968).

Cohen, Arthur A., ed., *Arguments and Doctrines: A Reader of Jewish Thinking in the Aftermath of the Holocaust* (Philadelphia: Jewish Publication Society and New York: Harper & Row, 1970).

Cohon, Samuel S., *Jewish Theology* (New York: Humanities Press, 1971).

Fackenheim, Emil L., *God's Presence in History: Jewish Affirmations and Philosophical Reflections* (New York: New York University Press, 1970).

——, *Quest for Past and Future: Essays in Jewish Theology* (Bloomington: Indiana University Press, 1968).

——, *Encounters Between Judaism and Philosophy* (Philadelphia, Jewish Pub. Society, 1973).

Herberg, Will, *Judaism and Modern Man: An Interpretation of Jewish Religion* (New York: Farrar, Straus and Cudahy, 1951; paperback edition, New York: Atheneum, 1970).

——, "Judaism as Personal Decision," in Alfred Jospe, ed., *Tradition and Contemporary Experience* (New York: Schocken-Hillel Books, 1970), pp. 77–90; also in *Conservative Judaism*, Vol. 22, # 4 (Summer) 1968.

——, *Protestant, Catholic, Jew,* second edition (Garden City: Doubleday Anchor Books, 1960).

Heschel, Abraham J.

——, *The Earth is the Lord's: The Inner Life of the Jew in East Europe* (New York: Henry Schuman, 1950). *The Earth is the Lord's and the Sabbath* (New York: Harper Torchbook, paperback edition).

——, *God in Search of Man: A Philosophy of Judaism* (New York: Farrar, Straus & Cudahy, 1956; Philadelphia: Jewish Publication Society, 1956; New York: Harper Torchbook, paperback edition).

——, *Israel: An Echo of Eternity* (New York: Farrar, Straus & Giroux, 1969; paperback edition).

——, *Man Is Not Alone: A Philosophy of Religion* (New York: Farrar, Straus, and Young, 1951; and Philadelphia: Jewish Publication Society, 1951; New York: Harper Torchbook, paperback edition).

——, *The Prophets* (New York and Evanston: Harper & Row, 1962; Philadelphia: Jewish Publication Society, 1962; New York: Harper Torchbook in 2 vols., paperback edition).

——, *The Sabbath: Its Meaning for Modern Man* (New York: Farrar, Straus, and Young, 1951).

——, *Theology of Ancient Judaism (Torah Min Ha-Shamayim Be-Aspaklaryah Shel Ha-Dorot)* in Hebrew (London and New York: Soncino, Vol. I, 1962; Vol. II, 1965).

——, *Passion for Truth* (New York: Farrar, Straus & Giroux, 1973).

Katz, S., ed., *Jewish Philosophers* (Part IV: Post-1945 Jewish thought; New York, 1975).

Louis Jacobs, *Principles of the Jewish Faith* (New York: Basic Books, 1964).

——, *We Have Reason to Believe,* third edition (London: Vallentine, Mitchell, 1965).

Rubenstein, Richard L., *After Auschwitz* (Indianapolis: Bobbs-Merrill, 1966).

Silver, Abba Hillel, *Where Judaism Differed* (Philadelphia: Jewish Publication Society. 1957; paperback edition, Schocken, New York, 1973).

Soloveitchik, Joseph B., "The Lonely Man of Faith," *Tradition,* vol. 1 # 2 (Summer 1965), pp. 5–67.

——, "Ish ha-Halakhah," *Talpiot* (1944), pp. 651–735.

——, *Al ha-Teshuvah* (ed, P. Peli; Jerusalem, 1975).

Steinberg, Milton, *Anatomy of a Faith,* edited by Arthur Cohen (New York: Harcourt Brace, 1960).

——, *Basic Judaism* (New York: Harcourt Brace, 1947).

——, *A Partisan Guide to the Jewish Problem* (Indianapolis: Bobbs-Merrill, 1945).

List of EJ Contributors

PART I—GOD

God in the Bible—Israel Abrahams
God in Talmudic Literature—Yehoshua M. Grintz
God in Medieval Jewish Philosophy—Marvin Fox
God in the Kabbalah—Gershom Scholem
God in Modern Jewish Thought—Marvin Fox
Names of God—Louis F. Hartman, Louis Isaac Rabinowitz and Marvin Fox
Attributes of God—Alexander Altmann
Providence of God—Yehoshua M. Grintz, Alexander Altmann and Gershom
    Scholem
Justice and Mercy of God—Lou H. Silberman
Manifestations of God
    Ru'aḥ Ha-Kodesh—Alan Unterman and Rivka G. Horwitz
    Shekhinah—Alan Unterman, Rivka G. Horwitz and Joseph Dan
    Logos—Daniel E. Gershenson
Anthropomorphism—Gershom Scholem

PART II—MAN

Man in the Bible
    A. Nature and Purpose of Man—Israel Adler
    B. Nature and Purpose of Woman—Anson Rainey
    C. Sin—Edward Lipinski
    D. Repentance and Forgiveness—Jacob Milgrom
    E. Death—Geoffrey Wigoder and EJ Staff
Man in Talmudic Literature
    A. Nature and Purpose of Man—Theodore Friedman
    B. Nature and Purpose of Woman—Louis Jacobs
    C. Free Will—Geoffrey Wigoder and EJ Staff
    D. Sin—Louis Jacobs
    E. Repentance—Louis Jacobs

F. Forgiveness—Alan Unterman
G. Death—Geoffrey Wigoder and *EJ* Staff

PART III—GOD AND THE JEWS

Judaism—Louis Jacobs

Covenant—Moshe Weinfeld

Chosen People—Lou H. Silberman

Revelation—Edward Lipinski, Jacob Joshua Ross, Lawrence V. Berman and Walter S. Wurzburger

Torah—Louis Isaac Rabinowitz and Warren Harvey

Mitzvot—Alexander Altmann and Gershom Scholem

Piety, Study, Charity and Prayer—Walter S. Wurzburger, Louis Jacobs, Raphael Posner, Haim Hillel Ben-Sasson and Israel Abrahams

Kiddush Ha-Shem ("Sanctification of the Name")—Norman Lamm and Haim Hillel Ben-Sasson

Much of the modern material and almost all the post-1945 material has been written especially for this volume by the editor Professor Steven Katz.

326